STATE AND GOVERNMENT IN ANCIENT INDIA

State and Government in Ancient India

A.S. Altekar

MOTILAL BANARSIDASS PUBLISHERS
PRIVATE LIMITED • DELHI

7th Reprint: Delhi, 2016
First Edition: Varanasi, 1949

ISBN : 978-81-208-1008-2 (Cloth)
ISBN : 978-81-208-1009-9 (Paper)

MOTILAL BANARSIDASS
41 U.A. Bungalow Road, Jawahar Nagar, Delhi 110 007
8 Mahalaxmi Chamber, 22 Bhulabhai Desai Road, Mumbai 400 026
203 Royapettah High Road, Mylapore, Chennai 600 004
236, 9th Main III Block, Jayanagar, Bengaluru 560 011
8 Camac Street, Kolkata 700 017
Ashok Rajpath, Patna 800 004
Chowk, Varanasi 221 001

Printed in India

by RP Jain at NAB Printing Unit,
A-44, Naraina Industrial Area, Phase I, New Delhi–110028
and published by JP Jain for Motilal Banarsidass Publishers (P) Ltd,
41 U.A. Bungalow Road, Jawahar Nagar, Delhi-110007

CONTENTS

CONTENTS

PREFACE TO THE THIRD EDITION

The work has been carefully revised and also enlarged when its third edition was prepared. Apart from the minor additions, made almost in all chapters, new sections have been added in Chap. XVI on North Indian Administration in the post-Harsha period and South Indian Administration in the first millenium of the Christian era. The problem of the date of the *Śukranīti* has been now discussed in detail in Chap. I and the contribution of some medieval works like the *Mānasollāsa* has been indicated. The question of the influence of religious and philosophical thought on the Ancient Indian Polity has been briefly discussed in Chap. III. The chapter on the kingship now discusses in clear-cut sections the position and status of the king in the early (i.e. before 500 B.C.) and later periods. Asoka's innovations in the administration are clearly brought out in Chap. XV.

It is hoped that in its third edition, the *State and Government in Ancient India* will be found to be as useful and comprehensive a work as a book of 400 pages can possibly become. The numerous footnotes giving original passages and others giving references to original sources will be found to be very useful by students who desire to pursue their studies further in the field. It is hoped that the general reader, the student and the research worker will all find the work authoritative comprehensive and stimulating.

PATNA, A. S. ALTEKAR
1.7.1958

PREFACE TO THE FIRST EDITION

There are a number of books already in the field, dealing with some of the aspects of Ancient Indian Polity, but a comprehensive work, explaining succinctly the Hindu political ideas, theories and ideals and describing the different features and aspects of the ancient Indian administration in its numerous branches is still a desideratum. The present work attempts to supply this need. It may not be inopportune to draw the reader's attention to some of its special features. It is based not merely on a study of the different Smṛiti books and Artha-śāstra works in Sanskrit, which give us the theoretical picture, but it also utilises fully all the data bearing on the subject available in Vedic and classical literature, Buddhist and Jain works, ancient books on history and accounts of foreign travellers and historians. Rich material supplied by inscriptions has been fully tapped and the discerning critic will not be unwilling to concede that no previous work on the subject attempts to give such a comprehensive synthesis of the divergent data supplied by theoretical and literary works on the one hand and by inscriptions and purely historical records on the other. The material has been arranged chronologically and also province-wise, whenever it was possible to do so. In each chapter, attempt has been made to trace the development of political theories and institutions from age to age, though the material in some cases was not quite sufficient to do so.

The oponing chapter gives a survey of the Literature on Polity, tries to settle the chronology of the principal works of this branch and seeks to account for the relative paucity of books of real merit in later times. The next two chapters (Chap. II and III) deal with the origin of the State, describe its different types and takes a stock of the ancient Indian speculations about the nature, aims and functions of the State. Wherever possible comparison is made with similar theories advocated in the West in ancient, medieval and modern times. The question as to how far the State of ancient India can be called theocratic has also been discussed at some length. The next chapter, Chap. IV, discusses the relationship between the State and the Citizen. How far the foreigners were differentiated from the citizens, how far the latter formed a homogenous group, how far there existed equality of all before the law, are some of the questions discussed in this chapter.

After thus discussing the main political theories in Chaps. II-IV, the book proceeds to describe the structure of the administration in ancient India. Chapter V deals with the Kingship; it describes its evolution from prehistoric times, discusses when and how far it was elective and when, how, why and to what extent divinity began to be associated with it. The different checks upon the king's powers are enumerated and their adequacy is critically examined.

Chapter VI deals with the Republics in Ancient India. When, how and where they came in existence, how far they were democratic in the modern sense of the term, what were the different types of their constitution, what were the relations between the Executive and the Central Assembly, when and why the republics declined and disappeared are some of the topics dealt with in this chapter. It is hoped that the reader will find a good deal of this chapter substantially new.

Chapter VII deals with the powers and functions of the Central Assembly or Popular Parliament. It shows how this institution existed in the Vedic times and gradually disappeared in the later period, when the state began to become more and more extensive. It is shown at the end that the Pauras and the Jānapadas mentioned in the literature and inscriptions of the post-Mauryan period do not denote any popular assemblies or parliaments.

Chapters VIII and IX deal with the machinery of the Central Executive. Chapter VIII deals with the evolution of the Ministry and the powers it exercised in the administration. Chapter IX describes the working of the Secretariat and of the various departments of the Central Government. Data scattered over a number of *Nīti* works and inscriptions have been corelated in order to give a detailed and synthetic account which will be found to be substantially new and original.

Chapters X and XI describe the Provincial, Divisional, District, Town and Village Government. Here also the evidence of the theoretical works is checked and supplimented with that of inscriptions scattered over the different provinces. As far as possible, an attempt is made to give developments in their chronological order; where possible, as in the case of the village councils, provincial variations in their constitution and functions are also indicated.

Chapter XII deals with Revenue and Expenditure. Principles of taxation have been discussed and the various aspects of the land tax have been extensively considered. The question of the ownership of land has been critically examined. Taxes on commerce and industry have also been considered. The chapter concludes with a discussion of the items of State expenditure. Epigraphical sources have supplied rich material for this chapter.

Chapter XIII deals with the Inter-State Relations both in times of peace and war and also discusses in details the relations between the suzerain and his feudatories.

The various chapters of the book isolate the different links of the administrative machinery like the king, the ministry, the secretariat and discuss their origin and trace their development during the different periods. This treatment is no doubt very useful and it enables the reader to trace the origin and development of the different institutions very clearly. It however does not give the picture of the whole administrative machinery from age to age.

This is attempted in the concluding chapter, which first gives a survey of the administration from age to age and then gives a general estimate of ancient Indian polity and its achievements. Lessons suggested by this general survey and the critical estimate are also stated at the end, so that they may be useful to us for the present as well.

The book is mainly a research work, which documents all important statements it makes and seeks to throw fresh light on several important and obscure points. The subject matter, however, has been presented in a manner calculated to be attractive and intelligible to the general reader as well. It is therefore hoped that the book will appeal both to the general reader and the scholar, as was the case with my books on *Education in Ancient India*, and *Position of Women in Hindu Civilization*.

The book is supplied with a detailed bibliography in Appendix I. Appendix II gives a chronological table of authors, kings and dynasties arranged alphabetically with a view to help the general reader. Appendix III gives an exhaustive Index.

Banaras Hindu University, **A. S. ALTEKAR**
15-5-1949

PREFACE TO THE SECOND EDITION

The hearty reception that was extended to the first edition of the *State and Government in Ancient India* showed that the observation made in the preface of its first edition that 'A comprehensive work explaining succinctly the Hindu political ideas, theories and ideals and describing the different features and aspects of the ancient Indian administration in its numerous branches was still a desideratum' was fairly correct. While preparing this second edition an effort has been made to make the work as comprehensive as possible by adding several new sections and chapters to it. Attention may be drawn to the following new features of the present edition :-

(1) A section has been added to Chap. I explaining the precise scope and meaning of the terms like the *Rājyaśāstra*, *Daṇḍanīti* and *Arthaśāstra* used to denote the political science. The chapter now contains a more exhaustive discussion of the problem of the authenticity of the *Arthaśāstra* of Kauṭilya and gives a critical discussion of the value of the different sources of ancient Indian polity.

(2) Chap. II contains a new section on the city states.

(3) In chap. III a section has been added on the distribution of functions and the vesting of the sovereignty.

(4) Chap. XII, dealing with Judicial Administration, is a new feature of this edition.

(5) Chap. XIV dealing with Interstate Relations now includes a discussion of the *Maṇḍala* theory, so frequently referred to by the ancient political writers.

(6) The last chapter of the first edition on Historical Survey and Estimate has now been expanded into three separate chapters. The historical survery in the first edition was rather brief, extending over seven pages only. It has now been made fairly exhaustive and covers 45 pages.

This subject has now separate sections dealing with

(1) Administration in the Vedic period.

(2) Administration in the Age of the Later Saṁhitās and Brāhmaāṇs.

(3) Administration during *c.* 600 B. C. to 325 B. C.

(4) Administration in the Mauryan Age.

(5) Administration during the Dark Period, 200 B. C. to 300 A. D.

(6) Administration during the Gupta period.

(7) Administration under Harshavardhana.

(8) Administration under the Rāshṭrakūṭas.

The second edition will thus give to the reader not only an idea of the origin and development of the several concepts and institutions of the Ancient Indian polity, but would put before him a concrete picture of the administration as a whole, as it was functioning and developing in the successive periods of Ancient Indian History from the Vedic age to about 1000 A. D.

'General Estimate' now forms a separate chapter, the last one (XVII), in the book. Some changes had to be made in this chapter also, especially in those portions of it that dealt with the lessons which modern India can learn from the ancient Indian polity. The original book was written when the Princely Order formed an effective part of the modern Indian Polity and the constitution of the Indian Republic had not been finalised. Some changes had to be made in the light of the new developments during the last six years.

This new, revised and enlarged edition of *State and Government in Ancient India* will be found to be as comprehensive as a book of 375 pages can be reasonably expected to be. It is hoped that it will appeal as an authoritative book both to the general reader as well as to the University student and teacher.

PATNA,
1-4-1955

A. S. Altekar

ABBREVIATIONS

A. Br. or *Ait. Br.*:—Aitareya Brāhmaṇa
Ap. Ś. S. :—Āpastamba Śrauta Sūtra
A. Ś. or *Artha.* :—Arthaśāstra of Kauṭṭilya
A. S. I., A. R.:—Archaeological Survey of India, Annual Report
A. V. :—Atharvaveda
B. D. S. :—Baudhāyana Dharmasūtra
B. G. :—Bombay Gazetteer
Br. Up. :—Bṛihadāraṇyaka Upanishad
B. S. S :—Baudhāyanā Śrauta Śūtra
Chā. U. :—Chhāndogya Upanishad
C. I. I. :—Corpus Inscriptionum Indicarum
E. C. :—Epigraphia Carnatica
E. I. :—Epigraphia Indica
Elliot :—Elliot and Dowson, History of India as told by her own Historians.
G. D. S. or *Gautama* :—Gautama Dharma Sūtra
I. A. :—Indian Antiquary
I. H. Q. :—Indian Historical Quarterly
I. M. P. :—Inscriptions from Madras Presidency
J. :—Jātaka
J. A. S. B. :—Journal of the Asiatic Society of Bengal
J. A. H. R. :—Journal of the Andhra Historical Society
J. B. B. R. A. S. :—Journal of the Bombay Branch of the Royal Asiatic Society
J. Br. :—Jaiminīya Brāhmaṇa
J. R. A. S. :—Journal of the Royal Asiatic Society
K. S. :—Kāṭhaka Saṁhitā
Manu :—Manusmriti
M. A. S. I. :—Memoirs of the Archaeological Survey of Ind'a
Mbh. :—Mahābhārata
M. N. :—Majhimanikāya
P. :—Purāṇa
P. Br. :—Pañchaviṁśa Brāhmaṇa

P. M. :—Pūrvamimānsā

P. R. A. W. C. :—Progress Report of the Archaeological Survey of India, Western Circle

Raghu :—Raghuvaṁśa

Rāshṭrakūṭas :—Rāshṭrakūṭas and their Times

R. V. :—Ṛigveda

Ś. Br. :—*Śat. Br.* :—Śatapatha Brāhmaṇa

S. I. I. :—South Indian inscriptions.

S. I. E. R. :—South Indian Epigraphical Report

Śukra :—Sukranītisāra

T. Br. :—Taittirīya Brāhmaṇa

T. S. :—Taittirīya Saṁhitā

V. D. S. :— Vasiṣṭha Dharma Sūtra

Vis. P. :—Vishnu Purāṇa

V. S. :—Vājasaneya Saṁhitā

Watters :—Watters : On Travels of Yuan Chwang

Yāj. :—Yājñavalkya Smṛiti.

TRANSLITERATION

The following are the main points to be noted in the scheme of transliteration followed in this work.

आ	ā	ई	ī	ऊ	ū
ऋ	ṛi	ए	e	ऐ	ai
ओ	o	औ	au	ङ्	ṅ
च	ch	छ	chh	ञ	ñ
ट	ṭ	ठ	ṭh	ड	ḍ
ढ	ḍh	ण	ṇ	श	ś
ष	sh	स	s		
Visarga	ḥ		Anusvāra	ṁ	

CHAPTER I.

NAME, HISTORY AND SOURCES OF THE SCIENCE OF POLITY

The Name of the Science

In ancient India the political science was known by several terms like the Rājadharma, Rājyaśāstra, Daṇḍanīti Nītiśāstra and Arthaśāstra. Some of these terms like the Rājadharma[1] 'Duties of the king' and Rājyaśāstra[2], 'Science of the state' require no explanation. Monarchy was the normal form of the state and the science of politics and government was therefore naturally called Rājadharma or Rājyaśāstra. The term Daṇḍanīti also is self-explanatory. Like many thinkers of the modern time, some Indian writers like Manu held that the ultimate sanction behind the state is force. If it is not used, the alternative is the law of the jungle (*mātsyanyāya*). It is Daṇḍa (physical force or physical punishment) which rules over all the subjects, it is Daṇḍa which protects them; when all else are sleeping, Daṇḍa keeps awake ; law is nothing but Daṇḍa itself.[3] Daṇḍa, however, must be wielded with discretion. If it is used too harshly, the subjects are distressed ; if it is used too lightly, the king will not be held in awe ; if it is used in the proper manner,[4] the subjects are happy and the realm progresses.

Some writers like Kauṭilya, however, do not understand Daṇḍa in a narrow sense. They point out that punishment or threat of punishment is not to be viewed only in its prohibitive aspect. It establishes law and order in society and thus

1. This term is used by Manu and other Smṛiti writers.
2. *Mbh.* XII. 1. 58-63 uses this term.
3. दण्डः शास्ति प्रजाः सर्वा दण्ड एवाभिरक्षति ।
   दण्डः सुप्तेषु जागर्ति दण्डं धर्मं विदुर्बुधाः ॥ VIII. 14.
4. तीक्ष्णदण्डो हि भूतानामुद्वेजनीयः। मृदुदण्डः परिभूयते । यथार्हदण्डः पूज्यः ।
Arthaśāstra, I, 1. Cf. also *Manu*, VII. 19,27.

indirectly brings about a natural tendency in the average individual to obey the law of the land, which renders the frequent use of force unnecessary. It ultimately secures proper progress in religion, philosophy and economic well-being,[1] so necessary for social stability. Daṇḍa enables the individual and the state to have new achievements to their credit, to protect and increase what has been acquired and to distribute the gains properly as between the state and the individuals, as also among the individuals themselves. The entire social well-being is thus dependent upon it. Daṇḍanīti thus deals with the totality of social, political and economic relationships and indicates how they are to be properly organised and integrated with one another. All relationship, says, Uśanas, is rooted in the Daṇḍanīti (*Mbh.* XII. 62. 28-9).

Manu goes to the extent of declaring that it is Daṇḍa who is the real king, the real leader and the real protector.[2] The rules about the functions and duties of the king and the welfare of the state were therefore naturally called Daṇḍanīti.

The works on the science of politics written by Uśanas[3] and Prajāpati were known as Daṇḍanīti ; it will be soon shown (p. 4) how the *Arthaśāstra* of Kauṭilya also was known by that term.

The next term we have to consider is Nītiśāstra. Nīti is derived from the root *nī* to lead ; Nīti therefore means proper guidance or direction. It was held that this would become possible by following the ethical course of conduct and therefore one connotation of the term Nītiśāstra was the science of ethics. Proper guidance or direction usually presupposes propriety, prudence and wisdom ; so Nītiśāstra also came to denote the science of wisdom and right course. Bhartṛihari used the term in this sense when he described one of his books as Nītiśataka. Greatest propriety, wisdom and circumspection have, however, to be

1. आन्वीक्षकीत्रयीवार्तानां योगक्षमसाधनो दण्डः। तस्य नीतिर्दण्डनीतिः। अलब्धलाभार्था लब्धपरिरक्षिणी रक्षितविवर्धनी वृद्धस्य तीर्थेषु प्रतिपादिनी। I. 4. Cf. also *Mbh.* XII 59. 78-9.

2. स राजा पुरुषो दण्डः स नेता शासिता च सः। VII. 17.

3. स च औशनस्यां दण्डनीतौ परं प्राविण्यमुपगतः। *Mudrārākshasa*, Act I.

shown in shaping and guiding the internal and foreign policy of the State, and so the term Nītiśāstra became very popular to designate the science of government from about the 5th century A. D. Kāmandaka and Śukra prefer to call their works as books on Nīti and not on Daṇḍanīti or Arthaśāstra. Lakshmīdhara (1150 A.D.), Annambhaṭṭa (1200 A.D.) Chaṇḍeśvara (1350 A.D.), Nīlakaṇṭha and Mitramiśra (1625 A.D.) call the relevant books of their digests as Nītikalpataru, Nītichandrikā, Nītiratnākara, Nītimayūkha and Nītiprakāśa respectively, and not as Arthaśāstra-Kalpataru or Rājadharma-ratnākara, Rājyaśāstra-mayūkha or Daṇḍanītiprakāśa. The aim of the government is to secure all round progress and prosperity of society and the same was taken to be the scope of Nītiśāstra. Śukra points out how Nītiśāstra is a *sine qua non* for the stability and progress of society in all directions and how it enables the realisation of the four-fold goals connected with Dharma, Artha, Kāma and Moksha.[1]

Arthaśāstra is the next term for the science of politics which we have now to consider. The usual meaning of the term Artha is money or wealth and so the term Arthaśāstra should connote the science of wealth or economics, and not the science of government. While conceding that Artha denotes the avocations of men, Kauṭilya contends that the term also can denote the territory where the people live together. Arthaśāstra, therefore, says Kauṭilya, is the science which deals with the acquisition and protection or governance of territory.[2] This explanation to justify the use of the term Arthaśāstra for the science of politics appears to be rather forced and far-fetched. But posterity has acquiesced in the term primarily because the most important book on the science of politics is known as Arthaśāstra. Thus the *Śukranītiśāra* states that the *Arthaśāstra* discusses instructions about the government along with the

1. सर्वोपनीतकं लोकस्थितिकृन्नीतिशास्त्रकम् ।
धर्मार्थकाममलं हि स्मृतं मोक्षप्रदं यतः ॥ I. 5.

2. मनुष्याणां वृत्तिरर्थः, मनुष्यवती भूमिरर्थः, तस्याः पृथिव्या लाभपालनोपायः शास्त्रमर्थशास्त्रमिति । Bk. XV, Chap. I.

acquisition of wealth (IV. 5. 56.). A perusal of the opening chapter of Kauṭilya's *Arthaśāstra* would show that the author had originally intended to christian his book as a Daṇḍanīti; later on he seems to have changed his mind and decided to call it as Arthaśāstra. The explanation and justification of the term Arthaśāstra occurs only in the last chapter of the work. In its colophon the work is called simply as Śāstra; it can be an abbreviation of Arthaśāstra as well as of Daṇḍanītiśāstra. It is interesting to note that the work was known to Daṇḍin as Daṇḍanīti[1] and not as Arthaśāstra. The *Amarakosha* also equates Daṇḍanīti with Arthaśāstra as also the *Mitāksharā* on Yājñayalkya I, 311 and 313.

To conclude, in the early stages of the development of the science, it was known as Rājadharma; Daṇḍanīti became a more popular term a little later, and Arthaśāstra was suggested as an alternative to it. In course of time, however, the word Rājanīti-śāstra, abridged into Nītiśāstra became most popular and gradually supplanted the other terms.

THE HISTORY OF NĪTIŚĀSTRA

We shall now proceed to describe the origin and development of the Nītiśāstra in ancient India. This will incidentally enable the reader to get an idea of the main sources available for reconstructing the picture of ancient Indian Polity and Administration and of the difficulties and limitations under which we have to work while engaged in this task.

Systematic literature on what we may call the Science of Polity does not go back to a time earlier than *c.* 500 B. C. This is but natural. Even semi-secular and semi-religious subjects like grammar, etymology and astronomy began to develop as independent treatises only from about the 8th century B. C. The science of polity, therefore, cannot be expected to have acquired an independent existence much before the sixth century B C.

1. अधीष्व तावद्दण्डनीतिम् । इयमिदानीमाचार्यविष्णुगुप्तेन मौर्यार्थे षड्भिः श्लोकसहस्रैः संक्षिप्ता । Book 1.

Though there was no systematic literature on the political science composed in the earlier period, usually called the Age of the Vedas and the Brāhmaṇas, there are scattered passages in the Vedic literature, which throw considerable light, sometimes dim, somtimes clear, on the theory and practice of government in the contemporary times. The material in the *Ṛigveda* is very scanty,[1] but that in the *Atharvaveda* is relatively more copious ; it however mostly refers to the institution of the kingship[2]. In the different Saṁhitās of the Yajurveda and in the Brāhmaṇa literature, we frequently come across the description of the coronation ceremony and of the different sacrifices laid down for the king either at the time of his accession or at some later time in his career. These give us valuable glimpses into the position of the king, the prestige he enjoyed, the taxes he collected and the entourage that surrounded him.[3] There are numerous passages in this literature which discuss the relative position and privileges of the different castes, especially the Brāhmaṇas and the Kshatriyas, which also are valuable to the student of the political institutions.

From about the 8th century B. C. an age of specialisation commenced and the specialists in grammar and etymology, prosody and astronomy began to form separate schools and compose special manuals for the beginners as well as the advanced scholars. The beginning of a school of politics, properly so-called, has to be ascribed to this age of specialisation; it is however certain that it was somewhat later in origin than the above sciences and probably contemporaneous with the school of the Dharma-śāstra. The earliest works on polity, which unfortunately have all been lost, were probably composed in *c.* 7th century B. C.

1. Particularly noteworthy are the following :—
X. 191 ; 173 ; 166 ; 124.8 ; 97.6 ; 78.1 ; IV. 42 ; IX. 92. 6 ; VII. 6.5 ; VI. 28.6 ; IV. 4.1 ; III. 43.5 ; I, 25.10-15 ; 67.1 ; 85.8 ; 130.1.

2. The following references are important :—
III. 4-5 ; VI. 88 ; V. 19 ; VII. 12 ; VI. 40.2; XX. 127; IV. 22; XIX. 31; VIII. 10. 8-13.

3. The following passages are important :—
T.S. 3.4.5; 8.9. 1. ; *K S.* XXXI. 10; XV. 4.; *S.Br.* 1. 7. 3. 4.; V. 3. 1. 1; 3. 3. 6-9; 4. 4. 7; IX, 3. 4. 5; XIII. 1. 9. 8. ; 2. 9. 2-5; 4. 4. 1. ; *A. Br.* 1. 14; II. 33; VIII. 10-12 ; 14; 23; 31; *P. Br.*, XIX. 4.

It is also but natural that in about the 7th century B. C. the science of politics should have begun to develop. The country was studded with small kingdoms and the advisers of kings, who were sages and scholars of mature judgement, were naturally expected to discuss problems of administration with them. It is interesting to note that in the Śāntiparvan of the *Mahābhārata*, while answering to some of the questions of Yudhishṭhira, Bhīshma does not give his own opinion, but suggests it by referring to the dialogues between kings and sages of hoary antiquity, who had discussed similar problems. While discussing the divinity of the king, Bhīshma refers to a dialogue between Māndhātā and Indra (chap 65); while emphasising the importance of Daṇḍa, he draws attention to a dialogue between king Vasuhoma and Māndhātā, (chapters 68, 122); while exhorting the king to be righteous, Bhīshma quotes from a dialogue between Yauvanāśva and Māndhātā (chapter 90); while emphasising the importance of the priest, he draws attention to a dialogue between king Aila and Kāśyapa (chaps 73); while warning a king against depletion of treasury, he referes to a dialogue between sage Kālakavṛiksha and Kośala king (chaps.82, 164); while referring to the problems of the republic, he quotes from a dialogue between Kṛishṇa and Nārada (chap. 81). It is quite obvious that these dialogues must not have been hanging in the air or in oral traditions only; some of them must have formed part of books on political science. The science of polity must have had a pretty number of books by about the 7th or the 6th century B.C.

Politics attained the status of an independent science in the west a couple of centuries later, when Aristotle composed his famous work, *Politics*, disentangling politics from ethics for the first time.

We are indebted to the *Mahābhārata* and the *Arthaśāstra* of Kauṭilya for an account of the works written and theories propounded by the pioneer writers in the field. It is interesting and important to note that these two works, which represent independent traditions and sources, agree with each other as far as the names of the early writers are concerned. The *Mahābhārata* account is semi-legendary and semi-historical. It states that a huge work on the science of polity extending over a lakh of verses was originally composed by Brahmadeva, the Creator, when he put an end to the prevailing anarchy and re-established the social order. It was then successively abridged by Śiva-Viśālāksha, Indra, Bṛihaspati and Śukra. Manu, Bhāradvāja and Gauraśiras are also mentioned by the epic as other authors on the science of polity.[1]

The names of well-known works like the *Manusmṛiti*, the *Yājñavalkyasmṛiti*, the *Parāśarasmṛiti* and the *Śukranīti* show that in ancient India authors often preferred to remain incognito and attributed their works to divine or semi-divine persons. We need not therefore suppose that works on polity attributed to Brahmadeva, Manu, Siva or Indra existed only in the imagination of a Kauṭilya or the author of the *Mahābhārata.*

This conclusion is supported by the data of the *Arthaśāstra* of Kauṭilya ; for in numerous places[2] it refers to and discusses the various views of Viśāslāksha, Indra (Bahudanta), Bṛihaspati, Śukra, Manu, Bhāradvāja, Gauraśiras, Parāśara, Piśuna, Kauṇapadanta, Vātavyādhi, Ghoṭamukha, Kātyāyana, Chārāyaṇa and other scholars of the Science of Polity that are referred to in the *Arthaśāstra* (Bk. VI chap. 5)[2].

As was the case with the other branches of knowledge, there were several schools among the students of the Science of Polity as well ; some of them claimed Manu (the father of the human race) as their founder, others Bṛihaspati, the teacher of the gods and others still Śukra or Uśanas, the rival teacher of the Asuras. Some chose to affiliate themselves to Brahmā, some to Indra and some to Śiva. In the beginning very probably handbooks for the use of the beginners were composed, which were later developed into comprehensive works. It is these books, written by human scholars but ascribed to super-human authors, which are referred to by the *Mahābhārata* and the *Arthaśāstra.*

1. XII. 57 and 58.
2. See pp. 6, 13-17, 27-29, 32-3, 63, 177, 192, 253, 255,322, 328-30, 375, 382 of the *Arthaśāstra*, 2nd Edi., by Dr. Shamshastri.

Unfortunately none of these books have survived to our times. It appears that the material contained in some of them was incorporated in the Rājadharma section of the Śāntiparvan of the *Mahābhārata* and that the others were superseded and thrown into the background by the masterly work of Kauṭilya. Some of them, however, existed down to the 9th century; for a verse of Viśālāksha has been quoted in the *Bālakrīdā*, a 9th century commentary of the *Yājñavalkyasmṛiti* by Sureśvarāchārya.

The references to the views of these authors made in the *Arthaśāstra*, however, enable us to get a fair idea of their contents.[1] The science of polity was a new one at this time and therefore many of these writers seem to have started their works with a discussion of its relative importance as compared to the Vedas, the philosophy and the economics. One of them, named Uśanas, went to the extent of advocating the extreme view that politics was the only science worth study. The polity which these writers were discussing was obviously a monarchical one, and they seem to have devoted considerable space to the discussion of the training of the prince and the qualifications of an ideal ruler. The relative importance that he should attach to the difficulties and calamities in connection with the treasury, forts and army were also exhaustively discussed. The constitution and functions of the ministry were described at length by most of them and they widely differed from one another about the number of the ministers and their qualifications. Principles of foreign policy also were debated upon, Bhāradvāja advocating submission to the strong when there is no alternative and Viśālāksha recommending a fight to the finish, even if it meant annihilation. Vātavyādhi did not subscribe to the theory of *Shāḍguṇya* but advocated that of *Dvaiguṇya*. Problems connected with taxation do not seem to have been discussed by these writers; at any rate the *Arthaśāstra* has no quotations from them bearing on that topic. The questions of the control over revenue and provincial officers were discussed, but the local government seems to have been left untouched. On the other hand these early works contained

1. Cf. especially the different views discussed at pp. 9, 68, 157, 161, 185, 192, 196, 198 (Shamsastri's ed.).

important sections dealing with civil and criminal law and laid down a scheme of fines and punishments for theft, robbery, misappropriation, etc. We would not be far wrong in concluding that the treatises of most of these writers were the precursors of the *Arthaśāstra* of Kauṭilya but dealing, of course in a much less exhaustive way, only with those topics dealt with in its Books I, II, III, IV, VI. and VII.

If the quotations from the works of his predecessors given by Kauṭilya can be taken as representative of their contents, we may well conclude that there was a fairly strong school of politics in India from c. 500 B.C. This school would be the counterpart of the Dharmsūtra school, which existed at this period. Whether the one school was Brahmanical and the other Kshatriya, it is difficult to state. It is, however, quite likely that some of the writers of the Nīti school may well have belonged to the class of the administrators of the age.

The *Mahābhārata* is an important source to the student of the science of polity. The Śāntiparvan has an extensive section devoted to the Rājadharma or the duties of the king and the government. It discusses the importance of the science of politics (Chaps. 63-64) and advocates its own theories about the origin of the state and kingship (Chaps. 56, 66, 67). The duties and responsibilities of the king are discussed at length in several chapters (Chaps. 55-57, 70, 76, 94, 96, 120), as also those of the different ministers (Chaps. 73, 82, 83, 85, 115, 118). Taxation is discussed in half a dozen chapters (Chaps. 71, 76, 87, 88, 120, 130), but the duties of the different officers are not laid down in detail as in Book II of the *Arthaśāstra*. Internal administration is briefly described only in one chapter (87). Problems connected with the foreign policy and peace and war naturally occupy a good deal of space (Chaps. 80, 87, 99, 100-103, 110 and 113). There is no doubt that the Rājadharma section represents a further advance over the works of the writers mentioned in it and in the *Arthaśāstra* ; it is not unlikely that it incorporates some of their theories and chapters.

Apart from the Rājadharma section of the Śāntiparvan, there are some other chapters in the work where problems of government are discussed. Sabhāparvan Chap. 5 gives us a very good idea of the ideal administration. Ādiparvan Chap. 142 contains a justification of Machiavellianism under certain circumstances. Sabhāparvan Chap. 32 and Vanaparvan Chaps. 25, 32, 33 and 150 contain interesting discussions on the emergency policy.

As the *Mahābhārata* has undergone several recensions, it is not easy to fix the time of the above chapters. The treatment of the topics however suggests that the above chapters may be belonging to a period earlier than that of the *Manusmṛiti*, i.e. to about the 4th century B. C.

The next important source is the famous *Arthaśāstra* of Kauṭilya. It belongs to the same category as the above works, but discusses the old topics with a remarkable thoroughness, referring to the views of the earlier writers and advancing its own theories. The setting of the work is secular. In Dharmasūtra works, Rājadharma forms but one section. Here on the other hand the study of the state is the main topic, though the king is expected to master the Vedas and philosopy. After discussing in Book I the various problems connected with the kingship, it gives an exhaustive picture of the civil administration in Book. II. The next two books deal with the civil, criminal and personal law. The Book V deals with the duties and responsibilities of the courtiers and retainers of the king and Book VI describes the nature and functions of the seven *prakṛitis* of the State. Then the work devotes its last nine Books to an exhaustive discussion of the problems connected with the foreign policy, the 'circles' of kings and the policy to be followed in connection with its different members, the ways and means by which to establish one's ascendancy among them, the occasions suitable for war and peace, the manner in which the warfare was to be carried on or dissensions were to be sown among the enemies, etc.

The *Arthaśāstra* is more a manual for the administrator than a theoretical work on polity discussing the philosophy and fundamental principles of administration or of the political science. It is mainly concerned with the practical problems of government and describes its machinery and functions, both in peace and war, with an exhaustiveness not seen in any later work, with the possible exception of the *Śukranīti*.

There is a great controversy about the date of the *Arthaśāstra*. Messrs. Shamasastri, Ganapatishastri, N. N. Law, Smith, Fleet and Jayaswal hold that the work proceeds from the pen of of the famous minister of Chandragupta Maurya, while Messrs. Winternitz, Jolly, Keith and D. R. Bhandarkar hold that the work is a much later one, written in the early centuries of the Christian era.[1] Conclusive evidence supporting either view is lacking and the question has become complicated owing to the work being occasionally retouched in later times. The second school points out that if the book was really written by Kauṭilya, the Mauryan premier, it is strange that it should not contain some references to the Mauryan empire and its administrative machinery, so well known to us from Greek sources. It ignores the boards of town officials, and lays down no rules for the care of foreigners, for escorting them to the border and looking after their effects if deceased. The fact that the views of Kauṭilya himself are quoted in the 3rd person would suggest that the real writer of the work was different from him.

Shamasastri and Jayaswal demur to these conclusions. They point out that the colophon of the work distinctly states that it was written by Kauṭilya, who had rescued the country from the Nandas. To say that the author was not acquainted with a wide empire is incorrect, for he states (at p. 340) that the sphere of the jurisdiction of a *chakravartin* extends from the Himalayas to the ocean. The aim of the book is to describe the machinery of a normal state ; the organization of a big empire which was only an occasional phenomenon in Indian history is not, therefore, discussed in detail. The *Arthaśāstra* no doubt refers only to the superintendents of the different

1. Important references are the following ; Shamasastri, Introduction to the *Arthaśāstra*; Jayaswal, *Hindu Polity*, Appendix C; N. N. Law, *Calcutta Review*, 1924; J.J. Meyer, *Das Alt-indische Buche vom Welt-und Staatsleben*, (Das Arthaśàstra des Kauṭilya) ubersetzt vom J. J. Meyer, 1925 Lepizic in support of traditional date ; Jolly, Introduction to the *Arthaśāstra* ; Keith *Sanskrit Literature*, pp. 458, and Winternitz, *Geschichte der Inder Literature*, Vol, III, pp. 519. ff. in support of a later date.

departments ; the boards of five may have been omitted because they were mainly non-official in character. It is quite a common practice among Indian authors to refer to themselves by their own name in the third person singular, rather than in the first person plural ; so the references to Kauṭilya in the third person need not necessarily show that he was not himself the author of the book.

It is true that the name Kauṭilya is not very complimentary ; we need not however on that account doubt his historicity, because a number of his predecessors like Vātavyādhi and Kauṇapadanta had equally unflattering names. Nor can it be argued that Kauṭilya is later than Bhāsa, because the verse *Navaṁ śarāvaṁ* etc. occurring in Book X Chap. 2 of the *Artha-śāstra* is to be seen in *Pratijñā-Yaugandharāyaṇa* of Bhāsa. Kauṭilya never fails to mention the names of his sources ; he has mentioned by name a number of earlier writers on polity ; had he borrowed the above verse from Bhāsa, he would also have mentioned his name. The *Arthaśāstra* introduces this verse along with another with the remark '*Apīha ślokau bhavataḥ*', 'There are these two verses', showing clearly that they were traditional ones ; both Kauṭilya and Bhāsa have obviously borrowed from the mass of floating popular verses. To argue that Kauṭilya was not a historical figure because his name is not mentioned by Megasthenes would have had some force, if the entire work of the Greek ambassador had come down to us ; as only fragments of the book are available, it is quite possible to presume that the name may have been mentioned in some of the lost chapters. Similarly Patañjali's silence about Kauṭilya cannot go against his historicity. It is true that he mentions Mauryas and also the *sabhā* of Chandragupta. But the point at issue is whether there was an occasion for Patāñjali to refer to Kauṭilya and whether he is still silent. No *sūtra* of Pāṇini or *vārtika* of Kātyāyana called for such a reference in the commentary. It may be pointed out that Patañjali is also silent about Aśoka and Bindusāra. Are we to conclude that they did not exist because of this silence ? The argument that the chemical and metallurgical knowledge presupposed by Book. II, Chap. 12 of the

Arthaśāstra is too advanced for the 3rd century B. C. will hardly carry any conviction when it is remembered how our knowledge of the development of these subjects in ancient India is very meagre.

The society depicted by Kauṭilya permits levirate and re-marriages of widows, as also post-puberty marriages and divorces (pp. 151-159). This was the state of affairs in the Mauryan age. Scant respect is shown to the Buddhists (p. 199) and persons are prohibited from becoming recluses without providing for their families (p. 48). This would indicate that the work was written at a time when Buddhism had not yet become strong enough to induce people to leave their families and join the order. The work frequently uses the word *yukta* in the sense of an official, as is done in the edicts of Aśoka. In later centuries this term went out of vogue.

The reference to the Madras, the Kambojas, the Lichchhavis and the Mallas as republics in Bk. XI, Chap. I of the *Artha-śāstra* would also support the view that the book belongs to the early Mauryan times, when these republics are known to have been flourishing. In the 4th century A. D. very few knew of their existence as republics. Like Yāska, who was a predecessor of Pāṇini, the *Arthśāstra* refers to only four parts of speech, and not to eight as has been done by the great grammarian. This would suggest that Pāṇini's grammar had not yet become very authoritative in the days of Kauṭilya. He should therefore be placed in the 4th century B. C. rather than in the 4th century A. D.

It is worth noting that there are several striking points of resemblance between the *Arthaśāstra* and the extant fragments of Megasthenes. Like Megasthenes, the *Arthaśāstra* refers to the royal procession at the time of hunting and religious ceremonies (Bk. I, Chap. 20) and to the necessity of guarding the road on the occasion (Bk. I, Chap. 18). Both authorities refer to female body guards of the king and to his habit of shampooing (Bk. I, Chap. 1 19). Megasthenes' account of irrigation canals and sluices reminds us of the observations on the *setubandha* in the *Arthaśāstra* (Bk. VII, Chap. 14). Megasthenes' overseers moving up and down and reporting to the king are obviously the spies of the *Arthaśāstra*.

Megasthenes' officials for the measurement of the land belong to the same service of which the *gopa* of the *Arthaśāstra* was a subordinate member. The great officers in charge of the markets and rivers, of cities and arts and crafts, mentioned by the Greek ambassador, remind us of some of the *adhyakshas* of the Bk. II of the *Arthaśāstra*.

There are no doubt some serious descrepancies between Kauṭilya and Megasthenes ; but in most cases it can be shown that the Greek ambassador's account is unreliable. The latter is, for some reasons unknown to us, drawing too rosy a picture of the Indian society when he states that theft, drinking and slavery were unknown in India. The data in the *Arthaśāstra* are not consistent with these statements, but are supported by the evidence of the Dharmasûtras written at about the 4th century B. C. ; we can therefore well place him in the Mauryan period, though his picture differs from that of Megasthenes. Megasthenes' statement that Indians did not know the art of writing and administered the laws from memory is now universally accepted as incorrect. His statement that the horses and elephants were the monopoly of the king is contradicted by Strabo and Arrian, who agree with Kauṭilya in recognising private ownership of these animals. When Megasthenes states that the state was the owner of land, he probably refers to the crown lands. Patañjali agrees with Kauṭilya in recognising the private ownership of arable land. The non-reference in the *Arthaśāstra* to the boards of five in the city and the military administration may be due to the fact that Kauṭilya perhaps wanted to refer to only the heads of the offices and not to their advisory councils

All things considered, it has to be admitted that there is a substantial agreement between the administrative and social picture as given by Kauṭilya and Megasthenes and we may well conclude that they were not far removed from each other in time.

The above facts as well as the colophon of the work would suggest that its kernel at any rate belongs to the Mauryan age and embodies the views of Kauṭilya. It was, however, retouched here and there in later times. Thus the reference to China could not have been in the original work, as the country was not known by that name in *c.* 300 B. C. It is probable that passages containing the term *suraṅga*, derived from the Greek term syrinx, may be later. At p. 255 the view of Bhāradvāja is placed after that of Kauṭilya. This may be an instance of opposite views being placed side by side in an impartial manner. But if it suggests that the view of Bhāradvāja was to be preferred to that of Kauṭilya, the passage would be a later addition.

Apart from a few such passages, the work seems to be substantially of the Mauryan age and may be taken to embody the views of the great minister of Chandragupta.

Kauṭilya was not only a famous statesman but also the founder of a school of politics ; hence the great respect in which his name and work have been held by the subsequent centuries. Both Bāṇa[1] and Daṇḍin[2] refer to the study of this work especially by the princes, and the Jain tradition, as recorded in the *Nandīsūtra* (p. 391) enumerates the work among the heretical books along with the *Rāmāyaṇa* and the *Bhārata*. Even south Indian epigraphs describe skilled administrators and diplomats like king Durvinīta (9th century)[3] and Mārashimha (10th century) of the Gaṅga dynasty[3] as incarnations of Vishṇugupta or Kauṭilya or as well versed in his statecraft.

The position of the *Arthaśāstra* in the realm of the literature on politics is analogous to that of Pāṇini's *Ashṭādhyāyī* in the field of grammar. Like Pāṇini, Kauṭilya superseded all his predecessors ; their works were, therefore, lost in the course of time. The excellence of Pāṇini's work was so great that very few among the later grammarians thought it possible to supersede the great master. The same apparently was the view of the later scholars in the realm of the political science.

1. येषामतिनृशंसं प्रायोपदेशनिर्घृणं कौटिलीयमर्थशास्त्रं प्रमाणम्। *Kādambarī.*

2. अधीष्व तावद्दण्डनीतिम्। इयमिदानीमाचार्यविष्णुगुप्तेन मौर्यार्थे षड्भिः श्लोकसहस्रैः संक्षिप्ता। *Daśakumāracharit*, Bk. I

3. Gumireddipura plates, *M. A. R.*, 1912 ; Vudlur grant, *M. A R.* 1942

That seems to be one of the reasons for the relative dearth of original works in the later history of the science.

There were also some other reasons for this phenomenon. The Smṛitis written during *c.* 200 B. C. to 200 A. D. like those of Manu (Chaps. VII-IX), Vishṇu (Chap. III) and Yājñavalkya (Chap. I, 304-67) took over the discussion of the topics like the duties of the king, the functions of the different officers, the rules of civil and criminal law and the different theories concerning the foreign policy. Of course their treatment of these subjects was not as comprehensive or systematic as that of the *Arthaśāstra*, but it was quite sufficient for every day purposes. They possessed the additional advantage of including a discussion of the rules of *varṇa*, *āśrama* and *prāyaśchitta* and thus appeared as more useful manuals to the public than the books on the pure *Arthaśāstra*, as they dealt with a number of religious, social and philosophical topics also, in which the age was more interested than in the pure discussion of the details of political theories or the problems of Government administration.

The Smṛiti works referred to above deal with the administrative problems in a general way. Their treatment would have been found inadequate and new books would have come into the field, had there been intense activity in the realm of the political thought. But there was no such activity. The general form of the works of the political science was determined by the *Arthaśāstra* and a few other manuals of similar nature. New political theories were not adumbrated in later centuries. The semireligious and semi-moral outlook of the writers of the time was responsible for this. Our writers, for instance, concede the principle that the king is the servant of the people and there is no sin in killing a tyrant. A good many theories and books could have come in the field, if the problem of rigicide had been viewed purely from the secular point of view. What are the duties of the king in his capacity as the servant of the people, what are the secular remedies for the people, if the king begins to behave autocratically, under what circumstances would people be justified in withholding allegiance or the payment of taxes, how public opinion was to make itself felt, what were the different milder remedies that people could adopt before they had recourse to rigicide, how were they to be made effective in the face of the police and military forces of the king,—these and similar questions would have given rise to a number of divergent theories, resulting in a rich literature extending over several centuries.But this could not happen, because our writers looked at the question from the religious and moral point of view. The king was to be a virtuous ruler, devoted heart and soul to the welfare of the people; if he was not such, then gods will punish him. The subjects had no secular remedies feasible in normal times ; gods were expected to destroy a bad king. Sometimes it is stated that he should be killed like a mad dog, but how, by whom, and under what circumstances is not explained. Abstruse thinking and daring speculation which is characteristic of Hindu thought in other departments like philosophy and poetics are strangely enough conspicuous by their absence in the works on the science of polity.

Epigraphical evidence shows that there existed considerable divergence in the country in the sphere of taxation and local government. New taxes were introduced by the different states in the course of time and the local government institutions developed on different lines in the various provinces of India. New books could have been written discussing these developments. But this did not happen, probably because taxation and local government were governed by local traditions, which were not usually incorporated in the standard works on polity.

The administrative machinery of the Guptas considerably differed from that of the Mauryas ; fresh developments took place in this sphere under Harsha, as also under the rule of the early medieval dynasties. Books could have been written bearing upon the changes that were taking place in the administrative machinery. But this also did not happen. Probably the students of the political science felt that these were minor changes of details which were not sufficiently important to warrant the composition of fresh books.

It has been suggested that the foreign invasions and alien

rule during *c.* 200 B. C. to 300 A. D. may have been responsible for the dearth of the political literature in the post-Kauṭilya period. This, however, appears improbable ; the dominions of the Greeks, the Scythians, the Parthians and the Kushāṇas did not extend beyond the Punjab for any appreciable time. Madhyadeśa and Bihar, which were the centre of Aryan culture from *c.* 500 B. C. remained practically unaffected by the foreign conquests.

To conclude, the relative sterility in political literature in the first millenium of the Christian era seems to be due to the great sway which the classical work of Kauṭilya continued to have over the public mind and the absence of any noteworthy development in the sphere of the political thought or government machinery. A few manuals, with no particular claim to originality, were of course composed during this period and we shall briefly refer to them after a few remarks about the state of affairs in South India.

South India in the early period did not produce any important works on polity. We get only occasional references on the government of the day from such literary works as the *Tirukkural*, and the *Silappadikaram*. But they usually refer to the king and his officers and hardly throw any light either on the political theories or on the administrative structure as a whole.

The great fascination which Kauṭilya had over his successors is well illustrated by *Kāmandakīya Nītisāra*, composed probably in the Gupta age (*c.* 500 A. D.). This book is nothing but a metrical summary of the work of Kauṭilya. Obviously its anonymous writer felt that the best service he could render to the students of politics would be to summarise this standard work in the popular Anushṭub metre, so that it could be easily memorised by the student. The work, however, does not at all describe the administrative machinery. The king and his courtiers dominate the picture, showing the great importance that monarchy had acquired by this time. Kauṭilya's chapter on republican states is omitted, probably because they were no longer in existence. Civil, criminal and personal law are completely left out, probably because the Smṛiti writers of this period had specialised in this branch. Jayaswal attributed the work to Ṣikharasvāmin, a minister of Chandragupta II ; his arguments however are not convincing. Vishākhadatta and Daṇḍin do not refer to the work but Vāmana (*c.* 800 A.D.) knows it. Its time may be somewhere between 500 and 700 A. D.

The *Nītivākyāmṛita* is also a colourless summary of earlier political thought ; it is somewhat interesting as it proceeds from the pen of a Jain author, Somadevasūri (*c.* 960 A. D.)

The *Śukranīti*, whose date is rather uncertain, is the next work to be considered. It is very important for the student of ancient Indian polity. Like other works of the class, it does not occupy itself with theoretical discussion of the principles of polity or government, but it gives us a more detailed and comprehensive picture of the administrative machinery than is given by any other work of the post-Kauṭilya epoch. Its polity is of course monarchical, republics having disappeared long before the date of the work. Besides discussing the duties of the king and the functions of his ministers and officers the work describes the problems of foreign policy and methods of warfare. Civil administration is described in very great details. We get a vivid picture of the judicial administration. The four popular courts are referred to ; substantive law is however not dealt with. The state as envisaged by Ṣukra was an organisation for the welfare of the subjects. It was not only to suppress crime and disorder, but to control gambling and drinking. It was to maintain hospitals and rest-houses and encourage learning and scholarship. It was to increase the resources of the country by encouraging trade, developing mines, forests and industries and executing schemes of irrigation.

In several respects the work supplies information not to be found in other works on polity. Interesting and minute details are given about the seating arrangements in the royal court on formal occasions (II, 70-71) and about different grades of feudatories and their incomes (I, 282-83). The portfolios of different ministers are given in this work for the first time ; it enables us to have a clear picture of the day to day working of ministry with the assistance of the secretaries and under the control of the king

(II, 109-10). Unlike any other work, Śukra gives us the percentage of the state income to be spent on different items (I, 316-17). The section dealing with the army administration (IV, Sect. VII) gives us the most comprehensive picture of the army organisation,—how the soldiers were to be recruited, trained and paid, how martial types of elephants and horses were to be selected, how weapons were to be manufactured or procured, etc.

Widely divergent views are held about the date of the *Śukranīti*. G. Oppert placed it even in the pre-Christian period; Dr. U. N Ghosal thinks that the work was written between 1200 and 1600 A. D. and the view of R. L. Mitra was similar. The fact is that the work is a composite one and was being retouched down to the 14th century; but its greater part has to be ascribed to the 11th or the 12th century A. D.. The statement that the Mlechchhas resided in the north-west of India, the reference to Sāmantas as both feudatories and officials, (I. 189), the information that the price of gold was 16 times that of silver (IV. 2. 92), as stated by Bhāskarāchārya, the inclusion of Deśabhāshās (vernaculars) as topics of study (IV.3.30), the reference to the Advaita Vedānta doctrine of Śaṅkara (IV. 3. 50), the injunction that peace should be made even with an Anārya, because otherwise he may uproot the kingdom (IV. 7. 243), the enunciation of the principle that the treasury should have a reserve equal to 20 years revenue (IV. 2. 23), which was obviously followed by Hindu kings of the 11th century as shown by the accounts of the plunder obtained from their treasuries by Muslim conquerors,—all these tend to show that the book as a whole belongs to the period between 900 and 1200. The verses dealing with firearms and gunpowder (IV. 7. 195-213; I. 231; II. 95 and 195) may have been added by the end of the 14th century, when gunpowder is known to have been used by the army of Vijayanagar.[1]

The *Bārhaspatya Arthaśāstra* is a small, unimportant and late booklet, doing justice neither to its subject nor to the reputation of

1. *E. C.* VIII Sa. 68; Sh. 433; Saletore, *Social and Political Life in Vijayanagar*, p. 430.

its supposed author. Like some of the earlier Smṛitis, a few later Smṛitis also occasionally deal with administration, but their treatment is quite perfunctory.[1] The Purāṇas of the Gupta and post-Gupta period also deal with State and Government, but disclose no originality of thought or treatment.[2]

From *c.* 1000 A. D. originality disappeared from most of the branches of Indian learning, and the science of polity was no exception. From *c.* 1000 A. D. to 1700 A. D. a number of compendiums were written giving a comprehensive treatment of Dharma in its different branches ; *rājanīti* or politics also formed a section of most of these works. As important works of this class, we may mention *Abhilashitārthachintāmaṇi* (1st four chapters) of Someśvara, *Yuktikalpataru* of Bhoja (*c.* 1025 A. D.), *Rājanītikalpataru* of Lakshmīdhara (*c.* 1125 A. D.), *Rājanītikāṇda* of Devaṇa-bhaṭṭa (*c.* 1300 A. D.), *Rājanītiratnākara* of Chaṇḍeśvara (*c.* 1325 A. D.), *Āmuktamālyada* of king Krishṇadevarāya of Vijayanagar dynasty, *c.* 1525 A.D. *Nītimayukha* of Nilakaṇṭha (*c.* 1625 A.D.) and *Rājanītiprakāśa* of Mitramiśra (*c.* 1650 A.D.). Most of these works are written from the theological rather than from the political point of view. Thus the *Rājanītiprakāśa* devotes as many as 100 pages to the description of the coronation ceremony. The *Nītimayūkha* gives detailed instructions to the king as to how he should cleanse himself, shave and bathe, what he should do if there are bad dreams and omens, and what different *śāntis* he should perform to avert different calamities. We have got sections in these works dealing with ministers, forts, treasury, foreign policy, war, etc. But there is nothing new about them. We usually get only a collection of quotations from earlier writers bearing upon these and similar topics.

Of the above mentioned works, we may review in detail the *Mānasollāsa or Abhilashitārtha chintāmaṇi*, as a typical work of the class; it was composed by the Chālukya king Someśvara (1125-1138 A. D.) Though written by a ruler, it is most disappointing as a book on Polity. Of its hundred chapters

1. See, for instance, *Vṛiddha-Hārita-Smṛiti*, Chap. VII, *Brihat-Pārāśara*, Chap. X.
2. See, for instance, *Agnipurāṇa*, Chaps. 218-42, *Garuḍapurāṇa*, Chaps. 108-115, *Matsya-purāṇa*, Chaps. 215-43 *Mārkaṇḍeya*, Chap. 24.

as many as 60 deal with the king's luxuries, amusements and pastimes (*upabhogas, pramoḍas* and *krīḍās*) and only the first forty deal with the aquisition of a kingdom and its stabilisation. But even here the viewpoint is more religious than secular. Among the best means of gaining a kingdom figure the telling of the truth, the observance of sex morality, the offering of Śrāddha and the going on pilgrimage. The royal author is more anxious to display his knowledge of other subjects than that of the science of politics and seizes every opportunity to make unjustified digressions. While dealing with the health of the king, he gives a long list of tonics; while referring to the duties of the treasurer, he gives the multiplication tables, rules of three and five, etc. (II. 99-123). The author is less anxious to give instructions about the training of war elephants and more particular to give details about their abodes and varieties (II. 172-331). While dealing with the army we have large sections on the medical treatment of horses and elephants (II. 529-674). The section on treasury gives less information about the principles of taxation and its varieties and more details about the qualities and types of pearls, diamonds, etc. (II. 361-516). While dealing with military operations, we have a very detailed discussion of good and bad omens to be inferred from the position of stars and planets and the notes and cries of crows, dogs and jackals (II. 753-948).

As to purely political topics, the qualities of the kings, the qualifications of ministers (I, 54 ff.) and the duties of the treasurer, chamberlain and royal physician are mentioned, but there is nothing noteworthy about them. The same is the case about the discussion of the foreign policy. Occasionally however we get some interesting information. We are told that it was the duty of the foreign minister to summon feudatories at proper intervals in order to check their actions and policies (II. 128). It appears that forts were provisioned with snakes (kept in jars), tigers and other carnivorous animals, which were let loose when the enemy beseiged them (II. 555). Detailed lists are given about the weapons of the army (II. 681 ff.). The author allows destruction of crops, burning of towns and villages, imprisonment of enemy citizens, etc, during the course of the war.

The book is on the whole quite disappointing as a treatise on political science and shows that the manual-writers of this period had hardly any genuine interest in the science of politics ; they were mainly occupied with the task of describing the hobbies, luxuries and pastimes of the king. The political science in the real sense of the term had ceased to be cultivated.

The same tendency is illustrated by a few works on polity written in vernaculars at this time. For instance, a manual on political science was written in Marathi in *c.* 1680 by Ramchandra Pant Amātya, a minister of Shivāji, for the guidance of the latter's son, but it shows no originality of thought. These works, therefore, possess very little intrinsic value to the student of the political science. Original thinking had come to an end for reasons already explained.

Other Original Sources.

Apart from the works on Nītiśāstra, there are a number of other books in Sanskrit, Pali and Prākṛita literatures that incidentally throw light on the science of polity. As shown already, (p. 5) a number of hymns in the *Ṛigveda* and the *Atharvaveda* and passages in the *Śātapatha*, *Aitareya*, *Taittirīya* and *Pañchaviṁśa Brāhmaṇas* are very valuable to the student of the subject. The importance of these passages is considerably enhanced by the circumstance that they refer to an early period when the literature on polity and administration had not yet come into existence. The Dharmasūtras and Smṛitis have usually important sections dealing with the duties of kings and the working of administration ; these, however, are usually written from the religious viewpoint. A few chapters on these topics occur in some Purāṇas ; but they usually summarise the Smṛiti views and are not therefore very important. Works like the *Pratijñāyaugandharāyaṇa*, the *Raghuvaṁśa* and the *Mālavikāgnimitra*, the *Pañchatantrà*, the *Hitopadeśa*, the *Kādambarī*, the *Harshacharit*, the *Daśakumāracharit* and the *Rājataraṅgiṇī* have important though often small passages giving us a valuable glimpse into the contemporary political theory or administration.

The *Ācharāṅgasūtra* (in Prākṛita) and the *Digghanikāya*, the *Chullavagga*, the *Divyāvadāna* and the *Jātakas* in Pāli have important passages throwing light especially on the nature and working of ancient Indian republics.

Stone and copper inscriptions of ancient India are an extremely important source of information to the student of the political science, though unfortunately they have not yet been adequately utilised by the previous writers on the subject. Being written by the court poets, they sometimes give an idealistic picture, but a discerning student can well differentiate between the courtly praise and prosaic facts. To a very great extent the inscriptions represent the actual state of affairs in the government machinery of the different administrations and enable us to ascertain facts and aspects sometimes altogether neglected in the works on Nitīśāstra. They are very useful in acquiring a correct picture of the territorial divisions and the official heirarchy of the different administrations. They give us a valuable insight into the taxation prevailing under different dynasties, when they enumerate the taxes from which the donees were exempted. They give us a graphic idea of the inter-state relations, as also of the relation between the suzerain and his feudatories. They often enunciate interesting maxims about the aims and ideals of government and the duties of kings and responsibilities of ministers. The reader of the following pages can easily visualise the important part they play in enabling us to get a realistic picture of ancient Indian administration.

The accounts of Greek historians, especially relating to the the invasion of Alexander the Great, are very valuable for getting a glimpse into city states and republics. Megasthenes' *Indica*, though fragmentary, is of very great value to the student of the Mauryan administration.

Numismatics or the science of coins is also not without some value to the student of polity. The coin legends often disclose the existence of a number of city states, not otherwise known to us. The existence of the republican constitutions of the Śibis, the Mālavas, the Arjunāyanas, the Kuṇidas, the Yaudheyas and the Lichchhavis is proved or confirmed by coin legends.

The sources above enumerated have now enabled us to fill a number of gaps in our knowledge of ancient Indian polity. We can give a tolerably realistic and comprehensive picture of the subject in the following pages.

CHAPTER II

ORIGIN AND TYPES OF THE STATE

Modern works on polity devote considerable space to the discussion of the question of the origin of the State. No contemporary evidence is available or is ever likely to be available to enlighten us on the point. While we possess ample evidence to show how some particular states originated among people already accustomed to political life, we have only the uncertain light of legends and mythology to visualise the circumstances under which men for the first time associated themselves into a political organisation. We are, therefore, left more or less to speculate on the problem. The modern speculation, however, is largely influenced by the scientific method and the theory of evolution, and seeks to fortify its conclusions by such analogies as can be drawn from the known condition of societies, which are more or less in an uncivilised condition at the present time. We should not forget that this line of approach was unknown to the ancients, whether of the East or the West. Most institutions were regarded in ancient India as due to divine agency or inspiration and the State was no exception to this rule.

We have occasional speculations on the origin of the State in the *Mahābhārata*[1] and the *Digghanikāya*,[2] and though these works belong to different centuries and religions, their version shows a marked similarity. They both aver that for a long time after the creation of society, there prevailed a golden age of harmony and happiness, when people led happy and peaceful lives on account of their innate virtuous disposition, though there existed no government to see that the laws of nature were respected and followed. Popular imagination has dreamt of a golden age in the dim and distant past not only in the East but also in the West. Plato's Republic may well be regarded as the idealisa-

1. Śāntiparvan, chap. 58.
2. Vol. III, pp. 84-96.

tion of such a Golden Age ; the actual state could be only a faint copy of the ideal one delineated by him. As late as the 18th century, Rousseau held that the era of the Golden Age had disappeared many many centuries ago ; the utmost that men could do today was to try to realise it to some extent in the present imperfect society[1]

The Śāntiparvan[2] goes on to narrate that society flourished without a king or law court for a long time, but later somehow there was a moral degeneration. People fell from rectitude; greed, selfishness and cupidity began to sway their mind and the earthly paradise which they had been enjoying was soon converted into a veritable hell. The law of the jungle began to prevail ; the strong devoured the weak, as is the order of the day among the fish (*mātsyanyāya*). Gods then became alarmed and decided to remedy the situation, when men went out in a deputation to pray for relief. Brahmadeva, the chief god, thought over the matter and came to the conclusion that human society can survive only if a code of law was framed and enforced through the instrumentality of a king. He composed a comprehensive code, created an asexual son named Virajas, appointed him king and men agreed to obey his orders.[2]

Elsewhere in the Śāntiparvan (Ch. 67) we have a slightly divergent account of the origin of the state, which seems to refer to an unsuccessful contract at one stage. People were tired of the law of the jungle which prevailed for a long time, and

1. It is averred by some observers that even during the 19th century there existed some primitive civilisations in the hearts of Africa and Australia, which led a happy and harmonious life in spite of the absence of any government among them. It is, however, not unlikely that the observations may have been incomplete and onesided owing to the difficulty of language or the shortness of the stay.

2. नियतस्त्वं नरव्याघ्र शृणु सर्वमशेषतः ।
यथा राज्यं समुत्पन्नमादौ कृतयुगेऽभवत् ॥ 58. 12.
न वै राज्यं न राजासीन्न च दण्डो न दाण्डिकः ।
धर्मेण च प्रजाः सर्वा रक्षन्ति स्म परस्परम् ॥
पाल्यमानास्तथान्योन्यं नरा धर्मेण भारत ॥ १४ ॥
दैन्यं परमुपाजग्मुस्तस्तस्मान्मोह आविशत् ।
प्रतिपत्तिविमोहाच्च धर्मस्तेषामनीनशत् ॥
कामो नामापरस्तत्र प्रत्यपद्यत वै प्रभो । १६ ॥

entered into a mutual contract that persons guilty of unsocial acts like misappropriation and adultery would be expelled from society. We are expressly told that in order to inspire mutual confidence, they entered into a universal social contract to guarantee the agreement. We are however told that people still continued to be unhappy, probably because there was no king or government to enforce the contract. They then approached the Creator with a request to appoint a king, who on the one hand, should be worth the reverence of the community and on the other, should be able to protect the people. The Creator straightway appointed Manu as the king.[1] To rule over a refractory populace was however distasteful to him and he did not like to undertake the job. Here the epic does not refer to the Creator solving the difficulty by composing a law code ; continuing the atmosphere of the theory of Social Contract it states that people themselves assured Manu that law would be followed and the sin would go the law-breakers and not to the king for punishing them. They further agreed to pay the necessary taxes.[2]

These divergent theories would show that the Great Epic is merely speculating about the origin of the state. According to both the theories God helped the humanity to escape from the law of the jungle by giving it a king. But one of theories refers to an apparently unfructuous earlier social contract, which however failed to put an end to anarchy before a God-appointed king appeared on the scene to restore law and order.

The accounts in the *Mahābhārata* show that the state was regarded as a divine institution; king's right to govern was partly due

1. वाक्शूरो दंडपुरुषो यश्च स्यात्पारजायिकः।
यः परश्चमथादद्यात्त्याज्या नस्तादृशा इति॥ 67. 18
विश्वासार्थं च सर्वेषां वर्णानामविशेषतः।
तास्तथा समयं कृत्वा समयेनावतस्थिरे॥
सहितास्तास्तदा जग्मुरसुखार्ताः पितामहम्।
अनीश्वरा विनश्यामो भगवन्नीश्वरं दिश॥ 20
यं पूजयेम संभूय यश्च नः प्रतिपालयेत्।
ततो मनुं व्यादिदेश मनुर्नाभिनन्दिताः॥

2. तमब्रुवन्प्रजा मा भैः कर्त्तॄ नेनो गमिष्यति।
घान्यस्य दशमं भागं दास्यामः कोशवर्घनम्॥ *Ibid* 23

to his divine creation and partly due to the agreement of the subjects to be governed by him in order to terminate the anarchy.

We may passingly note that the theory of the divine origin of State was widely held in Europe under the influence of the Christian dogma, especially in the Middle Ages, when the king was regarded as the annointed representative of God, ruling by divine right. Islam also shared a similar view, for it regarded king as the shadow of God.

The version of the *Dīghanikāya*[1] resembles the above account to a great extent. Buddhists did not believe in God and so Brahmadeva as the creator of the first king and code does naturally not figure in it. But we are told that in the dim and distant past, there was a golden age, when men who had ethereal and refulgent bodies, lived in virtue and happiness. Somehow there was a fall from this ideal state ; there arose anarchy and chaos, and people wondered how to put an end to it. Eventually there arose on the scene a person named Mahājanasammata (lit. one acceptable to the great community), who was born asexually. He was wise, virtuous and able, and the public requested him to become their king and to put an end to the prevailing chaos. He acceded to their request and people then elected him to be their king, agreeing to give him a part of their paddy in return for his services.

Jinasena, a Jain author of the 9th century, also holds that the earth was a paradise (*bhogabhūmi*) in the distant past, when all human wants were satisfied by desire-yielding trees (*kalpa-vṛikshas*). These latter, however, gradually disappeared and there was a chaos. But order was soon restored by the first Tīrthaṅkara, Ṛishabhanātha, who introduced kings, officers castes and professions.[2]

Let us now take a review of the opinions of other writers on politics. Kauṭilya refers to the problem of the origin of the state only incidentally during a discussion of spies among themselves. One party there argues that government came into existence to counteract the law of the jungle that prevailed in

1. Vol. III, pp. 84-6.
2. *Ādipurāṇa,* III. 30 ff.

society. People themselves selected Manu as their king and agreed to pay him the necessary taxes (I. 13). The work does not make any reference to any Golden Age existing in prehistoric times. Nārada (I. 1-2) and Bṛihaspati (I. 1-16) postulate the original existence of a Golden Age and point out that it soon came to an end and was succeeded by a social chaos. Government came into existence to put an end to it. They do not enter into any detailed discussion of the problem. Śukra has no useful observations to make about the origin of the state. He recognises a quasi-divinity in the case of a virtuous king ; this may suggest that he was not much inclined to believe in the theory of Golden Age or social contract.

A survey of the above passages shows that whatever may be the state of affairs in the mythical past, Hindu thinkers held that State was an indispensable institution for the orderly existence and progress of society in the imperfect world as known to us in historic times ; a country without government cannot even exist.[1] The idea of a primeval Golden Age is accepted only in some sections of the *Mahābhārata* and Buddhist literature. Writers on polity only toy with it for some time and hasten to point out that it was soon succeeded by a social chaos, which was terminated only when God gave a king to society. They thus regarded State as a divine institution, implying thereby that it is as old as society and owed its origin to that socio-political instinct which is twin-born with man.

The *Mahābhārata* implies that people accepted Virajas as king ; the *Digghanikāya* expressly states that Mahājanasammata accepted the people's request to put an end to anarchy and thereupon people elected him to be their king. There is no doubt a notion here of government coming into existence as a result of some implied contract. Some such idea seems to have been also in the mind of the Dharmasūtra writers, when they aver that the king is a servant of the people charged with the duty of protection, 16% tax being his wage.[2] Hindu writers,

1. अराजकं नाम रठ्ठं पालेतुं न सक्का । *Jātaka*, VI, p. 39.

2. षड्भागभृतो राजा रक्षेत्प्रजाम् ॥ *B. D. S.* I, 10, 6.

however, do not further develop the theory of contract, as was done in the West. Probably they had realised that it could not be fully applicable to the origin of government and society. These come into existence out of conditions primarily arising from the sociability inherent in human nature.

It is now generally recognised that the contract theory of the origin of government is bad history and worse logic ; it can no doubt explain the origin of a particular form of state among people who have already developed governmental institutions, but it cannot explain how the first agreement took place among the members of a community, which was still in the state of nature. Contract is possible only in a society where mutual rights and obligations are respected, and this is obviously impossible in a society where the law of the jungle prevails.

It would be, however, interesting to compare ancient Indian theory of contract with similar theories advanced in the west. The theory is rarely referred to by ancient thinkers of Greece and Rome ; it is worked out in detail only in the post-Reformation period. Hobbes and Locke are its important advocates.

Like most of the ancient Indian thinkers, Hobbes held that there was a state of anarchy in the beginning, the hand of each being against all. Tired of this state, people eventually agreed to surrender part of their rights to the sovereign. It was not, however, a contract between the sovereign on one side and the people on the other. It was merely an agreement among the people, which imposed no obligation upon the sovereign, who however got unlimited and irrevocable rights under it. Hindu writers also, like Hobbes, have presupposed a contract, which eventually put an end to the law of the jungle ; but it was not a contract which imposed obligations only on the people. The first king Virajas got no unlimited rights under it ; his powers were restricted by the Code of Law prepared by Brahmadeva for him. The same was the case with his son Kardama and grandson Anaṅga. The latter's son Vena was a tyrant, but the sages destroyed him by their supernatural powers. Vena's son Pṛithu was however brave and law-abiding and he willingly took the vow to rule righteously, as required by the sages. It would be thus seen that the king who came into power after the agreement among the people and at the intervention of divine power, was far from being a law unto himself, as was the case with the king as conceived by Hobbes.

According to Locke, the state of Nature in the pre-government period was more or less analogous to the Golden Age of the Hindu mythology. People as a general rule obeyed the laws of reason and nature, and respected one another's person and property. Society had thus come into existence, but not government. When, however, occasional breaches of law occurred, each individual could act both as a judge and executor of his own decrees, which created certain inconveniences. Though the law of Nature was known to all, still owing to difference of intelligence and conflicts of interests disputes arose as to the method of its enforcement, which gave rise to confusion and uncertainty in life. To put an end to it people entered into a covenant, surrendered their right to enforce the law of Nature and organised a government which was also bound by the terms of the original contract. Hindu writers vaguely suggest that somehow there was a fall from the Golden Age of the primeval period, owing to greed getting the upper hand in human nature. How the greed once absent from human nature began to warp it, they cannot explain, just as Locke cannot explain how in a society where the laws of reason prevailed, there were occasional breaches of its provisions and how, when they occurred, every party in the transaction could act both as the judge and the executor. Locke makes the provisions of the original contract binding on the king. Hindu writers seek to regulate his powers by the provisions of the original divine code.

It will thus be seen that the desire to put an end to anarchy and evolve a better type of society and government are stated to be the chief grounds for people entering into the original contract, that brought government into existence.[1] Western

1. Rousseau, however, is an exception in this connection. His State of Nature described in the *Discourse on Inequality* is as happy and idealistic as that of the Kṛita Yuga of the ancient Hindus; but he differs from them in postulating that the political organisation was introduced not as a means of escape from an intole-

thinkers, however, looked at the problem from a purely secular point of view; it is well-known how the views of some of them were unconsciously influenced by people's struggle against autocracy that was then in full swing in some countries. They, therefore, are anxious to thrash the idea of contract threadbare, initiate fundamental principles of political association, define the authority of the sovereign and prescribe the conditions under which popular obedience would be expected, and discuss whether the transfer of power by the people to the sovereign is irrevocable or otherwise. Ancient Indian writers did not live in an age of rationalism like Locke and Rousseau; they looked at the question from a semi-religious and semi-sociological point of view. They have, therefore, neither gone deep into the fundamentals of the problem, nor defined precisely the limits of the powers of the state and the people. They observe, for instance, that people offer obedience and taxation in return for the protection and services they expect from the government. If the king's government fails in its duty, they permit the people to remove the king, and even to kill him. But what precisely will constitute a breach of the contract on the part of government, and what is the secular constitutional machinery by which people can enforce the performance of the terms of the original contract is nowhere clearly described. The permission to remove a tyrant or to kill him no doubt assumes the ultimate soveriegnty of the people and invests them with supreme authority. This remedy, however, is drastic and difficult; it would have been more useful if our authorities had recommended a less extreme but more practicable remedy in the form of an everyday constitutional check. We should not, however, forget that such a remedy has been perfected even in the West only in the modern age.

There are various other theories advocated about the origin of State by modern writers. It is argued that people in the distant

rable condition, but as a means of conserving rights that were naturally enjoyed by men in the State of Nature. Cocker, *Readings in Political Philosophy*, p. 478.

The rise of the State was thus due according to Rousseau to the general will of the people; according to the *Mahābhārata* it was due to the Code of Brahmā and the willingness of the people and king to follow it.

past willingly entrusted government powers to an individual, either because he was a priest who could ensure divine help and favours, or because he was a magician who could command rain, or because he was a doctor who could cure patients. It is suggested that individuals who thus happened to gain ascendancy over the minds of their contemporaries, managed to retain it by the use of force, which they could exercise with ease owing to their pre-eminent position, already recognised on a large scale. It is quite possible that in some primitive societies government may have actually arisen owing to the operation of the above factors. But as far as the Indo-European communities are concerned, the institution of the patriarchal joint family seems to have been the germ out of which State was gradually evolved. The evidence of the comparative philology shows that even when the Aryans were in their original home, they were living in joint families consisting of the grandfather, father, uncles, nephews, sons and daughters-in-law.[1] The evidence of Homer shows that these joint families were sometimes so big as to include two or three hundred persons.[2] The patriarch of the joint family wielded very wide powers over its members ; he could pledge, sell, amputate and even kill any person under his potestas for an offence committed by him. The Roman patriarch possessed these powers ; some Vedic legends also show that the father could blind or sell a guilty son by virtue of his patriarchal authority.[3] The position of the patriarch in prehistoric times was more or less like that of a king amongst all the Indo-European communities. His jurisdiction increased, though perhaps his powers diminished, as the joint family expanded into a big federation of several natural families, springing from a common ancestor, real or imaginary, and living

1. Words for the uncle, the nephew, the father-in-law, the mother-in-law and the daughter-in-law are derived from common roots in most Indo-European languages.

2. Priam had fifty sons and twelve daughters ; they lived with their parents in a common home along with their wives, husbands and children.

3. *R V.* I. 116.16 tells us how Aśvins restored the eyesight of Ṛijrāśva, who was blinded by his father, exasperated to find that his son had permitted his hundred sheep to be devoured by a wolf. Śunaśśepa had been sold by his father to save the family from starvation (*A. Br.* VII. 15).

in the same village. The senior member of the senior-most family in such a village was regarded with great reverence by the whole community and used to be entrusted with most of the governmental functions to be discharged, no doubt, in consultation with other elder persons of the locality. The Ṛigvedic evidence shows that the Aryan society in that early period was divided into families, *janmans*, *viśas* and *janas*.[1] *Janmans* seem to have corresponded to a village consisting of people claiming a common descent, and a number of such villages joined together by a bond of kinship seem to have constituted a *viś* ; its chief was known as a *viśpati*. *Viśas* were closely knit together, and on the battle fields battalions were often arranged as per *viś* from which they had been recruited (*R. V.*, *X*, 84, 4). Several *viśas* made a *jana* or tribe, which had its own *janapati* or the king. This organisation among the Vedic Aryans shows a striking resemblance to the condition prevailing in Rome in early days. There the smallest unit, gens, consisted of a small number of families descended from a common ancestor; a number of these gens constituted a curia and ten curiae made a tribe. Vedic *jana* probably corresponded with the tribe, *viś* with the curia and *janman* with the gen.

The available evidence thus shows that as among other Indo-Aryan communities, State was evolved in India also in pre-historic times out of the institution of the joint family. The patriarch of the family was instinctively revered and obeyed ; and social traditions and atmosphere inspired a similar respect for, and evoked a similar obedience to the head of the village and tribe, who generally acquired the status of chiefs and kings. The power of the kings gradually became more and more extensive as states became larger and larger.

The institution of the joint family thus gradually led to the evolution of kingship. It also presupposed the rise and acceptance of the notion of family property, and also of the inviolability of the sacred family ties and relationships, especially connected with the institution of marriage. Molestation of women

1. स इज्जनेन स विशा स जन्मना स पुत्रैर्वाजं भरते धनानृभिः II. 26. 3.

had to be stopped and the peaceful enjoyment of property had to be ensured. This could be guaranteed only by the rise of the Institution of State. The institution of the family with the notion of the family property thus played its own part in the origin of the State.

TYPE OF STATES

Let us now see what were the different types of states existing in ancient India. Ancient constitutional writers hardly discuss this problem. This is probably due to their having flourished in an age when monarchy had become the prevailing type of State. Had a book on *daṇḍanīti* been written by a citizen of an aristocratic or republican state, we might have got some interesting discussion about the nature and types of different states like monarchy, aristocracy and republics and their relative merits and defects. But curiously enough this does not seem to have happened.

Our writers again and again revolve round the same type of state, viz., monarchy ; only a few of them passingly refer to the *Saṅgha* (republican) state. We have shown already how for a long time the state was tribal. Apart from the frequent references to *viśpatis* and *janapatis* the *Ṛigveda* (*c.* 2500 B. C.) frequently refers to specific tribes like the Yadus, the Purus, the Anus, the Turvaśas, etc. Viśvāmitra's prayers are said to have protected the Bharata people;[1] in the Rājasūya sacrifice, the king is announced as the ruler of the Bharatas or the Kuru-Pañchālas and not as the sovereign of a particular province or kingdom. The notion of a *rāshṭra* or a territorial state, however, was being gradually evolved in the later Vedic period ; we find it clearly referred to in the *Atharvaveda*.[2] The *Taittirīya Saṁhitā*[3] refers to a ritual, a partial performance of which could secure a king the over-lordship over his tribe (*viś*), but not over the country (*rāshṭra*). The Brāhmaṇa literature frequently refers to the

1. विश्वामित्रस्य रक्षति ब्रह्मेदं भारतं जनम् । III. 53. 2
2. XX. 127.9-10 ; XIX. 30. 3-4 ; III. 4, 2 ; VI. 98. 2
3. II. 3. 3-4.

emperors as the rulers not over all the tribes but over the whole earth bounded by the sea. It is clear that the notion of the territorial state was fully established at this time (*c.* 1000 B. C.)

Monarchy was the normal form of the State in the Vedic period, *rājā* (a king), *mahārāja* (a great king), *samrāṭ* (an emperor) are the different terms by which kings were designated according to their power and prestige. Some of them were also called *svarājas* and *bhojas* ; probably they were feudatories and zemindars.

In the description of the coronation, the ritual is sometimes described as securing *rājya*, *svarājya*, *bhaujya*, *vairājya*, *mahārājya* and *sāmrājya* to one and the same individual.[1] A doubt, therefore, naturally arises as to whether these terms really denoted different types of states or monarchies. It is, however, not unlikely that it is the desire to emphasise the omnipotence of the ritual that is responsible for the priest claiming that the king who is receiving the holy coronation from him, can attain to all the different positions referred to above. This conjecture becomes more probable when we remember that a passage in the *Aitareya Brāhmaṇa* states that the different types of States like *rājya bhaujya*, *vairājya*, and *sāmrājya* flourished in different provinces of the country.[2]

In the later Indian history we always come across a large number of kings, enjoying different degrees of autonomy and ruling as feudatories of an emperor (*samrāṭ*). It is not unlikely that such feudatories existed in the Vedic period as well ; they may have been known as *bhojas* and *svarājas* and their feudal lords as *samrāṭs*. The territorial extent of the dominion of a *samrāt*, as compared to that of *svarāṭ*, cannot be difinitely determined. Most of the states in Vedic period were small ; it is doubtful whether there was a state big enough to extend over a quarter of the Punjab. The dominion of a *samrāṭ* was perhaps not much bigger than that of an ordinary king. Military glory and achievements were probably more responsible for his

1. *A. Br.*, VIII, 2.6; VIII, 3, 13.
2. *A. Br.*, VIII, 3, 14.

higher title than the extent of his dominion. Rājya probably denoted a smaller but independent kingdom. The statement in the *Aitareya Brāhmaṇa* that kings were common in the Madhyadeśa and emperors in Eastern India would support our interpretation. *Vairājya* denoted a republic, a state which had no king.

States where the principal executive authority was vested in two rulers as in ancient Sparta were not unknown in ancient India. One such state existed at Paṭala in Sindh in Alexander's days, where the sovereignty was vested in two different kings hailing from different houses.[1] The *Arthaśāstra* (VIII. 2) also refers to such a state ; probably it used to come into existence when two brothers or cousins, being claimants to the same kingdom, preferred to rule it jointly instead of dividing it into two parts. But just as two swords cannot remain in the same scabbard, two kings can hardly rule in harmony ,when the power of each is unlimited and extends over the same kingdom. Such a state must have been often torn by factions and parties supporting the power of each ruler ; one can, therefore, well understand why the *Arthaśāstra*[2] does not approve of it, and why a Jain monk is advised not to travel through or stay in it. To avoid discord, very often the brother or cousin rulers of a *dvairājya* state would divide the kingdom between them, as was done in the *dvairājya* kingdom, created in Vidarbha by the Śuṅgas.[3] It would appear that though the kingdom was divided, the two rulers would hold joint consultations on all important matters. When the two kings were ruling in harmony, the state was called a two-kings-state (*dorajja* in Prakrit and *dvirājaka* in Sanskrit) ; when they were pulling in opposite directions, it was called a self-fighting state (*virudharajja* in Prakrit and *viruddharājya* in Sanskrit).[4]

1. Mc Crindle, *Alexander's Invasion*, p. 296
2. द्वैराज्यमन्योन्यपक्षद्वेषानुरागाभ्यां परस्परसंघर्षेण वा विनश्यति । VIII. 2
3. *Mālavikāgnimitra*, Act V, v. 13.
4. अरायणि वा गणरायणि वा जुवरायणि वा दोरज्जणि वा बेरज्जणि वा विरुद्धरज्जणि वा । *Āchārāṅga-Sūtra*, II, 3, 1, 10.

The Vedic literature sometimes refers to *kings* meeting together in an assembly;[1] we are also told that that person alone can become a *king* who is permitted to become one by other kings.[2] These passages probably refer to the existence of an oligarchy, where power was vested in a council of nobles, each member of which was entitled to call himself a kin and had a right to elect the chief of the state, who also was called a king. We shall see later how this type of the state continued to exist down to the 6th century B. C. in some parts of North-Eastern India.

Side by side with monarchical and oligarchical states, there also existed republican governments in ancient India as early as the Vedic age. A passage in the *Aitareya Brāhmaṇa* states that the people in the vicinity of the Himalayas like the Uttarakurus and the Uttaramadras have a *virāṭ* (kingless) type of the state and are, therefore, called *vi-rāṭ* or kingless. When it is remembered how the same passage earlier refers to the *kings* of the easterners and the southerners and the titles that were borne by them, and how it carefully states that it is the *people* among the Uttarakurus and Uttaramadras,—not their kings,—who were called *virāṭ*, it becomes quite certain that these people had a non-monarchical or republican form of government. This conclusion is further strengthened when we remember how Greek authorities tell us that in the territory above referred to, republican types of states were the order of the day as late as the time of Alexander the Great. Whether the non-monarchical states of ancient India were also republican will be discussed later in Chap. VI.

The city state was another feature of the political life in the early period. We get some account of its constitution and administration from the Greek writers. Arrian describes Nyasa as a free city state flourishing at the time of the invasion of Alexander the Great ; its President, when out to meet the Macedo-

1. यत्रोषधीः समग्मत राजानः समिताविव । *R. V.*, X. 97. 6.

2. यस्मै वै राजानो राज्यमनुमन्यन्ते स राजा भवति न स यस्मै न । *S. Br.*, IX 3. 2. 5.

nian hero with thirty deputies, said, 'Hcw Oh king, can a single city, if deprived of a hundred of its best men, continue to be well governed?' It is thus clear that Nyasa was not the capital of a kingdom, but a city state, almost entirely dependent upon its own resources. When Diodorus describes how the citizens from the Śibi state offered their submission, upon which Alexander permitted them to retain their freedom, he is obviously referring to the city state of the tribe. Several other city states are referred to by Greek writers; among them we may mention Pimprama of the Adraisti and Sangala of the Kathaians and Patala in Sindh. When the *Mahābhārata* refers to the powerful *grāmas* on the bank of the Indus, it is obviously referring to the powerful city states,[3] some of which are mentioned by the Greek historians. Coins issued by a number of cities like Tripuri, Mādhyamikā, Ujjayinī, Vārāṇasi, Kauśāmbī etc. have come to light.[4] It is quite probable that at some periods of their history they were city states, rather than capitals, issuing coins on their own authority. It was but natural that the city states should have brought under their control some of the outlying villages; but the government was usually carried on by the aristocratic classes in the city itself.

Composite and confederate states were not unknown to ancient India. The Kurupañchālas in the later Vedic period seem to have formed one composite state, ruled by a common king. The Kshudrakas and the Mālavas were separate states in the days of Pāṇini, but are very frequently mentioned together in the *Mahābhārata*. They had formed a confederation to meet the invasion of Alexander the Great, and it seems to have lasted for about a century. The alliance had been cemented by 10,000 intermarriages. The Yaudheya republican state seems to have comprised three sub-states. These confederations often lasted for short periods; in the life-time of the Buddha and Mahāvīra, the

1. McCrindle, *Invasion of Alexander the Great*, p. 81.
2. *Ibid*, p. 285.
3. सिंधकूलाश्रिता ये च ग्रामणीया महाबलाः II. 32. 9.
4. *J. N. S. I.*, XIII, pp. 40-45.

Lichchhavis had formed a confederation, once with the Mallas and once with the Videhas. The Lichchhavi-Malla federal council consisted of 18 members, nine being elected by each of the confederating state. We do not, however, possess sufficient information to indicate how these composite or confederate states were functioning,—what powers were retained by the federating units and what authority was delegated to the federal centre. It, however, seems very probable that the jurisdiction of the central government of the confederating states was confined only to foreign policy and the declaration and prosecution of war. Otherwise each state retained its sovereignty. The general for the joint army in a particular campaign was elected by the confederating states ; in the campaign against Alexander the Great, Kshudrakas and Mālavas had elected a Kshudraka generalissimo, who was famous for his skill and bravery.

Normally, however, states in ancient India were unitary in character. King was the fountain source from which the ministers and provincial governors derived their power. Village Panchayats, town-councils and trade-guilds also were under the general supervision and control of the central government. Long established tradition had, however, limited the state's intervention in the autonomy of these bodies only to those rare occasions when they were guilty of a breach of their traditional rules and constitutions. The unitary character of the the state in ancient India was, therefore, to a great extent modified by the presence of these autonomous bodies, which used to function on their own lines, though revolutions occurred at the centre.

CHAPTER III

NATURE, AIMS AND FUNCTIONS OF THE STATE

We saw in the last chapter how the state came into existence in ancient India and what were the different theories advocated about its origin. Let us now see what according to the ancient Indians were to be the nature, aims and functions of the state.

While discussing the origin of the state in the last chapter, we have passingly referred to the conception of ancient Indians about the nature of the state. They regarded it as essentially a beneficient institution evolved in prehistoric times for the efficient protection of human life and for the better realisation of its higher ideals. The idea that it was a necessary evil to be tolerated, as there was no other alternative, was not subscribed to by any ancient Indian thinker.

State was no doubt an unwelcome institution to evil-doers, but they had no right to expect that their convenience and feelings should be respected by society, which they were out to disorganise and destroy.

It is owing to the presence of this anti-social element that *daṇḍa* or force becomes the ultimate sanction of government. Ancient Indian thinkers do not desire that *daṇḍa* should make its appearance, every now and then ; on the other hand they regard that state as an ideal one where its exercise is rendered almost unnecessary by the willingness of the people to accept the scheme of a righteous life, determined by the code given to humanity by God. This code was binding alike upon the people and the king. If the people were to be guilty of its breach, they were to be punished by the king. If the latter contravened its provisions, he would forfeit his subjects' allegiance, who would be at liberty even to kill him if necessary. In the ideal state both the king and the subjects were expected to follow the provisions of the divine code for peace and prosperity both here and in the life to come.

The historic method being then unknown, the evolution of the state through various stages is not discussed by ancient Indian writers. The available evidence, however, shows that the state in the early Vedic period was still tribal. The Yadus, the Turvaśas and the Bharatas, for instance, who played a prominent part in the Vedic history, had for a long time no permanent territorial basis for their states ; the latter moved along with the peoples of their tribes and had thus only a tribal basis. In the later Vedic period, however, the state became territorial ; we have clear references to the different tribes settling down in the different parts of the country,[1] and to kings becoming masters both of their people as well as their country (*rāshṭra*).[2] In the later Vedic period the emperor is described as one who rules over the earth bounded by the oceans.[3] The different stages, however, by which the state gradually became territorial cannot be clearly visualised from the scanty evidence available to us at present.

What are to be the constituents of a territorial state and how are they inter-related and held together is the question that we have to consider next.

Vedic literature does not enable us to get any idea of what were the contemporary notions about this topic ; we, however, begin to get welcome light from *c.* 4th century B.C., when the political thought had become fairly developed. Both Kauṭilya (VI, 1) and Manu (IX. 294-7) held that the state was not a loose assemblage of parts, each having its own interests and moving at its own will ; it was characterised by an organic unity. The king, the ministry, the territory, the resources, the forts, the military forces and the allies constitute, according to these writers, the seven constituents of the state.[4] Later writers like Kāmandaka (I. 10) and Śukra (I, 122-4) regard this as a self-evident truth, and epigraphs also often describe

1. *A. Br.*, VII. 3. 14. 2. *T. S.*, II. 3. 3-4
3. *A. Br.*, VII. 3. 14.
4. Some of these seven constituents like the king, the ministers, and high officials (*ratnins*), forts (*purah*) and resources (*bali*) are no doubt mentioned in the Vedic literature, but their mutual relationship as well as their relation to the state have not been discussed there as in later works on the political science.

how the kingdoms acquired by the heroes, whom they eulogise, possessed all the seven constituents.[1]

Let us now compare these constituents of the ancient Indian state with those postulated by modern thinkers. According to the latter territory population and central government having a juristic personality, a common will and sovereign powers, are the main constituents of the state.

Let us now see how far any of these constituents find their counterpart in ancient Indian list of the seven constituents, given above.

Of the seven constituents, *svāmin* (king) and *amātyas* (ministers) constituted the central government, which exercised the sovereign powers and imparted the central unity. *Rāshṭra* (territory), *durgas* (forts), *bala* (army) and *kosha* (treasury) constituted the resources of the state. The stage of the tribal state had long passed,[2] and so territory was regarded as an essential element of the state. Forts and armed forces were vitally necessary to defend the very existence of the state and so are regarded as its essential constituents. The defence of the country and the proper discharge of the constituent and ministrant functions of the state required ample resources, and so *kosha* (treasury) is also regarded as indispensable to the very existence of the state. The inclusion of its allies among the constituents of a state strikes us as rather strange. The existence of a state, however, depends, as contemporary history has been showing in a forcible manner, upon its securing a proper balance of power by making suitable alliances. A large number of small states existed in the Indian sub-continent, and our political thinkers felt that the existence of none could be guaranteed for a long time unless a proper balance of power was secured by wise alliances. It is a little

1. *E. C.*, V. Channarayapattana, 149 (1183 A. D.).

2. The Mālava state was to the north-east of Multan in *c.* 325 B. C., in the Ajmer-Udaipur tract in *c.* 200 B. C. and in modern Mālwā about 400 years later. These migrations were however due to political pressure and were exception and not the rule for the contemporary times.

3. We must not forget that our writers wrote when aeroplanes and atomic bombs did not exist; forts could, down to the 19th century, defy mighty armies for a number of months and years.

surprising to note that population as such is not mentioned as one of the constituents of the state ; that was probably because it was realised that it was too evident a truth to be specifically mentioned.

The seven constituents of the state are regarded as the limbs (*aṅgas*) of the body politic by the Indian thinkers. Some of them like the king and the ministers may be more prominent than others like the forts and the allies.[1] Each limb, however, though by itself it may look unimportant, is indispensable to the body politic, for its functions cannot be efficiently discharged by any other.[2] The state can exist and function properly only if all the limbs of its body politic become mutally integrated and cooperate with each other.[3] No limb of the body politic can strictly be regarded as more important than any other. The body politic cannot stand if one of them is missing, just as three sticks poised properly against one another will collapse, if one of them is taken away.[4]

It is thus clear that ancient Indian thinkers regarded the state as an organic whole. They no doubt regarded the king and the government as the most important limbs of the organism, but others, if less important, were also indispensable for the proper functioning of the body politic. We should not also forget to note that the organic conception of the state is only partially true. The cells and limbs of an organism have no separate

1. It cannot be argued that this assumption militates against the organic conception of the state ; for in human body too, some limbs like the brain and the eyes, are more important than others like the ears or hands.

2. तेषु तेषु तु कृत्येषु तत्तदंगं विशिष्यते ।
येन यत्साध्यते कर्म तस्मिंस्तच्छ्रेष्ठमुच्यते ॥ *Manu*, IX, 297.

3. परस्परोपकारीदं सप्तांगं राज्यमुच्यते । *Kāmandaka*, IV, 1.
स्वाम्यमात्यजनपददुर्गकोशदंडमित्राणि प्रकृतयः ।
अरिवर्जाः प्रकृतयः सप्तैताः स्वगुणोदयाः ।
उक्ताः प्रत्यंगभूतास्ताः प्रकृता राज्यसंपदः । *Arthaśāstra*, VI, 1.

4. सप्तांगस्येह राज्यस्य विष्टब्धस्य त्रिदण्डवत् ।
अन्योन्यगुणवैशेष्यान्न किंचिदतिरिच्यते ॥ *Manu*, IX, 296.

existence of their own and cannot function independently. Such is obviously not the case with at least some of the constituents of the state. Forts and resources can exist independently and may be wielded into a new state by some groups of the subjects, who may not be able to see eye to eye with the old government.

Our authorities devote considerable space to describe the seven constituents of the state referred to above, and the excellences and strong points that should be developed in each. Of these the forts and the armed forces need not detain us, as they are constitutionally unimportant. The king, the ministry, the resources and the allies will be discussed in later chapters dealings with the Kinghsip (Chap. V), the Ministry (Chap. VII), Income and Expenditure (Chap. XIII) and Interestate Relations (Chap. XIV) respectively. As far as the territory is concerned, our authorities point out that the prosperity of a state will to a great extent depend upon the natural resources of its territory and the ease with which it can be defended. It must of course be populated by an energetic and industrious population, for the character of its people determines the destiny of a state more than any other fact or consideration. The territorial size of an ideal state is not discussed by our authorities. They, however, regarded the whole country from the Himalayas to the sea as the proper sphere for the activity of an emperor. As far as the smaller kingdoms were concerned, there were no natural boundaries in India to separate them in most cases ; they were usually small enough to be well-governed and large enough to be self-sufficient.

Whether an ideal state should consist of people of exclusively one nationality, having the same race, religion and language, or whether it can be a composite political unit of people of different nationalities, belonging to diverse races, professing many creeds and speaking several languages is a question which has not been discussed by ancient Indian thinkers. This need not surprise us, because it did not arise at all in the ancient period. It is true that a number of foreigners like the Greeks, the Parthians, the Scythians, the Kushāṇas and the Hūṇas invaded and conquered the country and settled down in it as its governors. But they did not remain foreign nationals with a different language, religion and culture for a long time. Within a generation or two all of them used to become completely Indianised and converted into Hinduism or Buddhism. They did not create any problems for the Indian states. The latter used to repose implicit confidence in their new Indianised subjects,[1] who also used to entertain no extra-territorial loyalties.

A state no doubt becomes homogenous if there is unity of language, race and religion among its subjects. Ancient Indian writers have not emphasised upon this point, because there was no necessity whatsoever to do so. Most of the states in ancient India did not differ from their neighbours either in race or in language or in religion. Hindus, Buddhists and Jains lived in all states peacefully and harmoniously. Sanskrit was the international language and Prakrits had not differentiated from one another to such a degree as to become mutually unintelligible. All the foreigners who were coming into the country, used to be rapidly Indianised and completely absorbed into the Hindu community. Thus the different states in ancient India did not at all differ in race, language or religion. Most of them had developed into separate entities primarily owing to individual ambition, administrative convenience or geographical considerations. It did not, therefore occur to our thinkers that they should emphasise upon the advisability of racial, linguistic or religious uniformity in the population of a state.

The Aims of the State

The Vedic literature does not specifically discuss the aims or ideals of the state. Incidental observations made therein, however, enable us to gather that peace, order, security and justice were regarded as the fundamental aims of the state. The king or the head of the state was to be like god Varuṇa,

1. Aśoka had appointed a Greek named Tushāspa as a viceroy over the frontier province of Kathiawar, though there was a Greek kingdom in Persia and Bactria at that time. The Scythian Rudradāman had appointed a Parthian named Suvishākha as his governor over the same province in *c.* 150 A. D., even though the Parthians were then in power in Persia.

the upholder of the law and order (*dhṛitavrata*) ; he was to punish the wicked and help the virtuous. Religion was to be promoted, morality was to be encouraged and education was to be patronised.[1] The state, however, was to secure not only the moral but also the material wellbeing of its citizens. The kingdom of king Parīkshit, idealised in the *Atharvaveda* (XX. 127), flowed with milk and honey. All round welfare of the public was clearly regarded as the chief aim of the state during the Vedic and Upanishadic ages, *i.e.* down to *c.* 600 B. C.

When the literature on politics proper began to be developed, we find that promotion of *dharma*, *artha* and *kāma* are usually mentioned as the aims of the state. The state was to promote *dharma*, not by championing any particular sect or religion, but by fostering a feeling of piety and religiousness, by encouraging virtue and morality, by extending help to the establishments belonging to all religions and sects, by maintaining free hospitals and feeding houses for the poor and the decrepits and last but not least, by extending patronage to literature and sciences. The promotion of *artha* was to be procured by encouraging trade, industry and agriculture, by developing national resources, by bringing fresh land under cultivation, by building dams and canals to make agriculture independent of rain, and by encouraging extensive and systematic working of mines. The state was to promote *kāma* by ensuring peace and order, so that each individual may enjoy life undisturbed, and by offering encouragement to fine arts like music, dancing, painting, sculpture and architecture in rder to promote aesthetic culture. The state was thus expected to maintain peace and order and promote moral, material and aesthetic progress of society.

Our writers have thus practically recognised the ideal of perfect development of the individual to the full development

1. न मे स्तेनो जनपदे न कदर्यो न मद्यपो नानाहिताग्निर्नाविद्वान्न स्वैरी स्वैरिणी कुतः। *Cha. U.*, V. 11. 5.

2. कृपणानाथवृद्धानां विधवानां च योषिताम्।
योगक्षेमं च वृत्तिं च नित्यमेव प्रकल्पयेत्॥ *Mbh*, XII, 86, 24.

of the society, when they laid down that it was the business of the state to promote Dharma, Artha, Kāma and Moksha ; only they have not used the modern terminology. The ideal of *sarvabhūtahita*, which is emphasised in several places, refers not only to the spiritual but also to the mundane sphere.

The inclusion of the promotion of *dharma* among the aims of the state has given rise to a considerable misunderstanding in modern times, which has been to some extent caused by the habit of later writers of describing the king as the champion of *varṇas* and *āśramas*. It is contended[1] that *varṇadharma* or the caste-system in particular is based upon iniquitous principles ; it exhalts the Brāhmaṇa and confers almost divine honours upon him, while it reduces the Śūdras and Chāṇḍālas almost to the position of slaves, denying them the most elementary rights of ordinary citizenship. The Śūdras were prevented from holding property and were subjected to more heavier punishments than those meted out to the Brāhamaṇas for identical offences. The Chāṇḍālas were treated worse than dogs. When the state became a champion of *varṇas* and *āśramas*, it became a party to all these iniquities. It enforced the iniquitous *varṇāśrma-dharma* at the point of the sword to the detriment of the lower classes. It was thus based upon social injustice. It confounded *dharma* with the existing iniquitous social order. It idealised the actual instead of trying to actualise the ideal.

The above criticism is mostly based upon a misunderstanding of the factors that have promoted the development of the Hindu social institutions. Customs and traditions changed in ancient India by the silent operation of social approval or disapproval and not by the noisy process of a legislative enactment or repeal. The state only enforced what had been previously approved by the social conscience. When society in early period was sanctioning intercaste dinners and marriages, the state had no objection to them. When later on it disapproved both these practices,

1. Anjaria, *The Nature and Ground of Political Obligation in Hindu State*, pp. 175-188.

the state did not propose to encourage them. In early days widows had no right of inheritance ; the property of a person having no heir other than a widow escheated to the state. Later on society decided to recognise widow as an heir of her deceased husband, and though this change adversely affected the interest of the excheqor, the state cheerfully sanctioned it. The recognition of the promotion of *dharma* as one of the duties of the state did not result in the apotheosis of the *status quo* ; every student of Hindu social institution will concede that changes were gradually and continously taking place in them. Levirate (*niyoga*), once approved, was later stamped out of existence ; not only the proprietary rights of women, but also those of the Śūdras were being constantly enlarged in spite of the opposition of the earlier writers.

It would, therefore, be unfair to attribute the existence of certain iniquities in the Hindu social order to *dharma* being considered as one of the aims of the Hindu state. The state no doubt claimed to be the champion of *varṇadharma*, but it did not support the Brāhmaṇas' claim to their exemption from the taxation and the capital punishment. It is extremely doubtful whether many cases had occurred in ancient India of the state punishing the Śūdras and Brāhmaṇa women for presuming to study the Vedas. The prohibition was regarded by the society, including the Śūdras, as divinely ordained, and as there was no material benefit whatsoever to be gained by its violation, there was no incentive to break it. The number of Brāhmaṇas themselves, who studied the Vedas, was microscopically small and provision was made to meet the needs of the religiously minded persons among the Śūdras and Brāhmaṇa women by throwing open the epics, the *Gītā* and the Purāṇas to them.

There is no doubt that some iniquities existed in the Hindu social order and their number increased in the first millennium of the Christian era. But that was due to the narrowmindedness of the Hindu society of that age and not to the state's making *dharma* as one of its aims. Of course it can be argued that the state should have given a lead in the matter by encouraging a more liberal policy. We should, however, not forget that legislation did not come within the normal activities of the state. Recent experience in our country about the Sharda Act also shows that legislation, far in advance of the social views on the point, tends to remain dead letter. The state was not interested in enforcing caste iniquities ; if any cases actually arose, they must have been decided by the caste or the village Panchāyats, which were purely non-official bodies. The state sought to encourage *dharma* by promoting piety and religiousness, by extending equal patronage to all sects and religions and their establishments and by financing works of public utility like tanks, canals, wells, poor houses and hospitals, and not by becoming an instrument in the hands of the church or the priests.

Was the ancient Indian State Theocratic ?

It would be convenient here to examine how far the ancient Indian state was under the influence of theology and to what extent it can be described as theocratic. A theocracy may arise when a king usurps the functions of the Church, as was the case with the Khalifas, or when the head of the Church becomes the king as is the case with the Dalai Lama of Tibet and the Pope of the Vatican kingdom. Or, the king may be a mere agent or instrument of the church, as was the case for some time in Europe during the 8th and the 9th centuries A. D. The Pope and the bishops at this time claimed the right to punish the king, if he was not ruling according to the will of God. Some rulers like Charles the Bold admitted the right and even the duty of the prelates to suspend the execution of the orders of the state regarded as objectionable by them. Orders of the Pope were to be regarded as of greater moment and validity than those of the Emperor, as they had the authority over the soul as well. Of course, the majority of the emperors were not disposed to recognise this claim and the early medieval European history presents an interesting tussle between the Church and the State.

Faint echoes of a similar conflict between the king and the church can be heard in the early Indian literature. *Gautama-Dharmasūtra* (*c.* 500 B. C.) claims that the royal authority does not touch the priest[1] and reminds the king that he can prosper only if supported by the latter. If he does not employ a qualified Brāhmaṇa priest, says the *Aitareya Brāhmaṇa*,[2] gods will not at all accept his oblations. At the time of the coronation, the king three times bows before the Brāhmaṇa ; he thereby accepts his subordinate position, and as long as he does so, he will prosper.[3] Priests like Vasishṭha exercised profound influence of the royal court. Rituals were also devised to ensure the subordination of the Kshatriyas and the Vaiśyas to the Brāhmaṇas.[4] In the *Ṛigveda* there is a clear passage to show that a king, who honoured his chaplain properly, could secure an easy mastery over his subjects and a smashing defeat over his enemies.[5] In Europe the Pope claimed the right to confirm thc election of the emperor made by the nobles ; we do not know whether such a right was advanced in ancient India.

The above evidence shows that down to the end of the Brāhmaṇa period (*c.* 1000 B. C.) the priests tried to extend their sway over the monarch and through him over the state. It is natural that many kings, should have opposed this tendency ; the bitter curses that are pronounced against the rulers who confiscate the cows, *i.e.* the wealth of the Brāhmaṇa[6], seem to be directed against those monarchs who were opposing the efforts of the priests to forge a theocratic state, where their voice was to reign supreme. Unfortunately we have no detailed information about any specific and individual cases, as we have in the case of early medieval Europe.

1. राजा वै सर्वस्येष्टे ब्राह्मणवर्जम् । I. 11.
2. न वै अपुरोहितस्य देवा बलिमश्नुवन्ति । *A. Br.*, VII. 5, 24.
3. स (नृपः) यन्नमो ब्रह्मणे इति······त्रिष्कृत्वो ब्रह्मणे नमस्करोति ब्रह्मण एव तत्क्षत्रं वशमेति तद्राष्ट्रं समृद्धं तद्वीरवदाह। *A. Br.* VIII. 1.
4. तद्यत्र वै ब्रह्मणः क्षत्रं वशमेति तद्राष्ट्रं समृद्धं तद्वीरवदाह । *A. Br.* VIII. 9 ब्रह्मणे क्षत्रं च विशं चानुगे करोति *P. Br.* XI, 11, 1.
5. तस्मिन्विशः स्वयमेवानमन्त यस्मिन्ब्रह्मा राजनि पूर्वमेति । स इद्राजा प्रतिजन्यानि विश्वा शुष्मेण तस्थौ अभि वीर्येण। *R.V.* IV, 50-7-9
6. *A. V.*, XII, 5; XIII. 3. 1-25.

In the course of time, however, the church and the state or the Brāhmaṇas and the Kshatriyas made up their quarrel. It was realised that the two could prosper only if they cooperated with each other. Each conceded a qualified divinity to the other, as both realised that they could prosper only if there was a complete harmony between them. It is interesting to note that this view agrees closely with that of Gregory VII, who maintained that the kingship and the Popedom were both divine, their position being comparable to that of the two eyes of the human body.

The general trend of the evidence of the Brahmanical literature is to show that the prince or the state was under the leading strings of the Brāhmaṇas or the church. The royal chaplain (*purohita*) knew rituals which could either promote or retard the welfare of the king and the state. The aim of the government, as shown already, was to promote *dharma*, and the laws which it enforced were regarded as divine in origin or inspiration. *Varṇāśramadharma*, which the state had to enforce, was largely moulded by the priests, who were the writers of the books on the subject. They not only claimed to be above the state, but they also put forth the right for exemption from taxation and capital punishment. The punishments that could be given to them were to be milder than those to be inflicted upon others. The appointment of the *dharmamahāmātras* by the Mauryas and the *vinayasthitisthāpakas* by the Guptas to regulate religious practices and moral conduct of the population would be a natural corollary of the swing towards theocracy.

There is, therefore, a considerable force in the view that the ancient Indian state was theocratic to a great extent. We should, however, note the limits to the theocracy and the period during which it was operative. The claims that have been put forth on behalf of the Brāhmaṇas in the Brahamanical literature are to a great extent exaggerated. They represent the wish more than the reality. There is no doubt that the influence of the royal chaplain over the king was great during the age of the Vedas and the Brāhmaṇas. Its extent, however, should not be judged merely by the implications of the passages referred to above. For there are other passages in the Brāhamaṇa literature itself, which give the other side of the picture. A passage in the *Taittirīya Brāhmaṇa* confesses that a king, at his sweet will, can lord it over the Brāhmaṇas.[1] Another in the *Aitareya Brāhmaṇa* admits that a king can expel the Brāhmaṇas at will[2]. The *Bṛihadāraṇyaka Upanishad* states that it is the Kshatriya or the king who enjoys the highest status in society ; the Brāhmaṇa sits lower than and next to him[3] When princess Śarmishṭhā suspected that Devāyanī, the daughter of the royal chaplain, was assuming an air of superiority, she sharply reprimanded her:—'Enough of presumptuousness. Sitting in a humbler place your father goes on flattering my father day and night. You are the daughter of him who begs and flatters, I am the daughter of him who donates and is praised.[4]

It would, therefore, be wrong to suppose that even in the Vedic period, the king or the state was under the leading strings of the Brāhmaṇa or the Church. Generally speaking the priest was treated with decorum ; the spiritual help offered by his rituals and sacrifices was welcome. But the king was far from becoming a mere instrument in the hands of the priest ; he could show him his proper place or even expel him, if he tended to become presumptuous. Brāhmaṇas no doubt claimed a number of privileges including exemption from the taxation and the capital punishment, but it will be shown in Chap. XIII how they existed more in their law books than in actual practice. In the course of time, the divinity of the king was re-

1. यदा वै राजा कामयते अथ ब्राह्मणं जिनाति । III. 9. 14.
2. (ब्राह्मणः) आदायी आप्यायी अवसायी यथाकामं प्रयाप्यः । VII. 29.
3. तस्मात्क्षत्रात्परं नास्ति तस्माद्ब्राह्मणः क्षत्रियमधस्तादुपास्ते । I. 4. 10.
4. आसीनं च शयानं च पिता ते पितरं मम ।
स्तौति बन्दीव चाभीक्ष्णं नीचैः स्थित्वा विनीतवत् ॥
याचतस्त्वं हि दुहिता स्तुवतः प्रतिगृह्णतः ।
सुताहं स्तूयमानस्य ददतोऽप्रतिगृह्णतः ॥ *Mbh.* I. 72. 9-10.

cognised as will be shown in Chap. V. This, however, did not make the king infallible or even the sole interpreter of the divine will. Laws, though regarded as divine, were really based upon social customs and traditions. By sanctioning their operation, the state did not become an instrument in the hands of the Church or the priests ; it rather became the mouthpiece of the social will.

From about the 4th century B. C. the influence of theology on the state began to decline further. The Vedic sacrifices themselves fell into disgrace and disuse, which naturally undermined the influence of the chaplain . Politics developed into a special science and princes naturally studied it assiduously in preference to the Vedic lore or the Upanishadic philosophy. Positive law began to be differentiated from religious rituals and traditional customs ; and the school of politics began to aver that the former was more important than the latter.[1] Hindu polity thus succeeded in emancipating itself from the leading strings of theology by the beginning of the Christian era. The king was no doubt regarded as the protector and enforcer of Dharma, but we have shown already how this did not make the state theocratic. His duty was to promote piety and religiousness by extending equal patronage to all sects and religions and to enforce customary laws approved by the social conscience ; he discharged this function through officers like the *dharmamahāmātras* and the *vinayasthitisthāpakas*. He was not to be an agent of a particular religion or sect working to promote its interests or seeking to carry out its commands. The crusade of a Hindu state against Bauddhism or Jainism is rarely met with in ancient Indian history.

THE INFLUENCE OF RELIGIOUS CONCEPTS ON POLITY

The influence of theological, religious and philosophical

1. धर्मश्च व्यवहारश्च चरित्रं राजशासनम् ।
विवादार्थश्चतुष्पादः पश्चिमः पूर्वबाधकः ॥ *Arthaśāstra* III. 1.
धर्मशास्त्रविरोधे तु युक्तियुक्तो विधिः स्मृतः ।
व्यवहारो हि बलवान्धर्मस्तेनावहीयते ॥ *Nārada* I. 41.

concepts on Hindu polity may be briefly noticed here. The concept of Dharma as the ultimate and supreme power was responsible for the king being struck by the Dharmadaṇḍa thrice on the occasion of his coronation ; it was also responsible for the exhortation to him to lead his whole life as dedicated to duty, *dhṛitavrata*. The duties of the king were conceived as Rājadharma. The violation of Dharma was ultimately punishable by God. So the king became ultimately accountable to God, who was to punish him in a suitable manner ; our political writers therefore usually did not encourage the subjects to seek to punish the king for his delinquencies. This concept of the supremacy of Dharma prevented the development of a reasoned philosophy of the rights of the people or opposition to tyranny.

The doctrine of Karman also has left some influence on the polity. At one stage of its development this doctrine believed in the possibility of an individual's *karman* being transferrable to another ; the political thinkers therefore regarded it as possible for the sages to pay off their dues to the state by transferring one sixth of their *puṇya* or merit to it. The threat that was held out to the king that if he misgoverned, the sin ofthe crimes of the subjects would be visited on him was also another corollary of the same doctrine. The usual view however was that a person reaps as he sows ; this was responsible for the threat of a long sojourn in hell held before a vicious king or a false witness. Three days' respite that Aśoka had granted to condemned criminals was for the purpose of enabling them or their relations to undertake pious acts, so that the criminals may benefit by them after their execution.

The theory of the supremacy of the moral order suggested the ideal of a moral state which should have no sinners or thieves among its subjects. It was also responsible for the enunciation of the code of righteous war, *dharma-yuddha*, which was followed to some extent at one stage of our history. The state was to strive for the realisation of the moral and religious ideals along with those in the spheres of social and economic life. It was thus to secure both the moral and material development of the people and the country.

The theory that God is omnipresent and is the giver of all good things has left its own influence here and there on the polity. The *Gītā* preaches that whatever is preëminent, striking or brilliant is particularly surcharged with the Divine Presence and illustrates the point by recognising the divinity in the king.

Alternatively the king began to be regarded as Divine Guardian. When the theory of incarnation became popular, the king was regarded as an incarnation of Vishṇu. Some kings (e.g. king Gautamīputra of the Bhita seal, *c.* 1st century A. D.) regarded their kingdom as a gift from God ; other states like the republic of the Yaudheyas regarded themselves as presided over by their favourite deity like Kārtikeya, though there is no evidence to show that the rulers in these cases regarded themselves as agents of God. All this was a natutal consequence of regarding God as the giver of all good things and protector of all good persons or states.

The gospel of *Aparigraha* is responsible for the ideal of self-denial placed before the king. The freedom from taxation that was conceded to pious and poor Brāhmaṇas was due to the view that those who practised *aparigraha* should not be made to bear avoidable economic burdens.

The Vedāntic doctrine that soul is identical with or similar to God should have led to the spread of the doctrine of social, economic and legal equality. Strangely enough this did not happen. The theory that every thing here is Brahman was effectively counterpoised by the gospel of the caste system, which permitted social and economic inequalities. Buddhism is sometimes assumed (though quite wrongly) to be opposed to the caste system ; but in the Lichchhavi republic which was under marked Buddhist influence, there were sharp economic and political inequalities.

To conclude, we have to admit that religious and philosophical dogmas and concepts did not deeply influence the Hindu political thought, practice or institutions.

FUNCTIONS OF THE STATE

Having finished our discussion of the nature and aims of the state, let us now consider its functions.

Modern writers usually divide the functions of the state into two categories, constituent and ministrant. Under the former class fall those functions of the state which are absolutely necessary for the orderly organisation of society, viz., defence against foreign aggression, protection of person and property, preservation of peace and order and adjudication. Under the latter class fall those activities of the state which it undertakes to promote the welfare of the people, to increase their wealth by a cooperative effort, and to add to their amenities of life. Education, sanitation, postal services, trade regulations, roads and communications, development of mines and forests, care of the poor and invalid, etc. would come under the ministrant functions of the state. The modern tendency of the state is to increase its ministrant functions.

The available evidence shows that for a long time the state in ancient India confined itself only to the constituent functions. The Vedic state protected citizens from foreign aggression. It also maintained internal order by enforcing respect for the traditional law. Like Varuṇa, the celestial king, the Vedic monarch was *dharmapati*,[1] the protector and enforcer of law, morality and *dharma*. Even the civil and criminal cases were decided by popular bodies (*sabhīs*) ; whether they were presided over by a royal officer is not definitely known.

With the development of the political literature from *c.* 4th century B. C. , we begin to get greater information about the functions of the state. The evidence of the *Mahābhārata*[2] and the *Arthaśāstra*[3] shows that the sphere of the state activity was very extensively extended between the Vedic and the Mauryan age ; we, however, are unable to trace the different stages of this development owing to the lack of evidence.

1. S. *Br.* V, 3. 3. 6 and 9.
2. Sabhāparvan, Chap. V.
3. Books II.

The activity of the state, as envisaged by the *Mahābhārata* and the *Arthaśāstra*, relates to all the aspects of human life,—social, economic and religious. The state was not regarded as a necessary evil, whose coercive activities were to be reduced to the minimum. The *laissez faire* theory, which advocates that the sphere of the state activity should be reduced to the narrowest functions consistent with the preservation of law and order, was not at all popular. The activity of the state was to embrace the whole of human life, both here and hereafter. The state was to offer facilities to religions and sects to develop on their own lines and foster and inculcate piety, morality and righteousness. It was to improve the social order and to encourage learning, education and art by subsidising learned academies and extending patronage to scholars and artists. It was to establish and maintain rest houses, charity halls and hospitals and relieve the distress due to floods, locusts, famines, pestilences and earthquakes. It was to see that the population is evenly distributed and encourage colonisation of fresh lands. It was to enrich the resources of the country by developing forests, working mines and constructing dams and canals in order to make agriculture independent of rain as far as possible. It was to offer active help to trade and industry, but also to protect the population against capitalistic selfishness, if merchant princes sought to corner the market and raise the prices. It was to regulate the vices of the community by appointing its own officers to supervise over wine booths, gambling houses and prostitutes.

The well-organised governments in ancient India like those under the Mauryas and the Guptas discharged most of the above functions. It is, however, possible that the smaller states may have confined themselves to a restricted sphere of state activities, especially in troubled times.

The jurisdiction of the state in ancient India thus extended over almost all the spheres of life. Did it not interfere with individual liberty? Did it become possible because the very conception of liberty was not properly developed[1] or because people were disposed to accept the state's claim to omniscience or infallibility?

State in ancient India was regarded as the centre of society and the chief instrument for its welfare, and hence it was permitted to have a wide sphere of activity. Individual liberty did not appreciably suffer in consequence, primarily because the state discharged its multifarious functions not exclusively through its own bureaucracy. The market superintendents and trade officers belonged to the state bureaucracy, as also the superintendents of morality, but these worked in close co-operation with trade guilds and Brāhmaṇa or Śramaṇa assemblies, where the voice of the people had the upper hand. The state and its officers only tried to harmonise the divergent interests after full consultation with the guilds and local assemblies, which were more stable institutions than the state itself and, therefore, enjoyed very considerable prestige and confidence. It encouraged education by liberal grants to colleges and universities, but never thought of controlling these institutions by its own Director of Public Instruction and his subordinate staff. It made liberal grants to Hindu temples and Buddhist monasteries, but never cared to dictate the dogmas or tenets that were to be encouraged under their auspices. The principle of decentralisation was carried to a very great extent and extensive powers were delegated to the village *Panchāyats*, city councils and trade guilds; and the state carried on its socialistic activities with the active cooperation of these popular bodies. There was hardly any encroachment on the individual liberty. Ancient Indians permitted the state a wide sphere of activity, not because they did not value individual liberty, but because they felt that state could organise them best by reconciling conflicting interests, if its bureaucracy worked in closer co-operation with well-established popular bodies like the trade guilds and village councils.

1. This is the view of Prof. Anjaria, *Nature and Ground of Political Obligation*, p. 245.

DISTRIBUTION OF FUNCTIONS

In the modern state, the executive, the legislative and the judicial powers and functions are usually distributed in different bodies. In theory the king in ancient India was like the President of the new Indian Republic, the final source of all the executive, legislative and judicial powers. In actual practice, however, the situation differed from age to age. In Vedic age, it would appear that the Samiti or the Parliament shared the executive powers with the king ; in some cases it could overrule him also. The king was the supreme judicial functionary in ancient India from the post-Vedic period ; but in actual practice considerable powers were delegated to the local popular courts or Panchāyats. Kings and Government officers usually declined to entertain a suit at first instance. The Parliament or the popular assembly disappeared as an effective body in the post-Vedic period ; this led to the increase in the influence and authority of the king in executive and administrative matters. Legislation in the modern sense of the term was not the function of the Samiti in ancient India ; laws, if secular, were sanctioned by custom and if religious, by the sacred texts. For a very long time the Ancient Indian State used to enforce laws which were not formally approved by any limb of its body politic. The scheme of taxation also was usually the one approved by the usage of the land, as codified in the Smṛitis. The Smṛitis however permitted a considerable variation in the incidence of taxation ; the land tax could be anything between 12 to 33%. The actual amount of the tax could thus be varied by the executive, which usually meant the king and the officers appointed by him and holding office during his pleasure. There is sufficient evidence to show that kings soon began to claim the power to make ordinances if not laws ; Śukra expressly concedes this power to the king. With the disappearance of the Parliament or Samiti, the executive, the judicial and the legislative powers (as far as they could be exercised by the state) tended to be concentrated in the hands of the king and the ministry nominated by him. The village councils and town corporations, which were largely popular bodies, could successfully contest with the king to some extetnt in the exercise of the judicial, executive and taxation powers in the limited sphere of their jurisdiction, during the Gupta and post-Gupta period.

VESTING OF THE SOVEREIGNTY IN ANCIENT INDIAN STATE

It would be convenient to make a few observations about the vesting of sovereignty in the Ancient Indian State. It has first to be noted that the modern conception of sovereignty was probably not fully developed. There is no Sanskrit term exactly corresponding to it, though *svāmitva* in the *Arthaśāstra* may be partly approaching its meaning. In the Vedic period sovereignty was probably vested jointly in the king and the Samiti; in the republican states it was vested in the Central Executive, which worked under the general superintendence of the republican Parliament, where however only the aristocracy was usually represented. When Samitis or Parliaments disappeared, the sovereignty became vested in the king alone. In the republican state, the presidents tended to become more and more powerful; their posts often became hereditary and they began to enjoy royal titles also. Republics however disappeared from India at *c.* 400 A. D.; and the king's position became very strong from this time.

One school held that the king was not above the law or Dharma; but that the latter constituted the essence of kingship. Dharma was the sovereign over the sovereign[1] and it may therefore be said that the sovereignty vested in it.

But though the king was below the Dharma and was bound by it, though it was the law (Dharma) which made the king, the ancient Indian polity provided no constitutional means or checks to call the king to account if he transgressed the law.

Another school however pronounced the king to be *adaṇḍya* or above punishment.[2] If he broke the law, the punishment

1. तत् (ब्रह्म) श्रेयोरूपमत्यसृजत् धर्मम् । तदेतत्क्षत्रस्य क्षत्रम् यद्धर्मः । तस्माद्धर्मात्परं नास्ति । *S. Br.* 1. 4. 14.

2. अथैनं पृष्ठतः तूष्णीमेव दण्डैर्घ्नंति । तं दण्डैर्घ्नंन्तो दण्डवधमतिनयंति । तस्माद्राजाऽदण्डयो यदेनं दण्डवधमतिनयंति । *Ibid*, V. 4. 7.

was left to God. In extreme cases extra-constitutional remedies like the rebellion or regicide were suggested ; but they were usually impracticable. Village councils and town corporations often enjoyed almost complete freedom in their local affairs ; the courts, whether royal or popular, usually administerd the traditional law as embodied in the *jātidharama* (caste rules), *śreṇidharma* (guild rules) and *janapadadharma* (local customs). But a wilful king could set all these at nought and rule in a tyrannical way, as is shown by the pages of the *Rājataraṅgiṇī* dealing with the history of medieval Kashmir. From *c.* 400 A. D. the sovereignty was vested in the king and it was not controlled by constitutional checks of the modern types. Of course it should not be forgotten that most of these checks were evolved in Europe only in the post-Reformation period.

Manu no doubt pronounces[1] that a king was to pay a fine of a thousand coins when an ordinary man had to pay that of one coin only, but he does not specify the offence, nor indicate the agency which was to try the king. The commentator Kullūka says that the fine was to be self-imposed and was to be given to Brāhmaṇas or to be thrown into water in the name of Varuṇa.[2] It is thus clear that Manu's statement is a merely idealistic one and hardly provides any real and practicable constitutional check.

1. कार्षापणो भवद्दण्डयो यत्रान्यः प्राकृतो जनः ।
तत्र राजा भवेद्दण्डयः सहस्रमिति धारणा । VIII. 336.

2. स्वार्थदण्डं त्वप्सु प्रवेशयेद्ब्रह्मणेभ्यो वा दद्यात् । ईशो दण्डस्य वारुण इति वक्ष्यमाणत्वात् ।

CHAPTER IV

THE STATE AND THE CITIZEN

The question of the relationship between the state and the citizen is undoubtedly an important topic. It was discussed in ancient times only by very few western political thinkers like Aristotle. Since the rise of democracy during the last two centuries, modern writers have begun to devote considerable space to the discussion of the mutual rights and responsibilities of the state and the citizen in the different spheres of the individual and communal life, enquiring whether there is any real conflict between the interests of the two, and if so, how it can be resolved.

Ancient Indian political thinkers have hardly devoted any space to the discussion of these problems, and no wonder. While discussing the relations between the state and the citizen the political science seeks mainly to define the mutual rights of the two parties. Hindu constitutional writers have approached the problem from quite a different point of view. They usually describe not the rights of the citizens, but the duties of the state ; the former are to be inferred from the latter. Similarly they discuss the duties of the citizens, from which we are to indirectly infer the extent of the control the state could exercise over its subjects. In our ancient works, therefore, there is no systematic discussion of the problem from the point of view of the rights of either party.

European writers, whether of the ancient or the modern times, further look at the question from a purely secular and constitutional point of view. They separate the civic and political life of the citizen from his religious and moral life, and define his rights as against the state, which is often assumed to be hostile to them. Ancient Hindu writers, on the other hand, considered the political duties of the citizen as part of his general duties (*dharma*) and assumed that normally there should be no conflict between the state and the citizen, necessitating a clear-cut definition of the rights and obligations of both. The very aim of the state was to promote the all-sided progress of the citizens both in this life and the life to come. If there is no state, there would prevail the law of the jungle. State is thus indispensable for the progress and happiness of the individual, and its main aim is to promote them. What is to be done if the state does not discharge its duties properly or the individuals do not carry out their obligations faithfully has received but scant attention from our ancient thinkers.[1] It was assumed that each party would normally abide by its own *dharma* or duty.

The ancient states in the west like those in Greece and Rome did not look upon all the inhabitants of the kingdom with the same eye. Those who had the right and privilege of actively participating in the government of the state and in making its laws and regulations were called citizens. They were sharply distinguished from the large body of inhabitants who were in a servile or semi-servile condition, hardly possessing any civic or political rights. Aliens formed another class, the members of which did, no doubt, not suffer from any disabilities, but nevertheless did not enjoy the privilege of participating in the constitutional life of the country.

The constitutional writers of ancient India have not made any differentiation among the residents of the country based upon the possession of franchise. We are quite in the dark about the details of the political life in the Vedic period. At that time popular assemblies (*samitis*) existed and controlled the king's activity and powers to a great extent. It is quite possible that not all the inhabitants had the right to become the members of the *samiti* ; only a small section of the population may have had this right, and it may have constituted a privileged class corresponding to the aristocratic order in the modern times or to that of the privileged class in ancient Greece. In the republican states, there existed a privileged aristocracy which appears to have been the custodian of the political rights.

1. See Chap. VII.

But as we have very little evidence to guide us, we can hardly say anything about the rights of this privileged class and its relation to the state on one side and the ordinary inhabitants on the other.

When the curtain rises to reveal to us the historic period from *c.* 500 B. C., we find the *samitis* or the Central Assemblies disappearing from the scene. Our constitutional thinkers, therefore, do not divide the inhabitants into two classes, citizens who possessed franchise for Central Assemblies and others who did not enjoy it. The village councils, town committees and district boroughs, however, developed in a remarkable manner during this period, and their members are frequently referred to. It was however the status, experience and seniority which raised individuals to the executive committees of these bodies, and not a popular election in the modern sense of the term. In south India we definitely know that the members of the village Panchāyats were selected by lot from among people possessing high moral, literary and property qualifications. The villagers, however, had a general assembly which is described as *pūga* in the Smṛiti literature. It consisted of all the village elders, variously described as *mahattaras*, *mahājanas* or *perumāls* in the different parts of the country. This was a truly democratic body because all castes and professions were represented in it, including even the untouchables.[1] As there was no distinction between privileged and non-privileged class in the sphere of the local government, it is not referred to by our constitutional writers.

Distinction between citizens and aliens, which was almost universal in the past and is very prominent in modern times, has not been made by Hindu jurists. This need not surprise us. There was a pervading cultural unity among the different states in the sub-continent of India, and, therefore, a Gauḍa (Bengali) did not appear as an alien to a Lāṭa (Gujarati) or a Kashmirian to a Karnataki. Provincial differences were no doubt developing, but they had not yet become strong enough to

1. See Chap. XI.

induce the independent states in the different parts of the country to impose the restrictions and disabilities of aliens on the inhabitants of adjacent states. Brāhmaṇas from Mahārāshṭra received land grants from the rulers of Gujarat ; poets from Kashmir became court poets in the kingdom of Karnatak ; and soldiers from the Deccan often enlisted in the armies of the rulers of northern India. All this became possible owing to the realisation of the cultural unity of the country, inspite of its division into separate sovereign states.

It is, however, interesting to note that no disabilities seem to have been imposed even upon foreigners as aliens. A Greek was serving as the viceroy of an important frontier province under Aśoka ; a Parthian was serving as a governor under the Śaka king Rudradāman I (*c.* 135 A. D.) and a Hūṇa officer was serving in an important post in the administration of king Yaśovarman (*c.* 725 A. D.) Muslims were permitted to settle down in Western India by the Rāshṭrakūṭas and allowed to have their own officers to administer their personal law.

The non-recognition of the aliens as a separate class was due partly to the catholic spirit of Hinduism and partly to its confidence of completely absorbing the foreigners in its body politic by means of its superior culture. The Greeks, the Scythians, the Kushāṇas and the Hūṇas were all absorbed into Hinduism, though they first came into the country as conquerors. Hindu constitutional writers, therefore, did not think it necessary to differentiate between citizens and aliens.

The right to make the laws, or to elect representatives who will make them, is regarded as an important privilege of the citizens. This notion, however, was not possible in ancient India, because laws, if religious, were regarded as revealed, and if secular, were believed to be determined by customs and traditions. Legislature of the modern type to enact laws in the modern sense of the term did not exist.

In modern times it is regarded as very essential that the state should afford equal opportunities to all its citizens. Very often, however, these opportunities are equal only in theory and rarely in practice. It is, however, contended that in ancient India the state failed to discharge this primary duty, because the different castes had no other alternative but to follow their predetermined professions. There was no doubt full freedom in the spiritual sphere; everybody could attain spiritual summum bonum. But there was hardly any freedom of action in the social sphere or in the selection of professions. There were, therefore, no equal opportunities for all.

This objection is, however, only partially true. The duties of the castes and the professions, which they had to follow, were determined not by the state but by social customs and traditions. When these were permitting full freedom in the choice of professions, as was the case down to *c.* 100 B. C., the state was not pinning down the different castes to certain predetermined professions. Even Kshatriyas and Vaiśyas could become teachers of the Vedas. Later on, however, professions became hereditary and the Smṛitis began to prescribe that the members of the different castes should normally restrict themselves to their ancestral professions. Smṛiti rules in this respect were based upon actual practice, and if there was an absence of equal opportunities to all, the blame lies not on the state, but on the society. It is possible to argue that the state should have carried on active propaganda against these restrictions, but that was hardly possible in an age which believed that they were based upon divine or semi-divine sanction. Epigraphical evidence, however, shows that in spite of the Smṛiti rules, there were many cases in actual practice, where individuals did not follow their hereditary professions; it is to the credit of the state that it did not use its powers to stop such practices and render individual choice altogether impossible. It appears that it was only in the case of the priestly profession that the prohibition was real and effective. No non-Brāhmaṇa was ever permitted to officiate as a priest or to teach the Vedas in the post-Upanishadic times; it is not unlikely that the state may have, on rare occasions, punished the delinquents in this connection. But it should not be forgotten that the privilege to become a priest or a Vedic teacher was really a privilege to beg; the priest's profession no doubt enjoyed a high status but brought a very low and insufficient income. Society further believed that the rule which confined this profession to the Brāhmaṇa caste was divine and its infringement would lead to eternal hell. If the state, therefore, became a party to the enforcement of the rule, which made priestly duty a monopoly for the Brāhmaṇas, it took a step which was acquiesced in by more than 99 per cent of the non-Brāhmaṇas themselves.

Equality of all citizens before the law is one of the fundamental features of a good state according to the modern notions. It has to be admitted that it did not exist in ancient India. Lighter punishments were recommended to the Brāhamaṇas in comparison to the other castes for the same offence. Smṛitis no doubt say that the sin of a guilty Brāhmaṇa is greater than that of a Śūdra and so its spiritual punishment in the other world would be heavier. Our respect for them, however, would have become greater, if they had laid down a heavier punishment for the Brāhmaṇa also in this life, proportionate to his higher sin. In fairness, however, it has to be admitted that this is too much to expect. Everywhere in the world till quite modern times, status determined the punishment of the culprit, if not in theory at least in practice. Only a nominal punishment was imposed on the citizen in ancient Greece and Rome for the murder of a slave. In the Anglo-Saxon times the *wergeld* for the murder of a serf was very small, as compared to that prescribed for the murder of a freeman or a knight. The legal inequalities in France down to the end of the 18th century were very glaring. It is, therefore, rather unreasonable to expect that equality of all before the law should have existed in ancient India in the full measure. Smṛitis have further exaggerated the picture to a great extent ; we know, for instance, that Brāhmaṇas were not in actual practice, exempt from the capital punishment, as Smṛiti-writers would like us to believe. The *Arthaśāstra* shows that they were executed by drowning, if found guilty of treason.

The state ensures protection for the person and property of the citizens and seeks to promote their all round progress. It, therefore, naturally expects the citizens to cooperate with it wholeheartedly by obeying its orders and laws, Ancient Indian thinkers have naturally emphasised this duty. The state in modern time further expects its citizens to fight for it, and even to die for it, if necessary. The ancient Indian state entertained no such expectation with reference to all its citizens in historic times owing to the emergence of the caste system. It was the duty of the Kshatriya to fight and protect ; it was an indelible stigma for him to run from the battle field to save his life. Other castes were to help the state not by fighting on the battlefield, but by providing the sinews of war by the fruits of their labour, trade and industry. The age did not believe in conscription, but in the division of labour.

Village communities, however, inspired intense local patriotism, and scores of cases are on record of people of all classes and castes dying in the defence of the village or its cattle. Numerous *vīrgals* or hero-stones, that are particularly common in the Deccan and south India, show that when the safety of the village was threatened, people from all castes came forward to fight and die for the community ; we sometimes find even women fighting and dying on such occasions.[1]

The normal type of government, envisaged by our constitutional writers, was monarchy. They, therefore, usually emphasise upon the duty of the soldier or the citizen to die for his king, rather than for his country. The same was the case in the west till the emergence of the national state in the modern period.

What may be described as patriotism for the state in the abstract did not much develop in ancient India for obvious reasons.[2] The large number of states into which the country was divided did not usually differ from one another in religion, culture, and language. For instance, the kingdom of Kāśī (Banaras) could hardly be differentiated from that of Kośala (Oudh), or the kingdom of Aṅga (Bhagalpur) from that of Vaṅga (Bengal). There were hardly any natural boundaries

1. *E.I.*, VI, 163 ; *S.I.E.R.*, 1921, No. 73; *E.C.*, I. No. 75.

1. It may be pointed out that the sentiment of national patriotism was practically unknown in Europe before the partition of Poland at the end of the 18th century. See Laski, *Grammar of Politics*, Chapter VI.

dividing the Gāhadwāl, the Chandella and the Chāhamāna kingdoms of the 12th century. The absence of natural boundaries and the presence of a common homogenous culture did not foster any feeling of intense local patriotism. Wars that were taking place were due more to dynastic jealousies or ambitions than to narrow local patriotism. The conqueror moreover was expected to enthrone a relation of the defeated king and respect the local laws and customs. People in general therefore, apart from the ruling classes and the army, did not take keen interest in the fortunes of the wars. From one point of view, it may be argued that they lacked patriotism, but from another point of view, it may be pointed out that they did not develop narrow provincialism. Had the people of about a dozen states, into which India used to be usually divided, developed intense feeling of territorial patriotism, driving them to fly to the throats of one another with the intense hatred of deep-rooted enmity, the cultural unity, which pervades the country at present, would have become impossible.

For India or Bhāratavarsha as a whole Indians did feel a great love and patriotism and whenever its religion, culture and independence were at stake, they came forward to lay down their lives in its defence. No body, who studies the opposition offered to Alexander the Great, can deny the existence of true patriotism in the Indians of the age. Brāhamaṇa philosophers were the leaders of the patriotic movement in lower Sindh and were hanged by the score by Alexander, whose task was becoming more and more arduous on account of the patriotic movement inspired by them.[1] One of them, when taken prisoner and condemned to death, was asked just before his execution as to why he had incited the people and the king to revolt. He boldly replied, 'Because I wished them to live with honour or to die with honour.'[2] Unfortunately we have no authentic account of the opposition offered to the Śakas, the Pahlavas and the Kushāṇas, but such scanty informa-

1. Mc. Crindle, *Ancient India, its Invasion by Alexander the Great*, p. 159-160.
2. *Ibid* p. 314.

tion as we possess shows that the states like those of the Kuṇindas, the Yaudheyas and the Mālavas continued their resistance movement for decades, till they were eventually able to regain ther independence. Important states in northern India joined their resources in order to oust the Hūṇas. When it became clear that the Muslim conquest was a serious threat to the culture and religion of the country, most of the important states in northern India made a common cause under the impulse of patriotism and offered a united front near Peshawar in 1008 A. D. 50,000 Hindus laid down their lives in the defence of the Somanātha temple before Mahmud of Ghazni could force his entry into it in 1024 A. D. Those who thus died for their religion and country no doubt believed intensely that Bhāratavarsha was so holy a land, that *svarga* and *moksha* is possible only by a birth in it and therefore even gods desire to be reborn within its territory.[1] A proverb states that the mother and the mother-country are even greater than heaven[2] and the history of the opposition to foreign aggression shows that Hindus did act up to it.

GROUNDS OF POLITICAL OBLIGATION

The citizen is bound to the state by a number of political obligations and we shall briefly state the grounds which, according to the ancient Indian thinkers, justified their imposition. State was regarded as the only agency that stood between the citizen and the anarchy ; it was, therefore, but meet that he should lend all his support to it and carry out the obligations imposed by its rules and regulations. If the power and prestige of the state were not there, says Manu (VII. 20-24), the strong will fry the weak like fish on the oven, most people will give up their appointed duties, and even dogs

1. कर्मभूमिरियं स्वर्गमपवर्गं च गच्छताम् ।
तत्पुण्यभूमिर्नान्यत्र संप्राप्तिः पुण्यपापयोः ॥
गायन्ति देवाः किल गीतकानि धन्यास्तु ते भारतभूमिभागे ।
स्वर्गापवर्गस्य च हेतुभूतौ भवन्ति भूयः पुरुषाः सुरत्वात् ।
Mārkandeya Purāṇa

2. जननी जन्मभूमिश्च स्वर्गादपि गरीयसी ।

will begin to lick the oblations intended for gods. Even gods discharge their divine functions because they are afraid of the punishment that would otherwise be imposed upon them by the Supreme Creator.

State is thus a necessary institution if the individual is to live according to his Dharma ; it is the coercive authority of the state which produces the automatic mental habit of following one's own Dharma. State in ancient India claimed absolute allegiance and there was no other civic corporate body to rival with it in this respect.

The divinity of the king was also regarded as justifying the political obligations of the citizen. The king is a veritable divinity, says Manu (VII. 8), and should, therefore, be obeyed. It will be shown in the next chapter how this theory of kings' divinity did not, however, impose an absolute obligation to obey, and how citizens were permitted to depose and even to execute a king, if he becomes guilty of gross misbehaviour and misgovernment.

Laws were also regarded as divine in origin and, therefore, the citizen was expected to obey the state which was an agency for their enforcement. The citizen, however, did not become a slave of antiquated laws, because the custom, if not the state, was permitted to change them in a gradual manner.

We have already shown how some of the thinkers of ancient India have advanced the contract theory for the origin of state. People agreed to obey the king and pay him the taxes because he undertook to protect them. Political obligations would thus arise out of the initial contract, express or implied. It must, however, be noted that our constitutionalists have laid down that if the king is unwilling or unable to carry out his part of the contract by protecting the people and ensuring a prosperous government, they should forthwith kill him like a mad dog.[1]

The *saptāṅga* theory of the state, already explained before (in chap. II), gives a further ground for political obligations.

1. अहं वो रक्षितेत्युक्त्वा यो न रक्षति भूमिपः ।
स संहत्य निहंतव्यः श्वेव सोन्माद आतुरः ॥ *Mbh.*, XIII. 96. 35.

Government and citizens are both limbs of the body politic; they can function only in cooperation with each other and will both perish if there is a conflict between the two. The state seeks to bring about the moral and material progress and prosperity of the citizens by its measures and efforts; it can succeed in its mission only if the latter offer it hearty cooperation by discharging their obligations to the state. Enlightened self-interest, therefore, demands that since the state is engaged in promoting the progress of its citizens in moral, economic and aesthetic spheres, the latter should make the state's onerous task easy by their hearty cooperation in discharging all their political obligations.

CHAPTER V

THE KINGSHIP

Although other types of state existed in ancient India, as shown in the second chapter, monarchy was the most common form of government. We shall, therefore, proceed to discuss the various problems connected with the kingship in this chapter.

The Vedic literature has some speculations about the origin of kingship. Once upon a time, we are told, there was a war between demons and gods, in which the latter were being constantly defeated. Gods, therefore, assembled to survey the situation with a view to remedy it. After analysing the position, they came to the conclusion that they were being overpowered because they had no king. They then decided to make Soma their king and leader, and then they succeeded in winning victory[1] Elsewhere we are told that Indra was made their king by gods because he was the most illustrious and powerful among them, as also the most senior[2] In a third place we are informed that Varuṇa wanted to be the king of gods, but the latter would not accept his leadership. He then learnt a particular chant from Prajāpati, his father, which made him superior to all other gods ; then his kingship was acknowledged by them.

The above parables indicate clearly that the ancient Indians believed that the kingship arose out of a military necessity, and that a king must be a capable general whose leadership is acknowledged by all. Success in war becomes easy only if the leader of the nation possesses strength, vigour, wisdom and energy. When a person is selected to lead his side on account of these qualities and eventually wins victory for his side, his position becomes stronger and stronger. He eventually attains the status of the king and if he has able sons, his office tends to become

1. अराजन्यतया वै नो जयंति राजानं करवामहै इति । *A. Br.*, I. 14.
2. *T. Br.*, II. 2. 7. 2.
3. *J. Br.*, III. 152.

hereditary. In the Vājapeya sacrifice performed at the coronation of a king there is a symbolical chariot race in which the king comes out first. This element in the ritual enables us to get a glimpse of that dim and distant past when the military capacity of a leader was sought to be tested by the chariot race,[1] before offering him the kingship.

We have seen already how the society in the Vedic period was patriarchal, and how several *kulas* (families) made a *viś* (a local community) and several *viśas* a *jana* (tribe). Those among the *kulapatis*, who were noted for their strength and leadership, used to become *viśpatis*. From among the *viśpatis*, one would rise to the position of the *janapati* for similar qualities, sometimes demonstrated in the chariot race.

Early Indian speculations and the known evolution of the Hindu family, therefore, show that kingship arose out of the patriarchal atmosphere prevailing in society. A *kulapati* who was prominent for his bravery and leadership[2] would become a *viśpati*. The usual tendency, however, was to assume these qualities in the leading member of the seniormost family ; an actual election would arise only in a doubtful case, where it was not clear as to who was the proper claimant.

The Aśvins, we are told, obtained divinity through their medical skill, but the Vedic literature does not refer to a physician becoming a king on account of his professional fame.

The Vedic literature is pre-eminently religious ; yet it does not suggest that kingship was connected with or originated from the priestly office. It is interesting to note that the Vedic king discharges no priestly functions, nor does he preside over any sacrifices performed for the community as a whole, as was the case with kings and magistrates in ancient Egypt,

1. What air-supremacy is in the modern warfare, supremacy in horsemanship and chariot-driving was in the Vedic period.

2. Alexander's historians have observed that the Kaṭhas, who enjoyed highest reputation for courage and skill in the art of war, used to choose the handsomest man as their king (Mc. Crindle, *Ancient India*, p. 38). If true, this may indicate that military qualifications being equal, the handsomer candidate was chosen ; it does not show that beauty was preferred to bravery.

3. *Kṛityakalpataru*, Chap. 2.

Greece and Rome. Nor is the Vedic king seen, like the Hittite monarch, participating in public rituals after his return from a military campaign.

The caste system had not become rigid in the Vedic period and so we cannot, strictly speaking, talk of the caste of the Vedic king. Later on when the caste system was fully evolved, the king usually used to belong to the Kshatriya caste. In the course of time however non-Kshatriya *viz.* Brāhmaṇas, Vaiśyas and Śūdras and non-Aryans *viz.* the Scythians, the Parthians and the Hūṇas established their own dynasties and the term *rājan* began to be applied even to non-Kshatriyas who were actually ruling over a kingdom.[1]

CEREMONY[2] CEREMONY

A few words may here be said about the coronation ceremony, which was performed at the time of the accession of the king since very early times. We are not very much concerned here with its ritualistic details ; as students of polity we have to understand its constitutional significance. The name of the coronation ritual was Rājasūya and its details are given in the Brāhmaṇa literature ; but they continue to be followed for a long time. The ceremony divides itself into three parts, preliminary rituals, the coronation itself and post-coronation ceremonies. Preliminary rituals mainly consisted of the *ratni*-oblations, which the king was usually to offer at the houses of his different *ratnins* or ministers and high officials[3] That the king is to visit the houses of these dignitaries for this purpose shows that the approval of his accession by the governing class and its representatives was regarded as essential in ancient times. The ritual performed in the houses of the *ratnins* also served to create a feeling of attachment and loyalty in their mind to the new king.

The actual coronation followed on the second day. The king was annointed and then seated on a throne covered with

1. तच्च राज्यमविशेषेण चत्वारोऽपि वर्णाः कुर्वाणा दृश्यन्ते । तस्मात् सर्वे राजानः । *Tantraı ārtika*, p. 580.
2. *Sat. Br.*, V. 2 and 3; Ait. *Br.*, VIII. 15.
3. *Sat. Br.*, V. 3, I.

tiger skin, where he was sprinkled with sacred waters brought from the holy rivers and seas. The priest, of course, first performed this ceremony with the proper Vedic Mantras, which prayed that God Savitṛi should endow the king with energy and driving power. Indra with ruling capacity, Bṛihaspati with eloquence, Mitra with truth, Varuṇa with the capacity to protect the law. The sacred texts emphasise that the protection of the law was the most sacred duty of the king.

It is interesting to note that later on a Rājanya *i.e.* a Kshatriya and a Vaiśya also took part in the king's annointment. The priest, the Rājanya and the Vaiśya were probably regarded as the representatives of the three main groups into which the Aryan society was divided at that time and the association of all of them in the ritual may have been intended to convey a general acceptance of the new king by the community. The *Mahābhārata* records the association of the representative of the Śūdra and lower castes also at the coronation of Yudhishṭhira.

There is no doubt that before the coronation the sacred texts require the king to take an oath. Some writers have argued that this corresponded to the coronation oath of the modern times, wherein the king bound himself to govern righteously and refrain from oppressing the people.[1] The text and context of the oath, however, make it quite clear that it was an oath by which the king bound himself not to do harm to the priest in view of the sacred powers which he was invoking at the time of the coronation for the prosperity and safety of the king.[2]

The coronation of Yuvarāja is referred to by some later writers like Śukra (II. 2.5). The Allahabad Pillar Inscription would suggest that it was performed in the Gupta dynasty; the Rāshṭrakūṭa records show that Govinda III was sanctified by this ritual

1. *E. G.* Jayaswal, *Hindu Polity*, 1st Edi., II, p. 28.

2. Cf. *Air. Br.* VIII. 15 :––एतेनन्द्रेण महाभिषेकेन क्षत्रियं शापयित्वाऽभिषिंचेत्। स ब्रूयात्सह श्रद्धया याञ्च रात्रिमजायेऽहं यां च प्रेतास्मि तदुभयमन्तरेण इष्टापूर्तं मे लोकं सुकृतमायुः प्रजां वञ्जीथा यदि ते द्रुह्येयमिति। 'ते' obviously refers to the priest performing the coronation ritual.

at the time of his formal selection as a crown-prince. Kalachūri king Karṇa himself performed the coronation of his crown-prince Yaśaskara in the 11th century (*C.I.I.*, IV, p. 294)

In Eastern Chālukya dynasty Bhīma II and Vijayāditya III had been coronated as Yuvarājas and were invested with a *kaṇṭhikā* or necklace in token thereof. Kings used to be invested with Paṭṭabandha or diadem.

There is nothing in the texts or their context to show that the officiating priest was regarded as a representative of the society. In later times, however, the king was formally required to take an oath at the coronation that he would never transgress provisions of Dharma.[1] What was to be done if this vow was not kept is nowhere indicated.

After the coronation ritual was over, the king went out for a state drive either in a chariot or on an elephant. On his return a Durbar was held where the representatives of the different classes came and offered their homage to the new king. This was followed by a game of dice and a chariot race in the Vedic period and by other suitable festivals in later times.

The coronation ceremony underwent considerable changes after about the 8th century A. D. The Vājapeya sacrifice, the chariot race and the oblations at the houses of *ratnins* were silently omitted from the ritual as a natural consequence of the disappearance of the Vedic culture. Instead the besmearing of the king's body with several auspicious types of earth-dusts and his bath with the waters of several sacred rivers became very important.[2] What is constitutionally very significant is that the ceremony no longer contained any oath to be taken by the king either with reference to his duties to the people or to the priest. The king's position had become stronger and

1. Compare the oath administered to king Vena; *Mbh.*, XII. 58. 115-6;

प्रतिज्ञां चावरोहस्व मनसा कर्मणा गिरा ।
पालयिष्याम्यहं भौमं ब्रह्म इत्येव चासकृत् ॥
यश्चात्र धर्म इत्युक्तो दण्डनीतिव्यपाश्रयः ॥
तमशंकः करिष्यामि स्ववशो न कदाचन ॥

2. *Kṛityakalpataru*, Rājadharmakāṇḍa, Ch. 2.

stronger, and so it was felt incongruous that he should be required to take any oath.

Pauranik religion was getting into ascendancy at this time and we find that many of the gifts recommended in the Purāṇas were given at the time of the coronation. The Rāshṭrakūṭa king Indra III gave away 400 villages at the time of his coronation. Kṛishaṇdevarāya of Vijayanagar weighed himself against gold, pearls and silver, besides giving the usual Mahādānas. We may well presume that such gifts had become the order of the day from *c.* 800 A. D.

WAS KINGSHIP ELECTIVE ?

There is considerable difference of opinion as to whether the kingship was elective in ancient India. There is no doubt that it was so *in some cases* in the early Vedic period. A passage in the *Ṛigveda* seems to refer to the people (*viśas*) electing a king[1]; another passage in the *Arthaśāstra* expresses the hope that the king to be coronated may be elected by the people.[2] But very probably not the whole population voted on these occasions. A passage in the later Vedic literature tells us that he alone becomes a ruler whose leadership is accepted by other kings[3]; a prayer at the coronation prays that the king should become preeminent amongst his peers.[4] It is, therefore, very likely that not the whole population but its leaders like the *kulapatis* and the *viśpatis* had a voice in the election of the king ; people in general, like the curiae in Rome, may at the utmost, have ratified the choice of *viśpatis*. The cases of election were, however, the exception rather than the rule ; the usual tendency

1. ता ईं विशो न न राजानं वृणाना बीभत्सवो अप वृत्रादतिष्ठन् । X. 124. 8. This passage no doubt expressly describes the people as *electing* the king, but its face value is to some extent disclosed by its describing the people as being afraid on the occasion. If the king was to owe his crown to the votes of the people, why should the latter be afraid of the former, as were the celestial waters of Vṛitra, their captor, even after his overthrow ?

2. त्वां विशो वृणतां राज्याय । III 4. 2.

3. यस्मै वै राजानो राज्यमनुमन्यते स राजा भवति न स यस्मै न । *S.Br.*, IX. 3. 4. 5.

4. Hence the absence of enthusiasm and the presence of some apprehension in their minds, as described in the Vedic passage quoted in note No. 1 above.

was to accept the leadership of the seniormost member of the seniormost family and formally elect him as the king.

This formal election of the king by the *kulapatis* and *viśpatis* was, however, getting antiquated even in the early Vedic period. Majority of the passages that are quoted in support of the election theory refer to a state torn by parties and factions among the aristocratic *kulapatis* and *viśpatis*, which often led to the expulsion of the king. They express the hope[1] that the king, who is *elected by his friends* may remain firm on the throne in spite of the challenge of the opponents ; or that the king, who is being restored after expulsion, may become *acceptable* to the people. These passages cannot prove that monarchy was really elective in the Vedic period in the modern sense of the term, though they no doubt show that it was to a much greater degree dependent on the support of the aristocracy than became the case in the later times. That the formality of the election had become antiquated in the Vedic period would become evident when it is remembered that in the vast majority of cases, kingship is seen to be hereditary even in the *Ṛigveda*. The kingship is known to have passed from the father to the son for at least four generations among the Tṛitsus and for a still longer period among the Pūrus. In the story of the Sṛiñjaya king Dushṭaṛitu Paumasāyana, there is a reference to a kingdom inherited through ten generations (*daśapurusham rājyam*),[2] and the formal proclamation at the time of the coronation, as described in the later Vedic literature, refers to the new ruler as himself a king and also the son of a king.[3]

There is thus no doubt that monarchy had become normally hereditary long before the later Vedic period. The arguments advanced to show that it continued to be elective in some states down to even the 8th century A. D. are hardly convincing.[4] The *rājakṛits* mentioned in the *Atharvaveda* (III. 6. 7) and *rāja-*

1. ह्वयन्तु त्वां प्रति जना प्रति मित्रा अवृषत । *A. V.*, III, 3. 6
2. *S. B.* VII 5. 3. 1-13
3. *Rājānam rājaputram, A. Br.* III. 12
4. R. C. Majumdar—*Corporate Life*, pp. 107-113
K. P. Jayaswal—*Hindu Polity*, Part II, pp. 10 ff

kartārah referred to in the *Rāmāyaṇa* (II. 67. 2) are not king-electors but the Brāhmaṇas, who were entrusted with the duty of offering the coronation ablutions to the king.[1] When kings Pratīpa and Yayati offer the crown to their younger sons Śantanu and Puru respectively, setting aside the claims of the elder brothers, people assemble before the palace and call for an explanation. This does not, however, lend any support to the view that they had a voice in the selection of their king. In each case they simply want to know why the claims of the eldest son, supported by the law of primogeniture, have been set aside, and they return home quite satisfied when a proper explanation is offered by the reigning king.[2] Both the incidents clearly show, not that the people had any voice in the election of the king, but that they had accepted primogeniture as the normal law for the succession to the throne. The chapters in the *Rāmāyaṇa* referring to the proposed installation of Rāma to the post of the heir-apparent (II. 1-2) do not also lend colour to the view that people had any voice in the matter. Daśaratha had summoned for the occasion not the notable citizens of his kingdom but his important feudatories and neighbouring monarchs.[3] They approved of the choice of Rāma as a mere formality ; that their consent had no practical value would become quite clear

1. Sāyaṇa explains *rājakritaḥ* as *rājānaṁ kriṇvanti, rājyebhishiñchanti.* The commentator on the *Rāmāyaṇa* explains *rājyakartāraḥ* as *rājābhishekakārtāraḥ.* That this explanation is correct becomes quite clear when we read the names of *rājakartāraḥ* given in the next few verses of the *Rāmāyaṇa.* They are the names of famous Vaidika Brāhmaṇas only ; no secular officers or leaders figure among them.

2. They were told that Devāpi, the elder brother of Śāntanu, was set aside because he was suffering from leprosy, and that the elder brothers of Pūru had been disinherited because they had declined to exchange their youth with the old age of their father.

3. समानिनाय मेदिन्याः प्रधानान्पृथिवीपतीन् ।
न तु केकयराजानं जनकं वा नराधिपः ।
त्वरया चानयामास पश्चात्तौ श्रोष्यतः प्रियम् ।
अथोपविष्टे नृपतौ तस्मिन्परबलार्दने ।
ततः प्रविविशुः शेषा राजानो लोकसंमताः । II. 1. 46-8

It is thus clear that the feudatory kings, were invited and not the notables of the realm ; the reading of the Calcutta edition समानिनाय मेदिन्याः प्रधानान्पृथिवीपतिः । is shown to be untenable by the verses following quoted above.

from the circumstance that it could not prevent the banishment of Rāma to the forest. The genealogy of the Ikshvāku family shows that for several generations both before and after the reign of Rāma, the crown was passing hereditarily and that people had no power to elect the king.

It is sometimes argued that Rudradāman (*c.* 130 A. D.), Harshavardhana (*c.* 606 A. D.) and Gopāla (*c.* 750 A. D.) owed their throne to their election by the people.[1] It is no doubt true that Rudradāman and Gopāla are expressly described as being elected to the kingship by their people[2]; but these statements occur in panegyric documents composed by their court poets and cannot be taken too seriously. Rudradāman's record, relied upon in this connection, elsewhere states that he had become a king by his own prowess[3] and describes how he had conquered and annexed a number of provinces. The claim put forth on behalf of such a famous conqueror by his court poet that he owed his throne to his election by the people can hardly be accepted by the historian. Gopāla, the founder of the Pāla dynasty, had put an end to the anarchy and restored law and order in Bengal; he was the founder of his dynasty and his claim to kingship is sought to be strengthened by the fiction of his being elected by his subjects. The crown used to pass hereditarily in his family and none of his successors cares to profess that he owed his throne to his people's votes. It is no doubt true that Harsha owed the crown to election; but it was the crown, not of his hereditary kingdom of Thāneshwar, but that of the Maukhari kingdom of Kanauj, which belonged to his deceased brother-in-law Grahavarman, and to which he had no claim. After the death of Grahavarman, there was no competent heir left for the Maukhari throne. The Maukhari ministers, therefore, decided to offer the crown to the brother of their widowed queen. This instance shows that

1. Majumdar, *Corporate Life*, p. 112
2. सर्वंवर्णैरभिगम्य रक्षणार्थं पतित्वे वृतेन । Junagad inscription ; मात्स्यन्यायमपोहितुं च प्रकृतिभिर्लक्ष्म्याः करं ग्राहितः । *E. I.* IV. p. 2
3. स्वयमधिगतमहाक्षत्रपनाम्ना रुद्रनाम्ना । Junagad Ins

when there was a failure of heirs, the ministers and other high dignitaries used to elect a suitable successor from among the relations of the deceased king.[1] There are some such instances in the Jātaka stories too.[2] But they cannot show that the kingship was elective in normal times. Epigraphic and literary evidence shows that almost all the dynasties subsequent to *c.* 600 B. C., of which we have any knowledge, were passing the crown on the principle of heredity. The very idea of the election of the king appeared totally strange to the historians of the 12th century.[3]

ROYAL SUCCESSION

We may now passingly refer to a few points of constitutional importance connected with a hereditary monarchy. In the case of ordinary families, property was divisible among brothers according to the Hindu law; the law of primogeniture, however, prevailed in the case of monarchy. It was realised that the division of a kingdom among different brothers would make it weak and lead to its eventual destruction.[4] The crown, therefore, usually passed to the eldest son,[5] but his brothers were generally appointed to responsible posts in the government like governor-

1. This holds good also of the so-called election of the Pallava king after the death of Parameśvaravarman II.

2. See Jātaka, Vol. I p. 470 ; Vol. V p. 187 etc.

3. When the Utpala dynasty came to an end in Kashmir in 939 A. D., one Kamalavardhana managed to get the effective control of the government machinery. When instead of crowning himself king immediately, he asked the Brāhmaṇas of the capital to elect somebody to the kingship, thinking that they would naturally support his claim, Kalhaṇa, the Kashmir historian, says that it was the most foolish procedure that could ever have been thought of, comparable to the conduct of a person who does not accept the love offer of a lady of exceptional beauty coming herself to his house under intoxication to beg to be accepted, but sends a messenger the next day to enquire whether she would come. In this particular case, the Brāhmaṇas went on arguing for five or six days without coming to any decision. In the meanwhile another claimant to the throne, Śūravarman, came and occupied the capital and the Brāhmaṇas then hastend to acclaim him as the king. *Rājataraṅgiṇi*, VII. 773 ff

4. राज्यविभजनाच्छ्रेयो भूपानां न भवेत्खलु ।
अल्पीकृतं विभागेन राज्यं शत्रुर्जिघृक्षति ॥ *Śukra*, I. 345

5. *Śukra*, I, 346-8

ships or viceroyalties.[1] We get several such instances both in the Jātaka stories and actual history.

Sometimes the status of the brothers of the ruling monarch was that of a sub-king which often produced the impression,—as in the Pāṇḍya state of the 13th century, of the kingdom being divided among the brothers or of several brothers ruling together. Hindu political thinkers did not approve of the division of the kingdom and the case of the Pāṇḍya kingdom mentioned above appears to be that of several brothers ruling as sub-king.

If the eldest son was unfit to rule owing to blindness, deafness, etc., then he was of course not allowed to succeed. Dhṛitarāshṭra and Devāpi were superseded under this rule.

The attraction of pomp and power was, however, often too strong, and younger brothers would sometimes seek to wrest the crown by starting internecine wars. These are known both to folk lore stories as well as to sober history. When, however, we take a survey of the ancient Indian history as a whole, we have to admit that they were rather an exception than the rule. Very often a compromise was effected by giving a small feudatory kingdom to the younger brother. The creation of the Rāshṭrakuṭa branch in Gujarat and the Chālukya branch in Veṇgi were due to this policy.

Great emphasis has been given to the proper training of the heir-apparent. Kingship may be divine, but it did not dispense with the necessity of proper training. Special schools were organised for the education of princes, though we sometimes see them being sent for training along with commoners to famous University centres like Takshaśilā. In early days the study of the Vedas and philosophy loomed large even in the princely curriculum,[2] but gradually economics and politics

1. C. इक्ष्वाकूणां हि सर्वेषां राजा भवति पूर्वजः
पूर्वजेनावरः पुत्रो ज्येष्ठो राजाभिषिच्यते । *Rāmāyaṇa* II. 110. 36
कथं ज्येष्ठानतिक्रम्य कनीयान्राज्यमर्हति *Mb* । I. 85. 22

2. *Arthaśāstra*, I. Chap. 2 : *Manusmṛiti*, VII. 43

became the main subjects of theoretical study.[1] Some writers go to the extent of declaring that princes need study no other subjects. One can understand this position, because society believed that its proper functioning and progress depended upon an efficient government machinery.[2] Practical education included training in administration and the military art and tactics. Above all the prince was to be a good bowman, a skilful horseman and an expert controller of the elephants.[3] The skill which some of the princes aquired in the military arts was often of a very high order. The *Śāstravinoda* section of the *Mānasollāsa* (12th century) shows that some of the kings were such noted experts in archery etc. that they would hold special functions to make a display of their skill. People were invited to a stadium in order to see the military feats of their rulers, who would show how they could pierce two objects by one arrow, or shoot through a target revolving over their head by merely looking at its reflection in a water basin below. There were similar displays of the mastery in the use of the sword, the spear and the mace. Probably not all the kings used to attain such high skill, but at least some did possess it.

When the training was complete, and the prince had attained majority, he was formally appointed as heir-apparent. He was then entrusted with considerable functions in the administration, which he discharged in consultation with his father.

South Indian polity attached great importance to the regent. It has been suggested that the expression *trairājya* that occurs in some south Indian inscriptions, refers to Mahārāja, the ruling

1. *Kāmandaka*, II. 2-5. Bārhaspatya school held that the study of the Trayī was undesirable, as it acted as a screen obscuring the vision of a king who should know the ways of the world.

2. Cf. सर्वा विद्या राजधर्मेषु युक्ताः सर्वे लोका राजधर्मे प्रविष्टाः ।
सर्वे धर्मा राजधर्मप्रधानाः । *Mbh.*, XII. 63. 26.

3. धर्मकामार्थशास्त्राणि धनुर्वेदं च शिक्षयेत ।
रथे च कुञ्जरे चैव व्यायामं कारयेत्सदा ॥
शिल्पानि शिक्षयेच्चैनं नाप्तैर्मिथ्याप्रियं वदेत् ॥

Agni P. Chap. 220, 2-3

It is interesting to note that Bāṇa agrees with the *Agnipurāṇa* on the scope of the raining of the prince. See *Kādambarī*, p. 55 (N. P. edition)

king, Yuvarāja, the heir-apparent and Muṭurāja the senior-male member of the royal family, who was the prospective regent in the case of necessity.

The regency had its own advantages and was an obvious necessity in the case of a minority administration. Many regents like Pātālamalla in the case of Rāshṭrakūṭa king Amoghavarsha I and Vijayāditya in the case of the Gaṅga king Śivamāra II discharged their duties disinterestedly. But some regents would try to usurp the throne for themselves, as happened in the case Maṅgaliśa, the regent of Pulakeśin I and Kṛishṇa in the case of the Yādava ruler Rāmachandra.

King Khāravela of Orissa was a minor at the time of the death of his father ; his formal coronation was postponed till his attaining the age of 24. It is however doubtful whether this practice was generally followed ; there are cases of formal coronation at a much earlier age. King Kārikāla of Saṅgama age is said to have been crowned king when he was only five. Avinīta Koṅganivarmā was crowned king when he was still a child in his mother's lap. Nandivarman Pallavalmalla was 12 at the time of his coronation. When the system of regency was developed, no objection was probably felt to the formal coronation of even a child.

When the heir-apparent was a minor at his succession, the administration was carried on by a council of regency. The evidence of the Jātakas,[1] dramas[2] and inscriptions shows that usually the dowager queen presided over this council. India can proudly point to several dowager queens like Nayanikā (*c*, 150 B. C.) and Prabhāvatīguptā (*c*. 380 A. D.), who successfully carried on the administration of extensive kingdoms during the long minority of their sons.

Hindu law, however, did not permit an only daughter to succeed her father as the ruling queen. Bhīshma, no doubt, advises king Dharma to sanction the coronation of the daughters

1 IV pp. 109, 487 In the last case the king of Banaras became a hermit and his subjects request the queen to undertake the royal duties. is was the usual practice ; cf. *Anno rājā no hoti*

2 During the captivity of king Udayana of Kauśāmbī, his mother carried on the administration ; *Pratijñāyaugandharāyaṇa*, Act I

of those kings, who had died in the war, and left no male issues behind.[1] This, however, was not the general opinion. The vast majority of the constitutional writers opposed the succession of women to the throne, because they felt that on account of their natural limitations, they cannot become efficient administrators.[2]

What therefore happened when the only heir to the throne was a daughter was that her husband succeeded to the kingdom of his father-in-law. In such cases, the daughter was sometimes regarded also as the regnant queen, as is suggested by the joint coinage of Chandragupta I and his Lichchhavi queen Kumāradevī. Usually however the heiress also became merely a queen consort.

In south India, especially under the Chālukyas and the Rāshṭrakūṭas, princesses in the royal family were appointed frequently to important administrative posts. We shall refer to only two cases by way of illustration ; Revakanimmaḍi, a daughter of Amoghavaraha I and the wife of Erragaṅga, was the governor of the important district of Edatore 2,000 in *c.* 850 A. D., and Akkādevī, an elder sister of Jayasiṁha III, was ruling over the district of Kinsukuda in 1022 A. D. Such cases, however, are not known to northern India.

We have a solitary case of an Alūpa ruler of south Kanara stating that he rules jointly with his Chief Queen. This however does not seem to have been a common practice even in the South.[3]

In conclusion we shall passingly refer to the position of the queen. In the Vedic period, she figured in the list of the *ratnis* or important state officers, but her function in the administration is not known. Constitutional writers do not allot to the queen any part in the administration, but in actual practice, it may have been often influenced by her views and personality. This was the case to a greater degree in south India, where we often find queens making land grants on their own authority

1. कुमारो नास्ति येषां च कन्यास्तत्राभिषेचय । *Mbh* XII. 32. 23
2. दुट्ठं तं जनपदं यत्थ इत्थि परिणायिका । *Jāt.* I. 155
अनवकाशं यमित्थी राजा अस्स चक्कवर्ती । *M. N.* III. 65-66
3. T. V. Mahalingam, *South Indian Polity*, p. 37

or functioning as viceroys over extensive provinces.[1] There is ample evidence to show that princesses and queens used to receive administrative and military training to be of use to them in the case of necessity.

DIVINITY OF THE KING

It is interesting to note that the doctrine of the divinity of the king, which became so popular in India in the first millennium of the Christian era, was unknown to the Vedic period. Kingship at that time was a purely secular institution. The king in his official or public capacity was not required to perform any sacrifices for the promotion of the public weal or the removal of a tribal or national calamity.

In the *Ṛigveda*, one king alone Purukutsa has been only once described as *ardhadeva* or semi-divine (IV. 42. 8-9) ; and one solitary and late passage of the *Atharvaveda* (XX. 127. 7) describes king Parīkshit as a god among men (*Yo devo martyān adhi*). These passages, however, do not prove the acceptance of the divinity of the king by the age ; Purukutsa was called semi-divine, probably because his widowed mother got him as a special favour of the gods Indra and Varuṇa. Parīkshit is called a god among men in a hymn which is out to panegyrise him ; as no other king is ever so described in the Vedic literature, we may take it that the theory of the king's divinity was yet confined to the imagination of a few grateful courtiers. When a Samiti (popular assembly) could depose a king, the theory of the latter's divinity was not likely to take root in society.

The growing sway of religious ideas and notions produced an atmosphere in the Brāhmaṇa period which was more favourable to the notion of the divinity of the king. Victories of the king began to be attributed to the favour of Indra, and very often the latter's epithet began to be transferred to the former.[2] At the time of the royal coronation the priest averred that it was at the command of god Savitar that the coronation ablution was being given, and that too, not with his human hands and arms,

1. A. S. Altekar, *The Position of Women*, pp. 186-8 (2nd Ed.)
2. *A Br.*, VIII. 2

but with the hands of god Pūshan and the arms of god Aśvins. Gods Agni, Savitar and Bṛihaspati were believed to enter the person of the king, when he was being annointed at the coronation. Some of the sacrifices he performed like the Aśvamedha and the Vājapeya were declared to enable him to obtain parity with gods [1] The mystery of the multitude obeying one king was sought to be explained by some on the ground that he was the veritable visible symbol of Prajāpati, the chief of gods.[2] Brāhmaṇas were claiming divinity (*bhūdevatva*) for themselves and were, therefore, not disposed to deny it to the king, who was expected to uphold their privileges. The political thinkers began to advocate that the age of anarchy came to an end, when at the request of the suffering humanity, the Creator made a Code of Law and appointed a king to administer it. This view about the origin of the state conceded a quasi-divinity to the king. The *Mahābhārata* states the god Vishṇu himself entered into the body of the first king (XII. 39. 128). It further maintains that if a person despises a king, his penance and sacrifices will bear no fruits. All these circumstances and factors created an atmosphere during the post-Vedic period, which was very favourable to the doctrine of the divinity of the king. The advent of the Kushāṇa dynasty in the 1st century A. D. further strengthened the tendency to regard the king as divine. Owing to the influence of the Chinese tradition, kings of this house claimed to be the sons of gods (*devaputra*) and represented themselves on their coins as descending from clouds and surrounded by divine flames.[3] Temples were also built by the Kushāṇa emperors in honour of their dead predecessors whose statues were worshipped there as gods or demigods.

Divinity has been definitely claimed for the king by some Smṛitis and Purāṇas. Manu avers that the king is verily a great divinity in the human form ; his very body is formed

1 *S. Br.*, XII. 4. 4. 3 ; *T. Br.*, XVIII. 10. 10

2. एष वै प्रजापतेः प्रत्यक्षतमं यद्राजन्यः। तस्मादेकः सन्बहूनामीष्टे । *S. Br.*, V. 1. 5. 14

3. *The Catalogue of Coins in the Punjab Museum*, Vol. I. Pl XVII. 31, 33

by the Creator by taking particles from the bodies of the divine guardians of the eight quarters.[1] The *Vishṇupurṇa*[2] and the *Bhāgavata* say that a number of divinities reside in the person of the king ; the latter goes to the extent of averring that Veṇa, the first king, had actually some of the marks of Vishṇu on the different limbs of his body.[3] The convention of regarding the king as divine has become quite general ; even the Buddhists in later times regarded the kings as *sammutidevas* (gods by convention or public opinion). Sanskrit dramatists use the word *deva,* when a king is to be addressed, and the efforts of the medieval dynasties to trace their origin to gods Brahmā, Rāma or Lakshmaṇa also presuppose a desire to emphasise their divine origin and character.

When the Avatāra theory became popular, kings began to be regarded as incarnation of gods. Thus kings Chandra and Govindachandra of the Gāhadawāla dynasty were regarded as the incranations of Brahmā and Hari respectively (*I. A.*, XVIII. 15 ; *E.I.* IX. 319) The *Prithvirājavijaya*, VII. 62 describes its hero as an *avatāra* of Rama.

The divinity of king was thus accepted by some Smṛitis and Purāṇas. It is, however, the view of only a small minority among them, which maintains that the king is the deity incarnate. The vast number of the Smṛitis and the Purāṇas merely content themselves by drawing attention to the *functional resemblance* between the king on one side and the various deities on the other.

1 यस्मादेषां सुरेन्द्राणां मात्राभिर्निर्मितो नृपः ।
तस्मादभिभवत्येष सर्वभूतानि तेजसा । *Manu*, VII. 5. 4

2. ब्रह्मा जनार्दनो रुद्र इन्द्रो वायुर्यमो रविः ।
हुतभुग्वरुणो धाता पूषा भर्मिनिशाकरः ।
एते चान्ये च ये देवाः शापानुग्रहकारिणः ।
नृपस्यैते शरीरस्थाः सर्वदेवमयो नृपः ॥ *Vishṇu P.*, I. 13-14

3 जातो नारायणांशेन पृथुराद्यः क्षितीश्वरः ।
वेणस्य दक्षिणे हस्ते दृष्ट्वा चह्नं गदाभृतः
पादयोररविदं च तं वै मेने हरेः कलाम् । *hāg.*, IV. 13. 23

Thus the *Mahābhārata*[1] (XII. 67. 40 ff.), the *Nāradasmṛiti* (XVII. 26 ff.), the *Śukranīti* (I.73 ff.), the *Matsya* (ch. 22), the *Mārkaṇḍeya* (27. 21. ff.), the *Agni* (225. 16), the *Padma* (I. 30. 45 ff.) and the *Bṛihaddharma* (Uttarakhaṇḍa, 3. 8) Purāṇas point out how the king *resembles* god Fire, because he burns the wicked by his power, the god Sun because he sees every thing through his spies the god Yama because he metes out just punishment, the god Kubera, because he showers wealth on the deserving, and so on.[1] The majority view thus points only to the functional resemblance between the king on the one side and the various divinities on the other. It does not say that the *king is himself a god*, but observes that *his functions are similar to those of some gods*. Most Hindu writers have thus advocated the divinity, not of the person of the king but of his office, because of the resemblance between his functions and those of some deities. *Varṇāśrama-dharma* which the king was expected to enforce was also regarded as divine and it was probably felt that the theory of the divinity of king would enable him to discharge this duty better. It was felt that the king's status would become higher and the tendency to obey the state's orders stronger, if its head was represented as divine. But when the question of the duties and responsibilities of the king was at issue, his divinity did not afford him any immunity or privilege. If he was bad in character and remiss in performing his duties, he became demoniac and not divine.

In Europe the doctrine of the divinity of the king was first

1 कुरुते पंच रूपाणि कार्ययुक्तानि यः सदा ।
भवत्यग्निस्तथादित्यो मत्युर्वैश्रवणो यमः ॥४१॥
यदा ह्यासीदतः पापान्दहत्युग्रेण तेजसा ।
मिथ्योपचरितो राजा तदा भवति पावकः । ४२॥
यदा पश्यति चारेण सर्वभूतानि भूमिपः ।
क्षेमं च कृत्वा व्रजति तदा भवति भास्करः ॥४३॥
अशुचींश्च यद्रा क्रुद्धः क्षिणोति शतशो नरान् ।
सपुत्रपौत्रान्सामात्यांस्तदा भवति सोऽन्तकः ॥४४॥
यदा त्वधार्मिकान्सर्वांस्तीक्ष्णैर्दंडैर्नियच्छति ।
धार्मिकांश्चानुगृह्णाति भवत्यथ यमस्तदा ॥४५।
यदा तु धनधाराभिस्तर्पयत्युपकारिणः ।
तदा वैश्रवणो राजा लोके भवति भूमिपः ॥४७॥ *Mbh.*, XII. 67. 41 ff.

advanced when Alexander the Great was deified in his life time in *c.* 324 B. C. Roman emperors were deified after their death and temples were built in their honour. Christianity conceded real divinity to the Pope and it was believed that he could transfer it to the king at the time of his coronation. The Reformation movement, which attacked the powers and privileges of the Pope, indirectly gave a fill-up to the divinity of the monarch. Later on the conflict between the Pope and the king came to an end and the kings started to utilise the theory of their divinity in their struggle against the people. In this connection four propositions were advanced, (1) that the monarchy is a divinely ordained institution; (2) that the hereditary right is indefeasible; (3) that kings are accountable to God alone; (4) that non-resistance and passive obedience are enjoined by God. King's divinity began to be advocated in defence of royal tyranny. In ancient India, Nārada is the solitary writer who at one place went to the extent of maintaining that the person of even a wicked king was inviolable because of his divinity.[1] His view, however, was not generally accepted. The wicked king Veṇa claimed exemption from punishment on the ground of his divinity, but angry sages killed him immediately after he had advanced this impious plea. It is further necessary to emphasise that only good and pious kings were regarded as divine by ancient Hindus; bad and impious ones were dubbed as demoniac.[2] The view of Gregory the Great that even bad kings are divine and responsible to God alone was clearly not acceptable to most of the ancient Indian thinkers. Even Manu, who advocates the divinity of the king in the extreme form,

1 राजनि प्रहरेद्यस्तु कृतागस्यपि दुर्मतिः ।
शूले तमग्नौ विपचेद् ब्रह्महत्याशताधिकम् । XVIII. 31
Rājataraṅgiṇī, 1.72 also enjoins regard for even a vicious king, cf.
नावगण्यः स दुष्टोपि विदुषा भूतिमिच्छता ।

2 गुणिजुष्टस्तु यो राजा स ज्ञेयो देवतांशकः ।
विपरीतस्तु रक्षोंऽशः स वै नरकभाजनः ॥ *Śukra* 1. 87
Cf also *Mbh*, 67,

3 दंडो हि सुमहत्तेजा दुर्धरश्चाकृतात्मभिः ।
धर्माद्विचलितं हन्ति नृपमेव सबान्धवम् । VII. 28

warns him that he will suffer and meet with punishment in this very life if he misbehaves and misgoverns. He further points out that the divinity of the king does not confer infallibility on him. As a matter of fact, says Manu (VII. 45), he is more liable to err and fall than ordinary men, as he is exposed to greater temptations ; he should, therefore, take greater precautions to see that he does not become a prey to different vices and calamities that arise out of *kāma* (passion) *krodha* (anger) and *lobha* (greed). A few kings misled by the surrounding flatterers, it seems, claimed infallibility on account of their so-called divinity ; how they became buts of public ridicule has been well described by Bāṇa,[1] the biographer of king Harsha.

The view of Blackstone that the king is not only incapable of doing wrong but also of thinking wrong was clearly not subscribed to by the ancient Indian thinkers. As a matter of fact they regarded him as more exposed to errors and temptations than ordinary human beings. Nor was king's divinity construed as necessitating passive obedience even to wicked kings. Bishop Bossuet contended that open impiety on the part of a prince did not exempt the subjects from the obedience which they owe to him ; Calvin held that kings, unworthy of honour, must nevertheless receive most respectful submission. Ancient Indian thinkers did not usually subscribe to such views ; they were not even prepared to recognise the divinity of unworthy kings. They have bluntly described them as demoniac and have permitted their subjects to rebel openly against them, as will be presently shown. The view of James I that the wickedness of a king can never make subjects that are ordained to be judged by him, to become his judges, was not acceptable to ancient India. It will be thus seen that Willioughby's observation that 'in all the vast Asiatic monarchies of the early days, the rulers claimed a divine right to control the affairs of the state and this

1 प्रतारणकुशलैर्धूर्तैः अमानुषलोकोचिताभिः स्तुतिभिः प्रतार्यमाणाः आत्मन्यारोपितालीकाभिभानाः मर्त्यधर्माणोपि दिव्यांशावतीर्णमिव सदैवतमिवातिमानुषमात्मानमुत्प्रेक्षमाणा प्रारब्धदिव्योचितचेष्टानुभवाः सर्वजनस्योपहास्यतामुपयांति । *Kādambarī*, Śukanāsa's advice to Chandrāpīḍa

was submitted to by people with but little question,' does not hold good of ancient India.[1]

It has been argued by Dr. Jayaswal that the theory of the Divinity of King was advanced by *Manusmṛiti* to support the Brāhmaṇa empire of Pushyamitra[2] and to counteract the Buddhist theory of the origin of state by contract. Our discussion above must have made it clear to the reader that the theory of the king's divinity was gradually gaining ground and it cannot be ascribed to Manu alone. The contract theory was also perfunctorily advanced by a few writers, both Hindu and Buddhist, and it was hardly suspected that it was in opposition to the theory of king's divinity.

Before concluding this topic, we may briefly survey the views of some ancient civilisations about the divinity of the king. In ancient Egypt Pharoha was regarded as the son of the god Sun (Ra). He officiated at public sacrifices and he alone could supplicate to God for favour or mercy. In ancient Babylonia and Assyria, kings were regarded as viceregents of God and were thus awarded divine honours. In ancient Greece king was believed to be descended from a divine ancestor ; he was Zeus-born and Zeus-nurtured. He alone possessed the knowledge of the divine infallible decrees. After 10 A. D. Rome began to deify her emperors ; they were proclaimed divine after their death and temples were built in their honour. The views of the 17th and 18th century thinkers of Europe have been referred to already.

We have so far examined the notion of king's divinity. Let us now examine some other notions associated with kingship in order to understand properly the position of the king.

KING AS UPHOLDER OF THE MORAL ORDER

From the Vedic times downwards, the king has been regarded as the supporter and upholder of the law. The Vedic age held that the ideal king was to be *dhṛitavrata*, dedicated to law and

1. *Nature of State*, pp. 42-3
2. *Hindu Polity*, Part II, pp. 54-7

piety like the great god Varuṇa. The king may be divine, but the law was still more so, and must, therefore, be respected by him. The essence of rulership lies in *dharma* ; the king should realise that there is nothing higher than *dharma* and always abide by it.[1] The first king Veṇa had to take the oath that he would scrupulously follow the *dharma* prescribed in the authoritative works on the subject and never act wilfully.[2] The responsibility of the the king was particularly great. He was the first citizen and his subjects were naturally prone to follow his example. His conduct, therefore, should be always exemplary. Unhappiness, misery and pestilence among the subject swere attributed to failure in duty on the part of the king. 'When kings are unjust' says one writer, 'even sugar and salt lose their flavour.'[3] The popular notion on this subject is well illustrated by the Jātakas. The ox of a ploughman is struck accidentally by his plough-share ; for this the king is to blame ; a milkman is killed by a vicious cow, the blame is assigned to the same quarter ; even a frog does not spare the king when it is bitten by hungry crows.[4] Happiness, it was believed, depended upon virtue and piety, and these could prosper only if the king set a proper example and standard. Under a good king prosperity will prevail.[5]

An early South Indian work, *Maṇimekhalai*, VII. 5. 8-12 expresses itself in a similar strain :—

> If the king did swerve from his righteous path
> The planets would all change their course ;
> If the planets errant turn,
> Would dearth of rain surely ensure.
> If dearth of rain there were,
> Nothing on earth would then survive.

1. तदेतत्क्षत्रस्य क्षत्रं यद्धर्मस्तस्माद्धर्मात्परं नास्ति । *Br. Up*, 1. 4. 14

2 यश्चात्र धर्म इत्युक्तो धर्मनीतिव्यपाश्रयः ।
तमशंकः करिष्यामि स्ववशो न कदाचन ॥ *Mbh.* XII. 59. 116

3. *Jātaka*, Vol. III, p. 111 4. *Ibid*, V, pp. 101-7.

5. सर्वत्र नो वार्तभवेहि राजन्नाये कुतस्त्वय्यशुभं प्रजानाम् ।
सूर्ये तपत्यावरणाय दृष्टेः कल्पेत लोकस्य कथं तमिस्रा ॥ Rv. V. 10

KING AS A PUBLIC SERVANT

The next important notion about the king was that he was *the servant of the people*. An early Dharmasūtra writer[1] observes that the king is really a servant, the 16% tax being his wage. Kauṭilya at one place points out how the king was on the same footing as his soldiers, both receiving their different wages and both being entitled to share the assets of the nation.[2] Nārada also regards the taxation as the king's pay for the protection of his people. No one ever makes a payment, says Aparārka, without expecting a return; the taxes, therefore, are paid only as a return for the protection expected from the king.[3] Since the people pay him the proper wage, the king must serve them as a servant, nay even as a slave.[4] This is of course a hyperbolic statement; the reality is hinted by Śukra when he describes the king both as a master and a servant of the people.[5]

KING AS A TRUSTEE

The notion of *the kingship as a trust* was also there in ancient India. The king was particularly enjoined to note that the treasury was not his private or personal property. It was a public trust to be utilised for public purposes. If a king misappropriated public funds and diverted them to his personal use, he would be guilty of sin and be condemned to hell.[6] To put

1. षड्भागभृतो राजा रक्षेत्प्रजाम् । *B. D. S.*, I. 10. 6.

2. निर्दिष्टकालो धर्मिष्ठः संहत्य ब्रूयात् । तुल्यवेतनोऽस्मि । भवद्भिः सह भोग्यमिदं राज्यम् । X. 3. (p. 367).

3. सर्वो हि धनं प्रयच्छन्नात्मसमवायि प्रयोजनमुद्दिशति । न च करदानस्य स्वगुप्तेरन्यत्प्रयोजनमस्ति । तस्मात्करमाददानेन प्रजापालनं विधेयमिति सिद्धम् । On *Yaj.* I. 366.

4. सर्वतः फलभुग्भूत्वा दासवत्स्यात्तु रक्षणे । *Śukra*, IV. 2. 130
पौरजानपदार्थं तु ममार्थो नात्मभोगतः । *Mbh.*, V. 118. 13

5. स्वभागभृत्या दास्यत्वे प्रजानां च नृपः कृतः ।
ब्रह्मणा स्वामिरूपस्तु पालनार्थं हि सर्वदा ॥ IV. 2. 137

6. बलप्रजारक्षणार्थं धर्मार्थं कोषसंग्रहः । परत्रेह च सुखदो नृपस्यान्यस्तु दुःखदः ॥ स्त्रीपुत्रार्थं कृतो यश्च स्वोपभोगाय केवलम् । नरकायैव स ज्ञेयो न परत्र सुखप्रदः ॥ *Ibid.*, IV. 2. 3-5.

it in a nutshell, the king must regard his own happiness as indissolubly connected with that of his subjects.[1]

According to some political thinkers, however, the duties of the king are even more onerous and exacting than those of a trustee. The latter is expected to take scrupulous care of the trust ; it is sufficient if he promotes the welfare of the trust and refrains from taking any direct or indirect advantage from his position as a trustee. He is not required or expected to make any self-sacrifice for promoting the interest of his trust. The ideal king, on the other hand, is required to do this. Just as an expectant mother sacrifices her own desires and pleasures, lest they should be harmful to the child to be born, the king must sacrifice his own conveniences, inclinations and pleasures in order to be of the maximum help and service to his people.[2] The body of the king is not meant for enjoyment of pleasures ; i has to put up with great troubles and worries while carrying out the royal duty of protecting the subjects and fulfilling the *dharma*.[3]

WAS THE MONARCHY LIMITED ?

There is thus no doubt that ancient Indian thinkers regarded him only as the ideal king, whose life was dedicated to service and welfare of his people. Human nature being what it is, the average king, however, was not likely to follow the ideal with a firm will and determination. What steps were devised to protect the people from the whims and caprices of a tyrannical king ? What checks were contemplated upon the royal power, if it tended to become unjust and oppressive ?

It must be admitted at the outset that no constitutional checks in the modern sense of the word were devised by our ancient thinkers. It is likely that the *samiti* or the Popular Assembly of the Vedic age functioned as a constitutional check upon

1. प्रजासुखे सुखं राज्ञः प्रजानां च हिते हितम् ।
नात्मप्रियं हितं राज्ञः प्रजानां तु प्रियं हितम् ॥ *Artha.* I. 19

2. नित्यं राज्ञा तथा भाव्यं गर्भिणी सहधर्मिणी ।
यथा स्वं सुखमुत्सृज्य गर्भस्य सुखमावहेत् ॥ *Agni-Purāṇa*, 222. 8

3. राज्ञां शरीरग्रहणं न भोगाय महीपते ।
क्लेशाय महते पृथ्वीस्वधर्मपरिपालने ॥ *Mārkaṇḍeya-P.* 130-33

the king ; there is evidence to show that a king could hardly maintain his position, if this Assembly was not in agreement with him. The powers of the Popular Assembly, however, declined as centuries rolled on ; it also disappeared from the scene by *c.* 500 B. C. ; and its place was not taken by any similar body. The king could punish his subjects for their breach of duty in his own law courts ; there was, however, no Popular Assembly or forum in the post-Vedic period, which could effectively control the king if he became oppressive. The ministry in normal times no doubt provided an efficient check ; but as ministers held their posts during the king's pleasure they felt powerless if a king was too self-willed and tyrannical to be amenable to the force of public opinion.

We should not, however, forget that the constitutional checks in the form of non-voting of supplies by Parliaments or Popular Bodies are recent developments, unknown to the ancient times. Courts to try kings for their oppressive acts were unknown in the ancient days not only in India but also elsewhere. Ancient Indians, therefore, naturally did not hit upon these remedies. They, however, devised a number of other checks, which were sufficiently effective in the normal times.

Religious and spiritual sanctions had the greatest terror in ancient India and our constitutional writers have made full use of them in order to curb the tyrannical tendency. The king, who oppresses his subjects or misappropriates public funds, is guilty of dereliction of duty ; Varuṇa, the chastiser of kings, would punish him severely. If a king levied an unjust fine, he was to offer thirty times that amount to Varuṇa as a fine by himself.[1] The threat of hell was also there, and it served as a great deterrent in ancient times.

1. अदण्डयदण्डने राज्ञो दण्डस्त्रिंशद्गुणोंऽभसि । वरुणाय प्रदातव्यो ब्राह्मणेभ्यस्ततः परम् । शास्ता हि वरुणो राज्ञां मिथ्या व्याचरतां नृषु । *Artha.* IV, 13. To medieval writers, this notion of a king fining himself appeared as strange; they therefore wrongly thought that it referred to a subordinate king or an officer; cf. तस्माद्राज्ञामिति अवान्तरनृपतीनामिति द्रष्टव्यम् । स्वस्य स्वयं दण्डानुपपत्तेः । *Daṇḍaviveka*, p. 55

The king was no doubt divine, but the established laws and customs were still more so. The king was required to take a vow at his coronation that he would scrupulously respect them. He had no power to change them at his sweet will.

Kings usually tend to become whimsical or arbitrary by the absence of proper training. Our writers, therefore, have laid particular emphasis on making adequate provision for the proper education and training of princes during their childhood and adolescence. They grow particularly eloquent in describing how a prince ought to be modest and self-controlled, pious and religious, sweet in speech and seemly in behaviour, eager to wait upon the elders and preceptors, careful to keep good company, sensitive to public opinion and criticism, and well-grounded in the military art and the science of public administration. It was hoped that a prince trained on the above lines would hardly ever go astray and become a source of troubles to his peoples.

It has been already shown above how very high ideals were placed before the king and how he was exhorted to regard himself as a public servant or a trustee of the people. He was to regard his subjects as his children and strive like a loving father, for their welfare. He was to realise that he can himself be happy only when his subjects are contented and prosperous. He could become stern only against the evil doers.

Our political writers realised that idleness is usually responsible for frivolity and have therefore prescribed a very exacting time table for the king, which hardly left him any leisure. In the king's time table as prescribed in the *Arthaśāstra* hardly six hours are allotted for recreation and sleep (I. 19). The time-table prescribed by Śukra is equally exacting (I. 275-283).

A king, however, may not receive such training, or his tyrannical disposition may be too strong to be curbed by it. If he is not amenable to the force of public opinion, if he does not listen to the advice of his elders, preceptors and ministers, if the horror of the hell has no deterrent effect upon his oppressive propensities and activities, what are the subjects to do?

We have already shown how our writers do not recommend passive obedience to wicked and tyrannical rulers. They want the people to take action, but it must be admitted that they do not give us any systematic exposition of the philosophy of resistance, indicating clearly the limits beyond which the king could not go and defining the circumstances that alone would justify the resistance on the part of the people. It is not unlikely that this may be partly due to an apprehension that an open and frank discussion of the topic may lead to the encouragement of anarchy.

Our ancient thinkers, however, do not contemplate that the subjects should take oppression lying down. It is recommended that they should threaten the tyrant that they would migrate from the country and go to another, which was better governed ;[1] it was probably hoped that the prospective loss of the revenue may bring the king to his senses. If this did not produce any effect, the subjects were to dethrone the king and enthrone a relative of his, who may appear to them as suitable.[2] This is not all ; the *Mahābhārata* expressly recognises subjects' right to tyrannicide, if there was no other remedy left to them.[3] Our works on polity carefully record the names of the tyrants who had thus lost their lives. Veṇa was one of them ; though he pleaded the inviolability of his person on account of his divinity, the sages, who were exasperated by his wickedness and tyranny, immediately killed him. Nahusha, Sudāsa, Sumukha and Nimi were other tyrants who lost their lives through the fury of their people, and it is interesting to note that this fact is pointedly brought to the notice of the king even by Manu,

1. अधर्मशीलो नृपतिर्यदा तं भीषयेज्जनः ।
धर्मशीलातिबलवद्रिपोराश्रयतः सदा ॥ *Śukra*, IV. 1. 3

King Kṛshṇadevarāya of Vijayanagar warns his officers that they should not allow subjects to migrate under such circumstances, but should try to remove their grievances.

2. गुणनीतिबलद्वेषी कुलभूतोऽप्यधार्मिकः ।
नृपो यदि भवेत्तं तु त्यजेद्राष्ट्रविनाशकम् ॥
तत्पदे तस्य कुलजं गुणयुक्तं पुरोहितः ।
प्रकृत्यनुमतिं कृत्वा स्थापयेद्राज्यगुप्तये ॥ *Śukra*, II. 274-5

3. अरक्षितारं हर्तारं विलोप्तारमनायकम् ।
तं वै राजकलिं हन्युः प्रजाः संनह्य निर्घृणम् ॥ XIII. 86. 35-6

who subscribed to his divinity. Jātakas also record a number of cases of subjects killing wicked kings as a punishment for their tyranny.[1]

The recognition of the subjects' right to depose or kill a tyrant no doubt shows that ancient Indians regarded sovereignty as ultimately residing in people. It could, however, be exercised only by a popular uprising and not through any peaceful means. It was thus not a constitutional, but rather an extra-constitutional right. It was a remedy very difficult to adopt. How can the people successfully defy the mighty power of a tyrant who has a trained and paid army to support his throne?

There is certainly a great force in the above line of argument. A less extreme but more practical remedy should have been devised against the tendency of the king's powers becoming oppressive. We should, howexer, note that in the ancient times it was not so difficult to dethrone or execute a tyrant, as it is in modern days; Jātakas often describe the people doing so with success[1] We should not forget that in olden days, on the one hand regularly paid and trained standing armies did not usually exist, and on the other hand, villages and towns had their own militias under popular control and armed with weapons in no way inferior to those of the king's army. The possibility of a successful rebellion was, therefore, not a remote one. The country was studded with a number of feudatories and sub-feudatories, and it was not difficult for people to find a leader from among them or from among ministers and high officials to put an end to tyranny. The last rulers of the Maurya and the Śuṅga dynasties and king Govinda IV of the Rāshṭrakūṭa house, for instance, lost their thrones because their misrule drove people, ministers and feudatories to rebel against them. People's right to rebel and invite a more virtuous ruler to the throne was a much more feasible and practicable right in ancient times than we can think it to be in the modern age, when governments are armed with tanks, aeroplane and atomic bombs and the subjects have to oppose them by fists, knives, and *lathis*.

1. See Sachchaṅkira and Padakusalamānava Jātkas, Nos. 73, 432

The normal checks on king's powers were, of course, not strong enough to compel a tyrant to respect the law, who had no apprehension of hell and no respect for public opinion. In their practicability and suitability, they were inferior to those devised by the modern democracies, where the Cabinet is responsible to Parliament. We should, however, not forget that when the states in ancient India were also small like the city states of ancient Greece, as in the Vedic period, the popular assemblies (*samitis*) did control the king more or less like a modern representative assembly. The greatest calamity for a king envisaged in that dim and distant past, was disagreement between him and his Popular Assembly.[1] When, however, states became larger and larger, a central popular assembly became impracticable owing to long distances and bad roads. We should also not forget that the principle of a representative democracy, where people are represented in a central parliament by their chosen representatives, is hardly more than 300 years old. It was no wonder that it did not exist in ancient India, as in ancient Greece or Rome.

It should not, however, be supposed that our ancient Indian constitutional thinkers had left everything to the fear of hell, the force of public opinion or the chances of a successful resurrection. They had advocated and brought about an extensive decentralisation of government functions and powers by investing village councils, town committees and district boroughs with very wide administrative powers and functions, as will be shown in Chap. XI.

Governments in ancient India could eventually reach the people and discharge their functions mainly through these bodies, and the representatives of the people had a decisive voice in them. Kings may impose any number of taxes; eventually those only could be realised which the village councils could agree to collect. The local bodies were also discharging judicial functions and that removed a powerful engine of oppression from the control of the king. They had also a prescriptive right to

1. नास्मै समितिः कल्पते । *A. V.*, V. 19. 15

a fair percentage of the land tax and other revenues collected in their jurisdiction, which they could utilise according to the wishes of the locality for the local works of public utility. The local executive officers were usually hereditary servants and not members of the central bureaucracy ; they, therefore, generally sided with the local bodies in their tussle with the central government. The village communities and town councils to a great extent resembled small republics, where the voice of the people prevailed. The activities of a tyrannical king, therefore, were not usually very effective much beyond his capital. The extensive decentralisation advocated and brought about in ancient India was thus the most effective and practical check upon the king's powers. The checks of the modern type were absent because the idea of the representative government was unknown both in the East and the West down to the 16th century.

THE POSITION OF THE KING BEFORE *c.* 500 B. C.

We shall conclude this chapter by making a brief survey of the position of the king in the different periods of the ancient history.

The position, powers and privileges of the king have varied from age to age. When in the prehistoric period, the king was only the seniormost member in the council of peers, when he often owed his position to an election, either real or formal, when there was a popular council (*samiti*) to actively supervise his administration, his position was often insecure and powers limited. He was often expelled from the throne and prayers were offered on his behalf that he may not have such a fate, as was actually the case with some kings like Dushṭartu, Dīrghaśravas and Sindhukshit.. It appears that taxation was also voluntary and the powerful nobles and patriarchs would give only occasional presents to the king, rather than regular taxes.[1] One great favour that India is supposed to confer at the time of coronation is to compel the subjects to pay the taxes regularly to the king.[2]

1 यत्र शल्को न क्रियते अबलेन बलीयसे । *A. V.* III. 29.3

2 अथा ते इन्द्र केवलीर्विशो बलिहृतस्करत । X. 173.6

The state in the pre-Vedic and early Vedic times was tribal and small, and a popular assembly used to function at the capital; so the king's powers were not extensive. In the course of time, when the state became territorial in character and extensive in size, the powers of the patriarchal barons like the *kulapatis* and *viśpatis* declined, as also those of the popular *samitis*, which could not meet frequently or regularly. These circumstances gradually tended to increase the powers and privileges of the king. Even in the *Ṛigveda* we have references to *ekarāṭs* (sole rulers), *adhirāṭs* (great rulers) and *samṛāṭs* (emperors).[1] It is no doubt true that some of these epithets are applied to gods, but there can be no doubt that their counterparts existed on the earth as well.

Considerable pomp and prestige surrounded the king in the later Vedic period. The panegyrics about the different kings show that they were rich and prosperous; probably they owned big herds of cattle and extensive areas of land and also received taxes from their subjects, which were tending to become more and more regular and obligatory. The *Atharvaveda* describes the king as lord of riches, the chief of the people and the most prominent among the warriors. It also prays that the king may have power, lustre and control over the nation.[2] In one ritual the Brāhmaṇa, the Kshatriya, the Vaiśya and the Śūdra each loses a cow to the king[3]; this shows that the king's sway was being regarded as encompassing all the classes of the population. His power, therefore, was getting more extensive: naturally his wrath also was being dreaded more and more.[4]

The king was pre-eminently the protector of his peoples[5] both against internal disturbances and foreign invasions. He was the upholder of law and order, of customs and traditions.

1. *R. V.*, II. 28. I ; VII 37. 3 ; X. 128. 9 ; I. 25. 10
2. IV. 22
3. *T. S.*, | 8. 16 ; *T. Br.*, I 7, 10
4. अन्यत्र राज्ञामभियातु मन्युः । *A. V.*, VI. 40. 2
5. गोपा जनस्य । *R. V*, III. 43. 5

He presided over the court at the capital,[1] which dealt with serious offences, though ordinary cases were disposed of by popular councils. He carried on the administration with the help of a number of officers like the generals (*senānīs*), *grāmaṇīs* (village headmen), *kshattris*, *saṅgrahītṛīs* and *sūtras*; the precise functions of the last three are not known at present.

THE KING'S POSITION AFTER *c.* 500 B. C.

States of fairly big size emerged into existence during this period and the power of the king was on the increase. The disappearance of the *samiti* or Popular Assembly naturally helped the process. The percentage of self-willed and tyrannical kings increased as centuries rolled on.

Considerable precautions were taken for the personal safety of the king. The *Arthaśāstra* (I. 21) narrates how streets were carefully guarded when the king was going outside and how a careful watch was kept over the visitors in the audience hall. A bodyguard of smart swordsmen was always on attendance on the king. The king used to often change his room of residence in the palace to upset possible plots of murder and his food was first tested to detect whether there was any poisoning.

Some writers of this period like Śukra and Someśvara give us a vivid picture of the audience hall, its seating arrangements and the etiquette followed in it. The king was seated in the centre on a richly decorated throne, attended by the parasol-bearer and the Chouri-wavers, a body-guard was posted at a suitable distance. Behind the king were seated his sons, grandsons and sisters' sons; the seats on the left side were allotted to relations like uncles' sons, daughters' sons, and officers like the commander-in-chief and those on the right to maternal grand-father, son-in-law and members of the ministry. The poet-laureate, the royal astrologer and the royal physician were given suitable places.

Bards and musicians occupied their allotted places and announced the entry of the king and chanted the songs describing his

1 तस्माद्राजन्येनाध्यक्षेण वैश्यं हंति। *Kāṭhaka Saṁhitā* 28. 4

exploits. The royal procession was headed by the king ; queens followed seated in their palanquins. Then came princes of the blood royal, ministers and high officials. These were followed by feudatories, heads of departments and such provincial governors, and officials who were in the capital on duty. When every body was properly seated, defeated kings were summoned ; they had to prostrate themselves first and were then allotted suitable seats. It is possible that the above plan may not have been followed in its exact details everywhere ; but it will give the reader an idea of the royal pomp and pageantry during the first millennium of the Christan era.

During this period theking became the effective head of the executive administration ; there was no popular assembly like *samiti* to check him. He controlled both the treasury and the military forces, though there were commander-in-chief and treasuerer under him. Foreign policy and peace and war were largely determined by him. Ministers were selected by the king and held office during his pleasure. The king presided over the council of ministers and its decisions had to receive royal assent. Taxation was to a great extent determined by the customary law, but the king could increase or decrease its incidence. Theoretically the king had no legislative power, but he could supplement the provisions of the customary law by his own ordinances, obedience to which was obligatory. Ordinances of kings like Aśoka and Kumārapāla are well known. The king used to go on frequent tours in the kingdom to inspect the condition of the people, to redress their grievances and to collect the tributes from his feudatories. When in the capital, he used to receive the reports of his spies to keep himself in contact with the latest developments. Foreign affairs took a large portion of his time. He was the supreme judicial authority and decided all appeals either himself or through his Chief Justice. He could also grant reprieve and order jail deliveries on the occasion of his birth day, the coronation, etc. It is not to be supposed that all kings of our period interested themselves in the above multifarious work. Personal ability and inclinations counted a good deal in determining the sphere of royal activities.

As there was no Popular Assembly functioning in our period, effective power in administration was usually shared by the king and his ministry. In some states and on some occasions the ultimate power rested with the king ; it was then described as an *ātmāyatta* or king centred administration ; in others it was vested in the ministry ; it was then called a *sachivāyatta* or ministry-dominated administration. In majority of cases however effective power was shared by the king and his ministry ; such an administration was called *ubhayāyatta*, dependent on the guidance of both the king and the ministry. The administrations during the first millennium belonged to one of these categories, the nature, capacity and ability of the two rival limbs of the body politic being the deciding factor.

CHAPTER VI

REPUBLICS

Monarchy, which was the prevailing form of government in the post-Christian period, has been discussed in the preceding chapter ; we shall now consider the various problems connected with the non-monarchical forms of the state, variously known as aristocracies or democracies or republics.

Some writers have averred that monarchy was the only form of government known to ancient India. They maintain that what are claimed to be republics were nothing more than tribal states. According to this view the Mālava-*gaṇa* and the Yaudheya-*gaṇa*, for instance, were not the Mālava and the Yaudheya republics, but the tribes of the Mālavas and the Yaudheyas respectively. This view, however, is obviously untenable ; for there is ample evidence to show that even if we grant that the Mālavas and the Yaudheyas were tribes, they had also a republican form of government. It can be proved beyond all doubt that *gaṇa* indicated a certain type of state, sharply distinguished from monarchy. When some merchants from Madhyadeśa, travelling in the Deccan, were asked by a local ruler as to who the kings were in their respective homelands, they replied, 'Sir, in the countries of some of us there are kings, but in those of others, there is *gaṇa* or republican government.'[1]. A Jain work warns a monk that he should avoid visiting a country which has no king, or has a crown prince as the ruler, or two kings fighting with each other, or is governed by the *gaṇa* form of government.[2] These two passages make it clear that *gaṇa* had a definite constitutional meaning and denoted a form of government, where the power was vested not in one person, but in a *gaṇa* or group of people. Saṅgha was another term used precisely in the same sense, because it

1. देव केचिद्देशा गणाधीनाः केचिद्राजाधीनाः । *Avadānaśataka* II.p. 103
2. अरायणि वा गणरायणि वा जुवरायणि वा दोरज्जणि वा वेरज्जणि वा विरुद्धरज्जणि वा । *Āchārāṅgasūtra* I. 3. 160

was sharply distinguished from monarchy.[1] When,t herefore, we get coin legends on hundreds of coins, referring not to the kings of the Yaudheyas, the Mālavas and the Arjunāyanas, but to their *gaṇas* it is clear that they refer not to their tribes but to their *gaṇa* or republican states, which had authorised the coin issue.

Apart from the evidence of coin legends and technical constitutional terms, we have also the valuable testimony of some contemporary Greek writers to show that there were many forms of non-monarchical states in ancient India. The account of Greek writers is held at discount in some quarters ;[2] it is impossible not to suspect, they say, that the account of the State machinery given by them was not deliberately assimilated to the forms of government prevailing in Greece. It is very difficult to accept this line of argument. The political sense was nowhere more developed and state institutions better studied than in ancient Greece. Greek historians found both monarchical and non-monarchical forms of the state prevailing in India. They themselves liked democracy better than monarchy, and there is no reason to believe that they would have gone out of their way in making a false statement about the prevalence of democracy among Indians, who were their bitter political opponents for a long time. A study of their writings shows that they have taken particular pains to distinguish the different forms of government. Amphi was a king and so was Porus ; when the latter became a faithful subordinate ally of Alexander the Great, we are told that the Greek conqueror added a large province to his kingdom, 'subduing inhabitants whose form of government was republican'.[3] The government of the city of Nyasa was in the hands of an aristocracy.[4] The Sabaracae was a powerful Indian tribe, 'where the form of government was democratic and not regal'.[5] To the east of the Beas was a powerful kingdom 'in which the multitude was governed by

1. क्षत्रियादेकराजात संघप्रतिषेधार्थम् । Kātyāyana on Pāṇini IV. 1. 160
2. Beni Prasad, *State in Ancient India,* 168-9
3. M'Crindle, *Invasion of Alexander the Great,* p. 308-9
4. *Ibid,* p. 81
5. *Ibid,* p. 252

the aristocracy, who exercised their authority with justice and moderation.[1] There were a number of non-monarchical states in the Indus valley, but when the Greeks came across a monarchy in that region, their historians do not fail to mention it. They are careful to point out that the kingdom of Mausikanos was governed by a king and that of Patala, by two kings belonging to two different families, but ruling simultaneously with the help of the popular council. When such minute facts about the variations in the forms of the state and administration have been carefully noticed by the Greek writers, we cannot brush aside their account on the fanciful plea that their imagination, which incited them to see Hellenistic things in non-Hellenic countries, was mainly responsible for their references to Indian republics. M 'Crindle's view that the independent or autonomous states mentioned by the Greek writers refer to village communities is equally untenable.[2] Greek authors in fact have rarely referred to the village life or village government. Nor can we accept the opinion of Fick that the autonomous states of the Greek writers were individual cities or small states that maintained their independence in the neighbourhood of great monarchies like that of Magadha.[3] The fact is that there was no such big monarchy in the Punjab in the days of Alexander the Great ; as a matter of fact non-monarchical states were more extensive and powerful than the monarchical ones in that province at the time.

It must have been noticed that the states under discussion have been so far described by us negatively as non-monarchical. We must now proceed to ascertain their real form. They have been sometimes described as mere tribal organisations, sometimes as oligarchies, sometimes as aristocracies and sometimes as republics. Let us see what term will correctly describe their constitution.

It is argued that to describe these states as republics or democracies would be hardly justifiable. Power was vested in these states not in the whole body of the citizens but in a

1. M'Crindle, *Invasion of Alexander the Great*, p. 121
2. *Ibid*, p. 115, n. 2.
3. Fick, *Social Organisation in the North-Eastern India*, p. 137.

small aristocratic class. Thus among the Yaudheyas, we definitely know that the government was vested in a college of 5,000 persons, each of whom was required to present an elephant to the state.[1] It is clear that the governing class of this state consisted of a rich aristocracy, members of which could afford to present an elephant to the state; common people had no voice in its administration. The same was also the case with the Śākyas and Koliyas; the question of peace or war, which vitally affected the fortunes of the man in the street, was decided there by the Śākya and Koliya aristocrats, (*rājās*), who were a few hundreds in number; the commoners like the farmers and the workers had merely to wait for and carry out the decisions of the privileged order.

It can be at once conceded that the *gaṇa* states of the Yaudheyas and the Śākyas, the Mālavas and the Lichchavis were not democracies or republics in the sense in which we understand these words today. Supreme and ultimate power did not lie vested in the whole body of adult citizens, as is the case with most of the well developed modern democracies. We can, however, still describe these states as republics. Standard works and authorities on the political science define republic as a state, where the sovereign power vests, not in a single person as in monarchy, but in a group or college of persons, more or less numerous. Oligarchies, aristocracies and democracies have all been labelled as republics. Thus Sparta, Athence, Rome, medieval Venice, the United Netherlands and Poland have all been described as republics, though none of them possessed that full democratic character, which we are at present inclined to consider as the most distinguishing feature of a republic. In the republics of ancient Greece and Rome, the franchise was confined to a small minority, who governed a vast majority, consisting of slaves as well as persons like mechanics and artisans who were personally free and yet had no franchise. Democracy was a reality only with reference to the small class of full fledged citizens, and not the whole population. In the

1. M'Crindle, *Invasion of Alexander the Great*, p. 121

medieval republic of Venice, after the closing of the council, the franchise was confined to a strictly limited aristocracy, which itself was dominated by a small oligarchy. The republic of the Seven States of Netherlands was no doubt governed by an elected Stateholder, but he was raised to that position by the votes of a very small body of burghers, who only had the franchise. And even in modern times in the U.S.A. millions of Negroes had no franchise for a long time and England had a number of pocket boroughs till the middle of the 19th century. In the 20th century France, nearly half the population has no franchise, for women in that country cannot yet vote in elections.

With this theoretic background and historic evidence, we can certainly describe ancient Indian *gaṇa* states as republics in the same sense in which the ancient states of Greece and Italy were given that designation. Sovereignty in these states was vested not in one individual, nor in a small number of persons, but in a fairly numerous class. In the beginning this class consisted only of the descendants of the Kshatriya families, who had colonised the land, brought it under cultivation and founded the new state. It appears that even the Kshatriya families, who arrived later, did not enjoy the privilege of admission to the ruling class for a long time. The descendants of the original Kshatriya families, whose heads were called *rājās*, were known as *rājanyas*, while the rest of the Kshatriyas were known as *rājans*. In the famous Andhaka-Vṛishṇi republic, the descendants of Śvāphalaka, Chaitraka, Vāsudeva and Śini could be called *rāj nyakas* ; the rest were all *rājans*.[1] The coin legend *Vṛishṇi-rājanya-gaṇasya jayaḥ* would show that in the Vṛishṇi republic the power was vested in the original Kshatriya founder families. It may be interesting to note that in the eastern states of the U.S.A. the distinction between the descendants of the original settlers' families and those who arrived later, was for a long time recognised in the sphere of social life.

The Kshatriya settlers had inherited monarchical traditions

1. *Pāṇini*, VI. 2. 34. The *Kāśikā* describes *rāyanaya* as *Abhishikta-vamisya-kshatriyas*.

and the leaders of the colonising families claimed and enjoyed the privilege of royal coronation and royal title. Kauṭilya (Bk. XI.I) undoubtedly uses the term *rājaśabdopajīvinaḥ* with reference to such republics where this usage prevailed. When Yudhishṭhira in the *Mahābhārata* points out how in some places there were kings in every house,[1] he obviously has small republics in view where this custom prevailed. We can now well understand the statement in the Buddhist literature about the Lichchhavi Saṁgha or republic having 7707 kings in it. The traditional number of the original Kshatriya settlers, who had colonised Muzaffarpur district was 7707 ; each one of them enjoyed the title of *rāja* and claimed the privilege of ablution in the coronation tank (*abhisheka-pokaraṇī*), which is referred to in the Jātakas[2] and is still remembered at Vaiśāli. He also had his own crown-prince, general and treasurer. Vaiśāli was a small republic, covering not more than the area of one district, and if it had 7707 kings, one can well understand the taunt in the *Lalitavistara* that everybody at Vaiśāli considered himself to be a king.[3]

In course of time, political power became more broadbased in the republics. The *Amarakośa* distinguishes between two types of the Kshatriya republic ; *Rājanyaka-gaṇa* or republic was one where power was vested in the descendants of the original founder-families enjoying the title of the *rājā* ; whereas *rājaka-gaṇa* or republic was one where it was vested in all the Kshatriya families, whether descended from the original founders or not.[4] We can therefore well understand how the Śāntiparvan in one place describes the members of a republic as equal to one another in their caste and family status.[5]

Brāhmaṇas enjoyed high social privileges in ancient India. Some of them used to take to the military profession also and would often found their own republican states ; one such state

1. गृहे गृहे तु राजानः । II. XV. 2
2. वेशालीनगरे गणराजकुलानां अभिषेकमंगलपोखरिणी । Jātaka, IV. 148
3. एकैक एव मन्यते अहं राजा अहं राजेति ।
4. अथ राजकम् । राजन्यकं च नृपतिक्षत्रियाणां गणे क्रमात् । II. 8. 9. 3
5. जात्या च सदृशाः सर्वे कुलेन सदृशास्तथा ॥ XII. 107. 29

existed in Sindh at the time of the invasion of Alexander the Great. In Brahmaṇa republics they enjoyed the privileged position, but whether they had the same in Kshatriya republics, we do not know.

The *Arthaśāstra* XI. 1 would show that in some republics, both the military and trading classes shared the political power.[1]

The governing class in the Gaṇa state was thus a fairly large one, probably as numerous as the corresponding class in the ancient republics of Greece and Italy.

We can, therefore, legitimately describe the ancient Gaṇa states as republics in the same sense in which the standard works on the political science describe the states of Athens, Sparta or Venice as republics, remembering at the same time that they were not democracies of the modern type, where the franchise is vested in as large a number of citizens as possible. Political power was mainly in the hands of the Kshatriyas. In ancient Greece, there was often a conflict between aristocracy, which wielded the power, and the common people, who wanted to have it. We do not know whether there were such conflicts in ancient India.

There is sufficient evidence to show that in the Gaṇa states the non-Kshatriyas were sharply distinguished from the ruling aristocracy. This distinction was so well established that special terms were devised to indicate it. Thus in the Mālava and Kshudraka Gaṇa states, the terms Mālava and Kshudraka denoted only the members of the privileged Kshatriya order; those, who were neither the Kshatriyas nor the Brāhmaṇas, were called, not Mālavaṣ or Kshudrakas, but Mālavyas and Kshudrakyas respectively. It seems that the Brāhmaṇas could get exemption from being designated as Mālavyas and Kshudrakyas under certain circumstances, which, however, are not quite clear.[2]

1. काम्बोजसुराष्ट्रक्षत्रियश्रेण्यादयो वार्ताशस्त्रोपजीविनः । XI. 1

2. आयुधजीविसंघाञ्ञ्यड्वाहीकेष्वब्राह्मणराजन्यात् Pāṇini, V. 3. 114 वाहीकेषु य आयुधजीविसंघस्तद्वाचिनः प्रातिपादकाद् ब्राह्मणराजन्यवर्जितात् स्वार्थे ञ्यट्प्रत्ययो भवति। ब्राह्मणे तद्विशेषग्रहणम्। राजन्ये तु स्वरूपग्रहणमेव। क्षौद्रक्यः क्षौद्रक्यौ। क्षुद्रकाः। मालव्यः। मालव्यौ। मालवाः। *Kāśikā*, on V. 3. 114

Let us now trace the history of our republics. As shown already, monarchy was the normal form of government in the Vedic age. It was a period of Aryan expansion and the advantages of a capable and unitary leadership were naturally valued. Curiously enough a tradition narrated to Megasthenes in the 4th century B. C. also averred that monarchy was the earlier and democracy the later form of government.[1] The Madras, the Kurus, the Pāṇchālas, the Śibis and the Videhas, who figure as republics in the 6th century B. C., were all monarchies in prehistoric times as shown by the pre-Buddhist genealogies of their dynasties preserved in the Purāṇas.

The concluding hymn of the *Ṛigveda* prays that the deliberations of the *samiti* should be harmonious and the minds of its members well-disposed towards one another and its conclusions unanimous.[2] It is not impossible to argue that the hope and the desideratum expressed in the hymn refers to the deliberative and administrative activity of a republican state. Usually, however, the *samiti* is associated with a king and served as a check upon his power. It is, therefore, doubtful whether it denoted the Central Assembly of a republican state. The hymn by itself cannot conclusively prove the existence of a republican state.

In one place we get a reference to several kings meeting together in one *samiti*.[3] In another place we get the significant statement that he alone becomes a king whose leadership of the state is assented to by *other kings*.[4] The *kings* here referred to were probably the heads of the Kshatriya families, entitled to coronation and the state contemplated by this passage is one which was the prototype of the later republics already described above. The sovereign power of course rested not in the populace in general

1. Cf. 'At last after many generations had come and gone, the sovereignty, it is said, was dissolved and a democratic government set up in the cities'. Arian, Chap. IX.

2. समानो मंत्रः समितिः समानी समानं मनः सह चित्तमेषाम् । X. 191. 2

3. यत्रौषधीः समग्मत राजानः समिताविव । *R. V*, X. 97. 6

4. यस्मै वै राजानो राज्यमनुमन्यन्ते स राजा भवति न स यस्मै न ।
S. Br., IX. 3. 2. 5

but in the aristocratic leaders of the cantons who were fairly numerous. If the kingship or leadership assented to by them became hereditary in the course of time, the normal monarchy of the later period was evolved. If, on the other hand, power was delegated to their leader by the members of the aristocracy for a short time, and if the leadership was not allowed to become hereditary, then circumstances were created which were to develop into the Kshatriya republics of the later times known as *gaṇas* or *saṁghas*. It is interesting to add that the kingship that is disclosed in Homer was similarly replaced by aristocracy at *c.* 700 B. C. on account of the power passing into the hands of a relatively small number of privileged persons.[1]

A well-known passage in the later Vedic literature[2] observes that the kings of the easterners were known as *Samrāṭs* or emperors, those of the Sātvatas as *Bhojas*, those of the Nichyas and Apāchyas as *Svarāṭs*, while the countries to the north of the Himalayas like the Uttaramadras and Uttarakurus had a *vairājya* state and their *people* were called *virāṭs*. There is some difference of opinion about the meaning of the terms *Svarāṭs* and *Bhojas*,[3] but there can be no doubt that the *vairājya* states of the Uttarakurus and the Uttaramadras were kingless (*vairājya*) states, where people, that is the heads of founder families, were consecrated for the rulership.[4] It is worth noting that the Punjab, which was near the homeland of the Uttarakurus and

1. Dunning, *Political Theories*, I. pp. 7-8

2. ये के च प्राच्यानां राजानः साम्राज्यायैव तेऽभिषिच्यन्ते । ये के च परेण हिमवन्तं जनपदा उत्तरकुरव उत्तरमद्रा इति वैराज्यायैव तेभिषिच्यन्ते विराडित्येतानभिषिक्तानाचक्षते । *A. Br.*,VII. 3. 14

3. Dr. Jayaswal contends that they denote republican states (*Hindu Polity*, I, pp. 90-1); but this does not seem probable.

4. Sāyaṇa's explanation of वैराज्य as इतरेभ्यो भूपतिभ्यः श्रैष्ठयम् is due to his ignorance of a democratic state. The *Mbh.* XII. 67. 54 describes a *virāṭ* as one of the synonyms of the word king. But just as we can explain *virāṭ* as a *viśesheṇa rājā*, we can as well explain *Vairājya* state as one, which is devoid of (*vi*) the king. The *Vedic Index* explains *Vairājya* as a form of royal authority, but if in that state, the whole people, and not the kings only, were consecrated to the rulership, is it not reasonable to assume that the sovereignty in the *Vairājya* state was vested not in one individual, but in a large class, if not in the whole population ?

the Uttaramadras, continued to have republican states down to the 4th century A. D., as will be soon shown.

In historic times republics were flourishing in ancient India in a north-western and in a north-eastern zone. Curiously enough south India, where democracy was more effective in the realm of local government than in north India, does not seem to have developed any democratic state or republic. We shall now briefly notice the different republics that flourished in historic times. We shall start from the north-west.[1]

The Punjab and the Indus valley were pre-eminently the land of republics from *c.* 500 B. C. to 400 A. D. Unfortunately in the case of some of them, we know nothing but their names fortunately preserved by some grammarians. To this category belong the Vṛikas, the Dāmaṇis, the Parśvas and the Kambojas. The Trigarta-shashṭhas, according to Pāṇini (V. 3. 116), formed confederation of six states which, according to the *Kāśikā* (composed about a thousand years later), were Kauṇḍoparatha, Dāṇḍaki Kraushṭaki, Jālamāni, Brahmagupta and Jānaki. Coins issued with the legend *Trakatajanapadasa*, coinage of the Trakata (Trigarta) country, seem to have been issued by them.[2] It is likely that this confederation flourished in the Jullandar Doab and later became a unitary state under the name of the Kuṇindas, coins issued by whom, but belonging to a later period, have been found in large numbers.[3] In the course of the description of Arjuna's conquests in the Punjab, *the Mahābhārata* mentions[4] the Pañchagaṇa and

1. Our chief sources of information about the republics of ancient India are the Greek writers for the north-western zone and the Buddhist works for the north-eastern one. Very valuable evidence is also obtained from grammarians like Pāṇini, and Patañjali, which has been lucidly utilised by Dr. V. S. Agrawala in his work, *India as known to Pāṇini*, Chap. VII. The *Mahābhārata* has two valuable chapters, written from a sympathetic point of view, directly describing some aspects of the working of the constitution of these states (XII. 81 and 107). The *Arthaśāstra*, Bk. XI, is mainly interested in describing measures to break the power of the *gaṇas* and *saṁghas*, but while doing so, it gives us some glimpses of the working of their consitution.

2. Allan *Coins of Ancient India*, Pl. XXXIX, 10. The legends on the coins issued by this and other republics afford very valuable and concrete evidence to prove their existence.

3. R.C. Majumdhr and A.S. Altekar: *Th Age of the Vākāṭakas and the Guptas.* Chapter II. It may be pointed out that the Kuṇinda republic flourished down to the 3rd century A. D. and offered valuable cooperation to the Yaudheyas in driving out the Kushāṇas.

4. II. 27. 12, 16

Saptagaṇa republics. These were probably federations of five and seven republics. The federating units may have been some of the Punjab republics mentioned by Pāṇini.

The Arjunāyanas flourished as a republic in the Agra-Jaipur tract from *c.* 200 B. C. to *c.* 400 A. D. Their coins have been found, which do not bear the name of any king or general; the legend is simply *Arjunāyanānāṁ jayaḥ*. 'victory to the Arjunāyanas.' The coins belong to *c.* 100 B. C., but the Arjunāyana state must have been much more ancient, for the ruling class believed that it was descended from Arjuna, the epic hero. They worked in close cooperation with the Yaudheyas, their northern neighbours, who believed themselves to be the descendants of Dharma, the eldest brother of Arjuna.

The Yaudheya republic was a fairly extensive state. The findspots of its coins show that it extended from Saharanpur in the east to Bahavalpur in the west, from Ludhiyana in the north-west to Delhi in the south-east. It was a confederation of three republics. Rohtak in the Punjab was the capital of one of them, and northern Pañchāla, known as Bahudhānyaka (rich in corn) country, was the centre of power of the second. Northern Rajputana seems to have been in the jurisdiction of the third. The powerful trans-Beas state, mentioned by Alexander's historians, which possessed fertile territory and virile inhabitants, and which was governed by an aristocracy exercising its power with justice and moderation, is obviously the Yaudheya republic. The Yaudheyas had an unsurpassed reputation for bravery, and no wonder; for they were the devotees of Kārttikeya, the generalissimo of gods. They were, therefore, also known as Mattamayūrakas, peacock (*mayūra*) being the vehicle of Kārttikeya.[1] It was this reputation of their bravery and the report about the rich resources of their state that made Alexander's soldiers lose their heart and refuse to advance further. The Yaudheyas continued to flourish down to the end of the 1st century A. D., when they were temporarily overpowered by Kanishka I. But they soon became 'insubordinate', as a record

1. *Mbh.*, V. 35. 3-4

of their enemy puts it, 'owing to their pride due to their valour being respected by all the Kshattriyas',[1] and rebelled against the Kushāṇa hegemony. They not only reasserted their independence in *c.* 225 A. D., but dealt a powerful blow to the Kushāṇa empire from which it could not recover.[2] They were flourishing as a republic down to *c.* 350 A. D. Their subsequent history is unknown.

The Madras in the Central Punjab were a republican state during the 4th century A. D ; they seem to be identical with the Kaṭhas whose republic is mentioned by Alexander's historians with its capital at Sialkot. They disdained to purchase peace by surrender and fought against the Greek invader to the bitter end. This republic continued to flourish down to the 4th century A. D.

The Mālavas and the Kshudrakas were among those republics, which offered stoutest resistance to Alexander the Great. The region between the Chenab and the Ravi along with some territory further south was the homeland of the Mālavas at this time, and the Kshudrakas were their southern neighbours.[3] In order to meet Alexander's invasion, they formed an alliance, but before their armies could effect a junction, Alexander struck against the Mālavas. The Mālavas, who could muster an army about 1,00,000 strong, offered bitter opposition, and Alexander almost lost his life while trying to capture one of their forts. Eventually both the Mālavas and the Kshudrakas were compelled to sue for peace. The two states, however, became wiser by this defeat and formed a confederation which lasted for a few decades. In the *Mahābhārata*, the Mālavas and the Kshudrakas are always mentioned together,[4] and grammarians refer to a peculiar dual compound formed from the names of the two states. Later on the Kshudrakas seem to have completely merged in the Mālavas, who eventually migrated to Ajmer-Chitor-Tonk area in *c.* 100 B. C., and to the modern province of Mālwā

1. Junagad inscription of Rudradāman I.
2. R.C. Majumdar and A.S. Altekar : *The Age of the Vākāṭakas and the Guptas*, pp. 28-33.
3. M,Crindle, *Invasion of Alexander the Great*, pp. 138 ff.
4. II, 79, 90 ; V. 57, 18

about 400 years later. They were for a time subjugated by the Scythians in *c.* 150 A. D., but they reasserted their independence in *c.* 225 A. D. They claimed descent from the illustrious Ikshvāku stock of Śrī-Rāmachandra. They have left a very copious copper currency, whose legends do not mention any king but commemorate the victory of the Mālava republic.

The precise location of the Agesinae and the Śibis, who were in the nieghbourhood of the Mālavas at the time of Alexander's invasion, is not known. The Śibis had a monarchy in the earlier days but became a republic later. By *c.* 100 B. C. they migrated to Mādhyamikā, near Chitor in Rajputana, where a large number of their coins, issued in the name of their republic, and not that of any king, have been found.[1]

In the neighbourhood of the Kshudrakas there was another republic, that of the Ambashṭhas (Sambastai of the Greeks). Curtius expressly describes their form of government as democratic. They had an army of 60,000 foot, 6,000 cavalry and 500 chariots, and had elected three generals to oppose Alexander the Great. Eventually, however, they decided to submit to him following the advice of their elders. Their later history is not known

The Andhaka-Vṛishṇis, the Yādavas, the Kukkuras and the Bhojas are described in the *Mahābhārata* as having their full confidence in the leadership of Kṛishṇa. Probably they, formed a federal republic at least for some time.[2] The *saṁgha* states of Kathiawar mentioned by the *Arthaśāstra* (Bk. XI) appear to have continued the ancient republican tradition.

The Buddhist canon and the Jātakas and their commentaries disclose the existence of a large number of republics flourishing in the Gorakhpur division of U. P. and in northern Bihar. Of course the Bhaggas, the Bulis, the Koliyas and the Moriyas were very small states, hardly more extensive than a tehsil or

1. The legend is '*Majhamikāya Śibi-janapadasa*' (The coinage) of the Śibi country or commonwealth (issued in the city) of *Majhamikā* or Mādhyamikā. Allan, *Coins of Ancient India*, p. cxxiv

2. यादवाः कक्कुरा भोजाः सर्वे चान्धकवृष्णयः ।
त्वय्यासक्ता महाबाहो लोका लोकेश्वराश्च ॥ XII.81.29

two of the modern times. The Śākyas, the Mallas, the Lichchhavis and the Videhas were relatively larger, but the total extent of the territories of all these four states did not cover an area of more than 200 miles in length and 100 miles in breadth, between Gorakhpur in the west and Darbhanga in the east, between the Gangā to the south and the Himalayas to the north.[1] Of these four states, that of the Śākyas was the smallest and occupied a portion of Gorakhpur district. The Mallas were to their east and occupied the territory round Kusinagar. Then came the Lichchhavis and the Videhas.

Some doubts arise as to the nature of the Śākya state. Some references in the Buddhist canonical literature suggest that the Śākyas had a monarchy. Bhaddiya, who was a king in Buddha's time, takes a week to arrange for the succession to his kingdom when he decides to enter the Holy Order. We, however, know that each member of the Kshatriya aristocracy, which ruled these eastern states, was entitled to call himself a *rājā*, and Bhaddiya may have been a *rājā* in that restricted sense of the term. Jātaka evidence shows that the Śākyas had an Assembly Hall, where all of them used to meet and decide important questions of peace, war and alliance. It does not refer to a hereditary king ruling over the whole state.

There is no doubt that the Mallas, the Lichchhavis and the Videhas were republics during the life time of the Buddha. Their neighbours, the kings of Magadha and Kośala, were anxious to conquer them, and so we find these republics often forming confederation among themselves. Sometimes we find the Lichchhavis confederating with the Mallas and sometimes with the Videhas. The latter two, however, disappear from history from *c.* 500 B. C., when they were conquered by Magadha. The Lichchhavis had also to bow before the Magadhan imperialism, but they reasserted their independence by *c.* 300 B. C. They were a powerful state at the beginning of the 4th

1. It will thus be seen that these republics were not much larger than the city states of ancient Greece. Sparta, the biggest state, had an area of 3360 sq. miles; the area of the Lichchhavi state was approximately the same. Athence at the time of its greatest prosperity ruled over 1060 sq. miles, which seems to have been the area of the Śākya republic.

century A. D. and it was by an alliance with them that the Guptas could rise to the imperial position.

We shall now proceed to consider the constitution and the administrative machinery of ancient Indian republics. Our main handicap is the absence of sufficient evidence to enlighten us upon the point. We shall have to consider disconnected data, often belonging to widely distant centuries and referring to different states and draw a composite picture. This method has its own obvious limitations and dangers, but there is no other procedure possible in the present state of our knowledge.

It is clear that the constitutional machinery of small states like those of the Moriyas, the Koliyas and the Śākyas, which included hardly a few score villages in their jurisdiction, must have been different from that prevailing in big states like those of the Yaudheyas and the Mālavas, which covered extensive territories including dozens of cities and thousands of villages. It appears that in the small states of north-eastern India, most of the members of the Central Assembly lived in the capital where they used to meet frequently in the Assembly Hall (*santhāgāra*) to transact business of the state. Each member of the aristocratic order was known as a *rājā* and his son as an *uparājā*.[1] Probably the *rājā* held some zemindari land in the moffusil which he managed through his local agents. Besides the governing class, the population consisted of a large number of artisans farmers, servants and serfs. When a quarrel arose between the farmers and servants of the Koliyas and the Śākyas about the distribution of the water of the Rohiṇī, they reported it to the officer of their own state, who in turn appraised their *rājās* about it. It is the latter, who decided to go on war with the opposing

1. This is, as shown above, the correct interpretation of the statement, तत्थ निच्चकालं रज्जं कारेत्वा वसंतानं येव राजूनं सत्तसहस्सानि सत्तसतानि सत्त च राजानो होंति तत्तका येव उपराजानो तत्तका सेनापतिनो तत्तका भंडागारिका। *Jātaka*, I, p. 504

Dr. Bhandarkar's view that this statement suggests that the Lichchhavi state was a confederation of 7707 principalities, each having full authority under its *rājā*, *uparājā* etc., does not seem probable. *Carmichael Lectures*, 1918, p. 135. Such a big confederation is impracticable.

For Dr. R. C. Majumdar's interpretation, see *Corporate Life*, pp. 53-4 (1st edition).

state. This incident, therefore, shows that the commoners had not much voice in the momentous decisions of the central government on important topics like peace or war, which affected the whole population. There were, however, a number of small towns and villages in the Śākya state, which had their own Assemblies meeting in their Assembly Halls (*santhāgāras*).[1] It is very likely that in these village assemblies the non-privileged classes may have had an equal voice in local affairs.

The administration of bigger states like that of the Yaudheyas or the Mālavas was naturally organised in a different way. They were divided into provinces, each under a separate governor, probably recruited from the privileged class. The numerous cities of the state constituted separate government units, completely autonomous, and administered by their leading men. Unfortunately we do not know how these city councils were constituted. It is likely that the members of the privileged order may have dominated in them, but what we know of other city councils functioning in monarchical states enables us to infer that traders, artisans and agriculturists also belonging to the general population, may have had their own representatives on that body. In the village councils of the hundreds of villages that were situated in these states, the average population must have had the dominating voice. It is likely that the headman of the village may have been a member of the ruling class; the bureaucracy also may have been largely recruited from it. But the vast majority of the members of the village councils must have belonged to the different trades and professions which were recruited from all classes and castes.

The sovereignty in these republics was vested in a very large Central Assembly. Its membership is stated to have been as high as 5,000 among the Yaudheyas and 7,707 among the Lichchhavis. The Kshudrakas had sent 150 of their leading men to negotiate peace with Alexander; the number of the members of their Central Assembly may have been probably much larger.

2. The assembly hall of the village Chatuma is expressly mentioned in the Buddhist canonical literature; *M. N*, I. 457

These figures no doubt strike us as very large; but we should not forget that in contemporary Greece, the Athenian Assembly consisted of 42,000 citizens, each of whom had a right to attend its meetings. In actual practice, however, not all the members cared to attend. The country people did not like to spend time and money to attend all the meetings. The normal attendance was 2,000 to 3,000, hardly 7 or 8 per cent of the total membership. The Central Assembly of 7,707 members of the Lichchhavis or of 5,000 of the Yaudheyas probably consisted of the heads of the families of the descendants of the founder members of the privileged aristocracy, who were all entitled to the honorific title *rājā*.[1] Some of them stayed at the capital and some were scattered in moffusil or serving there as important government officers. They were all entitled to attend, but at ordinary meetings of the Assembly hardly 10 per cent members may have attended, as in ancient Athens. If a city like Nyasa had an Assembly of 30 councillors, a big state like that of the Yaudheyas might well have had one of 5,000. We should not forget that the membership depended upon belonging to the privileged order, and no one who belonged to it by his birth and extraction could be excluded from it; each member was extremely jealous of his proud position and extraction. There was no question of the possibility of a number of them being represented by one representative, even if the principle of representation had been known at the time, which of course was not the case. In ancient Indian republics, there was then no electoral role giving a list of qualified voters; nor were there any periodical elections. Had any such existed, they would have been referred to in the literature bearing upon the science of polity.

to in the literature bearing upon the science of polity.

Dr. Jayaswal has suggested that in some of these states there were two Houses, an Upper and a Lower House.[2] This seems

1. One Jātaka states that there were twice eighty four thousand nobles at Vaiśāli (I. 271). Probably the total population of the ruling class was 1,68,000 and the Assembly probably consisted of the heads of big joint families, each consisting of about 20 persons.

2. *Hindu Polity*, I, p. 84. The grammatical *Sūtra*, *Saṁghe chānauttarādharye* (Pāṇini, III. 3. 42), does not at all refer to the higher and lower hourses of a legislative assembly. It does not refer to a political constitution but to the groups of monks, Brāhmaṇas and herds of swine and points out that in the first two cases there is a difference among their members and in the last one there is none.

to be very improbable. The members of the privileged classes, who constituted the Assembly, were very jealous of their status and extraction, and would hardly have tolerated an Upper House. The elders, on whose advice the Ambashṭhas decided to make peace with Alexander, were not the members of a House of Elders, but the senior persons of their own order.

Sovereignty was vested in these large Central Assemblies, which were very jealous of their rights and powers. They elected not only the members of the executive, but also the military leaders. When reports reached about the impending invasion of Alexander the Great, the Ambashṭhas elected three generals renowned for their bravery and military skill to lead their armies. It seems that like the Roman Senate, the Assemblies of these republics elected their own generals for the different campaigns.[1] The election in the beginning at any rate was for a specific campaign ; this was a precaution against a general seizing all the powers of the state. What was true of the Ambashṭhas of the 4th century B. C. was true also of the Yaudheyas of the 4th century A. D., for an inscription of the Gupta period refers to a general elected, *puraskṛita*, by the Yaudheya *gaṇa*.[2] Gradually these tended to become hereditary. The Mālava general, who regained the independence for his state in *c.* 225 A.D., belonged to a family which was entrusted with the military leadership for three generations.[3]. Its leaders, however, were not permitted to have any regal title like *rājā* or *mahārāja*.

The evidence of the Buddhist literature shows that the Central Assemblies of the republics controlled foreign affairs, entertained ambassadors and foreign princes, considered their proposals and decided the momentous issues of peace and war.[4] On grave occasions the latter power was entrusted to a smaller

1. In ancient Athens also generals were elected by the people. Dunning, *Political Theories*, I. p. 15

2. Fleet, *C. I. I.*, III. p. 152

3. Cf. जयसोमपुत्रस्य सोगिनेतुः श्रीसोमस्य । II. 15-16. Nandsa inscription, *E. I.*, XXVII, p. 252

4. *Jātaka*, IV. p. 145 (No. 465) ; Rockhill, *Life of the Buddha*, pp. 118-9

body ; the 150 'ambassadors' deputed by the Kshudrakas to Alexander the Great, were obviously the leading members of their Central Assembly ; they had been entrusted with full powers to conclude the treaty.[1] Some writers were of the opinion that it is in the interest of the *gaṇas* themselves that they should not discuss delicate questions like peace and war in the General Assembly, but should leave them to the decision of the Executive.[2] It is quite possible that this policy might have been followed in some states in order to ensure secrecy, so necessary for the success in foreign policy. But their number was not large, for one of the weaknesses of the Gaṇa state frequently emphasised by constitutional writers is its incapacity to preserve political secrets.

Generally speaking the Executive was under the complete control of the Central Assembly in the republican states. Śrī Kṛishṇa, who was the President of the Andhaka-Vṛishṇi state, bitterly complains to Nārada that he is not the master but the slave of the Central Assembly, as he has to listen patiently to the bitter criticisms of the different parties.[3] The *Arthaśāstra* (Bk. XI) shows that if the President of the *Saṁgha* (*Saṁghamukhya*) or the members of the Executive Council were guilty of the mismanagement of the public funds or violating the ordinary laws of the land, they could be dismissed and punished by the state tribunals. The Executive was thus under the complete constitutional control of the Central Assembly. Though there is no specific evidence on the point, it is almost certain that the appointments to the state services and the governorships of the provinces must have been made by the Central Assembly. That must have been one of the reasons for the keen contest for power that was often going on in that body.

The Assembly Hall also served the purpose of a social club, where social and religious topics were also discussed at times.

1. M'Crindle, *Invasion of Alexander the Great*, p. 154
2. न गणाः कृत्स्नशो मंत्रं श्रोतुमर्हन्ति भारत ।
गणमुख्यैस्तु संभूय कार्यं गणहितं मिथः । *Mbh*, XII. 107. 24
3. दास्यमैश्वर्यभावेन ज्ञातीनां वै करोम्यहम् ।
अर्धभोक्तास्मि भोगानां वाग्दुरुक्तानि च क्षमे । *Mbh*, XII. 81. 5

The Mallas of Kusinagar discussed the problems about the funeral of the Buddha and the disposal of his ashes in their Assembly Hall. They, as well as the Lichchhavis, are known to have requested the Blessed One to perform the opening ceremonies of their new Assembly Halls by first using them for delivering a sermon to a congregation assembled therein.

The meetings of the Assembly held for such religious or social functions may have been peaceful ; but such was not very often the case when political matters of moment had to be discussed and decided. Many of the Assemblies of these republics, like the Parliaments and municipalities of the modern age, were torn by party factions ; in fact the Buddhist literature, the *Arthaśāstra* and the *Mahābhārata* point out that family quarrels, party factions, lure of corruption, internal dissensions and mutual recriminations among the members of the Assembly constitute the main weaknesses of the Gaṇa states. Bhīshma emphasises again and again that the danger from foreign invasion is not at all so great as the danger from the internal quarrels.[1] The latter were often carried to such an extent that leaders and members of different parties would not even speak with one another. The language used by Bhīshma to describe the strained relations among the republican parties is almost a paraphrase of the words in Buddhist literature used to describe the conditions of the Lichchhavis after the seeds of dissentions were successfully sown among them by spies and agents of their enemy, king Ajātaśatru. The Buddha and Nārada, who viewed the republics with a sympathetic eye, warn them against these dissensions and give helpful suggestions as to how they were to be avoided.[2] Kauṭilya, who was unsympathetic to them, suggests several

1. आभ्यन्तरं भयं रक्ष्यभसारं बाह्यतोभयम् ।
आभ्यन्तरं भयं राजन्सद्यो मूलानि कृन्तति ॥ XII. 107. 28

2. Cf. भेदमूलो विनाशो हि गणानामपलक्षये ।
मंत्रसंवरणं दुःखं बहूनामिति मे मतिः ॥
कुलस्य कलहा जाता मंत्रवृद्धैरुपेक्षिताः ।
गोत्रस्य नाशं कुर्वन्ति गणभेदस्य कारकम् ॥
भेदाच्चैव प्रदानाच्च भिद्यन्ते रिपुभिर्गणाः ॥ *Mbh*, 107.27-32
See also *Dialogues of the Buddha*, II. p. 80.

crooked methods by which the internal feuds could be further intensified (Bk. XI).

Personal rivalry and greed for power were usually at the root of party factions. As in modern times, so in ancient days, members used to form groups of their own in order to get power for themselves. Those, who were energetic in habits and skilful in organisation and noted for successful oratory, usually succeeded in gaining power in their hands.[1] When two parties were more or less evenly balanced, small groups of members made or unmade the governments as in modern days. Some members had a nuisance value; they were equally a source of trouble whether they were included or excluded from the party. Ahūka and Akrūra had the unenviable reputation of belonging to this class in the Andhaka Vṛishṇi state[2]. As in modern times so in ancient days, it was usually found to be a difficult task to oust the party in power.[3] When the Assembly was torn by factions, the task of its President was very difficult. Often he was furiously attacked by both the parties, neither of whom was usually entirely in the right. Under such circumstances, like the mother of two sons who are gambling with each other, the impartial President, anxious for the welfare of the state, could wish success to neither party. Keeping himself unruffled, he would try to restore a calm atmosphere to ensure a proper consideration of the points at issue.

In the ideal Gaṇa state, there were no parties and matters were not pressed to a vote. Meetings were characterised by concord and harmony and the opinions of the elders and not the vote of the majority decided the issue. This was the usual practice

1. अन्ये हि सुमहाभागा बलवन्तो दुरासदाः ।
नित्योत्थानेन संपन्ना नारदान्धकवृष्णयः ॥
यस्य न स्युर्न वै स स्याद्यस्य स्युः कृत्स्नमेव तत् ॥ *Mbh*, XII.81.8-9
अन्योन्यं नाभिभाषंते तत्पराभवकारणम् । *Mbh*, XII.107. 29-30

2. स्यातां यस्याहुकाक्रूरौ किं नु दुःखतरं ततः ।
यस्य चापि न तौ स्यातां किं नु दुःखतरं ततः ॥ *Mbh.*, XII. 81. 10

3. बभ्रूग्रसेनतो राज्यं नाप्तुं शक्यं कथंचन ।
ज्ञातिभेदभयात्कृष्ण त्वया चापि विशेषतः ॥ *Mbh.*,XII.81.17

among the Lichchhavis during the golden period of their republican constitution.[1] The Assembly of the Ambashṭha republic first appointed generals to oppose Alexander the Great, but later accepted the advice of their elders and decided to make peace proposals.

Chap. 107 of the Śāntiparvan gives us a good picture of the internal condition of an ideal republic. The rising generation was properly educated and the youths were taught proper manners and made to realise that they must follow the path of virtue and the lead of the elders. Experienced statesmen noted for their valour, intelligence and prompt dispatch were entrusted with the responsible posts in the administration and they usually enabled the republic to tide over serious crises. Delicate questions of policy, internal or external, were left to be tackled by them ; they were not publicly discussed in the parliament. Members of the government worked in harmony and concord to achieve the interests of the state. Spies and ambassadors were selected with great care and particular attention was paid to the development of a sound economic policy to ensure the prosperity of the state and the people.

Normally the republican government was a government by parties. We have already explained above how they came into existence. The party system was so common among the republics, that it is referred to even by the grammarians. The term *dvandva* was used to denote the rival parties and the term *vyutkramaṇa* to their rivalry.[2] As in modern parliaments, members of the parties sat in separate groups.[3] *Vargya*, *gṛihya* and *pakshya* were the technical terms used to denote party members. Parties were usually named after their leaders; *Vāsudeva-vargya* was the name to denote a member of the party of Vāsudeva or Kṛishṇa, *Akrūrapakshya*, a member of Akrūra party, and so on.

It is but natural that some rules of procedure should have been evolved as far as the debates and working of the Assembly

1. *Dialogues of the Buddha*, II. 80 2. Pāṇini, VIII. 1. 15

3. व्युत्क्रमणं भेदः पृथगवस्थानम् ।
द्विवर्गसम्बंधेन पृथगवस्थिता द्वन्दं व्युत्क्रान्ता इत्युच्यन्ते ।
Kāśikā on Pāṇini, VIII, 1. 15

were concerned. But unfortunately they are not anywhere described by our political writers. We can get, however, some idea in the matter if we assume, as is very probable, that the rules of the procedure and the debates in the meetings of the Buddhist *saṁgha* were modelled on those of the Assemblies of the *Gaṇa* or *Saṁghas* states. A Buddhist chapter required a quorum of 20 ; it is very likely that a similar rule may have prevailed in the meetings of the political *Saṁgha*, especially when we remember that usually there were parties keen in getting power in their own hands. Pāṇini refers to *gaṇa-titha* as the person whose attendance completed the quorum in a *Gaṇa* and to *Saṁgha-titha* as one who completed the quorum of the *saṁgha*. The person who acted as a 'whip' to secure the quorum is described as a *gaṇapūraka* by the *Mahāvagga* (III. 3. 6.) There was an officer who was in charge of the allotment of seats; probably the executive had the seats on a dais and other members were grouped partywise in their front. The *saṁghamukhya* or the President of the State presided over the Assembly and regulated its debate. He was to observe strict impartiality ; otherwise he was furiously criticised. The resolution was formally moved by its mover and then the debate followed. In the Buddhist *Saṁgha* the practice was that those in favour of the proposal kept silent, while those who were against it expressed their dissent. It is, however, very likely that in the political *Saṁgha* where passions often ran high, both sides must have voiciforously expressed their votes. In the Buddhist *Saṁgha*, as in some modern legislatures, a motion was thrice proposed and passed. One may doubt whether this procedure was followed in the meetings of the political Assemblies. In the case of difference of opinion votes were taken and the majority view prevailed. When the ultimatum was received by the Śākyas from the Kośala king, who was besieging their capital, their Assembly assembled to deliberate whether they should open the gates or not. Some favoured the proposal, others opposed it. Eventually, therefore, votes were taken to ascertain the majority view, which it was discovered favoured capitulation.[1] Accordingly action was taken. This

1. Rockhill, *Life of the Buddha*, pp. 118-9

procedure, being the obvious and natural one, must have been followed everywhere.

In the Buddhist Saṁgha the voting was sometimes done by the secret method (*gūḷhaka*), sometimes by the whispering method (*sakarṇajapakam*) and sometimes by the open method (*vivatakam*).[1] Voting tickets were in the form of sticks of different colours and a person called *śalākā-grāhaka* collected them; later they were counted by the President. The technical term for vote was *chhanda* which meant free choice. We may well presume that the above procedure in the Buddhist Saṁgha was followed in the Republican Assemblies, since the latter served as the model for the former.

It is almost certain that there must have been clerks of the House, who must have kept records of its proceedings. Matters when once properly and finally decided, were not allowed to be reopened. (*Diggha-nikāya*, II. p. 220).

Let us now consider the Central Executive of the *Gaṇa* state. Its membership varied with the size and traditions of each state. The Malla state, which was small, had an executive of four members only, all of whom are known to have taken a prominent part at the funeral of the Buddha. The Lichchhavis, whose state was a bigger one, had a council of nine, though the membership of their Assembly numbered 7,707. The confederation of the Lichchhavis and the Videhas had an executive of 18. We have no information of the strength of the executive of the larger states like the Yaudheyas, the Mālavas and the Kshudrakas, but their number could not have been much bigger.

The evidence of the grammarians also points to the same conclusion. When Patanjali refers to a Saṁgha as *pañchakaḥ* or *daśakah* or *viṁśakaḥ*,[2] he probably has the strength of its executive in mind, which consisted usually of five or ten or twenty persons. When the *Anatagaḍadasao*[3] refers to ten principal Daśārahas headed by Samudravijaya and to Baladeva and his four deputies, it obviously has the number of the executives of the republics in view. The *Mahāvagga* also speaks of five different

1. *Chullavagga*, IV. 14. 24 2. V. 1. 58-59

3. समुद्दविजयपामोरवाणं दसण्हं दशार्णानं, p. 4. (P. L. Vaidyas' edition).

kinds of Saṁghas, namely those who had a *vagga* (executive)[1] of four, five, ten, twenty or more.

We may therefore well conclude that normally speaking the executive of a republic consisted of 4 to 20 members. The 150 eminent men of tall stature and stately appearance that were sent by the Kshudraka republic to negotiate peace with Alexander were probably the notables of the state and not members of its executive; an executive council of 150 is too large a body to work promptly and efficiently.

The Central Assembly must have elected the members of the Executive Council. Whether the election could be made from among the members of a few leading families, or whether anybody could offer himself as a candidate, we do not know. Gradually in the course of time, the posts of the councillors became more or less hereditary, though a formal election was probably necessary before the son could succeed the father. The family of Śrīsoma, who succeeded in recovering the independence of the Mālavas, was at the head of its executive and military affairs at least for three generations.[2] The *Arthaśāstra* shows that the sons of councillors, if not permitted to succeed to the posts of their fathers, would often create commotion in the body politic by joining the enemy. Among some republics, like those of the Lichchhavis and the Yaudheyas, the councillors were given regal title. The Mālavas however, did not permit this procedure; even the great leader, who re-established their independence in *c.* 225 A. D. is seen not to take any royal titles in the document of the official proclamation of his victory.

The Gaṇa states were famous for their military traditions. We may, therefore, take it for granted that the members of their Executive must have been normally capable captains and dauntless leaders, competent to guide the state on occasions of emergency. In addition they were to be men of tact and experience, energetic in action, firm in resolution and well grounded in the laws,

1. IX 4

2. Cf. समुद्धृत्य पितृपैतामहीं धुरम्। line 4, *E. I. XXVII.* 252

customs and traditions of the country.[1]

The President of the Executive Council was probably the President of the Assembly also. Besides supervising the general administration, one of the chief concerns of the President was to ensure internal harmony by promoting concord and preventing quarrels.[2] For internal dissension was the main weakness of a Gaṇa state, which often contributed to its downfall. Foreign affairs constituted the portfolio of one member; he used to receive the reports of spies and members of the secret service. Treasury was in charge of a second member; he was also authorised to invest the state funds and to realise the state debts.[3] Justice was the portfolio of a third member; he was to decide civil and criminal cases, probably as an applellate court, according to the laws of the land.[4] The *Arthaśāstra* describes how hostile kings would try to bring him into disrepute by sending young widows to him, ostensibly for the purpose of pleading for their rights to property, but really for leading them astray into the path of vice. The police and revenue must have been the portfolios of two members, as also trade and industry; we should not forget that many of the republics were as much noted for their military traditions as for their commercial pre-eminence.[5]

It is not unlikely that the status and privileges of all the members of the Executive Council were not exactly alike.[6] The same is the case in some modern cabinets.

1. प्राज्ञान् शूरान्महोत्साहान्कर्मसु स्थिरपौरुषान् ।
मानयन्तः सदा युक्तान् विवर्धन्ते गणा नृप ॥
द्रव्यवन्तश्च शूराश्च शस्त्रज्ञाः शास्त्रपारगाः ।
कृच्छ्रास्वापत्सु संमूढान् गणान्सन्तारयन्ति ते । *Mbh.*, XII. 107. 20-1

2. *Mbh.* XII. 81 gives a graphic account of the efforts of Śrī Kṛishṇa, the president of the Vṛishṇi republic, in this connection.

3. चारयन्त्रविधानेषु कोषसंनिचयेषु च ।
नित्ययुक्ता महाबाहो वर्धन्ते सर्वतो गणाः ॥ *Mbh.* XII. 107.19
See *Arthaśāstra* Bk. XII for investment powers.

4. धर्मिष्ठान्व्यवहारांश्च स्थापयन्तश्च शास्त्रतः ।
यथावत्प्रतिपश्यन्तो विवर्धन्ते गणोत्तमाः ॥ *Ibid.* 17

5. Cf. वार्ताशस्त्रोपजीविनः *Arthaśāstra*, Bk. XI

6. This often afforded opportunity to the enemy to foment internal quarrels. *Arthaśāstra*, Bk. XI

The different departments had their own officers of diverse grades, who must have worked under the orders of their ministers. In small states like those of the Śākyas and the Koliyas, they could directly report unusual incidents to the supreme authorities ; in bigger states, they must have reported through the proper channels.

The big republics like those of the Yaudheyas and the Kshudrakas had a number of cities which had full internal autonomy. How were their councils usually elected, we do not know. It is not unlikely that not only the privileged Kshatriya class but also trades, industries and professions were represented on these bodies. This was the practice in the monarchical states,[1] and there is no reason to think why it should not have been followed in the republics. Only future discoveries can show how the city councils were controlled by the central executive, and whether they had any representation in the Central Assembly.

The villages in the Gaṇa states must have had their own Panchāyats and there is no reason to believe that their powers were less than those of the Panchāyats under monarchies. It is hardly likely that the membership of the village Panchāyats was confined to the members of the privileged aristocracy ; most of the latter must have been staying in cities and the capital. As in other states, all the village interests like agriculture, trade, industry, etc. must have been represented on the village council. This is of course a conjecture, but a very likely one.

Want of adequate reliable data handicaps the historian perhaps in no other sphere so much as in the case of the republics. We get only a dim and blurred picture of their constitutions and their working. But what little we know shows that the states were fairly efficient and prosperous. They offered much more stubborn resistance to Alexander the Great than that put forth by the contemporary monarchies. Patriotism and appreciation of liberty were much more genuine among them than among the monarchical states. Trade and industry

1. Compare the evidence of the Damodarpur plates for the Gupta empire ; *E. I.* XV. pp. 129. ff

also prospered under their regime; the Punjab and Sindh republics were studded with numerous and prosperous cities. They encouraged freedom of thought, which in its turn resulted in philosophical progress. This is particularly noteworthy about the Eastern Republics, whose citizens have made rich contributions to the philosophy as developed in the Upanishads, Buddhism and Jainism. In the Indus valley also there were many philosophers who impressed the Greeks by their theories and views.

Most of the republics had a clan origin and the members of the privileged aristocracy believed themselves to be members of one stock or descended from one eponymous hero. Membership of the Central Assembly seems to have been confined to them. In the city councils and village assemblies, however, all the leading classes and interests had their proper representation and voice. There is no sufficient evidence to suggest that there was any serious clash of interests between the members of the privileged order and the rest. We should not here forget that inter-marriages were fairly common down to the 5th century A. D. and so the Kshatriyas could not have formed a water-tight privileged order. Members of the Vaiśya and the Śūdra classes, who entered into the army and rose to high positions in it, could hardly have been denied the privileges of the Kshatriya status. A *sūtra* of Pāṇini suggests that the status of the Brāhmaṇas was the same as that of the Kshatriyas.[1]

The consciousness of a clan origin seems to have played a great part in the formation of republics. Where it did not exist, such a state did not usually come into existence. It further appears that the political horizon and influence of these states could not usually extend to territories where their own clan was not in ascendancy. It is no doubt true that these states often formed federations to present a stronger front to a common enemy, but they could not expand into a strong and big state like the Mauryan or the Gupta Empire. Their horizon was limited to their nomelands. If its freedom was threatened, they would

1. आयुधजीविसंघाञ्ञ्यड्वाहीकेषु अब्राह्मणराजन्यात् । Pāṇini, V.3. 114 Here Brāhmaṇas and the Kshatriyas are grouped together.

die fighting for it, but it did not occur to them that they might found a big north-western federation embracing the Punjab, Rajputana and Sindh, which could stand as a bullwork against the foreign invader. The presence of the clan spirit in each state, the internal dissensions that often disfigured its politics and the love of freedom that characterised its inhabitants naturally did not favour the development of a strong central government, which must have necessitated the transfer of considerable power to its Central Executive.

Let us now examine the causes for the disappearance of these republics by *c.* 400 A. D. Dr. Jayaswal has attributed their eclipse and destruction to the imperialism of the Guptas. 'Samudragupta, like Alexander, killed the free spirit of the country. He destroyed the Mālavas and the Yaudheyas, who were the nursery of freedom and many others of their class.' This does not seem to be true. The republics of the Mālavas and the Arjunāyanas, the Yaudheyas and the Madras had only accepted in a general way the imperial position of Samudragupta. They offered him tribute, but retained their autonomy. Their territories were never directly administered by the Guptas, and so their republican institutions could not have been much affected. It should be remembered that their independence had been completely eclipsed under the Mauryas and the Kushāṇas, but they once more emerged as republics when the above imperialism declined. The Gupta imperialism had not interfered with their autonomy and it is, therefore, difficult to understand how it could have been fatal to their democratic institutions.

The Nandsa inscriptions show that early in the 3rd century the leadership of the Mālavas had already begun to pass into hereditary families, which were claiming to be as respectable as the Ikshvāku race. The leaders of the Yaudheyas and the Sanakānīkas had assumed the titles of Mahārājas and Mahāsenāpatis in the 4th century. The same probably was the case with the Lichchhavi republic, for Kumāradevī was an heiress to their dominion. Varāhamihira of the 7th century refers to the king of the Yaudheyas (*Bṛihatsaṁhitā*, X. I). When the leadership of republics thus passed into the hands of hereditary presidents, who were military leaders and claimed royal titles, they could no longer be distinguished from monarchies. Why the democratic traditions were allowed to be weakened, and why the republics permitted the new developments to take place is still an unsolved problem. The growing tendency to regard monarchy as divine may have induced the republics to accept the leadership of hereditary presidents, styled as Mahārājas. Probably it was felt that the unitary leadership facilitated by the kingship was a better protection against invasions than that offered by the group leadership possible in a republic.

CHAPTER VII

CENTRAL ASSEMBLY

In the modern state, the Central Government consists of the Head of the Executive,—King or President—, his Council or Cabinet, and a Legislature or Central Assembly, largely if not entirely popular in composition, to control the executive and enact the laws of the state. The problems connected with the Chief Executive Head have been already discussed in the course of the last two chapters. We shall now consider those connected with the Central Assembly. Did a Central Assembly, more or less similar to a modern democratic Parliament, function in the different states of Ancient India? Was it existing in all the periods of her history or was it confined to particular ages or to particular types of states? How were the members of the Assembly elected? Could they control the Executive? If so, to what extent? Were they the custodians of the legislative powers of the state or could the Executive pass laws independently of their sanction? These are the questions that will be engaging our attention in this chapter.

We have shown already in the last chapter that Central Assemblies, more or less similar to modern Parliament, did exist in republics. The nature of the interests they represented and the control they exercised over the Executive have also been discussed. In this chapter we have now to see whether similar bodies existed in monarchical states.

A perusal of the Vedic literature makes it quite evident that Popular Assemblies controlling the kings of the numerous small states with which Afghanistan and the Punjab were then studded, were a prominent feature of the Vedic polity. The average state of the Ṛigvedic period consisted of only a few square miles like the city state of ancient Greece. It had a capital, not much larger than the few dozen villages comprised in it. Villages had their own popular asemblies known as *sabhās* and the capital had the Central Assembly for the whole state, which was called a *samiti*.

Sabhās and *samitis* enjoyed a high prestige in the Vedic age. They are in one place[1] described as the twin daughters of Prajāpati, the Creator. This suggests that the people regarded both the assemblies almost as divine institutions of hoary antiquity, and almost coeval with the political life of the community, if not with the community itself. The India of the Vedic age was studded with scores of such assemblies and the hope of the rising scholar and politician was to distinguish himself in their meetings.[2] Nay, the hope was also expressed on behalf of every bride at the time of her marriage that she would in due course be able to command the attention of the Assembly by her powers of speech and persuasion.[3]

The Vedic literature refers to the popular assemblies of the age by three different terms, *vidatha*, *sabhā* and *samiti*. The precise meaning of these terms is difficult to determine and it seems not improbable that it may have differed from age to age and locality to locality. Modern scholars also have not been able to agree on the point. Ludwig, for instance, holds that the *sabhā* was something like the Upper House, where the priests and rich men were represented, while the *samiti* was something like the Lower House, where ordinary commoners had their proper place. Zimmer on the other hand thought that *sabhā* was the village assembly and *samiti* the Central Assembly of the whole tribe. Hillebrandt thought that *sabhā* and *samiti* were much the same, *samiti* being the assembly and *sabhā* its meeting place. Jayaswal's view was that *samiti* was probably the national assembly and *sabhā* was its standing body ; he however candidly admits that the exact relation between these two bodies cannot be deduced from the available evidence.

It is not possible to discuss here the various arguments in favour of the above divergent views. It is quite possible

1. सभा च मां समितिश्चावतां प्रजापतेर्दुहितरौ संविदाने । *A.V.* VII. 12. 1
2. ये ग्रामा यदरण्यं याः सभा अधि भूम्याम् ।
ये संग्रामाः समितयस्तेषु चारु वदाम्यहम् ॥ *A. V.*, XII. 1. 56
3. वशिनी त्वं विदथमावदासि । *R. V.*, X. 85. 26

that these terms were used in different senses in the different parts of Vedic India or in different decades or centuries. Council, Assembly and Chamber have been used to denote different types of bodies during the last fifty years in modern India.

Vidatha[1] seems to be derived from the root *vid* to know and probably indicated a religious or sacrificial gathering, rituals at which required the highest knowledge. Apparently it was a big assembly, probably representing the entire tribe, because there are references to people being arranged there by groups, and singing and dancing. Women took an active part in the Vedic sacrifices in early time and they are seen to be prominent in the *vidatha*. Though in some rare passages kings are represented as attending the *vidatha*, the latter body is rarely seen taking any active part in the administration. We need not therefore further discuss its nature.

The view of Hillebrandt that *sabhā* did not denote a different body, but only the place of meeting of the *samiti* is also unacceptable ; a passage in the *Artharvaveda* (VII. 12. 1), already quoted, clearly states that the *sabhā* and the *samiti* were two different bodies and compares them to *two* daughters of the Creator. Another passage states how *vrātya* was followed by the members of the *sabhā* , *samiti* and the army.[2].

It is, therefore, clear that *sabhā* was not the meeting place of the *samiti*, but was a separate body. An early Vedic passage describes how the talk in the *sabhā* often veered round the cows and the wonderful nourishment which they supplied to humanity;[3] and another describes how the gamblers assembled at the hall of the *sabhā*, challenged one another and played to the last penny, often staking the freedom of themsleves and their wives.[4] The connection of *sabhā* with gambling is referred to

1. See *J. B. R. S.* 1952 pp. 429 ff for a learned article on the nature of the *Vidatha*, by Dr. R. S. Sharma. His view that *Vidatha* also transacted military business is however untenable, nor did it do every distributive work.

2. तं च सभा च समितिश्च सेना चानुव्यचलन् । *A. V.* XV. 9

3. यूयं गावो मेदयथा कृशं चिदश्रीरं चित्कृणुथाः सप्रतीकम् ।
भद्रं गृहं कुणुथा भद्रवाचो बृहद्वो वयं उच्यते सभासु ॥ *R. V.*, VII. 28. 6

4. सभामेति कितवः पृच्छमानः जेष्यामीति तन्वा शोशुभानः ।
Ibid, X. 34. 6

also in the Brāhmaṇa literature.[1] It would thus appear that the *sabhā* was primarily the village social club, but the few items of the simple village government of the age were also transacted there by its members, when it was necessary to dispose of them. These probably included steps for the communal safety and decisions in the matters of the village disputes. For, the member of a *sabhā* is associated with the sacred law in the Purushamedha sacrifice.

It is, however, likely that in some localities or states, *sabhā* was associated wth the king and was more a political than a social gathering. A passage in the *Atharvaveda* describes how the *sabhāsadas* (members of the *sabhā*) of god Yama were royal in status and entitled to share the 16th part of the merit accruing to that deity.[2] It is possible to argue that the status of the members of the terrestrial *sabhā*, like that of the celestial one, was also almost as high as that of the king and that they too were entitled to receive a small share of the tithes and tributes that were paid to the ruler. It is, however, not impossible that the *sabhā* referred to may be the cabinet or ministry of the earthly king also ; and the description of a member of the *sabhā* as a person possessing considerable wealth (consisting of kine of course) and going to the *sabhā* in his full paraphernalia, riding on a charger or seated in a carriage, would confirm that hypothesis.[3] The balance of available evidence, however, tends to show that the *sabhā* was usually the village assembly, meeting for social as well as political purposes.

In the concluding hymn of the *Ṛigveda*, *samiti* no doubt seems to be referring to a social or learned gathering,[4] but an earlier hymn of the same book refers to the plans of an aspirant for political power, which include the domination of the

1. *T. Br.*, I. 1. 10. 6 ; *S. Br.*, V. 3. 1. 10
2, यद्राजानो विजभन्त इष्टापूर्तस्य षोडशं यमस्यामी सभादः ॥
A. V., III. 19. 1
3. अश्वी रथी सुरूप इद्गोमाँ इदिन्द्र ते सखा । *R. V.*, VIII. 4. 9
4. संगच्छध्वं संवदध्वं सं वो मनांसि जानताम् ।
समानं मंत्रः समितिः समानी समानं मनः सह चित्तमेषाम् ॥
X 191.2-3

samiti.[1] The *Ṛigveda* refers to a 'true' king paying visit to his *samiti* and the most important significant hope expressed in the *Atharvaveda* on behalf of an exiled king, who has succeeded in his restoration, is that his *samiti* may for ever be in agreement with him.[2] Conversely the bitterest curse pronounced upon a king guilty of misappropriating a Brāhmaṇa's property is that his *samiti* should never be in agreement with him.[3]

The above passages make it clear that while *samiti* sometimes denoted a social gathering, usually it referred to a political assembly at the central government. It was a powerful body wielding what may be conveniently described as sovereign powers, for very often the fate of a king depended upon his ability to carry his *samiti* along with him. If the *samiti* assumed an obstructive attitude, the life of the king became miserable ; the partisans of a restored king felt that their work was likely to be enduring only if his *samiti* was prepared to co-operate with him. It is quite clear that the *samiti* exercised considerable control over the military and executive affairs of the Central Government ; but how exactly it was exercised and how the *samiti's* powers were co-ordinated with that of the king we do not know.

We are also completely in the dark as to the constitution of this important body. The modern reader may well ask, was the *samiti* an official or a popular body? If the latter, was it elective? If so, who enjoyed the privilege of electing its members, the whole population or a select class? How long did the members, once elected, function in the *samiti*,—for a certain number of years or for life? Were their rules of procedure similar to those in the republican Assemblies of later times? Was quorum insisted upon? Did the majority carry the day? We have at present no data to answer these and similar questions in an authoritative manner. Since, however, the Central Assemblies of the republican states were aristocratic bodies, it may be permissible to suggest that the same was probably the case with the *samitis* functioning under the monarchies. The Vedic state

1. आ वश्चित्तं आ वो व्रतं आ वोऽहं समितिं ददे ॥ X. 166. 4
2. ध्रुवाय ते समितिः कल्पतामिह । *A. V.*, VI. 88. 3
3. नास्मैः समितिः कल्पते न मित्रं नयते वशम् । *A. V.*, V. 19-15

was a small one like the city state of ancient Greece ; and the *samitis* probably consisted of the heads of the few military and aristocratic families which occupied a prominent position in the the political and social life of the community. Priests in these days played an important part even on the battle-field and, therefore, it is not unlikely that they also may have been represented in the *samiti* at least by the king's chaplain, if not by others as well.

Members of the *samiti* were men of substance and exercised considerable influence over the administration. Their status must have been high in society ; they must have, like the members of the *sabhā*, gone to the meetings in their full grandeur riding their horses or carriages.

Debates and discussions naturally loomed large in the proceedings of the Assemblies. The ambition of a new careerist was to shine as a debator in these bodies.[1] One could succeed in the *samiti* only if one could capture the mind and sway the feelings of its members. When there were parties in the *samiti*, the proceedings became enlivened and often bitter. Hot words were exchanged often leading to violent party quarrels. One can well understand the sincerity of the prayer offered in the *Ṛigveda* that the deliberations of a *samiti* should be cordial, its members well disposed towards one another, and their minds in perfect harmony.[2]

It is rather sad and surprising to find that the *samiti*, which exercised so much influence over the king and administration in the days of the *Ṛigveda* and the *Atharvaveda*, should completely disappear from view in the period of the later Saṁhitās and the Brāhmaṇas. *Sabhā*, however, figures in this literature, but in a new sense. It is no longer a popular village assembly, but comes to stand for the king's court or Privy Council, a sense in which the word was destined to be used for several centuries. The *sabhā* met frequently and had its own president ;[3] the status

1. ये संग्रामाः समितयस्तेषु चारु वदाम्यहम् । *A. V.*, XII. 1. 56
2. *Ante*, p. 142, Note 4
3. *V. S.*, XVI. 24

of its members was as high as that of the high priest or chamerlain.[1] Dependent kings are often mentioned as attending the *sabhā*,[2] making it quite clear that it was being transformed from a popular body into king's court. The word also began to be used to denote the highest judicial court. The historian of the Central Assembly or the Parliament need no longer follow its history. The *samiti* once more makes its appearance in the Upanishadic age ; we find Śvetaketu visiting the *samiti* of the Pāñchālas after his educational course. The king is present in this assembly on the occasion and puts him some questions to test his scholarship. The passage thus shows that *samiti* in the Upanishadic period denoted a learned body rather than a popular assembly ; it was sometimes presided over by the king, especially when it was going to test the knowledge of new graduates. The king was perhaps only the ceremonial head of the gathering, as the Governors are of the modern convocations. There can be no doubt that *samitis* and *sabhās* both ceased to function as political bodies much earlier than the days of the Dharmasūtras (*c*. 500 B. C.) ; for the latter never mention them while describing the duties of the king or the machinery of the administration. The term *samiti* is altogether unknown to them ; the word *sabhāsada* is used, but it denotes a member either of the Privy Council or of judicial assembly, but never of a Popular Assembly.

Central Popular Assemblies, however, continued to function in the republican states, as shown already in Chap. VI. Why they disappeared from the monarchical states it is difficult to state. Republics as a rule continued to be small states even in later times ; monarchies, on the other hand, developed into big states in the Brāhmaṇa period (*c*. 1500-1000 B. C.) . Emergence of extensive states with large rural areas and dispersed population rendered the meeting and functioning of a central popular assembly difficult. Representative system was unknown, and so an assembly could meet only when it was a small body with members living not far from the capital. This was no longer possible

1. *A. Br.* VIII. 21
2. *S. Br.* III. 3. 4. 14

in a large state. While members found it difficult to meet and work in the new circumstances, the kings of the ever-growing kingdoms were always eager and anxious to grab all power in their own hands. It was but natural that under such circumstances *sabhās* and *samitis* should have gradually died down.

THE PAURA-JĀNAPADA THEORY

K. P. Jayaswal has, however, argued at great length[1] that the *sabhā* and *samitis* of the Vedic age did not disappear without leaving their successors in the body politic of the later period. They were known as Paura-Jānapadas and figure frequently in literature and sometimes in inscriptions. The true significance of this expression was, however, altogether missed by modern writers. While it is true that Paura-Jānapadas often denote the inhabitants of towns and villages that comprised a kingdom, it should be remembered that the expression, when especially used in the neuter singular as Paura-Jānapadam, denotes a constitutional body consisting of the representatives of the capital and the country. Such a body is known to the *Rāmāyaṇa* and functioned under the administration of king Khārvela of Orissa in the 2nd century B. C. It is presupposed by the laws of *jānapadas* referred to by Manu and other Smṛiti-writers, who also refer to their presidents. The prestige of this popular body was so great that the state would often refuse to grant any relief to a person who was working against its interest.[2]

The above theory of the Paura-Jānapada body has been put forth brilliantly, but a careful analysis of the evidence advanced by Jayaswal and an impartial consideration of other data available on the point, make it fairly clear that there were no popular twin-assemblies known as Paura-Jānapadas in ancient India. It is worth noting that the expression Paura-Jānapada is generally used in the plural, sometimes in the singular, but never in the dual. If Paura and Jānapada really constituted two houses of Parliament, one fails to understand why the dual number should never have been used in referring

1. *Hindu Polity*, Part II, Chaps. XXVII-XXVIII. (1st. Ed.)
2. *Ibid*, Part II, pp. 66 ff

to them. The grammatical argument relied upon to show that the term Paura-Jānapada should really have been in the singular in the *Rāmāyaṇa* II. 14. 54 and would then denote a representative body of the citizens is weak and untenable.[1] The epic generally uses the term *paura-jānapadāḥ* in the plural and it denotes the citizens in general and not any constitutional or representative body of theirs. Thus the *Rāmāyaṇa* II. 14. 40 refers to the notables among the *paura-jānapadas*,[2] and the *paura-jānapada* people to whom Bharata refers in II. 111. 19 are obviously the ordinary citizens who accompanied Bharata to see whether Rāma could be persuaded to return to Ayodhyā.[3] Even if we assume that *paura-jānapadas* here denote a constitutional body of citizens, it is clear that it wielded no effective powers ; it could neither veto Daśaratha's plan to banish Rāma nor induce the latter to return home as desired by them. It is significant to note that when making the final appeal to Rāma to return to Ayodhyā, Bharata refers to the prayer of himself and his ministers and not to that of any Paura-Jānapada body.[4] Rāma also, bidding adieu to his brother, urges him to carry on the administration in consultation with friends, officers and ministers ; here again the Paura-Jānapadas are conspicuous by their absence.[5] This omission is difficult to explain if we assume that the Paura-

1. The verse in question is :—उपतिष्ठति रामस्य समग्रमभिषेचनम् । पौरजानपदश्चापि नैगमश्च कृताञ्जलिः ॥ Jayaswal's argument is that because the verb उपतिष्ठति is in the singular, therefore each of the subjects joined by the particle *cha* should also be in the singular ; hence it follows that the first word in the next line should be read as *jānapadaḥ* and not *jānapadaḥ* ; it would then denote the Jānapadah Assembly and not merely citizens. Grammar, however, lays down no such rule ; on the contrary it states that even if each of the words joined by the particle *cha* is in the singular, the verb will be in the combined number, dual or plural.

2. पौरजानपदश्रेष्ठा नैगमगाश्च गणैः सह ।
अभिषकाय रामस्य तिष्ठंति ब्राह्मणैः सह ॥ II. 14. 40

3. आसीनस्त्वेब भरतः पौरजानपदं जनम् ।
उवाच सर्वतः प्रेक्ष्य किमार्यमनुशासथ ॥ II. 111. 19

4. एभिश्च सचिवैः सार्धं शिरसा याचितो मया ।
भ्रातुः शिष्यस्य दासस्य प्रसादं कर्तुमर्हसि ॥ II. 104. 16

5. अमात्यैश्च सुहृद्भिश्च बुद्धिमद्भिश्च मंत्रिभिः ।
सर्वकार्याणि संमंत्र्य सुमहान्त्यपि कारय ॥ II. 112.17

Jānapadas constituted a regular constitutional popular assembly, wielding considerable power over the administration.

The Hathigumpha inscription of Khāravela also does not refer to any Central Popular Assembly. Line 7 of the record states that the king conferred many favours (*anugraha*) amounting to or numbering hundreds of thousands on the Paura and Jānapada.[1] Jayaswal contends that *anugrahas* here are constitutional privileges conferred upon the City-Corporation and the Realm-Corporation.[2] Constitutional privileges conferred upon a legislature by the king can never be described as amounting to hundreds and thousands. It is clear that the sentence rather refers to numerous favours conferred upon the city and country population, the monetary value of which amounted to hundreds and thousands of rupees or contemporary coins. If a king orders several wells, roads, hospitals, and rest-houses to be constructed out of the central revenues, or abolishes a number of taxes payable by the villagers and citizens to the exchequer, he can well be described as conferring several favours, amounting in value to hundreds of thousands. An analysis of the Hathigumpha inscription further makes it quite clear that Khāravela's administration and policy were not in the least controlled by any City or Realm Corporation. The record refers to his organising several military expeditions to the distant parts of India, and not in a single case is it stated that the City and Realm Corporations were consulted by the king on any occasion. The king could decalare war and make peace without the consent of the *Paura-Jānapadas*, supposing such a body did exist.

Nor do the *Jānapada-dharmas* referred to by the Smṛitis prove the existence of a Jānapada as a central law-making popular parliament. The *jānapadadharmas* referred to by Manu in VIII. 14 are the customs of the country and not the enactments of its legislature. A comparison of this verse with Manu. I. 118[3] would show that *janapadadharmas* are identical with *deśa-*

1. अनुग्रहानेकानि सतसहसानि विसजति पोरं जानपदम् । *E.I.* XX. 79
2. *Hindu Polity*, II. p. 64.
3. Both verses refer to the sources of Dharma and the comparison shows that *jānapadadharma* of VIII. 41 is equal to *deśadharma* of I-118. cf. *P.T.O.*

dharma. Katyāyana defines the latter as those customs of a country which are generally accepted and which do not go counter to the rules of Śruti and Smṛiti.[1] It is such provincial customs that are referred to as *deśadharma* in the *Arthaśāstra* or Kauṭilya also.[2] The laws of inheritance, marriage, food and professions differed in different parts of the country ; widows were heirs in some places but not in others ; marriage with maternal uncle's daughter was approved in the south, but not in the north ; wine drinking was tolerated in the north but condemned in the south. While deciding cases in the court, Manu and other Smṛiti-writers point out that *deśadharmas* or *jānpadadharmas i. e.* the customs of the province concerned should be taken into consideration by the court. They were, however, mere customs and not any laws passed by the legislature like a Jānapada body.

Nor can we accept the contention of Jayaswal that the breakers of the *samayas* of *grāma* and *deśa*, referred to by Manu, were the persons who violated the laws or resolutions of the corporate assemblies of the villages or the country. Manu VIII. 19, quoted below, expressly shows that *samayas* or *saṁvids* do not refer to resolutions or laws, but to agreements arrived at in good faith with the village or country authorities.[3] If out of pure

(Contd. from the last page)

जातिजानपदान्धर्मान्श्रेणीधर्मांश्च धर्मवित।
समीक्ष्य कुलधर्मांश्च स्वधर्मं प्रतिपालयेत॥ VIII. 41
देशधर्मान्जातिधर्मान्श्रेणीधर्मांश्च शाश्वतान्।
पाषण्डगणधर्मांश्च शास्त्रस्मिन्नुक्तवान्मनुः॥ I. 118

See also the following passages throwing light on the point :—

देशजातिकुलधर्मा आम्नायैरविरुद्धाः प्रमाणम्। *Gautama* D. S., XI. 20
पंचधा विप्रतिपत्तिः दक्षिणतस्तथोत्तरतः। तत्र तत्र देशप्रामाण्यमेव स्यात्।
B. D. S., I. . 17-22

1. यस्य देशस्य यो धर्मः प्रवृत्तः सार्वलौकिकः।
श्रुतिस्मृत्यनुरोधेन देशदृष्टः स उच्यते॥ quoted in *VMS.*, p. 13

2. देशस्य जात्या संघस्य धर्मो ग्रामस्य वापि यः।
उचितस्तस्य तेनैव दायधर्मं प्रकल्पयेत्॥ Bk. III. Chap. 7

3. अत ऊर्ध्वं प्रवक्ष्यामि धर्मं समयभेदिनाम्।
यो ग्रामदेशसंघानां कृत्वा सत्येन संविदम्।
विसंवदेन्नरो लोभात्तं राष्ट्राद्विप्रवासयेत्॥
निगृह्य दापयेच्चैनं समयव्यभिचारिणम्।
चतुःसुवर्णान् षण् निष्कान् शतमानं च राजतम्॥ *Manu.*, VIII. 18.20

selfishness, a person resiles from such agreements Manu says that he should be fined. The *Arthaśāstra*, Book. III chap. 10, which deals with the violations of the *samayas* or agreements made with the village, country, caste, or family, makes the point still clearer ; for the agreements are actually illustrated by Kauṭilya. If a farm labourer does not carry out the work undertaken for the village, or if a person refuses to pay subscription for a show and still sees it stealthily, if a villager declines to carry out the instructions of a leader who is acting on behalf of the village and in its interest, there is a violation of *grāma-samayas i.e.* agreements, explicit or implicit, made wth a village, and the person guilty becomes liable for punishment. The *Arthaśāstra* adds at the end that the violation of *deśasamayas* is also to be similarly understood.[1] It is thus clear that the violations of *deśasamayas* were not non-compliance with the resolutions of a Central Parliament, but non-fulfilment of agreements made with the chief executive of the province or the country, who was called *Deśādhyaksha*. *Deśādhyaksha* or *Deśādhipa* did not denote the President of the Parliament of the country, as Jayaswal contends (p. 67) ; the passages from the *Vishṇu-smṛiti* and *Śukra-nīti* quoted below make it quite clear that they denoted the executive heads of districts.[2]

There is nothing whatsoever in the Smṛiti literature to show, as contended by Jayaswal (p. 68), that a suitor who was hostile to Paura or the City Assembly could get no relief in a law-court. The passage quoted in the footnote below, upon which Jayaswal relied, simply states that if the claim in a suit ran counter to a custom or convention regarded as universally valid in a town or a country, it cannot be decreed by the local

1. कर्षकस्य ग्राम पभ्युपेत्याकुर्वतो ग्राम एवात्ययं हरेत् ।
प्रेक्षायामनंशदः सस्वजनो न प्रेक्षेत ।
प्रच्छन्नश्रवणेक्षणे च सर्वहिते च कर्मणि निग्रहेण द्विगुणमंशं दद्यात् ।
सर्वहितमेकस्य ब्रुवतः कुर्युराज्ञाम् । अकरण द्वादशपणो दंडः ।
तेन देशजातिकुलसंघाना समयस्यानपाकर्म ब्याख्यानम् ॥
Book III. Chap. 10

2. तत्र स्वस्वग्रामाधिपान्कुर्यात् । दशाध्यक्षान् शताध्यक्षान् देशाध्यक्षांश्च ।
Vishṇu, III. 7-10
चतुर्दिक्ष्वथवा सदा देशाधिपान् कुर्यात् नृपः । *Śukra*, I. 347

courts.[1] The passage enunciates a sound legal principle, and has no reference whatsoever to the denial of any relief to a person who was hostile to the City-Assembly.

The theory that an ex-member of the Paura-Assembly, though belonging to the Śūdra caste, was entitled to respect even from a Brāhmaṇa, is based upon a misunderstanding of the original texts, which simply refer to the courtesy to be shown to one another by the different citizens of the same city. Gautama says that one must get up as a mark of respect when one meets a priest or maternal uncle, though junior in age. The same courtesy is to be shown to an aged Śūdra citizen above 80 by a junior person.[2] Paura denotes the resident of a city and not the member of any City-Assembly.[3]

Let us now examine Jayaswal's views about the constitutional powers of the so-called Paura-Jānapada Assembly. His contention that it had the power to nominate the heir-apparent is based upon the casual reference to the citizens in the *Rāmāyaṇa* in connection with Rāma's selection as heir-apparent. But the epic expressly states that the selection was made by the king in consultation only with his ministers.[4] The view that Pauras were consulted is based upon the wrong translation of the word *āmantra*, which means 'to bid farewell'

1. The passage in the *Viramitrodaya* is as follows :—

यत्र नगरे राष्ट्रे च व्यवस्था पुरातनी तद्विरोधापादको व्यवहारो नादेयः । पौरजानपदक्षोभापादकत्वात् । *Vyavahāra-prakāśa* p. 44

Apararka, while commenting upon *Yāj.* II. 6, expressly explains पौरराष्ट्रविरुद्धः पौरराष्ट्राचारविरुद्धः ।

2. ऋत्विक्श्वशुरपितृव्यमातुलानां तु यवीयसां प्रत्युत्थानमभिवादनाद्याः ।
तथाऽन्यः पूर्वः पौरः अशीतिकावरः शूद्रोऽप्यपत्यसमेन । *G.D.S*, VI. 9-10

3. Cf. *V. M. Sanskāra-prakāśa*, p. 466, while explaining Manu, II, 134, दशाब्दाख्यं पौरसंख्यं पंचाब्दाख्यं कलाभृताम् ।
expressly says एकपुरवासिनां अधिकतरविद्यादिगुणरहितानां दशाब्दपर्यंतं ज्येष्ठे सत्यपि सख्यत्वमभिख्यायते न तु अभिवाद्यः । पुरग्रहणं प्रदर्शनार्थं तेन एकग्रामवासेपि एवं भवति ।

4. निश्चित्य सचिवैः सार्धं युवराजममन्यत । II. 1. 41

and not 'to offer advice'. The verse in question, quoted below,[1] states that the citizens went home after bidding farewell to the king, not after offering him advice. Any body acquainted with the *Rāmāyaṇa* episode knows full well that it was the palace intrigue, and not the wishes of the citizens, which determined the fate of Rāma.

The view that the Paura-Jānapadas could depose the king is also based upon a queer misunderstanding of the 10th Act of the *Mṛichhchakaṭika*. The wicked king Pālaka is killed by Śarvalika, who offers the crown to Āryaka, a friend of his. Paura-Jānapadas have nothing to do with the transaction. Śarvalika carries the news of this revolution not to the *Corporate Association of the Jānapadas* but to the *concourse of the people*, who had assembled to witness the public execution of Chārudatta. For a time he wonders where possibly this place can be. After thinking a while, he concludes that it should be at a certain street, because there was a concourse of people there, which he presumes must have assembled to witness the execution.[2] The *Mṛichchhakaṭika* does not at all refer to any Realm or Citizen Assembly in any of its Acts.

Another important function of the Paura-Jānapada Assembly, according to Jayaswal, was to sanction extra-taxes at the time of a state crisis. He quotes a passage from the *Mahābhārata*, which he contends is an address from the throne begging extra taxes from the Paura-Jānapada Assembly. The last verse of the passage however states, "A king who knows how to act properly, should send his *messengers* among the people with a sweet, attractive but cunning message of the above type".[3] The passage is not at all a speech from the throne, but contains the argument with which king's messengers were to try to convince the people in general of the dire necessity which was compelling the state to demand extra taxation.

1. ते चापि पौरा नृपतेर्वचस्तच्छ्रुत्वा तदा लाभमिवेष्टमाशु।
नरेन्द्रमामन्त्र्य गृहाणि गन्त्वा देवान्समानर्चुरतिप्रहृष्टाः। II. 3. 48
2. भवतु अत्र तेन भवितव्यं यत्रायं जनपदसमवायः । Act. X (after v. 47)
3. इति वाचा मधुरया श्लक्ष्णया सोपचारया ।
स्वरश्मीनभ्यवसृजद्योगमाधाय कालवित् ।। *Mbh.*, XII. 87. 24

The view that the Paura-Jānapada Assembly had the power to present bills to the king for the losses sustained in the kingdom by theft and dacoities is also incorrect.[1] In ancient Indian polity, the state was held responsible for such losses if the stolen property could not be recovered, and Yajñavalkya calls upon the authorities to recompensate the aggrieved citizen (*jānapada*).[2] That Jānapada here does not refer to the Realm Assembly would become quite clear if we compare the verse in Yājñavalkya to the corresponding verse in Manu, where it is expressly stated that the compensation was to be given to members of all the castes.[3] It is thus clear that *Jānapada* in Manu denotes the citizen in general, irrespective of his caste, and not to any Jānapada-Assembly.

It will be shown in Chap. X how the towns and cities had their own non-official councils exercising considerable powers. But Jayaswal is wrong when he suggests that capitals as such had their own Paura-Assemblies, which were distinct from those of the Realm-Assemblies (Jānapada bodies). As far as the latter are concerned, there is no evidence whatsoever to show that they existed and functioned in the post-Buddhist period. All the evidence of Jayaswal about their existence is literary in nature and we have shown above how it does not at all prove the existence of a twin torganisation, the Paura-Jānapada Assembly, which could depose the king, nominate his successor, give or withhold sanction for new taxes and demand and obtain industrial, commercial and financial privileges for the country (*Hindu Polity*, II, p. 108). It is contended that this organisation flourished from 600 B. C. to 600 the A.D., but it is very strange indeed that it should be referred to nowehere in the contemporary inscriptions. We can get a fairly detailed picture of the Mauryan administration from the account of Megasthenes and the inscriptions of Aśoka, but neither source refers to any Central Parliament like the

1. *Hindu Polity*, II. 98.
2. देयं चौरहृतं राज्ञा द्रव्यं जानपदाय तु । II. 36
3. दातव्यं सर्ववर्णेभ्यो राज्ञा चौरैर्हृतं धनम् । VIII. 40

Paura-Jānapada Assembly of Jayaswal.[1] Nor is such a body known to the *Arthaśāstra* of Kauṭilya.[2] It is strange that it should not have been included among the *sapta-aṅgas* of the state by a *single* work on polity. Gupta inscriptions and seals refer to scores of officers, but the Paura-Jānapada body is conspicuous by its absence. Jānapada seals have been discovered in large numbers at Nālandā, but they are the seals of the Panchāyats of the respective villages whose names they bear, and not of any Central Popular Assembly.[3] We have discovered hundreds of copper plate grants belonging to the different dynasties ruling in northern and southern India from *c.* 500 to 1300 A. D. While assuring a peaceful possession of the villages granted in them, kings refer to all possible officers and authorities from the crown-prince to the village headman, who were likely to disturb the peaceful possession of the donees and charge them to refrain from doing so. But the Paura-Jānapada Assembly of Jayaswal does not figure *even in one single record*. If such an assembly

1. The Pauras of Takshaśilā, referred to in the *Divyāvadāna*, pp. 407-8, are the citizens of the city and not the members of its Assembly. The work describes them as decorating the roads and beautifying the houses of the city ; this is what ordinary citizens do at the visit of a prince, and not the members of their Representative Assembly, Cf. श्रुत्वा च तक्षशिला पौरा अर्धत्रिकानि योजनानि मार्गशोभां नगरशोभां च कृत्वा पूर्णकुम्भैः प्रत्युद्गताः ।

2. Jayaswal's view (Part II. p. 84) that the *Arthaśāstra* refers to the Sectional Sub-assemblies of the Paura in charge of the sacred places and public buildings and of trades and manufactures, is also untenable. What the *Arthaśāstra* states is this : the spies should visit the concourse of people (*jana-samavāya*) at *tīrthas* or holy places, public halls (*sabhā-śālās*) and markets (*pūgas*) and cunningly start a discussion there with a view to ascertain the views of the people in general about the king and the administration. Could it ever have been possible for spies to start discussions in the Sub-committees of the City-Assembly, of which they could hardly have been members? The state also could have learnt of their views from their general debates ; there was no necessity of spies being sent to induce them to start discussion. The original passage of the *Arthaśāstra* is given below :—

सत्रिणो द्वन्द्विनस्तीर्थसभाशालासमवायेषु विवादं कुर्युः सर्वगुणसंपन्नश्चायं राजा श्रूयते न चास्य कश्चिद् गुणो दृश्यते यः पौरजादपदान् दण्डकराभ्यां पीडयति । Bk. I. Chap. 13

3. Cf. पुरिकाग्रामजानपदस्य ; वारकीयग्रामजानपदस्य ; श्रीनालंदा-प्रतिबद्धमंनयिकाग्रामजानपदस्य *M. A. S. I.* No. 66. pp. 45-6

existed during all these centuries, and had effective control over taxation and expenditure, as contended by Jayaswal, is it not reasonable to expect that the kings who made the land grants should have formally stated in the preambles of their charters that they had secured the necessary sanction of the Paura-Jānapada Assembly? If all the officers of the realm were charged not to interfere with the future enjoyment of the revenues granted, should not this request have been made to the Paura-Jānapada Assembly also, since it controlled the finances of the state? The fact that the Paura-Jānapada Assembly figures not even in one out of the thousands of copper plate grants, where all possible authorities, who could have disturbed the possession of the donees are exhaustively mentioned wth a meticulous care, is in our opinion the most convincing proof that no such Assemblies existed during the first millennium of the Christian era. The *Rājataraṅgiṇī*, which gives a detailed picture of the life and administration of Kashmir, is also unaware of the existence of any Popular Assembly in that province. It may further be noted that not a single inscription or work on polity refers to or describes any rules of election to the Paura-Jānapada assemblies.

As will be shown in Chaps. X and XI, village Panchāyats, and town and city councils flourished down to the end of the 18th century and possessed considerable administrative powers. But there is no evidence whatsoever to show that a Central Assembly flourished in the post-Buddhist period in monarchical states and exercised powers attributed to it by Jayaswal. The reasons for the disappearance of this body are already explained before (pp. 145-6). Popular will sought to influence the administration through other devices, which are indicated already in Chap. V.

STATE AND THE LEGISLATIVE POWER

It will be convenient to discuss the legislative powers of the state in ancient India in the present chapter. In modern times, the Central Assembly of the State usually wields these powers; let us see whether such was the case in ancient India, when *sabhās* and *samitis* were flourishing in the country.

The modern reader will be surprised to learn that neither

the king nor the *samitis* claimed and exercized legislative powers in the Vedic period. In the modern age, laws as enactments of the sovereign legislature, are becoming all powerful, gradually displacing the customary, the traditional and the case law. Such, however, was not the case in the ancient times. Laws were either sacred or secular ; if the former, they were based upon the sacred texts, if the latter upon the customs and traditions. Neither the king nor the *samiti* nor the Central Assembly, it was felt, had any jurisdiction in the matter. If the state had ever proceeded to bring about a forcible change in the customary law, it would have been overthrown in a very short time. Traditional law was as sacred as the divine law. Of course it also did change in the course of time ; but the change was gradually and inperceptibly brought about by the silent operation of custom and not by the noisy process of legislation. A deliberate change in the customary law at the dictation of a legislature, it was apprehended, would spell disaster for the community.

Neither the king nor the *samiti*, therefore, claimed or exercised any legislative functions in the Vedic period ; and the same continued to be the case down to the age of the Smṛitis. This need not surprise us. For in the West also early philosophers like Plato did not regard legislation as a function of the ideal government. It was held that no actual man or group of men could ever possess so much of the spirit of true political science as is embodied in written laws and national customs of the people, which therefore must be obeyed unquestionably.[1]

The Dharmaśāstra literature is particularly emphatic in pointing out that it is the king's duty to enforce the *dharma*, as determined by the sacred texts and accepted customs,[2] and not to enunciate it on the authority of himself or any state

1. Dunning, *Political Theories*, I, pp. 35-6

2. देशजातिकुलधर्मान् सर्वानेवैताननुप्रविश्य राजा चतुरो वर्णान्स्वधम प्रतिष्ठापयेन् । *V. D. S.*, XIX.4

जातिजानपदान्धर्मान्श्रेणीधर्मांश्च धर्मवित् ।
समीक्ष्य कुलधर्मांश्च स्वधर्मं प्रतिपादयेत् । *Manu*, VIII. 41

organisation. The Dharmaśāstra as well as the Nītiśāstra are promulgated by the Creator ; it is the king's duty to enforce the rules laid down in them, and not to introduce any changes on his own authority.[1]

In the course of time, however, as the administration became more and more developed and life more and more complex, it began to be felt that the state should have powers to make its own rules and regulations. The rules in the old Dharmaśāstra and Nītiśāstra works, it was realised, had not provided for all possible contingencies, and changes were necessary both in the interest of the state and the subjects. The *Manusmṛiti* invests the king with the power to pass administrative orders which were to be obeyed by the subjects.[2] These orders were, however, to be in consonance with the Śāstra and tradition.[3] Yājñavalkya also maintains[4] that king's orders were to be enforced by the law courts. *Śukranitī* (I. 292-311) shows that these orders mostly related to well-established laws and customs and exhorted the subjects to respect the elders, to cultivate concord in family, not to cause interference in boundaries, not to use false weights or make false accusations, not to commit misappropriation of property, not to give asylum to theives, not to fabricate false evidence or documents, etc. Sometimes they referred to the proper discharge of duty by government servants and often warned the subjects against talking about the king's vices or divulging his line of policy.

1. यश्चापि धर्म इत्युक्तो दंडनीतिव्यपाश्रयः ।
तमशंकः करिष्यामि स्ववशो न कदाचन ॥ *Mbh.* XII. 59. 116

2. तस्माद्धर्मं यमिष्टेषु स व्यवस्येन्नराधिपः ॥
अनिष्टं चाप्यनिष्टेषु तं धर्मं न विचालयेत् ॥ VII. 13

3. Medhātithi on the above :—
यतः सर्वतेजोमयः स राजा तस्माद्धेतोरिष्टेषु वल्लभेषु मंत्रिपुरोहितादिषु कार्यगत्या यं धर्मं कार्यव्यवस्थां शास्त्राचाराविरुद्धां व्यवस्येत् न विचालयेत् ।

4. निजधर्माविरोधेन यस्तु सामयिको भवते ।
सोपि यत्नेन संरक्ष्यो धर्मो राजकृतश्च यः ॥ II. 186

Aśoka's edicts also contain not merely moral exhortations but create new offences like the killing of animals on forbidden day's. They sanction a respite of three days to persons condemned to death and exhort the emperor's successors not to follow a policy of aggression.

The works on polity, however, declare that the orders of the state were to be regarded as more authoritative and binding than even the rules of the Dharmaśāstra.[1] The same is the view of Bṛihaspati (II. 27). Nārada decalres that a person, who does not obey the rules enjoined by the king, should be immediately punished for the offence of showing contempt to the royal decrees.[2] Śukra states that the king should publish his ordinances at importtant places by pasting them on the wall for the information of the public.[3]

It is thus clear that though the state was usually expected to enforce the customs and laws mentioned in Dharmaśāstra, it began to be invested with some powers to make its own regulations from about the 3rd century B. C. At the time when these powers were granted, *samitis* or Popular Assemblies had already disappeared from the scene, and so they came to be exercised by the king in consultation with his ministers.

The power of issuing *rājaśāsanas* or royal decrees was however not as extensive as the modern power of legislation. Personal, civil and criminal laws were usually determined by custom and the Smṛiti rules and were hardly affected appreciably by the royal power to issue ordinances. But in the realm of administration and taxation, kings could introduce several changes and reforms by the new powers conceded to them. They could create

1. धर्मश्च व्यवहारश्च चरित्रं राजशासनम् ।
विवादार्थश्चतुष्पादः पश्चिमः पूर्वबाधकः ॥ Book III, Chap. I

2. राज्ञा प्रवर्तितान्धर्मान्यो नरो नानुपालयेत् ।
दण्डयः स पापो वध्यश्च लोपयन्राजशासनम् ॥ I. 13

3. लिखित्वा शासनं राजा धारयीत चतुष्पथे ।
इति प्रबोधयन्नित्यं प्रजाः शासनडिंडिमैः ॥ I. 131

new offices and departments, promulgate (like Aśoka) their new policies and tap fresh sources of taxation. This resulted in the considerable enlargement of the royal powers and the curtailment of the rights of the people, since they were not effectively represented at the Central Government by a Popular Assembly, when kings came to be invested with these new semi-legislative powers.

CHAPTER VIII

MINISTRY

In modern times, the machinery of the Central Government consists of the King or the President, the Central Legislature, Ministers usually selected from the latter, Heads of the Departments, and the Central Secretariat. In chapters V-VII we have already discussed the position and functions of the king, the Executive of the Republican States and the Central Assembly. In this and the next chapter we shall proceed to consider the Ministry, the Departmental Heads and the Secretariat; this will complete the survey of the central government.

Ministry

Ministry or a Council of Advisers has been regarded by ancient Indian political thinkers as a very vital organ of the body politic. The *Mahābhārata* observes in one place that the king is as vitally dependent upon ministers as animals are upon clouds, Brāhmaṇas on the Vedas and women upon their husbands (V. 37. 38). The *Arthaśāstra* reminds the king that he can succeed only if assisted by competent councillors; one wheel alone does not move the carriage.[1] Manu points out that even a simple thing appears as difficult if one is to do it single-handed; why then attempt to run the complex machinery of the administration without the assistance of ministers[2]? Śukra observes that even an all-round king cannot know everything; different persons have different aptitudes. The king therefore should enlist the help of competent ministers. Otherwise he will ensure

1. सहायसाध्यं राजत्वं चक्रमेकं न वर्तते ।
कुर्वीत सचिवांस्तस्मात्तेषां च श्रृणुयान्मतम् । Bk. I. Chap. 3

2. अपि यत्सुकरं कर्म तदप्येकेन दुष्करम् ।
विशेषतोऽसहायेन किंनु राज्यं महोदयम् ।। VII. 53

the destruction of himself and his kingdom.[1] Hindu political thinkers, it is thus clear, always regarded ministry as indispensable for the king.

Let us now see whether such was actually the case in practice. In the *Ṛigveda* and the *Atharvaveda* we find no mention of king's ministers, probably because there was no occasion to refer to them. The *saṁhitas* of the *Yajurveda* and the Brāhmaṇa literature, however, mention in several places some high functionaries, known as *ratnins*, (jewels), who probably formed the king's council.[2] The list of these 'jewels', however, is not the same in the different sources, nor are we yet in a position to interpret with confidence the functions of all of them. It is, however possible to state in a general way that the *ratnins* consisted of royal relatives, departmental heads and courtiers. To the first of these categories belong the Crowned Queen and the Favourite Queen, who are invariably mentioned by all our authorities. This would suggest that queens in the Vedic age were not merely the consorts of kings, but played some part in the administration. The heir-apparent may have been included in the council of the king; he does not figure among the *ratnins*, because at the time of a coronation, the king's eldest son is not likley to be old enough to take active part in the administration.

Purohita, the royal chaplain, figures in all the lists of *ratnins* and naturally. Gods, it was believed, would not accept the oblations of a king, who had no competent chaplain ; the presence of this personage in the ministry was indispensable in an age which believed that victories on the battlefield depended largely upon the favour of gods to be secured through proper sacrifices,

Among the departmental heads included in the list of the *ratnins* figure *senānī*, *sūta*, *grāmaṇi*, *sangrahitā* and *bhāgadhuk*. Of

1. पुरुषे पुरुषे भिन्नं दृश्यते बुद्धिवैभवम् ।
आप्तवाक्यरनुभवैरागमैरनुमानतः ॥ 5.
न हि तत्सकलं ज्ञातुं नरेणकेन शक्यते ।
अतः सहायान्वरयेद्राजा राज्याभिवृद्धये ॥ 7
विना प्रकृतिसंमंत्राद्राज्यनाशो भवेद् ध्रुवम् ।
रोधनं न भवेत्तस्माद्राज्ञस्ते स्युः सुमंत्रिणः ॥ *Śukra*, Chap. II.

2. *P. Br.*, XIX. 1. 4 calls them *vīras* or heroes.

these *senānī* is the commander-in-chief. *Sūta* was probably the commander of the chariot corps of the royal army, who might have also acted as the honorary charioteer to the king. *Grāmaṇī* in a small state may have been the most prominent among the village headmen of the kingdom, who might have been selected to serve on the council of the *ratnins*. One text expressly calls him Vaiśya ; he seems to have usually belonged to that class. *Bhāgadhuk* was obviously the tax-collector or the finance member and *saṅgrahitā* the treasurer.

Kshattā, *akshāvāpa* and *pālāgala*, included among the *ratnins*, seem to have belonged to the class of courtiers. *Kshattā* was probably the Royal Chamberlain.[1] *Akshāvāpa* was the king's companion at the game table and *Pālāgala* was probably the king's bosom companion, corresponding to the *vidūshaka* of the later period. It has also been suggested that he might have been the ambassador of the neighbouring state,[2] but this seems improbable. Some texts[3] add *govikartana* or *govyachha*, *takshā* and *rathakāra* to the list of the *ratnins*. Wealth in the Vedic age consisted mostly of cows, and *govikartana* might have been some high officer connected with the royal herd of cattle. *Takshā* means the carpenter and *rathakāra* the chariot-maker. Chariots played as important part in the Vedic warfare as the aeroplanes do in the modern one. It is therefore not unlikely that the chief of the guild of the carpenters or the chariot-makers might also have been represented on the council of the *ratnins*.

The council of the *ratnins* of the Vedic age thus appears to have consisted of (*a*) king's relations like the queens and perhaps the crown-prince (*rājanya*), (*b*) king's courtiers like the chamberlain, his bosom companion and his playmate at the game table and (*c*) important officers of the state like the commander-in-chief, the commander of the chariot corps, the chief tax-gatherer, the treasurer, the principal officer in charge of the royal stable,

1. This is the sense of the word in later literature. Dr. Ghoshal, however, suggests that *kshattā* may have been food-distributor ; *History of the Hindu Public Life*, I, p. 109. Whether there was such an office in the Vedic period may well be doubted.

2. Ap. Ś. S. XVII. 10. 26

3. Ś. *Br.*, V. 3. 1. 1. ; *K. S.*, XV. 4

the principal village headman and the head of the carpenters' guild.

The status of the *ratnins* was fairly high; at the time of the Vājapeya sacrifice, the king had to repair to their houses and not they to his palace in order to offer the so-called *ratnin* oblations. They are in one place expressly described as bestowers of kingdom upon the king.[1] *Samiti* in the Vedic age was a powerful body, and it is not unlikely that the *ratnins* might have been selected from among its members ; but we have no positive evidence to support this probable conjecture. Nor do we know how they functioned ; whether they met as a council to advise the king or whether the latter consulted them in their individual capacity.

With the gradual disappearance of the Vedic sacrifices, the conception of *ratnins* also faded away from society. We occasionally get references to the *ratnas* of the king, but they do not denote only his advisers. Thus, for instance, the *Vāyupurāṇa* divides the *ratnas* of the emperor into two categories animate and inanimate. To the former group belong not only the queen, the *purohita*, the commander-in-chief, the charioteer and the councillor but also the horse and the elephant, and to the latter class the *maṇi* (amulet), the sword, the bow, the lance, the jewels the banner and the treasure.[2] It is clear that the nature of the *ratnins* was clearly misunderstood in the later period; their council had ceased to function as a part of the administration.

The evidence of the Dharmaśāstra and the Nītiśāstra, however, shows that the *ratnins* did not disappear without leaving a more effective body to discharge their functions ; this was the council of ministers, variously described as *mantrins*, *sachivas* and *amātyas*.[3] We have shown already how the ministry was regarded as indispensable for good government by our cons-

1. एते वै राष्ट्रस्य प्रदातारः । *T. Br.* I. 7. 3

2. Chap. 57. vv. 68-71.

3. The connotation of these terms was not uniform. The *Rāmāyaṇa* sometimes identifies *mantri* with *sachiva* (II 112. 7) and sometimes differentiates between them (I. 7. 3 and I. 8. 4.). The *Amarakosha* states that the *amātya*, who is a *dhīsachiva*, is called a *mantrin* ; others are mere *karmasachivas*. According to Kauṭilya *mantrins* were to be selected from among *amātyas* (I. 8).

titutional thinkers and the available evidence shows that it functioned in historic times in most of our states. In the earliest historical dynasty of Magadha, Vassakāra figures as the premier of Ajātaśatru;[1] his contemporary in Kośsala, king Prasenajit, relied upon the advice of his ministers Mṛigadhara and Śrīvṛidha in carrying out important schemes.[2] The Jātakas frequently refer to ministers.[3] The Mauryas and the Śuṅgas had a regular council of ministers known as *Mantri-parishad*, which figures both in inscriptions and literature.[4] The Śaka rulers of Western India ruled with the assistance of a council of *mati-sachivas* (councillors) and *karma-sachivas* (administrative heads of departments)[5]. *Mantrins* (ministers) figure frequently in the Gupta inscriptions. The ministers under the Maukharis wielded great power, for it was their council which offered the Maukhari crown to Harsha, when the last Maukhari king died suddenly without leaving an issue.[6] Ministry was a regular feature of the medieval Hindu dynasties as well. Mahāpradhāna (prime - minister) Purushottamadeva figures in one record of the Paramāra king Yaśovarman.[7] Mahāmātyas (chief ministers) figure in almost all land grants of the Chaulukyas of Gujarat, and *mantrins* (ministers) in those of the Gāhadawālas of U. P. Mahāmātya (chief minister) usually heads the list of the officers mentioned in the grants of the Chāhamānas of Nadol[8]. Several ministerial families are mentioned in the records of the Chandellas of Mahobā.[9] The *Rājatarangiṇī* shows how ministers played a very important part in the administration of Kashmir. The same was the case with the Rāshṭrakūṭa, the Chālukya and the Śilāhāra adminstrations of the Deccan, as shown by a number of their records. One Yādava grant states how it was made by the king after

1. *Dialogues of the Buddha*, II, p. 78
2. *Uvasagadasao*, II, Appendix p. 56
3. Nos. 528, 533
4. *Arthaśāstra*, Bk. I. Chap. 15 ;
Aśoka rock-edicts, Nos. 3 and 6 ;
Mālavikāgnimitra, Act V
5. Junagad inscription of Rudradāman I,. *E. I.* VIII. p. 42
6. Watters, *On Yuan Chwang*, I. p. 343
7. *I. A.*, XIX, p. 349
8. *E. I.* XI, p. 308
9. *E. I.* I. p. 157 ; p. 208

previous consultation wth the ministry.[1] The Deccan records further show that ministers often enjoyed the status of the feudatories and were granted the coveted title of *mahāsāmantas* and *mahā-maṇḍaleśvaras*.

Ministry was regarded as so very essential for good government that crown-princes and viceroys used to have their own councils of ministers in their own courts. Under the Mauryas, the viceroys at Taxila had their own ministers. Agnimitra, the crown prince and viceroy of Mālwā under Pushyamitra, had his own council of ministers (*c.* 150 B. C.). *Yuvarājapadīya Kumārāmātyas* constituted the ministry of the crown-prince under the Guptas.[2] Jaitugi, the crown-prince of the Yādava ruler Bhillama V (1190-1210 A. D.), had his own ministry. The same was the case with Tikkamadevarasa, the viceroy of the south, under the Yādava ruler Rāmachandra.[3] The Yuvarājas and viceroys had the status of feudatary rulers and it was, therefore, but natural that they should have had a ministry of their own, as was the case at the imperial court.

Let us now see what was the strength of the ministry. Manu holds that the ministry should consist of 7 or 8 members ;[4] the latter number is prescribed by the *Mahābhārata*.[5] The *Arthaśāstra* quotes different views on the topic, from which we learn that the Mānava, the Bārhaspatya and the Auśanasa schools were in favour of a ministry of 12, 16 and 20 respectively.[6] The *Śukranīti* recommends a ministry of ten,[7] but also refers to another view which was in favour of a smaller body of 7 or 8 persons ; the view was shared by the *Mānasollāsa* of Someśvara and adopted by Shivaji in 1674. The *Nītivākyāmṛita* is in favour of a smaller ministry consisting of 3, 5, or 7 members only.

1. श्रीसेउणारव्येन नृपेणप्रधानयुक्तेन विचार्यं हट्टद्वयं दत्तम् ।
I. A., XII. p. 127
2. *A. S. I.*, *A. R.*, 1953-4, p. 107
3. *S. I. I.*, IX. Nos. 367 and 387
4. सचिवान्सप्त चाष्टौ वा कुर्वीत सुपरीक्षितान् । VII. 54
The *Mānasollāsa* adopted this verse, only changing the last word into मतिमान्नृपः । II.2.57
5. अष्टानां मंत्रिणां मध्ये मंत्रं राजोपधारयेत् ॥ XII. 85
6. Bk. I. Chap. 15
7. II. 70

It is clear that this difference of opinion on the question is due to the differing needs of the different states which our writers had in their mind. Manu[1] and Kauṭilya[2] agree with each other in stating that the actual number of ministers should depend upon the needs of the situation in the state concerned. If the state was a small one or if its activities were limited in their scope, a small ministry of 4 or 5 would suffice. Such, for instance, was the case under the Śilāhāras, whose kingdom was a small one.[3] In the age of the Jātakas, when the activities of the state were limited, we find that the ministry usually consisted of 5 members only.[4] But in big empires the number of ministers was large. The foreign office itself had several ministers in charge of its different sections. Thus in the Śilāhāra administration, there was one chief foreign minister along with another minister in charge of the foreign affairs of Karnatak only, having also the full ministerial status.[5] If a small kingdom like that of the Śilāhāras had two foreign ministers, larger states like the Maurya, Gupta, and Rāshṭrakūṭa empires must have had several. The traditional number of ministers, however, seems to have been eight ; if more persons were necessary to discharge the duties properly, they must have been usually appointed as secretaries to the ministers concerned, as recommended by Śukra[6].

To ensure despatch and secrecy, there often used to be a smaller cabinet of important ministers consisting of three or four members only. When Rāma exhorts Bharata to decide his policy after consulting three or four ministers (II. 100. 71) or Kauṭilya or Bhīshma lay down that the king should hold consultation with three or four ministers,[7] it is clear that the smaller cabinet of the ministry is being referred to.

It appears that in addition to the ministry of eight or ten, the members of which were usually called *mantrins*, there was

1. *Manu*, VII. 61
2. यथासामर्थ्यमिति कौटिल्यः । Bk. I. Chap. 15
3. *I. A.*, V. p. 278 ; IX p. 35
4. *Jātaka* No. 528
5. *I. A.* V. 277
6. II. 109-110
7. मंत्रिभिस्त्रिभिश्चतुर्भिर्वा सह मंत्रयेत् । I. 15

also a large body of advisers corresponding to the modern Privy Council, the members of which were usually known as *amātyas*. The council of 36 *amātyas* referred to by the *Mahābhārata*[1] seems to have corresponded to such a Privy Council rather than to the ministry. The *Arthaśāstra* also shows that the *amātyas* were no doubt high officials and departmental heads but inferior in status to and much larger in numbers than *mantrins*.[2] They were however, summoned for consultation on grave occasions along with the ministers.

The scope of the work of the ministry included the whole administration. It was to enunciate new policies, to ensure their successful working, to remove any difficulties that may crop up, to supervise and direct the state policy regarding taxation and expenditure, to take steps for the proper education and training of the princes, to participate in their coronation, and to direct the foreign policy, both with reference to internal feudatory kings and external independent states.[3]

It is but natural that this work should have been divided among themselves by the ministers, each one taking one department. Our early writers, however, do not enlighten us about the different portfolios assigned to the members of the ministry. It is only Śukra, a writer of about the 11th century A. D., who gives us some idea of their portfolios. According to him, the ministry, whose strength was to be 10, was to consist of (1) *Purohita*, (2) *Pratinidhi*, (3) *Pradhāna*, (4) *Sachiva*, (5) *Mantrin*, (6) *Prāḍvivāka*, (7) *Paṇḍita*, (8) *Sumantra*, (9) *Amātya* and (10) *Dūta*. The status and pay of each succeeding minister were lower than those of the preceeding one.[4]

1. XII. 85. 7-8.

2. *Mantrins* had a salary of 48000 a year ; the *amātyas* received only 12,000. A person qualified to become an *amātya* was not regarded as necessarily fit to become a *mantrin*.

विभज्यामात्यविभवं देशकालौ च कर्म च ।
अमात्याः सर्व एवैते कार्याः स्युर्नतु मंत्रिणः ॥ I.8.

3. मंत्रो मंत्रफलावाप्तिः कर्मानुष्ठानमायव्ययकर्म कुमाररक्षणमभिषेकश्च कुमाराणां आयत्तममात्येषु । *Artha*. Book VII. Chap. I

See also Book I. Chap. 6 .*Jātaka* No. 257 shows that the ministers would often exercise their discretion in deciding when the heir-apparent should be invested with ruling powers.

4. II. 70-72.

Though earlier authorities do not mention the names of the different portfolios, we may take it that ministers usually divided the departments on the lines suggested by Śukra ; for many of the ministers mentioned by him figure in inscriptions, either with the same or equivalent titles. We shall now briefly survey the duties and functions of the different ministers.

Purohita or the Royal Chaplain figured prominently in the council of *ratnins* of the Vedic period, and he continued to be a member of the ministry for several centuries. He stood in the relation of a spiritual preceptor (*guru*) to the king. He was to protect the nation by counteracting the magical charms of the enemy and ensuring its prosperity by performing the requisite rituals (*purohitikarmas*) recommended in the *Atharvaveda*.[1] He consecrated the war elephants and horses of the state army in order to enhance their military efficiency,[2] and even accompanied the king to the battlefield in the Vedic times in order to ensure his victory by his prayers, sacrifices, charms and incantations.[3] He was expected to be well-versed both in *śastra* (military art) and *śāstra* (religious rituals), as also in the political science. When the king, consecrated for a long sacrificial session, could not direct the administration, it was the *purohita* who deputised for him.[4] The *Rāmāyaṇa* shows that when the monarchy was in abeyance owing to the absence of a suitable heir to ascend the throne, it was the *purohita* Vasishṭha, who carried on the administration. Among the ministers, *purohita* alone enjoys the distinction of having a ritual prescribed for his installation ; it was known as *Bṛihaspatisava*, and was in vogue in the Vedic age.

Purohita must have wielded considerable influence during the period of the ascendancy of the Vedic sacrifices. When the

1. पुरोहितं षडंगे वेदे दैवे निमित्ते अभिविनीतमापदां दैवमानुषीणामथर्वभिरुपायैश्च प्रतिकर्तारं कुर्वीत । तमाचार्यं शिष्यः पितरं पुत्रो भृत्यः स्वामिनमिवानुवर्तेत । *Arthaśāstra*, Bk. I, Chap. 9

2. Susīma Jātaka.

3. Viśvāmitra was with his king Sudās throughout the campaign against the 10 kings. It was at his prayer that the Vipāś and the Śutudru rivers agreed to reduce the depth in order to facilitate the movements of the king's armies (*R. V.*, II. 33).

4. *Ap. S. S.*; XX. 2. 12. 3. 1-3 ; B. *Ś. S.*, XV. 4

popular faith in them declined with the rise of the Upanishadic, Jain and Buddhist movements, the influence of *purohita* must have declined. In the Jātakas, he is seen still occupying an important position ; he is *sabbātthaka* minister or minister plenipotentiary. But later on, there is no doubt that his influence declined. Post-Gupta inscriptions usually distinguish him from ministers, showing that he was no longer a member of the ministry.[1] *Śukranīti* is probably following the old tradition, rather than reflecting the contemporary practice, when it places the *purohita* at the head of the ministry. It however admits that he had no place in that body according to the views of others (II. 72). Though *purohita*, generally speaking, ceased to be a member of the ministry from *c.* 200 A. D. he continued to exercise considerable moral influence upon the king ; the frown of an ideal *purohita* was sufficient to keep the king on the path of virtue and rectitude.[2]

The second minister of Śukra is *pratinidhi*. It was his duty to deputise for the king when he was ill or absent on an expedition It is very likely that this duty must have devolved upon the Crown-prince, when he had become old enough to assume the reins of his office. The *uparājā* of the Jātakas seems to have corresponded with the *pratinidhi* of Śukra. It however appears that the portfolio of *pratinidhi* was not generally included in ministry ; inscriptions do not refer to his office and Manu states that the premier should deputise for the king, and not the *pratinidhi*.[3] In the Maratha cabinet also there was usually no Pratinidhi, but the post was created by king Rajaram when he had to leave Mahārāshṭra and take refuge in Jinjee.

Pradhāna or the Premier was the most important member of the ministry. According to Śukra, he was to be *sarvadarśi*[4] *i. e.* the superintendent of the whole administration.[5] Jiyanta,

1. राजराज्ञीयुवराजमंत्रिपुरोहितप्रतीहारसेनापति... in Gāhadawāla records. The Śilāhāra records also differentiate him from *Mantrins* and *Amātyas*. *E. I.* IX. p. 24.

2. यत्कोपभीत्या राजापि धर्मनीतिरतो भवेत् । Śukra, II. 99

3. VII. 141

4. सर्वदर्शी प्रधानस्तु । II. 89

5. *I. A.*, VI. p. 24

in who is called *sarvasya anushṭhātā*, the performer of everything, a 6th century record of the Kadamba dynasty,[1] Kṛishṇambhaṭṭa, who was a *mahāmātya* under king Dantivarman (*c.* 880 A. D.) of the Gujarat Rāshṭrakuṭa branch,[2] Babhiyaka, who is styled as *mahāpradhāna* in an 11th century Yādava record,[3] *mantrīndra* Vatsarāja of the Chandella king Kṛishṇavarman, (*c.* 1090 A. D.),[4] Sallakshapāla, who figures as a *mahāmantrin* of the Chāhamāna ruler Viśāladeva (*c.* 1160 A. D..), the *mahāmātyas* who figure in several Paramāra and almost all the Chaulukya grants,—these were all discharging the duties of the prime-minister. This office existed under Shivaji and its holder was known as Mahāpradhāna. The status of the premier was naturally very high; our epigraphs often state how the nails of their toes were brightened by the rays in the crowns of the feudatories. As in modern times so in ancient India, premiers used to take a particular portfolio as well; the premier of the Śilāhāra king Anantadeva was also the Lord High Tresurer in 1085.[5]

The War-minister was the next important member of the ministry. The title *sachiva*, given to him in the *Śuktranīti*, was, however, not the usual designation by which he was known. He was known as *senāpati* under the Mauryas and the Marathas. *Māhābalādhikṛita* under the Guptas,[6] *Kampana* in Kahmir,[7] and *Mahāprachaṇḍadaṇḍanāyaka* under the Yādavas. The *Nītivākyāmṛita* is opposed to the inclusion of the commander-in-chief in the ministry,[8] but it seems that the normal practice was to include him in that body. The war minister was to be an expert in the theory and practice of war and well versed in the art of organisation. It was his duty to see that all forts were properly garrisoned and all the branches of the army were properly equipped and were kept at their highest efficiency.[9]

1. *E. I.*,VI. p. 287
2. *E. I.* II. p. 225
3. *I. A.*, XVIII. p. 238
4. *I. A.*, XIX. p. 218
5. *I. A.*, XII. p. 127
6. *E. I.*, X. 71.
7. *Rājataraṅgiṇi*, VII. 365
8. Chap. X. 101-2
9. *Śukraniti*, II. 95

The Foreign Minister is the next important member of the ministry. He is designated as mantrin by Śukra, but the inscriptions give him the more significant title of *mahāsandhivigrahika*, 'the highest officer in charge of peace and war'. This minister was known as Sumanta (Sumantrin) under Shivaji. India was usually studded with a large number of states, some independent ansd some feudatories. Most of them used to entertain the secret hope to attain the imperial status one day. The work of the Foreign Minister was therefore both heavy and exacting. It was divided state-wise; even the small Śilāhāra kingdom of Chittarājadeva (*c.* 1025 A. D.) had one chief Foreign Minister and another Foreign Minister in-charge of Karnatak affairs.[1] If such a small kingdom required two officials at the foreign office, both of the status of a minister, one can well conclude that the ministries of big kingdoms like those of the Mauryas, the Guptas, the Rāshṭrakūṭas and the Gurjara-Pratīhāras must have had several foreign ministers or secretaries working under the directions of a Chief Foreign Minister.

The Foreign Minister was to be well versed in the four-fold policy of *sāma* (conciliation), *dāma* (appeasement), *daṇḍa* (war), and *bheda* (causing dissentions in the enemy's camp).[2] Numerous inscriptions show that he was also usually in charge of drafting the copper plate charters, granting lands and villages to Brāhmaṇas, temples and monasteries. This appears rather strange, but when we remember that the charters had usually to describe the genealogy of the dynasty with the exploits and achievements of each ruler, one can at once realise that the Foreign Minister was the best person to draft the texts of the grants. It is interesting to note that there is an agreement in this respect between the epigraphical practice and the dicta of contemporary Smṛitis; an anonymous text quoted in the *Mitāksharā*, expressly states that the *sandhivigrahakārī* should draft the copper-plate charters.[3]

1. *I. A.*, V. p. 277.
2. *Śukra*, II. 95.
3. संधिविग्रहकारी तु भवेद्यस्तस्य लेखकः। On *Yāj.*, I. 319

The next minister *prāḍvivāka* was in charge of the judical department ; he was also the chief-justice.[1] He was to be well-versed in the traditional and Smṛiti law, and an expert in evaluating evidence. He presided over the highest court of appeal in the absence of the king. He figures rather rarely in inscriptions.[2]

The next minister *paṇḍita* was in charge of religion and morality. He was to be well-versed in Dharmaśāstra and to find out which religious views and practices were actually current and popular, which were prescribed in Śāstras but had become obsolete and which were opposed both to the dictates of the Śāstras and the practice of the people. It was his duty to take a wide and comprehensive view in the matter and advise the government upon its socio-religious policy. We have shown already how the state was to be the gaurdian of *dharma*. This, however, did not mean that it was to blindly enforce whatever was prescribed in antiquated texts. It was the duty of one of its ministers, *viz.* the *paṇḍita,* to find out which practices had become antiquated and to discourage and not enforce them. He was also to advise the government about suitable changes that could be introduced in consonance with the spirit of *dharma* and culture.[3] One of Shivaji's ministers, bearing almost the same name, Panditrao, discharged similar functions. The *dharmamahāmātras* of Aśoka, the *śramaṇamahāmātras* under the Sātavāhanas,[4] the *vinayasthitisthāpakas* under the Guptas,[5] the *dharmāṅkuśas* under the Rāshṭrakūṭas[6] and the *dharmapradhānas* under the Chedis, all seem to be the officers working under this department. Grants to temples and monas-

1. In the cabinet of Shivaji he was known as Nyàyàdhiśa.
2. He is mentioned in the Sanjan Plates of Amoghavarsha I as the drafter of the record. *E. I.*, XVIII. 235

3. वर्तमानाश्च प्राचीना धर्माः के लोकसंश्रिताः ।
शास्त्रेषु के समुद्दिष्टा विरुध्यन्ते च केऽधुना ॥
लोकशास्त्रविरुद्धाः के पण्डितस्तान्विचिन्त्य च ।
नृपं संबोधयेत्तैश्च परत्रह सुखप्रदैः ॥ *Śukra*, II. 100

4. *E. I.*, VIII. p. 91
5. *A. S. I.*, *A. R.*, 1904-3 p. 109
6. *I. A.*, XVIII, p. 230

steries, as also to schools and colleges, must have fallen primarily within the province of this department.

The next minister mentioned by Śukra is Treasurer. He designates him as *sumantra*, but the Vedic term *saṁgrahītā* (collector) or the Kauṭiliyan expression *samāhartā* (bringer together) are more expressive. Inscriptions often describe him as *bhāṇḍāgārika*, the officer in charge of treasury and stores ;[1] this phrase correctly describes the duties of his office. It was his duty to find out what were the total collections and disbursements for the year, and what was the balance at its end.[2] Taxes were collected mostly in kind ; the duty of the treasurer was, therefore, an exacting one. He had to sell old corn and replace it by new one every now and then, lest it should become useless.

The Treasurer was an important minister. In 1094 A. D. the Śilāhāra ruler Anantadeva had a small ministry of only three and yet the Treasurer was included in it. The *Mahābhārata* (XII. 130.35), *Kāmandakanītisāra* (XXXI. 33) and *Nītivākyāmṛita* (XXI. 5) declare that the treasury was the very root of the state and must be properly looked after. The Treasurer figures invariably among the officers mentioned in the Gāhadawāla copper plate grants ; his non-mention in other records may be regarded as purely accidental.

The Revenue Minister now remains to be considered. He is called *amātya* by Śukra, and bore the same title in Shivaji's cabinet ; it was his duty to have a correct inventory of villages, towns, mines and forests in the country and of the income expected from them. His office also had an accurate account of the land under cultivation, and land lying fallow, as also of the expected produce from the different mines.[3] He figures rather rarely in inscriptions.[4]

The salaries of ministers are given only by Kauṭilya. Puro-

1. *I. A.*, IX. p. 33
2. इयच्च संचितं द्रव्यं वत्सरेऽस्मिंस्तृणादिकम् ।
   व्ययीभूतमियच्चैव शेषं स्थावरजंगमम् ।
   इयदस्तीति वै राज्ञे सुमंत्रो विनिवेदयेत् ॥ *Śukra*, II. 101
3. *Śukra*, II. 103-5
4. An 11th century Yādava record mentions him ; *E. I.* I. p. 225. The *mahāmātyas*, who figure in Chàulukya records, are Premiers.

hita and Senāpati were to receive 48,000 Paṇas a year, Revenue and Treasury ministers were to receive 24,000 Paṇas, and the rest 12,000 Paṇas. It is quite possible that the salaries varied with the size and revenues of the state, but the data in the *Arthaśāstra* may perhaps indicate the relative importance of the different portfolios.

It is unfortunate that we should possess no detailed evidence about the actual working of the ministry either from our constitutional writers or from inscriptions. Under normal conditions the king presided over the council and is advised not to lose his temper, if a different view is taken by his advisers.[1] The *Arthaśāstra* however refers to the President of the Council as a separate officer (I. 12). The Rock Edict VI of Aśoka records his order that a difference of opinion among the ministers should be at once reported to him. It is therefore clear that on some occasions not the king but one of his ministers presided over the cabinet meeting. Manu recommends (VII. 57) that the king should consult the ministers both jointly and separately. A minister may not choose to divulge his real views in the presence of others; hence individual consultation was also recommended. Śukra apprehended that the presence of the king in the council may often induce ministers not to express their real views, that may be unpalatable to the king; he therefore recommends that ministers on such occasions should be asked to send their views in separate memoranda, explaining fully the grounds for their advice.[2] Kauṭilya was in favour of joint consultation with three or four ministers, whose portfolios may have been connected with the matter.[3] The *Rājataraṅgiṇī* shows that all these alternatives were followed by the Kashmirian kings as required by the particular situation.[4]

1. मंत्रकाले न कोपयेत् । *Bārhaspatya-Arthaśāstra*, II. 53
2. रागाल्लोभाद्भयाद्राज्ञः स्युर्मूका इव मंत्रिणः।
न ताननुमतान्विद्यान्नृपतिः स्वार्थसिद्धये ।
पृथक् पृथक् मतं तेषां लेखयित्वाससाधनम् ।
विमृशेत्स्वमतेनैव यत्कुर्याद् बहुतसंमतम् ॥ I. 363-4
3. Bk. I. Chap. 15
4. At VII. 1043 and 1415, we find king Harsha having a joint consultation with all his ministers. King Jayasiṁha often preferred to consult only a few ministers (VIII. 3082-3)

Under normal circumstances, we may, however, presume that the ministry acted in a body and was jointly consulted. A unanimous decision of the ministry arrived at after full discussion and in consonance with the dictates of the science of polity was highly valued.[1] Kauṭilya recommends that even on critical occasions, the king should usually accept the advice of the ministry or the view of its majority, though it was open for him to adopt a course which he thought to be most advantageous.[2]

Rock edicts III and VI of Aśoka throw further light upon the working of the council of ministers. The third edict shows that the council's orders were to be duly recorded and expounded to the public by local officers. The sixth edict discloses that the oral orders of the emperor, as well as the decisions of the departmental heads taken in urgent cases, were subject to review by the counci of ministers. It was not merely a recording body, for very often it used to suggest amendments to the king's orders or even recommend their total reversal. Aśoka says that when such a contingency arose, or when the council was divided on any topic, the matter was to be at once reported to him.[3] There can be no doubt that the emperor himself must have taken the final decision, but the fact that the council used to suggest revision of royal orders, necessitating their reconsideration by the king, shows that its powers were real and extensive.

The council of ministers continued to flourish under the Śuṅgas as well, even in the courts of their Crown-princes. Agnimitra had such a council to assist him in his provincial capital. The council could meet and transact business even in the absence

1. ऐकमत्यमुपागम्य शास्त्रदृष्टेन चक्षुषा।
मंत्रिणो यत्र निरतास्तमाहुर्मंत्रमुत्तमम्॥ *Rāmāyaṇa*, VI. 12

2. तत्र यद्भूयिष्ठाः कार्यसिद्धिकरं वा ब्रूयुस्तत्कुर्युः।
Arthaśāstra, Bk. I. Chap. 6

3. यं किंच मुखतो आणपयामि अहं दपक श्रवक व येन पन महामंत्रेण अचयिकं आरोपितं होति तये अथाये विवदे निझति वा संतं परिषयं अनंतरियेन पटिवेदितवो मे। Rock Edict VI (Shahabazgarhi)

of their Crown-prince ; its decisions were later communicated to him for final acceptance.[1]

The ministerial council existed also under the Śakas of the Western India. The Junagad inscription of Rudradāman shows how important financial projects like the rebuilding of the Girinagar dam were first referred to it for consideration. It is a pity that we should have no information about its functioning in northern India in the Gupta and post-Gupta administrations. We have, however, already shown how ministers were integral parts of all these administrations. It is but natural to presume that they usually worked in a corporate capacity as a council and continued to exercise the same great influence upon the administration as under the Mauryas, the Śuṅgas and the Śakas. This inference is strengthened by what we know of the Chola administration of the 11th century. The records of this dynasty show that the ministry functioned under the Cholas in southern India exactly in the same way as it did under Aśoka 1300 years earlier in northern India. The oral orders of the Chola king were subject to review by his council, as was the case with the oral orders of Aśoka. It was only when they were thus scrutinised that they were entered into official registers.[2]

Details of the routine working of the ministry can be gathered only from the *Śukranīti*. Though this is a late work, we may well presume that its account held good of the earlier periods as well. Śukra recommends that each minister should normally have two secretaries, but their number may be increased if the work of the department demands this step. Conversely if a department was very small, the secretary was often dispensed with.[3] A secretary was often promoted to the position of the

1. *Mālavikāgnimitra*, Act. V
2. *S. I. I.*, III, No. 21 ; *E. C.*, X. Kolar No. 111
3. एकस्मिन्नधिकारे तु पुरुषाणां त्रयं सदा ।
नियुञ्जीत प्राज्ञतमं मुख्यमेकं तु तेषु वै । 109
द्वौ दर्शकौ तु तत्कार्यं हायनैस्तान्निवर्तयेत् ।
त्रिभिर्वा पंचभिर्वापि सप्तभिर्दशभिश्च वा ॥ 110
अधिकारिबलं दृष्टवा योजयेदर्शकान्बहून् ।
अधिकारिणमेकं वा योजयेदर्शकर्विना ॥ 115 (Chap. II)

minister in due course, if he had proved his capacity by his work and achievements. Śukra recommends the occasional transfer of ministers from one portfolio to another. This was intended partly to offer scope to able ministers to get the charge of departments, more important than those to which they were originally appointed. That such changes in portfolioes were often taking place in practice is shown by the case of Pṛithivishena, who was first an ordinary minister, but was later promoted to the post of the War Minister[1] under Kumāragupta I.

Capable and ambitious ministers often held more than one portfolioes, a phenomenon not unknown in our own times. Thus in the cabinet of king Jayasiṁha of Kashmir, Sujji was both the Judicial and Military member. A little later Alaṁkāra was appointed to the post of both the Commander-in-Chief and Chief Justice.[2] It was, however, only in exceptional cases that the portfolioes were thus allowed to be combined ; normally each minister held the charge of one department only.

When a matter was decided, the minister to whose department it primarily belonged, used to write a minute, containing the decision, with a note at the end that it had his full approval. The minute was then sealed and sent to the king for his sanction. The king used to sign the final order in token of his approval or ask the Crown-prince to do so on his behalf. When the order thus received the royal approval, it was duly announced or sent to the department or officer concerned for execution.[3]

Let us now see what qualifications were expected in ministers. The *Arthaśāstra* and other works show that opinion was not unanimous upon the point. Some regarded ability and others loyalty as the most important criterion. Some held that the selection should be made from among the king's school-companions, others thought that the choice should be restricted to members of certain loyal and tested families. Kauṭilya opined that there was truth in each of the above views and recommended the selection of persons combining as many qualifications as possible.

1. *E. I.*, X, p. 71
2. *Rājataraṅgiṇi*, VIII. 1582-4 ; 2925
3. *Śukra*, II. 363-7

According to him an ideal minister should be a native of the country, born of high family, influential, well-trained in arts, possessed of foresight, wise, strong in memory, bold, eloquent, skilful, intelligent, possessed of enthusiasm, dingnity and endurance, pure in character, affable, affectionate, firm in loyal devotion, endowed wtih excellent strength, health and bravery, free from procrastination and fickle-mindedness and such defects as excite hatred and enmity.[1] The picture of the ideal minister, according to other writers also, is almost the same.[2] In actual practice, all these qualities could not be ensured in every minister; it was, therefore, recommended that an effort should be made to make the selection in the light of the ideal. Manu and Kauṭilya (I. 10) lay down that before being appointed to the ministry, the king himself should test him to find out whether he was above the temptation of wealth, wine and women and possessed the minimum qualifications.

Let us now see how far ministers conformed to this high standard in actual practice. When weak, vicious and fickle-minded kings were on the throne, ministers selected by them were often worthless sycophants. Thus in Kashmir king Unmattāvanti is known to have selected his ministers from among musicians, and king Chakravarman from among the *dombas*, who were the relations of his newest love. Probably the same was the case under the rulers like Bṛihaspatimitra Maurya, Devabhūmi Śuṅga, Govinda IV Rāshṭrakūṭa, and other rulers of their type who were weak, vicious and wicked. Such cases, however, were occasional and did not frequently disfigure the administration. A perusal of the epigraphical and literary evidence shows that effort was usually made to select capable persons, well-versed in the political science. Śāba, a minister of Chandragupta II, is expressly described as well grounded in the science of politics and reasoning.[3] Nārāyaṇa, a minister of of Rāshṭrakūṭa king Kṛishṇa III, is known to have been a past-

1. Bk. I, Chap. 5
2. *Mbh.*, XII. Chaps. 82-5 ; *Kāmandakanītisāra*, IV. 25-31 ; *Śukranīti*, II. 52-64; *Kural*, Chaps. 51-2
3. शब्दार्थन्यायनीतिज्ञः कविः पाटलिपुत्रकः । *C. I. I.*, III. 35

master in the political science.[1] Nāgarasa, the premier of the Yādava ruler Krishṇa, was a statesman whose intellect had become versatile owing to the study of various works on the science of polity.[2] We can well conclude that in normal cases ministers were appointed only when they were known to be well versed in the theory and practice of administration and political science.

The view of the Smṛiti writers that the sons or relations of a minister should, if possible, be selected while making new appointments to the ministry, was also very frequently given effect to. Under the Guptas, the families of Śāba and Pṛithvīsheṇa were holding different ministerial appointments for more than one generations[3] In the Parivrājaka administration, Śūryadatta was a minister in 482 A. D. and his son Vibhudatta 28 years later.[4] Under Uchchkalpa dynasty, Gallu was Foreign Minister in 496 and his brother Manoratha in 512 A. D.[5] Under the Chandellas five generations of one family, Prabhāsa, his son Śivanāga, his son Mahīpāla, his son Ananta and his son Gadādhara, are known to have worked as ministers or prime-ministers under seven generations of the dynasty represented by Ḍhaṅga, his son Gaṇḍa, his son Vidyādhara, his son Vijayapāla, his son Devavarman, his brother Kīrtivarman, his sons Sallakahaṇavarman and Pṛithvīvarman and the former's son Jayavarman.[6] A little later under the same dynasty, Lahaḍa was minister under Madanavarman and his son Sallakshaṇa and grandson Purushottama under Paramarddideva, the grandson of Madanavarman.[7]

It is thus clear that when the Smṛitis and Nītis recommend that ministers should be selected on the hereditary principle, they were enunciating a theory that was widely followed in actual practice. If, however, the son of a minister was incompetent,

1. पारगो राजविद्यानां कविमुख्यः प्रियंवदः । *E. I.*, IV. p. 60

2. अनेकराजनीतिशास्त्रोक्तविवेकवर्धितबुद्धिकौशलः । *I. A.*, XII. p. 126

3. Śāba is described as अन्वयप्राप्तसाचिव्यः । Pṛithvīsheṇa was a minister under Kumāragupta I and his father Śikharasvāmin under the latter's father Chandragupta II. *E. I.*, X. p. 71

4. *C. I. I.*, III, pp. 104-108

5. *Ibid*, p. 128

6. *E. I.*, I. p. 197

7. *Ibid*, pp. 208-211

it is expressly laid down that he should not be appointed to the ministerial post ; he may be offered some inferior post.[1]

Sometimes ministers were selected also from the members of the royal family. Thus king Harsha of Kashmir had appointed two sons of a former ruler as his ministers[2] and the premier of the Chāhamāna ruler Visaladeva was his own son Sallakshanapāla.[3] Selection of ministers from the distant scions of the royal family could not, however, have been very common ; for there was also the danger in such cases that the minister may try to usurp the throne for himself.

Curiously enough Smṛiti and Nīti writers do not emphasise military leadership and ability in the minister.[4] A perusal of the epigraphical evidence, however, shows that they were usually military leaders as well. Harisheṇa, the Foreign Minister of Samudragupta, was also a general (*mahābalādhikṛita*). Provincial governors under the Ikshvākus and the Vākāṭakas were military commanders, and the same was the case probably with many of their ministers. Chāmuṇḍarāya, the minister of the Gaṅga king Mārasiṁha, had won the battle of Gonur for his king.[5] In 1024 A. D. the Minister of Records of the Later Chālukyas was a *mahāprachaṇḍadaṇḍanāyaka* ; clearly he was a high military officer as well. All the ministers of the Kalachuri king Bijjaladeva were *daṇḍanāyakas* or generals.[6] One is surprised to find that even the minister Hemādri, who had spent so much of his time in writing about *vratas* and rituals, should also have been a general ; he was not only well aquainted with the theory and practice of training war-elephants, but had led a successful expedition against a

1. यदि मौलाः कुलीना अपि तथा पितृपैतामहपदयोग्यगुणहीनास्तान् यथायोग्येषु कर्मसु नियुञ्जीत न तु तत्तत्पितृपैतामहपदेषु तत्र तत्र तेषामयोग्यत्वात् । *Rājanītiprakāśa*, p. 176

2. *Rājataraṅgiṇī*, VIII. 874

3. *I. A.*, XIX. p. 218

4. Kauṭilya, Kāmandaka and Somadeva passingly observe that ministers should be brave, but do not emphasise upon military qualifications and leadership.

5. *E. I.*, V. p. 173

6. *I. A.*, XIV. p. 26

rebel chief in Jhandi district[1]. Nāgarasa, the premier of Yādava king Krishṇa, was as great a scholar as a soldier.[2]

Smṛitis prefer that ministerial appointments should normally go to Brāhmaṇas. How far such was actually the case, we do not know. Epigraphs do not refer to the castes of the ministers mentioned in them. It is, however, likely that most of the castes and interests were represented on the ministry. According to the *Mahābhārata*, the Privy Council of the king was to consist of only four Brāhmaṇas, but eight Kshattriyas, twenty one Vaiśyas and three Śūdras.[3] Śukra states that it is only on the occasion of dinner and marriage that one should enquire about the caste, not when making appointments to the ministry.[4] Somadeva recommends that the ministers should be selected from all the three regenerate castes[5] and Śukra has no objection to the military portfolio being under a Śūdra, if he is capable and loyal.[6] Majority of kings in ancient India were non-Brāhmaṇas, and it is very likely that the same was the case with the majority of their ministers, exspecially because they were also expected to be military leaders.

Ministerial appointments were made by the king. We have shown already how there existed no popular Central Assembly in historic times to which ministers could have become res-

1. *J. R. A. S.*, V. p. 183
2. *I. A.*, XIV. p. 70
3. चतुरो ब्राह्मणान् वैद्यान्प्रगल्भान्स्नातकाञ्शुचीन् ।
क्षत्रियान् दश चाष्टौ च बलिनः शस्त्रपाणिनः ॥
वैश्यान्वित्तेन संपन्नानेकविंशतिसंख्यया ।
त्रींश्च शूद्रान्विनीतांश्च शुचीन्कर्मणि पूर्वके ॥ XII. 85. 7-8

No other writers give such a preponderence to Vaishyas; the specific inclusion of the Śūdras in the ministry is also unusual.

4. नैव जातिं न च कुलं केवलं लक्षयेदपि ।
कर्मशीलगुणाः पूज्यास्तथा जातिकुलेन च ।
न जात्या न कुलेनैव श्रेष्ठत्वं प्रतिपद्यते ।
विवाहे भोजने नित्यं कुलजातिविवेचनम् ॥ II. 545

5. *Nītivākyāmṛita* p. 55
6. स्वधर्मनिरता नित्यं स्वामिभक्ता रिपुद्विषः ।
शूद्रा वा क्षत्रिया वैश्या म्लेच्छाः संकरसंभवाः ।
सेनाधिपाः सैनिकाश्च कार्या राज्ञा जयार्थिना ॥ II. 139

ponsible. They were, therefore, directly responsible to the king and only indirectly to the public opinion. Influence of ministers, therefore, largely depended upon personal factors and not upon the constitutional backing of a popular assembly. When there was a powerful and self-willed ruler upon the throne, like Bimbisāra, he would dismiss some ministers for giving bad advice, degrade some for inefficiency and promote others for their good service.[1] The position of ministers under such rulers was difficult. They, like Rāvaṇa, expected their ministers to concur with them; if they offered unwelcome advice, they were often in the danger of being dismissed.[2] Sometimes they were even banished and their property confiscated for their daring to displease the king by their unwelcome advice.[3] The other side of the picture comes before us when kings were weak and ministers ambitious to usurp the throne. Then also their mutual relations were strained ; the ministers would conspire to multiply the difficulties and calamities for their rulers.[4] The father of Satyavān, the husband of Sāvitrī, had lost his kingdom owing to the machinations of his ministers ; the same was the case with the last ruler of the Śuṅga and the Later Chālukya dynasties in historic times.

Cases above referred to were, however, unusual. Normally kings had a high regard for their ministers and the latter were loyal to them ; they also regarded themselves as trustees of the interest of the people. Ministers were the pillars of the state[5] and normally the kings used to accept their advice,

1. *Chullavagga*, V. 1

2. संपृष्टेन तु वक्तव्यं सचिवेन विपश्चिता ।
वाक्यमप्रतिकूलं तु मृदुपूर्वं हितं शुभम् ।
सावमर्दं तु यद्वाक्यं मारीच हितमुच्यते ।
नाभिनंदति तद्राजा मानार्हो मानवर्जितम् ।
एतत्कार्यमवश्यं मे बलादपि करिष्यसि । *Rāmāyaṇa*, III 43. 9-10, 25

3. *Rājataraṅgiṇī*, II. 68; VI. 342

4. सदैवापद्गतो राजा भोग्यो भवति मंत्रिणाम् ।
अत एव हि वाञ्छंति मंत्रिण: सापदं नृपम् ।। *Panchatantra*, p. 66

5. अंत:सारैरकुटिलैरच्छिद्रै: सुपरीक्षितै: ।
मंत्रिभिर्धार्यते राज्यं सुस्तंभैरिव मंदिरम् ।। *Panchantantra*, p. 66

though the ultimate responsibility rested with thc crown.[1] It was the first and foremost duty of the minister to control the king and to see that he did not follow the wrong path.[2] They are the real friends of the king, says Kāmandaka, who prevent him from following a dangerous path.[3] Ministers, worth their name, must inspire the king with awe ; they must devote themselves wholeheartedly to the proper performance of public duties and never think of pandering to the whims of the ruler.[4] As ministers occupied so important a place in the body politic, it was but natural that some thinkers should have held that the ministerial debacle was the greatest calamity that could fall upon a kingdom.[5]

Personal factors counted for a good deal in derterming the position and powers of ministers. Our constitutional writers point out that when kings were strong and powerful, they were the centres of power and the administration was known as 'king-centred' (*rājāyatta-tantra*) ; when they were weak and incapable, ministers were the virtual rulers and then the administration was known as ministry-controlled (*sachivāyatta-tantra*). In normal times, however, power was shared by both and the administration was known as *ubhyāyatta*,[6] dependent equally both on the king and the ministry.

There is sufficient evidence to show that normally ministers were held in high regard by kings, and that their advice was followed by them. Nārāyaṇa, the foreign minister of the Rāshṭrakūṭa emperor, Kṛishṇa III, (*c.* 950 A. D.) is described as his right hand ;[7] king Parabala of Pathari (*c.* 850 A. D.)

1. तद्यद्भूयिष्ठाः कार्यसिद्धिकरं वा ब्रूयुः तत्कुर्यात् । *Arthaśāstra*, Bk. I. Chap. 15
2. ये एनमपायस्थानेभ्यो वारयेयुः । *Ibid*, Bk. I. Chap. 3
3. नृपस्य त एव सुहृदस्त एव गुरवो मताः ।
   य एनमुत्पथगतं वारयंत्यनिवारितम् ॥ IV. 14
4. सा मंत्रिता च यद्राज्यकार्यभारैकचिन्तनम् ॥
   चित्तानुवर्तनं यत्तदुपजीवकलक्षणम् ॥ *Kathāsaritasāgara*, XVII 46
5. This was the view of Bhāradvāja; *Arthaśāstra*, Bk. VII. Chap. 1
6. *Mudrārākshasa*, Act II ; *Kathāsaritsāgara*, I. 58-9
7. तस्य यः प्रतिहस्तोऽभूत्प्रियो दक्षिणहस्तवत् । *E. I.*, IV. p. 60

used to regard his minister as worthy of salutation by his own head.[1] A record of the Yādava king Kṛishṇa compares his prime-minister to his own tongue and right hand.[2] Another document of the same dynasty states that wealth of the country, the contentment and prosperity of its inhabitants and the increase in virtue and piety among the population all depend upon how the ministers discharge their duties.[3]

We had pointed out earlier how sometimes ministers were reduced to mere figure heads when kings were strong, able or self-willed, that is to say, when the state was king-centred (*rājāyatta*). The reverse used to be the case when kings were weak and ministers strong and capable, and able to work in a team-spirit. Tradition asserts that Chandragupta Maurya was completely in the hands of his prime-minister Kauṭilya. Aśoka's extravagant charity was curbed by his ministers, and eventually he could present only half an *āmalaka* fruit to the Church;[4] a *stūpa* was built over this valued gift which was seen by Yuan Chwang. This pilgrim further informs us how kings Vikramāditya of Śrāvasti had proposed to sperd five lakhs daily in charity, and how he was opposed by his ministers ; they pointed out how fresh taxes would have to be imposed upon people, when the treasury was emptied out by this procedure, and said, 'Your Majesty will indeed get credit for charity, but your ministers will lose respect of all'.[5]

In Pādāñjali Jātaka (No. 247) we find that ministers could successfully veto the accession of the heir-apparent Pādāñjali because he was lacking in intelligence and commonsense. These are more or less traditional accounts, but the *Rājata-*

1. परबलनृपतेर्मूर्ध्नि वन्द्यः प्रधानः। *E. I.*, IX. p. 254
2. यो जिह्वा पृथिवीशस्य यो राज्ञो दक्षिणः करः। *I. A., XIV*, p. 70
3. राष्ट्रस्य पुष्टिः स्वजनस्य तुष्टिर्धर्मस्य वृद्धिः सकलार्थसिद्धिः।
नंदंति संतः प्रसरंति लक्ष्म्यः श्रीचंगदेवे सति सत्प्रधाने ॥
I. A., VII, p. 41
4. भृत्यैः स भूमिपतिरद्य हृताधिकारः।
दानं प्रयच्छति किलामलकार्धमेतत् ॥ *Divyāvadāna*, p. 432
5. Watters, Vol. I. p. 211

raṅgiṇi gives historical instances showing the great powers wielded by ministers. The deposition of Ajayāpīḍa was due to the decree of his ministers Mamma and others (IV. 707). Śūra could become king because the crown was decided to be offered to him by the ministry, which had concluded that he was most qualified for it (IV. 715). When on his death-bed, king Kalaśa wanted to inaugurate his son Harsha as Yuvarāja, he could not do so owing to the determined opposition of his ministry (VII. 702). There is ample evidence to show that when a king died without leaving a competent heir, it was the ministry which settled the question of succession. When king Vijaya of Ceylon died, ministers took over the administration in their own hands till the return of his nephew from India after one year, when they duly invested him with the ruling powers.[1] It was the Maukhari ministers who offered the crown of Kanauj to Harsha.

Generally speaking, however, in normal times and under normal administrations the ultimate responsibility of decision lay with the king,[2] but he was usually guided by the advice of the council of his ministers. The relations between the king and his ministers were also cordial. Kings had high regard for their ministers and confided in them as implicitly as in their own heart.[3] They regarded them to be as indispensable as their right hands and paid as much regard to their views as to their own.[4] Kalhaṇa describes how king Jayasiṁha kept by the side of his ailing minister till the last moment of his life (VIII. 3329), and we need not suppose that this was an exceptional case.

Very often even powerful kings like Lalitāditya would leave standing instructions with their ministers that they should not execute their orders if they were unreasonable or given when they were not in their full senses ; they would not fail to thank

1. *Mahāvṁśā*, Chap. 9
2. घृतेऽपि मंत्रे मंत्रज्ञैः स्वयं भूयो विचारयेत् ।
तथा वर्तेत तत्वज्ञो यथा स्वार्थं न पीडयेत् ॥ *Kāmandaka*, XI. 60
3. विश्वासे हृदयोपमम् । *J. B. B. R. A. S.*, XV. p. 5
4. यो जिह्वा पृथिवीशस्य यो राज्ञो दक्षिणः करः । *I. A.* XIV. p. 70

them for such disobedience.[1] Ministers on their part also were usually loyal to the king and also solicitous about the interest of the people. When king Jayāpīḍa had been imprisoned, one of his ministers committed suicide in order to enable the imprisoned king to escape by crossing the river over his bloated corpse.[2] In the Deccan we get many cases of ministers taking the vow to die with their kings and carrying it out when the occasion arose. Lakshama, a minister of Hoysala king Ballāla II, had taken this vow and when the king died, both he and his wife mounted a stone pillar and committed suicide by jumping down. Inscriptions from Karnāṭak refer to many such cases.[4]

Of course the combination of an appreciative and wise king and a devoted and capable minister between whom there would never arise any misunderstanding and quarrel was an ideal one.[5] But the ideal was more frequently approached in practice than we may be *prima facie* inclined to believe. The available evidence shows that the ministry usually exercised a wholesome influence upon the administration and though not constitutionally responsible to the people, sought to protect and promote their interests and welfare to the best of its ability.

1. कार्यं न जातु तद्वाक्यं यत्क्षीबेण मयोच्यते ।
   तान्युक्तकारिणोऽमात्यान्प्रशंसन्निति सोऽब्रवीत् ॥ *Rājataraṅgiṇī*, IV. 320
2. *Rājataraṅgiṇī*, IV. 575
3. *E. C.*, V. Belur No. 12
4. *E. C.*, V. Arkalgad, Nos. 5 and 27; *E. C.* VI. Kadur No. 146 *E. C.*, X. Kolar No. 129; Mulbagala. Nos 77 and 78, etc.
5. कृतज्ञः क्षांतिमान्क्ष्माभृन्मंत्री भक्तः स्मयोज्झितः ।
   अभंगुरोयं संयोगः सुकृतैर्जातु दृश्यते ॥
   परस्परमनुत्पन्नमन्युकालुष्यदूषणौ ।
   न दृष्टौ न श्रुतौ वान्यौ तादृशौ राजमंत्रिणौ ॥ *Rājataraṅgiṇī*, V.463-1

CHAPTER IX

SECRETARIAT AND DEPARTMENTS

In the preceding chapters, we have already seen what were the powers and functions of the king and his council of ministers, who together constituted the brain centre of the government organism. But just as the brain can function through the instrumentality and cooperation of a number of senses and organs, so also the king-in-council requires the assistance of a central secretariat and the heads of a number of departments. We shall describe in the present chapter the organisation of the secretariat and of the different departments of the central government. Here again we have to observe that the data are very meagre ; we shall have to generalise from a few disconnected facts that we can gather from different dynasties flourishing in widely different provinces and centuries.

The art of writing was either unknown or was not much in use in the Vedic period. It is therefore natural that a secretariat should not have been developed in that age. Government orders must have been orally issued by the king or the Assembly (*samiti*) and communicated to the outlying villages by messengers through the word of mouth. The states were usually small and this procedure could not have been found inconvenient. Of course there was no other alternative method as well.

We have no data to draw a picture of the secretariat, as it might have gradually evolved in the post-Vedic period. The art of writing was coming into more extensive use ; kingdoms were developing into empires ; functions of government were becoming more numerous ; some kind of a Central Secretariat must, therefore, have existed in the courts of legendary kings like Yudhishṭhira and Jarāsandha, or historical emperors like Ajātaśatru or Mahāpadma Nanda. We however have no data to ascertain its nature.[1]

1. It may be pointed out that Rome developed the Central Secretariat only in the days of Hadrian (2nd century A. D.). In India it was developed at least by the 3rd century B. C.

The *Arthaśāstra*, however, shows that the secretariat had developed into a full-fledged and well-developed organisation in the Mauryan period. The senior officers of departments were called *lekhakas* or writers. These *lekhekas*, however, were not mere clerks, as one may perhaps be inclined to think. For, Kauṭilya lays down that the *lekhakas* were to be of the status of *amatyas*, whose position and pay were to be inferior only to those of ministers (*mantrins*).[1] The status of the secretariat officials (*lekhakas*) was equally high under the Sātavāhans; we often find them so rich as to construct and donate costly caves to Buddhist monks.[2]

The efficiency of the administration depended to a great extent upon the ability of the secretariat officers and the accuracy with which they drafted the orders of the Central Government. 'Government is writ and writ government'[3] says Kauṭilya, 'royalty does not reside in the person of the king but in his sealed and signed orders" says Śukra. We have already shown how in ancient as in modern times, ministerial appointments often went to senior and experienced secretaries of proved capacity. Government, therefore, used to take great care in the selection of the secretariat officers; they were required to possess alomost as high qualifications as ministers, as far as education, ability and reliability were concerned. Above all they were to be experts in drafting; it was their business to listen to the oral orders of the king or ministers and to draft them properly and accurately in as short a time as possible. They were to look into the previous files, assure themselves that there was no contradiction of earlier views or orders and then frame the wording of the new communique, which was to be characterised by relevancy, completeness, sweetness, dignity and lucidity. Redundancy was to be avoided, facts were to be stated either in their chronological sequence or according to their importance; the description was to be impressive, and cogent reasons were to be adduced

1. *Arthaśāstra*, Bk. II. Chap. 10
2. *E. I.*, VII. Nasik inscriptions Nos. 16 and 17
3. शासने शासनमित्याचक्षते । Bk. II., Chap. 10

for the action that the government was taking.[1] When the communique was ready, it was to be shown to the minister or head of the department concerned and then submitted to the king for his final approval and signature. After the royal signature, the office used to seal the document and forward it to its destination.

It is very probably the high officials of the secretariat who are referred to by Greek writers as the members of the seventh class, consisting of councillors and assessors. To them belonged the highest posts of the government and they took prominent part in the administration of public affairs. Their class was small in number but distinghished for its superior wisdom and justice. Greek writers observe that this class enjoyed the prerogative of choosing governors, chiefs of provinces, deputy governors, superintendents of treasury and agriculture, generals of the army and admirals of the navy. It is thus clear that it was from out of the senior officials of the secretariat that these posts were usually filled.

We have unfortunately no information about the working of the secretariat in the Śuṅga, Sātavāhana and Gupta administrations. But we may well infer that it worked on lines more or less similar to those outlined above ; for it was a regular feature of government even in Kashmir in medieval times, where the standard of administration was by no means high. The *Rājataraṅgiṇī* records several cases of royal orders being reduced to writing by the secretariat officers. The secretariat was known as *śrīkaraṇa* under the Chāhmānas and Chaulukyas.

The Chola records, as usual, give us most detailed information about the secretariat and its working. When the king used to pass his orders upon a matter, all secretariat officers connected with it used to be present on the occasion. The order was written out by one secretary and compared and attested by two or three others. It was entered into the necessary registers by the secretaries of the departments with which its subject matter

1. *Arthaśāstra*, Book II. Chap. 10. Śukra II. 172 also prescribes similar qualifications

2. *E I.*, III. p. 206

3. *E. I.*, IX.., p. 64

was connected, and then despatched to its destination in the mofussil.[1]

The secretariat had naturally a big record office. Ordinary or routine orders were not naturally preserved for a long time, but those which granted lands or assigned revenues were kept with great care for future reference. Sometimes donees wanted to exchange villages ; original grants had to be consulted and amended on such occasions.[2] In all cases of land grants, therefore, the entry of the transaction was made at the secretariat as soon as possible ; the delay in this connection was regarded as irregular and officers responsible for it were censured.[3] Ordinary individuals had to pay a fee registering transfers of property in the secretariat registers ; king Yaśaskara of Kashmir could detect a fraudulent transaction on account of the unusually high fee paid when it was registered at the secretariat.[4]

Very often kings used to pass verbal orders. These were taken down by a personal secretary, who is described as Tiruvāyakkkelvi in some south Indian records (*S. I. I.*, II. pp. 125, 276). Literally the designation of this officer means one who hears what comes from the sacred mouth of the king. The officer, who took down the orders of the king-in-council, was known as Tirumundir Olai in South India. What his designation was in the North is not known.

Inspector-General of Records, who was in charge of the Record Office, was called *akkshapaṭalika* or *mohākshapaṭalaka* in the Gāhadawāla and Chaulukya[5] administration. It is but natural that he should be sometimes found composing the copper plate charters.[6]

One of the most important duties of the Central Government and secretariat is the supervision and control of the provincial, district and local administrations. Let us now see how this work was done in ancient India.

1. *S. I. E. R.*, No. 185 of 1915
2. For such a case under the Paramāras, see *E. I.*, II. p. 182
3. *Rājataraṅgiṇī*, V. 397-8. In the case of one Chola grant, there was a delay of 12 years, probably due to disturbed conditions created by foreign invasion. *S. I. I.*, III. p. 142
4. *Rājataraṅgiṇī*, VI. 38
5. *E. I.*, XIV., p. 193
6. *I. A.*, VI. p. 194

Tours of inspection have been recommended to the king and his officers by several writers. Manu observes that royal officers have a natural tendency to be come corrupt, oppressive and partial, the king should, therefore, go on tours every now and then to find out whether people are pleased or displeased with them.[1] Śukra recommends annual tours for this purpose, during which the king or the higher officers should visit all villages and towns to ascertain first hand their real condition and the feelings of their residents.[2] These recommendations were followed in practice ; we find many of the charters issued when the kings were on tours in the different sections of their dominions.

The Central Government used to have its own reporters and informers to keep it in touch with the developments in the provinces. These appear to have acted independently of the officers of the local government. Local officers were often summoned to the capital for explanation, when reports about them were not satisfactory.

Kauṭilya (I. 11-12) gives us a very detailed desription of the spy system. Some spies moved in the guise of students, some in that of ascetics and some in that of merchants. Recruitment was also made from the classes of nuns, prostitutes and astrologers. Spies were to report on the conduct of both officials and non-officials. Care was taken to see that one spy did not know the others. Spies were punished if their reports were found to be false or inaccurate. The Government usually took action in the matter, when the report of one spy was confirmed by that of another.

Many governments used to appoint special inspection officers. Thus under the Kalachuris of Karnāṭak there used to be five imperial censors, known as *karṇams*, who are described as five senses of the Supreme Government. It was their duty to see that public funds were not misappropriated, justice was properly administered and sedition promptly punished.[3]

1. VII. 122-44, Cf. also *Arthaśāstra*, Bk. II. Chap. 9
2. I. 374-5
3. *E. C.*, VII, Shikarpur Nos. 102 and 123

The Chola government used to send every year its special inspectors and auditors from the central scretariat to check the accounts of temples and local bodies. It is quite likely that what the Kaḷachuri and Chola governments did was usually done by other governments as well. A Pratīhāra record, for instance, incidentally refers to the visit to Ujjayanī of a touring officer, who is seen investigating into certain affairs as desired by the king.[1]

The decisions of the central government were communicated to the local authorities by the secretariat through its special messengers. The work being responsible, was usually entrusted to high officers. They are described in the Deccan Vākāṭaka records as *kulaputras* (youths of noble birth), who carry the commands of the Central Government.[2] The Pallava records of south India call them premier's messengers.[3] An Assam officer of this service proudly describes himself as one who had conveyed hundreds of royal commands.[4]

The reader, it is hoped, will get a fair idea from the foregoing account of the manner in which the Central Governnment and secretariat tried to supervise and control the provincial and local administration.

We now proceed to consider the different departments, their officers and their functions. The departments were presided over by heads, who were called *adhyakshas* in the Mauryan age and *karmasachivas* in the Śaka administration. Curiously enough Smṛitis refer to them in a very general and vague way;[5] it is the *Arthaśāstra*, which supplies detailed information, which is very largely confirmed by inscriptions.

Modern governments usually differentiate between the head of the department and the minister in charge of it. This distinction is primarily due to the ministers being drawn from among the eminent persons in public life, returned by the electorate to the council or parliament. In ancient times

1. *E I*, XIV. pp. 182-88
2. *E. I.*, XXII. p. 167
3. *I. A.*, V. p. 155
4. *E. I.*, XI. p. 107
5. *Manu*, VII. 81 ; *Yaj.* I. 322

however it did not exist in most countries. In ancient India we sometimes find a minister rising to the position of a commander-in-chief; thus Pṛithvīsheṇa, who was first only a minister, later became the commander-in-chief under Kumāragupta I.[1] It is very likely that the chief justice and the minister for law, the commander-in-chief and the minister for war, were not always different.

The number of departments must have been naturally few in early times or in small states. The *Vishṇusmriti* refers to only four of them,—mines, customs, ferry and elephants.[2] In pre-historic Kashmir the number of departments was only seven; one of the reforms introduced by Jalauka, the son of Aśoka, was to increase their number to 18. This number was raised to 23 by king Lalitāditya about ten centuries later.[3] The epics usually refer to eighteen departments only, which are called *tīrthas*.[4] Their names, however, have not been given; they have to be gathere from the commentators who flourished several centuries later, and whose explanations therefore may not be quite reliable. The *Arthaśāstra* also refers to this traditional number of departments',[5] but it does not hesitate to increase their number by five or six. The number of departments contemplated by Śukra seems to be twenty.[6]

Epigraphs disclose some further departments not mentioned by the Smṛiti or *nīti* writers. It would be inconvenient and tedious to enumerate these departments, as they are given in our source books. We shall, therefore, group them together under the heads of administration well-known to the modern reader.

1. *E. I.*, X. p. 71
2. III. 16
3. *Rāj.* I. 188-20.; IV. 141 ff
4. *Rāmāyaṇa*, II. 100 36; *Mbh.*, IV. 5. 38
5. Bk. I Chap. 8. Book II, describing the functions of the different departments, is known as अध्यक्षप्रचार. It was well-known for a long time and is referred to in medieval inscriptions. Cf. अन्यांश्च सकलराजपादोपजीविनोऽध्यक्षप्रचारोक्तानिहाकीर्तितान् । Betwa Plates of Bhoja, *E. I.*, XII. p. 40; Barrackpur plates of Vijayasena, *E. I.*, XV. p. 283.
6. II. 17

Monarchy being the normal form of government, the department of the Royal Household may well engage our attention first. The palace and its precincts were in charge of a trusted and experienced officer called *āvasathika* in Bengal[1] and *saudhagehādhipa* by Śukra.[2] The ingress into and the egress from the palace and royal camp were naturally controlled very strictly by an officer known as *dvārapala* ; passports were usually necessary for this purpose which were issued by an officer known as *mudrādhipa*. Visitors and ambassadors were ushered into the royal presence by an officer known as *pratīhāra* or *mahāpratīhāra*. The king had a bodyguard of his own, the English term being almost the same as the Sanskrit word *aṅgarakshaka*;[3] sometimes its variation *śirorakshaka*[4] was also in vogue. This officer was called *anganigūhaka* in the Chaulukya administration.[5] There was a comptroller of Royal Household known as *sambhārapa*; the officers in charge of the royal treasury, kitchen (*pākādhipa*), museum and menagerie[6] must have worked under him. The management of the kitchen was a very responsible duty ; the officers had to take particular precautions to see that no attempt was made to poison the king.

There used to be a royal physician at the king's court corresponding to the royal surgeon of modern times. He figures in the Gāhadawāla records,[7] and is probably referred to as *ārāmādhipa* by Śukra.[8] When astrology became popular after *c.* 600 A. D., the court used to maintain a royal astrologer also, whose advice was often taken when starting on a military expedition. This officer figures in the records of the Gāhadawālas, the Yādavas, the Chāhamānas and the Chaulukyas.[9] Poet-laureates used to be maintained at the royal courts since very early times. Many of the famous Sanskrit poets were con-

1. Majumdar, *History of Bengal*, p. 284
2. II. 119
3. Majumdar, *History*, p. 285
4. *Ibid.*, p. 285
5. *Bhavanagar Inscriptions*, p. 158
6. *Śukra*, II. 117-120
7. *E. g.*, *I. A.*, XVIII. p. 17
8. II. 119
9. *I. A.*, XVIII. p. 17 ; *E. I.*, I. p. 343 ; *I. A.*, XIX. p. 218

nected with one court or another. A large number of learned men also got some kind of preferment or other at the royal court or in the king's administration.

The management of the harem was entrusted to a special officer known as *kañchukin*. He was usually old in age and enjoyed great confidence of the king.

Military department was undoubtedly the most important department, the expenditure on the fighting forces often being as high as 50% of the central revenues.[1] The department had an elaborate organisation, the infantry, the cavalry, the elephant corps, the chariots, the transport, the labour corps, boats, spies and instructors being looked after by a different branch.[2] The head of the department was variously known as *senāpati*, *mahāsenāpati*, *mahābalādhikṛita*[3] or *mahāprachaṇḍadaṇḍanāyaka*[4] in different times and administrations. *Mahāvyūhapati*, corresponding to the modern chief of the staff, worked under him.[5] The army consisted of four arms, infantry, cavalry, elephant corps[7] and chariot corps;[6] they were under the immediate charge of four officers known as *pattyadhyaksha*, *aśvapati* (also *bhaṭāśvapati* and *mahāśvapati*), *hastyadhyaksha* (also known as *mahāpīlupati* under the Guptas) and *rathādhipati*[7]. *Aśvapatis and rathapatis* had masters of stables under them, who were known as *sāhaṇiyas* in Rajputana under the Chāhamānas[8]. *Daṇḍanāyakas*, who figure freqhently in Gupta inscriptions,[9] seem to have been

1. *Śukra*, I. 316-7 ; see also Chap. XII

2. रथा नागा हयाश्चैव पादाताश्चैव पांडव ।
विष्टिर्नाविश्चराश्चैव देशिका इति चाष्टकम् । *Mbh.* XII. 59. 41

3. Under the Parivrâjakas, 5th century ; *C. I, I.*, III. p. 108
4. In the Deccan, under the Yâdavas ; *I. A*, XII. p. 120
5. *History cf Bengal*, p. 288

6. Chariots which were most important in the Vedic period are hardly ever mentioned in the *Harshacharit*. Elephants, which hardly played any part in the Vedic and epic battles, later assumed very great importance ; Cf. हस्तिप्रधानो विजयो राज्ञाम् । *Artha.* II. 2. नागेषु हि क्षितिभृतां विजयो निबद्धः । Kâmandaka, XIX. 62

7. *Arthaśāstra*, Bk. II ; *Śukranīti*, I. 117-120 ; *A. S. I., A. R.* 1903-4, pp. 107 ff. All these officers figure with slightly varying titles as late as the Gâhadwâla period ; E. I., XIV p.p. 193-6
8. *E. I.*, XI. p. 29
9. *E. g.*, in Bhita seals, *A. S. I. A. R.*, 1911-2. p. 152

officers of the status of colonels, stationed in different districts in charge of the local units. The army had its own quarter-master-general as in modern times to look after the commissariat ; department ; his office was known as *raṇabhāṇḍāgārādhikaraṇa* under the Guptas.[1] *Āyuḍhāgārādhyaksha*, who was in charge of the weapons of the forces, must have worked under him. The same must have been the case with the Officer in charge of elephant-forces, who had to supply elephants to the army. The Commissariat department also supplied boats and labour necessary for the army. It received the cooperation also of merchants, who accompanied the camp to get lucrative business (*Śiśupālalvadha*, XII, 26). Forts constituted an important link in the scheme of national defence. Each of them was in charge of an officer variously known as *durgadhyaksha* or *koṭṭapāla*; probably there was an inspector general of forts at the capital. *Dvarapalas* or wardens of the marches kept watch over the frontier and the roads and passes leading to the kingdom. They worked in close cooperation with the superintendents of forts in their vicinity. Very often the same officer worked in both capacities, as was the case under the Pratīhāras at the fort of Gwalior whose commandant was also *maryādādhurya*, or the officer in charge of boundary.[2]

In the 19th century the Indian army used to be organised and located territorially ; there was the Bombay Army, the Madras Army and the Northern Army. Such an organisation was almost inevitable in the pre-railway period. In ancient times also the big empires like those of the Pratīhāras used to have a southern army to watch the Rāshṭrakūṭas, an eastern army to check the Pālas and a western army to oppose the Muslims. The same principle is known to have been followed by the Rāshṭrakūṭas.[3] The Mauryas and Guptas must have followed the the same principle, although we have no definite evidence on the point at present.

One Rāshṭrakūṭa record refers to an officer who is described

1. *A. S. I.*, *A. R.*, 1903-4., pp. 107 ff
2. *E. I.*, I. pp. 154-60
3. *Rāshṭrakūṭas and their Times*, pp. 247-48

as a marvel in training horses.[1] It is clear that the training of the fighting forces was the special duty of a section of the army officers. Not much training must have been required in the case of *maula* or hereditary forces, which formed the crack divisions of the ancient Indian army. In their case fighting was the hereditary profession and soldiers were paid by assignment of villages. Other soldiers however received payment sometimes daily sometimes, monthly, sometimes after three months, and sometimes after six months (*Mānasollāsa*, II. 6. 568-9).

The army had naturally its own complement of doctors, nurses and ambulance staff, fully equipped with instruments, bandages, medicines and ointments. The ambulance corpse rarely figures in inscriptions but is referred to by the *Arthaśāstra* and the *Mahābhārata*.[2] It is known to have formed part of the Kashmir army.[3] Veterinary doctors for the army are mentioned in the *Vishṇudharmottara Purāṇa* (V. 26. 278).

The corpse of sappers, miners and labourers was as indispensable as the ambulance organisation. It is referred to by Kauṭilya (Bk. X. Chap. 4) as a service whose duty it was to examine camps, roads, bridges wells and rivers. It must have had its own superintendents and officers. The army was naturally accompanied by a contingent of spies and secret service men to gather all possible information about the strength of the enemy forces and their plans,. Cavalry units were also used for this purpose.

We may refer briefly to the weapons used by soldiers. They were bows and arrows, spears, battle-axes, knives tridents, maces, etc. Someśvara refers to weapons impelled by machines (*yantramuktāyudha*), but their nature is not known. The firearms are mentioned only in the *Śukranīti* in some later passages. The earliest reference to their use in India perhaps

1. *Rāshṭrakūṭas and their Times*, p. 252

2. चिकित्सकाः शास्त्रयंत्रागदस्नेहहस्ताः स्त्रियश्चान्नपानरक्षिण्यः पृष्ठतस्तिष्ठेयुः । Bk. X. Chap. 3. उपातिष्ठन्नथो वैद्याः शल्योद्धरणकोविदाः । *Mbh.*, VI. 120.55 ; see also XII. 95.12

3. *Rāja*. VIII, 741

occurs in Vijayanagar inscriptions of the 14th century A. D. (*E. C.*, VIII, p. 81, 1.282).

The enemies whom Indian states had to face usually operated with land forces; many kingdoms had no coast line at all. Navy, therefore, rarely figures in Smṛitis and inscriptions. The Mauryas had a naval force administered by a board of its own. The Vaṅgas of Bengal were knwon as a naval power to Kālidāsa,[1] and the Pālas also used to maintain a strong naval force.[2] Tamil states since early days had their own navies, powerful enough to protect their extensive trade with the West and the East. In the 11th centrury the Cholas had a powerful navy; which enabled them to conquer a number of islands. The Śilāhāras of Western India had also naval forces of their own. We, however, possess very little information about the organisation of the navy and its administration.

The department of foreign affairs was in charge of a minister known as *mahāsandhivigrahika* in inscriptions and *dūta* in Smṛitis. Usually it had to deal with a large number of feudatories and foreign powers, and so its work was divided among several officers who worked under the Foreign Minister. As usual, the Foreign Minister had a large staff of the intelligence department under various guises in different countries, members of which used to send their reports to their chief. *Mahāmudrādhyaksha* and his subordinates, who granted visas to foreigners for entering the country, must naturally have worked under the supervision of this department. The same must have been the case with the officers in cities like Pāṭaliputra, whose duty it was to watch the movements of the foreigners residing in the country.

The Revenue Department, which was under a cabinet minister, had a large number of superintendents working under it. One was in charge of the crown-lands. He was called *sītādhyaksha* and his duty was to cultivate them either directly through labourers or indirectly through tenants by leasing them out.[3] A second superintendent was in charge of forests and is

1. *Raghu.*, IV. 36
2. Majumdar, *History of Bengal*, p. 286
3. *Arthaśāstra*, Bk. II. Chap. 24

styled as *aranyādhikṛta*[1] in Pallava records and *aranyadhyaksha* in Smṛitis. It was his duty to develop the forest resources of the state. Superintendents of the state herds (*godhyaksha*)[2] consisting of cows, buffaloes and elephants, for whose grazing a portion of the state forests was assigned, must have worked in close cooperation with the superintendent of forests. In pre-historic times herds constituted a very important item of the wealth of the state ; in historic times also it did not neglect this source of income. These officers figure as *gokulikas* down to the 12th century in some Paramāra and Gāhaḍawāla records.[3] There was also a superintendent of waste lands (*vivītādhyaksha*),[4] whose duty it was to develop and sell them, and also to prevent them from being used by undersirable persons for their nefarious ends. The superintendent of land records, usually called *mahākshapaṭalika*, who kept an accurate record of the different fields and their boundaries, must have worked under the supervision of the revenue department. Officers working under this superintendent are known as *Simākarmakaras*[5] in Bihar, *Pramātṛis*[6] in Bengal and *sīmāpradātṛis* in Assam.[7] The principal tax collected by the Revenue Department was the land tax ; its officers, who collected it, were sometimes known as *shashṭhādhikṛitas*[8] and sometimes as *audraṅgikas*.[9] The land tax being usually collected in kind as a certain share of the actual produce, the revenue department had to employ a large army of officers to supervise its collection ; they were known as *dhruvas* in Gujarat.[10] Some taxes were also collected in cash ; the officers entrusted with this work were known as *hiraṇyasamudāyikas* in Bengal.[11]

1. *E.I.*, I. p. 7
2. *Arthaśāstra*, Bk. II. Chap. 29
3. *E. I.* XXI. p. 71 ; XIV. p. 193
4. *Arthaśāstra*, Bk. II. Chap. 34.
5. *C. I. I.* III. p. 261
6. *History of Bengal*, p. 286
7. *E. I*, XI. p. 107
8. *History of Bengal*, p. 278
9. *Ibid*, p. 284
10. *C. I. I.*, III, p. 168
11. *History of Bengal*, p. 277

When the work of the Revenue Department terminated, that of the Treasury Department commenced. It was much more arduous in ancient times, for it was not merely the question of striking a bank balance and keeping the bullion in safe custody. A good deal of the sate revenue was collected in kind,—corn, fuel, oil, etc.,--and careful steps had to be taken to keep the stocks properly and renew it periodically, so that old articles may be replaced by new ones. The head of the Treasury Department was known as *Koshādhyaksha*[1] and a number of superintendents worked under him. Among them the officer in charge of the granary, known as *koshṭhāgārādhyaksha*,[2] was most important.

It was the uniform policy of the ancient Indian state to have a full and flowing treasury by insisting upon the allocation of a large percentage of the annual revenues to the Special Reserve Fund which was never to be touched except on occasions of grave calamities. The treasury superintendent, therefore, had large quantity of bullion, diamonds and jewels under his custody.

Officers of the finance department in charge of the allotment of revenues rarely figure in Smṭitis or inscriptions. They are referred to as *vyayādhikārins* or *kṛtyākṛityeshu arthaniyojakas* by Nilakaṇṭha, the commentator of the *Mahābhārata*.[3] It appears that the king, the premier and the *dānādhipati* (minister for charity) jointly performed the duty of the finance department. In the Chaulukya administration, however, there wss a separate officer in charge of disbursements known as *vyayakaraṇamahāmātya*.[4]

The activity of the ancient Indian state in the realm of industry and commerce was considerable and the department in their charge engaged large staff to supervise and carry on its activities. Cloth industry was the most flourishing industry of the country and the state used to have its own weaving department, partly as a means of poor relief and partly as a source of revenue. The employees of this department used to send cotton to the homes of weak and destitute persons, and get

1. *Śukra* (II. 118) calls him *vittādhipa*.
2. *Arthaśāstra*, Bk. II. Chap. 34. He is called *dhānyādhyaksha* by Śukra (II. 117-120) and *bhāṇḍāgārādhikṛita* in inscriptions (*E. I.*, XI. p. 107).
3. On II. 9. 38
4. *J.B.B.R.A.S.*, XXV. p. 322

the yarn spun through them at agreed rates.[1] Of course the department must have had its own compliment of able-bodied workers as well. The officers of this department are designated as *sūtrādhyaksha* by Kauṭilya and *vastrādhyaksha* by Śukra (II. 119). The state used to have its own distilleries, which were under the charge of *surādhyaksha*.[2] Private persons were also allowed to manufacture wines under licenses on the payment of prescribed fees. It was the duty of the officers of this department to supervise the drinking houses and to see that no cheating was practised in their premises. The state also tried to control prostitution through another department, whose officers were known as *gaṇikādhyaksha*.[3] Prostitutes were required to give full information about the persons who visited them ; it often helped the police department to detect crimes. They were also used as spies and often sent to other states in that capacity ; very often feudatories were compelled to entertain some dancing girls of the imperial court at their capitals.[3] In big towns there used to be state slaughter houses, where animals could be slaughtered, of course after the payment of a fee. There was a prohibition against the slaughter of calves, bulls and cows. Superintendents of slaughter houses used to be appointed to supervise the arrangement in this connection. They were also to see that animals in the game forests were not killed by outsiders.[4]

The state claimed proprietary rights in all the mines. It had a special department, which engaged geologists and metallurgists to examine the prospective sites. The state would itself work out such mines as appeared promising and give the rest to private industrialists, who were required to surrender a certain portion of the mineral yields to the state as its royalty.[5] The offices of this department figure as late as in the Gāhadawāla records.[6]

A survey of the *Arthaśāstra* shows that Kauṭilya was in favour

1. *Arthaśāstra*, Bk. II. Chap. 23
2. *Arthaśāstra*, Bk. II. Chap. 25
3. *E. I.*, VI. p. 102
4. *Arthaśāstra*, Bk. II. Chap. 26
5. *Arthaśāstra*, Bk. II. Chap. 12
6. *E. I.*, XIV. p. 193

of state control of important and lucrative trades and industries. Mines, pearl fishery and the production of gold were under state control and management ; private individuals could come in only as lessees. Cotton industry, forest development and salt and wine production were controlled by the state. In the industries in private sector the state was keen to ensure that the labour was not exploited and the public was not cheated.

Sometimes state used to license goldsmiths for the manufacture of silver and golden wares and ornaments. Coinage also was often entrusted to them when the state cared to issue it. This department was under a superintendent known as *suvarṇādhyaksha*.[1]

Department of commerce also required a large number of superintendents. In the first place markets themselves were in charge of government officers, called *paṇyādhyakshas* in the *Arthaśāstra*, *haṭṭapatis* in Bengal and *drāṅgikas* in Kathiawar.[2] It was their duty to put the government products in the market under favourable conditions, to organise the import of goods required in the locality and to supervise their sales at reasonable rates and to export merchandise when this could be done at a profit. Rates were also controlled by them and cornering of articles was prevented.

This department also engaged a number of toll superintendents (*śulkādhyaksha*).[3] Thieir offices were naturally located at the town gates, where all merchandise had to be shown for the assessment of toll dues before it was imported into the town for sale. Sometimes the sales were effected at the toll office itself. Superintendents had the power to punish different kinds of frauds usally practised by cunning merchants to escape the customs duties. There were also superintendents of weights and measures, who tested and stamped the weights used in the market.[4] It is quite likely that the duties of the superintendents of the market, the tolls and the weights and measures might have

1. *Arthasastra*, Bk. Chap. 13 ; *History of Bengal*, p. 282; *E. I.*, XIII. p. 239
2. *Arthaśāstra*, Bk. II. Chap. 16
3. *Ibid.*, Bk. II. Chap. 21; They are called *śaulkikas* in Pāla and Paramāra records. *E. I.*, XIX, p. 71
4. *Ibid.*, Bk. II, Chap. 9

been combined in one officer in small places. In villages, the headman alone might have probably discharged these duties.

Let us now pass on to consider the organisation of the Judicial Department. King was the fountain source of justice and was expected to decide all cases brought before him either at the first instance or in appeals. He often discharged this duty himself, but when he was too busy to attend to it, the Chief Justice (*prāḍvivāka*) deputised for him. The state policy, however, was to encourage decentralisation in the department; the village *pañchāyats* and town councils were not only encouraged but required to try and decide all local civil cases. Complainants were not permitted to file their suits at the first instance in the official courts. This naturally reduced the volume of the work of government courts. It is therefore but natural that the royal courts should figure rather rarely in inscriptions. Government courts also existed in important towns and citites and are referred to both by Nārada and Bṛihaspati.[1] They were known as *dharmāsanādhikaraṇas*[2] in the Gupta administration and were situated in big towns only. Presiding judges were called *dharmādhyakshas* or *nyāyakaraṇikas*.[3] Whether the *dharmalekhins*, who figure in some Chandella records,[4] were judges or pleaders who wrote the complaints, it is difficult to say.

The Chief Justice had to be well grounded in Smṛiti literature; it is therefore no wonder that sometimes the royal chaplains, who were often well grounded in it, were appointed to the post. Such was the case under the Chandella king Dhaṅga in 1003 A. D.[5] Petty criminal cases were tried by local bodies, but serious ones were decided in royal courts. Judges of the criminal courts were probably known as *daṇḍādyakshas*. It is rather strange that jail officers should figure so very rarely both in Smṛitis and inscriptions. This may be probably due to imprisonments being not quite common. It appears that fines

1. I. 26-31
2. *A. S. I.*, *A. R.*, 1903-4, pp. 107. ff
3. In Assam, 7th century, *E. I.*, XI. p. 107
4. I. *A.*, XVI. p. 208; *E. I.*, IV. p. 160 and X. pp. 47-49
5. *E. I.*, I. pp. 140 ff

were more usually imposed ; officers in charge of their collection are designated as *daśāparākdhikas*[1] in some Pāla records.[2]

The officers of the police department are usually referred to in inscriptions as *choroddharaṇikas* 'the exterminators of thieves' or *daṇḍapāśikas* 'the carriers of nooses to catch (thieves)'. The latter designation occurs in Pāla, Paramāra and Pratīhāra records.[3] Higher officers of this department do not figure in epigraphs. It is not unlikely that their duties might have been entrusted to the officers of the milittary department, who were stationed at different centres of the kingdom to preserve law and order. We should not forget that ordinary thefts were very unusual ; only desperadoes attemped to commit dacoities and carrry away cattle and property. They could be effectively dealt with only with the help of the militia or military forces. The village headman was the chief police officer of the village and had the village militia under his control. When, however, dacoits could not be effectively dealt with by the local force, police and military soldiers were sent by higher authorities to apprehend them. When they came for this work, the townsmen and villagers had to meet their boarding and lodging expenses. Donees of *agrahāra* villages were usually exempted from this liability. The state was ultimately responsible for making up all losses due to thefts. It fastened this liability upon the village community, if it could not prove that the thieves had escaped out of the village. If they could be proved to have taken shelter in another village, the responsibility was shifted to it. If it appeared that the thieves had taken shelter in forests or waste lands, their superintendents were called upon either to apprehend them or to make up the loss. If the responsibility could not thus be shifted, the state had to compensate itself.

What may be conveniently designated as the eclesiastical department must now engage our attention. The royal chaplain (*purohita*) and the minister known as *paṇḍita* were both concerned

1. *History of Bengal*, p. 285
2. For further details of Judicial Administration, see Chap. XII.
3. *History of Bengal*, p. 285; *E. I.*, XIX. p. 73; *E. I.*, IX. p. 6. Sometimes they were called *daṇḍoddharaṇikas* also ; *E. I.*, IX. p. 6

in directing and supervising its different activities. The state in ancient India was the preserver of religion and morality and the different steps that were to be adopted in this connection were taken under the guidance and advice of these officers. If certain socio-religious customs became obsolete, they were discouraged ; if new changes were necessary and deemed desirable by public opinion, learned Brāhmaṇas were requested to compose new Smṛitis, commentaries or digests, advocating the needed changes, which were encouraged and gradually enforced.

The officers of this department were known as *dharmamahāmātras* under the Mauryas, *śramaṇamahāmātras* under the Sātavāhanas, *vinayasthitisthāpakas* under the Guptas and *dharmāṅkuśas* under he Rāshṭrakūṭas. Their duty was to encourage all religions impartially ; no distinction was usually made between the followers of Hinduism, Buddhism and Jainism when distributing state patronage. The officer directly in the charge of state grants for religious purposes is called *dānapati* by Śukra (II. 119). Learned Brāhmaṇas, Buddhist monasteries and Hindu temples and *maṭhas*, which usually received these grants, used to organise schools, colleges, hospitals and poor houses. The donations given by the state to them may to a certain extent well be regarded as grants in aid of hospitals, education and poor relief as well. The villages assigned to temples, monasteries and learned Brāhmaṇas became fairly numerous from *c.* 400 A. D.; a special officer came to be appointed to look after their administration. He is called *agrahārika* in the Gupta and Pāla records.[1] It was his duty to see that there were no difficulties created in the enjoyment of grants given to the donees. If intervening anarchy had interfered with their enjoyment,[2] the possession was to be restored. Very often conditions were imposed when grants were given ; in some cases they were tenable only as long as the recipients or their descendants continued to be learned

1. *C. I. I.*, III. p. 45 ; *History of Bengal*, p. 284. The niew that *agra harika* can be the donee of the *agrahara* village is untenable ; in Bihar stone inscription (*C. I. I.*, III. p. 45) the term appears in a passage, which enumerates different officers ; it should therefore denote a government officer.

2. For such a case under the Pratīhâras, see *E. I.*, XIV. pp. 19-17 ; for a similar case under the Châhamânas, see *E. I.*, XI. p. 308.

and pious scholars. The *agrahārika's* duty was to see that these conditions were duly fulfilled. Sometimes counterfeit grants were produced by fraudulent Brāhmaṇas;[1] it was the duty of this officer to detect and punish the fraud. In south India, the Chola administration used to send special auditors to see that temple funds and properties were duly utilised.

We have now finished the survey of the different departments and their activities. It will not be correct to maintain that all these departments existed even among the tiny feudatory states that existed by the dozen in ancient India. But the evidence adduced will make it clear that most of them existed in the administrations of moderate-sized states of the ancient period. The evidence of the *Arthaśāstra* is strikingly confirmed by the data of inscriptions in several respects.

The *Arthaśāstra* gives us detailed information about the pays of different dignitaries and officers. The queens, the crown-prince and the important ministers like the commander-in-chief received 48,000 Paṇas a year ; the chamberlain, the treasurer and revenue minister received 24,000 ; ordinary members of the ministry and wardens of the marches, 12,000 ; superintendents of horses, chariots and elephants, 8,000 Paṇas; army doctors and horse trainers 2,000, etc. It is difficult to state whether the Paṇas were silver or copper coins. The salaries must have varied with the size and resources of the state also, as is clear from a scheme given in the *Śukranīti*, under which in a state of the income of a lakh a year all ministers put together received only 300 a month. Probably 300 here refers to silver coins worth equal to modern six annas (IV. 7. 24). Even then the pay of the minister would be rather small.

In conclusion, we shall say a few words about the recruitment of officers to these different departments. Many of them, *e..g*, those who worked in the commerce or mining departments, required high technical qualifications and Smṛitis emphasise that only those who were specially qualified for them should be

1. For such a case under the Gâhadawâlas, see *J. R. A. S.*, VI. 547-48.

appointed after a thorough test.[1] Śukra goes a step further and suggests that the state should give scholarships for training young men for the different techinical posts.[2] Birth and high connection must have counted then, as they count now, in the selection to posts where no special training was necessary; the subsequent career must have depended largely on the merit of the new entrant.

Whether there were grades of service like the Central, Provincial and Subordinate services of the modern times, we do not know. It however appears very probable that the *mahāmātyas* of the Mauryan age or the *kumārāmātyas* of the Gupta period formed a class of officers, similar to the modern I. C. S. or I. A. S.; the members of this class used to serve sometimes as district and divisional officers, sometimes as secretariat officials and sometimes as cabinet ministers. Persons who belonged to this service were usually of high birth, often recruited from the members of ex-royal families, which had been superseded by the empire. Their posts often used to become hereditary, as those of the ministers.

Officers of the status of provincial and subordinate grades of the modern time were probably recruited from local areas; means of transport being slow and unsatisfactory, their transfers could not have been common. The system of paying these officers by the assignment of lands or of government revenues must have made many of these posts hereditary.

1. यो यद्वस्तु विजानाति तं तत्र विनियोजयेत् । *Kāmandaka*, V. 76
2. सर्वविद्याकलाभ्यासे शिक्षयेद् भृतिपोषितान् ।
समाप्तविद्यं तं दृष्ट्वा तत्कार्ये तं नियोजयेत् ॥ I. 317

CHAPTER X

PROVINCIAL, DIVISIONAL, DISTRICT AND TOWN ADMINISTRATION

Before we consider the provincial, divisional and district administration, it would be necessary to understand the scheme of territorial divisions in vogue in ancient India. It has to be observed at the outset that there was no uniformity in this respect. As in modern so in ancient days, some districts and divisions were small, while others were large. This was partly due to difference in population and fertility and partly to political causes. If a feudatory had a small fief, which was later annexed to an empire, it would normally constitute a separate and, therefore, a small district. On the other hand, a frontier district may become large owing to gradual enchroachment and expansion. The growing importance of a place would also lead to the incorporation of larger number of villages in it ; thus Karhāṭaka district (*vishaya*) in Mahārāshṭra had 4000 villages in it in 768 A.D. but 10,000 in 1054 A.D.

Small kingdoms like those of the Pallavas, the Vākāṭakas and Gahaḍawālas had naturally fewer types of territorial divisions than big empires. In the case of the former we usually find reference to only one territorial division, the district, variously called *vishaya* or *rāshṭra*[1]. The administrative divisions of a big empire like the Mauryan one were almost similar to those of the Union Government to-day. It was divided into provinces often as big as any in modern India. These provinces were divided into Divisions, whose heads, like the modern Commissioners, ruled over large tracts of land. The Divisions were divided into districts or *vishayas* and the latter into subdivisions variously termed as *pathakas*, *peṭhas* or *bhukits*. These latter were divided into smaller groups of villages, each one containing from 10 to 50 villages.

1. *E.g.*, *E.I.*, XXIV, p. 260 ; *E.I.*, XV, p. 297; *E.I.*, IX. p. 304

Ancient Indian history extends over several centuries, and we need not be surprised if we do not find a uniformity in the nomenclatures of the different territorial and administrative divisions in the various kingdoms flourishing in different centuries and provinces. Thus *bhukti* denoted administrative division even smaller than a modern Tehsil or Taluka in the Deccan and M. P., but in northern India under the Guptas and Pratīhāras it denoted a unit as large as the Commissioner's Division in modern times. Thus *Pratishṭhanabhukti* consisted of only 12 and Koppārakabhukti of 50 villages in the Deccan under the Rāshṭrakūṭas,[1] whereas under the Guptas the Puṇḍravardhanabhukti comprised of the districts of Dinapur, Bogra and Rajshahi, and Magadhabhukti included the districts of Gayā and Pāṭaliputra.[2] Śrāvastibhukti under the Pratīhāras included several districts in northern U. P. *Rāshṭra* was used in literature to denote a kingdom, but it was the name of a Commissioner's Divisions under the Rāshṭrakūṭas.[3] In south India, however, under the Pallava, Kadamba and Sālaṅkāyana administrations, it denoted only a district, if not a Tehsil.[4] Sometimes, these terms were used with a certain amount of looseness; thus one Rāshṭrakūṭa document describes Nasik as a *vishaya*, and another, issued only 29 years later, calls it a *deśa*.[5] It would, therefore, be dangerous to draw a precise and *prima facie* conclusion about the extent of an administrative division merely from its name.

PROVINCIAL GOVERNMENT

Provincial administrations in the modern sense of the term existed only in big kingdoms. The Mauryan empire was divided into several provinces. Five of them are known at present, Uttarāpatha, Avantirāshṭra, Dakshiṇāpatha,

1. *Rāśhṭrakūṭas*, p. 137; see also *E. I.*, XXV, p. 269
2. *E. I.*, XV. pp. 125. ff. When the *Mitāksharā* on *Yaj*. I. 315 states that only a king can make the grant of land and not a *bhogapati*, it is obviously referring to the head of this territorial division.
3. *Rāshṭrakūṭas*, p. 136
4. *E. I.*, XV. p. 297; *E. I.*, XVI, 271; *I. A.*, V. p. 179
5. *Rāshṭrakūṭas*, p. 137

Kaliṅga and Prāchya with Taxila, Ujjainī, Survarṇāgiri, Tosali and Pāṭaliputra as their respective capitals. It is not unlikely that Uttarāpatha and Dakshiṇāpatha may have had several provinces under them. Under the Śuṅgas, in the beginning at any rate, the administration of Mālwā had the status and powers of a Provincial Government. The Kaṇva kingdom was probably too small to have any viceroys. The Sātavāhana empire extended over the whole Deccan, but we know very little about its provincial administration. The status of *mahākshatrapas* ruling at Banaras, Mathurā and Ujjayinī in the empire of Kanishka was undoubtedly similar to that of provincial governors. In the Gupta empire, Kathiawar, Mālwā and Gujarat had provincial administrations. In the home territories of the Rāshṭrakūṭa empire, there do not seem to have been any officers with the viceregal status, but Gujarat, Banavāsi and Gaṅgavāḍī, which were new additions to the empire, had viceroys to govern them. The *Bhuktis* under the Pratīhāra empire appear to have been rather Commissioners' Divisions than provinces. The Pālas, the Paramāras, the Chaulukyas, the Chandellas, the Gāhaḍawālas and the Cholas ruled over relatively smaller kingdoms ; the bigger ones amongst them like the Cholas had two grades of administrative divisions, *maṇḍala* which was roughly equal to about two or three modern districts, and *nāḍu*, which usually covered two Tehsils. Smaller kingdoms were divided only into districts and their sub-divisions.

Heads of the provincial administrations were officers of very high status. Very often princes of the blood royal were appointed to them. Thus under the Mauryas, Bindusāra, Aśoka and Kuṇāla had all served as viceroys in the different provinces of the empire[1]; under the Śuṅgas, the crown prince Agnimitra was serving as viceroy in Mālwā.[2] Ghaṭotkacha-gupta, the Gupta viceroy of the same province in *c.* 435, was a prince of the royal family. The Gujarat viceroys under the Chālukyas and the Rāshṭrakūṭas were scions of the royal family,

1. *Divyāvadāna*, p. 371.
2. *Mālavikāgnimitra*, Act. V.

who eventually managed to establish practically independent houses. The province of Gaṅgawāḍī in the Rāshṭrakūṭa empire had the emperor's eldest son as viceroy in *c.* 790 A. D. Of course princes of the blood royal were not always available for appointment to the viceregal posts ; then they went to the most senior and trusted officers of the empire, who were usually military generals as well. Thus Nahapāṇa and Chashṭaṇa, the Deccan viceroys of the Kushāṇas, were capable generals, as also Baṅkeya, the Banavāsi viceroy of the Rāshṭrakūṭa emperor Amoghvarsha I. Military leadership was regarded as an essential qualification not only for ministerial but also for viceregal posts. Viceroys enjoyed high and wide powers ; they had to maintain internal order and protect the empire against the external enemies contiguous to the territories under their charge. So military leadership was essential to them.

Provincial viceroys, being often royal princes, had their own courts and ministers. It is against the oppressive ministers that the people of Taxila had their grudge when they rose in rebellion in *c.* 280 B.C. Agnimitra, the viceroy over Mālwā, had his own ministry ; the same was the case with the southern viceroys of the Rāshṭrakūṭas and the Yādavas, who usually had the status of *mahāsāmantas* or feudatory rulers.[1] Viceroys were required to follow the policy of the Central Government as communicated to them either by imperial writs or through special messengers. Communications being difficult, they naturally enjoyed considerable autonomy. Like the provincial governors of the East India Company before the Regulating Act of 1773, we sometimes find them declaring their own wars and dictating their own peace, as did Agnimitra with reference to the kingdom of Berar.[2] This was to some extent inevitable, because there was the tacit understanding that they would try to extend the extent of the empire. They had their own military forces, and the Central Government would often summon some of their battalions to put down rebellions in other parts of the empire. Thus the Kushāṇa emperor summoned his Deccan viceroy Rudradāman

1. *S. I. I.*, IX. Nos. 367 and 387
2. *Mālavikāgnimitra*, Act I

to put down the revolt of the Yaudheyas in northern Rājputānā ; Baṅkeya, the viceroy of Banavāsi, had to repair to Gujarat to put down the revolt there, when the Rāshṭrakūṭa emperor Amoghavarsha I could not cope with the situation.

We have no definite evidence about the part which the viceroys played in the civil and revenue administration of the province. They must obviously have been in charge of its supervision and guidance in the light of the orders received from the capital. Divisional Commissioners must have worked under their instructions. In the Gupta administration, however, the latter appear to have been directly responsible to the emperor. Thus the Divisional Commissioner of Puṇḍravardhana was appointed by Kumāragupta I and appears to have worked under his direct instructions.[1] It is, however, doubtful whether there was a viceroy between him and the emperor.

Besides maintaining law and order and supervising revenue collection, the viceroys had to take steps for developing the resources of their provinces by constructing and repairing works of public utility like irrigation tanks and canals and to strengthen the foundation of the empire by ensuring good government and promoting public confidence. Almost all the departments mentioned in the last chapter, that existed at the imperial capital, must have had their replicas in the provincial headquarters.

The government taxes and revenues must have been first collected at the provincial headquarters. The balance that remained after meeting the charges of the provincial administration must have been sent to the imperial capital.

DIVISIONAL ADMINISTRATION

The next administrative unit roughly corresponded to the size of a Commissioner's Division consisting of three or four districts. It was called a *bhukti* under the Guptas and Pratīhāras, *rāshṭra* under the Rāshṭrakūṭas and *maṇḍala* under the Cholas and Chāulukyas. Sometimes the term *deśa* also was

1. *E. I.*, XV. pp. 130, 133 etc

loosely used to denote it. *Rajjukas*, who ruled over several hundred thousands of persons in the Mauryan administration, might have corresponded to the modern Divisional Commissioners, but there is some evidence to show that they might have been known as *Prādeśikas*.

Aśoka had followed a policy of decentralisation and granted large powers to the *rajjukas*. Subject to the general imperial policy, they had full administrative powers in civil, revenue and criminal affairs. They could confer favours or impose punishments as demanded by the situation.[1] Under the Rāshṭrakūṭas, on the other hand, their powers appear to have been restricted ; even Baṅkeya, the favourite Banavāsi viceroy of Amoghavarsha, had to take the imperial sanction for alienating a village in favour of a Jain temple.[2] Hardly any data are available to determine the powers of the officers over *bhuktis* under the Pratīhāras.

Divisional Commissioners had extensive powers over their subordinate officers. If the latter became disloyal or disaffected, they were arrested by them and sent up for further action. District officers had small forces under them ; so very often departmental action against them meant a small military expedition as well. The Divisional Commissioners, therefore, had sufficiently strong military forces under their command, which were used for controlling subordinate officers and local feudatories.[3] When a big campaign was planned by the king, a greater part of these forces were naturally sent to the capital.

Divisional Commissioners were also at the head of the revenue administration. They are usually mentioned among the officers who are requested not to interfere with the peaceful enjoyment of the lands or revenues assigned to donees. The term *rajjuka* used to denote them (or the district officers) implies an intimate connection with the measurement and assessment of lands. Revenue settlement of villages or their reassessment

1. Pillar Edict No. IV
2. *Rāshṭrakūṭas*, p. 179
3. *Rāshṭrakūṭas*, pp. 174-9

necessitated by causes like the drying up of canals must have been carried under their supervision.

Aśoka's exhortation to his *rajjukas* to follow a uniform policy in punishments[1] implies that they had judicial powers as well ; the same must have been the case with the Commissioners of the Divisions. Probably they constituted the highest court of appeal of the division.

The patronage which the Divisional Commissioners exercised must have varied with different administrations. It must have been considerable under the Mauryas. Under the Guptas they had sometimes the power of appointing district officers,[2] but sometimes the emperor also exercised it. Under the Rāshṭrakūṭas not only the district officers, but even the Tehsildars were often appointed by the emperor himself.[3]

We have shown already how in historic times, there used to be no Central Assembly at the capital of the kingdom. It will be shown in chapter XI how popular village councils functioned almost all through the ancient Indian period and exercised considerable powers. It is very difficult to say whether popular councils existed at the Divisional head-quarters. The term *mahattara* denoted the members of the village councils, as will be shown in chapter XI. Among the officers requested not to disturb the peaceful enjoyment of land grants we sometimes come across *Rāshṭramahattaras* ;[4] sometimes their *adhikārins* or executive officers are also mentioned.[5]

It is, however, difficult to say whether there was a regular popular council of *rāshṭramahattaras* to guide and advise the Divisional Commissioners. They are mentioned only in two records, and it is therefore not safe to generalise from them. It is not unlikely that the *Rāshṭramahattaras* mentioned in the above records may have been simply the notable citizens of the Division, who may not have been members of a consti-

1. Pillar Edict IV

2. *E. I.*, XV. p. 130

3. *Rāshṭrakūṭas*, p. 176

4. *E. I.*, VIII. p. 186 (under the Rāshṭrakūṭas in Khāndesh).

5. *E. I.*, XII. p. 130 (under the Kaḷachuris in Mālwā).

tutional popular council. The point, however, cannot be settled, until more evidence becomes available.

District Administration

The *vishaya* of our ancient records usually corresponded with the district of the modern administration, consisting of about a thousand to two thousand villages. This administrative unit was known as *āharaṇī* in Kāthiawār and *rāshṭra* in M. P., Andhradeśa and Tamil country in the early centuries of the Christian era[1]. The head of the *vishaya* was naturally called *vishayapati* or *vishayādhyaksha* in the Mauryan administration, since he is mentioned in Aśokan inscriptions immediately after the *rajjuka* and is also required to go on tour like him. *Sahasrādhipa* of the Smṛitis,[2] who was in charge of a thousand villages, is probably to be identified with him. The *nāḍu* was a smaller division in Tamil country, but the powers of its head were probably similar to those of a *vishayapati*.

The district officers like the modern collectors were responsible for maintaining law and order in their districts; they had also to supervise the collection of government taxes and revenues. They were naturally assisted by a large subordinate staff; the *yuktas*, *āyuktas*, *niyutas* and *vyāpṛitas* who are exhorted in numerous records[3] not to disturb the peaceful enjoyment of alienated villages, were most probably the members of the subordinate revenue staff. Some of them were known as *gopas* in the Mauryan age[4] and as *dhruvas* in Gujarat in the post-Gupta period.[5]

In order to maintain law and order, the *vishayapatis* used to have a small military force under them. The *daṇḍanāyakas*, who figure so frequently in inscriptions and seals, were probably the captains of the military units quartered in the different places to work under the orders of the district officers. The officers of the police department, known as *daṇḍapāśikas*

1. *E. I.*, XVI. p. 18; *E. I.*, XXIV, p. 261; *I. A.*, V. p. 155
2. *Manu*, VII. 115; *Vishṇu*, III. 70 ff.
3. *E. g.*, *C. I. I.*, III. p. 165; *I. A.* XIII. p. 15
4. *Arthaśāstra*, Bk. II. Chap. 36
5. *C. I. I.*, III. p. 105

or *chorod dharaṇikas*, probably worked under the directions of the district officers. There is no definite information as to whether the different officers of the commerce, industry and forest departments were subject to the immediate general supervision of the *vishayapati*, though working under the direct orders of the heads of their respective department at the capital. Whether the *vishayapatis* exercised any judicial powers is also not known at present. It is, however, not unlikely that they may have presided over the district court.

The popular element had a large voice in the district administration at least in the Gupta period. The chief banker, the chief merchant, the chief artisan and the chief Kāyastha (writer) figured prominently in the council, which helped the *vishayapati* of Koṭivarsha in Bengal in the 5th century A. D. It should not be, however, supposed that only the big business dominated the district administration ; the persons mentioned above were only the prominent members of the district council, which consisted of a large number of other members as well. The Faridpur Plate III[1] shows that there were about 20 members in this body, some of whom like Kulasvāmin and Śubhadeva were Brāhmaṇas and some like Ghoshachandra and Guṇachandra probably non-Brāhmaṇas. Whether the council looked after the administration of the headquarter of the district alone or of all the territories included in the district is not known. Probably the latter was the case.

Unfortunately we have no information as to how the members of the district council were elected or selected. As far as the bankers and merchants were concerned, they were obviously represented on the council by the president of their guilds, as their designation *prathama-śreshṭhin* and *prathama-sārthavāha* would show. The same was the case with the writers' class. As far as the remaining members of the council were concerned, we shall not be wrong in assuming that persons of different classes, who had by their age, experience and character, acquired a preeminent status, were coopted to the

1. *I. A.*, 1912, pp. 195 ff.

council by a general consensus of opinion. Most probably the district council was dominated by the urban interests, but probably a few members might have hailed from the rural areas.

We get no detailed picture of the district council from pre-or post-Gupta records. But *vishayamahattaras* or members of the district council figure in a 6th century Vishṇukuṇḍin record from Andhradeśa[1] and a 9th century Rāshṭrakūṭa document from Gujarat.[2] We may not be, therefore, far wrong in assuming that they existed and functioned in the post-Gupta period as well, more or less on the lines similar to those obtaining at Koṭivarsha under the Guptas.

The district administration was well organised in the Gupta period. It had its own Records Office in charge of a *pustapāla* (record keeper), who kept accurate records of the dimensions and ownership of not only cultivated but also the waste lands, and also of house sites in towns and villages. Even when waste lands, the ownership of which was vested in the state, were to be sold, the sanction of the popular council was necessary. Some of the land-grant charters even bear the seals of the district administration.[3] Sealings of the district administrations of Rājagṛiha and Gayā were found at Nālandā, showing that their communications to outsiders bore the impress of their official seals[4]. All business was transacted methodically ; even when the *vishayapati* himself wanted to purchase some waste lands in order to gift it for religious purposes, he had to appear before the council and take its permission.[5]

Sub-Divisional Administration

Between the district and the village there were some administrative divisions, whose nature and dimensions varied widely from age to age. Manu recommends[6] that ten villages

1. *J. A. H. R. S.*, VII. p. 17
2. *E. I.*, I. p. 55
3. *I. A.*, 1910, p. 195; p. 204
4. *M. A. S. I.*, No. 66. pp. 45. ff.
5. *E. I.*, XXII. p. 54
6. VII. 115; see also *Vishṇu*, Chap. III. Kauṭilya however refers to group of five villages as the smallest administrative division. Its officer was called *Panchagrāmi*.

should form one administrative unit, and ten of the latter should constitute a bigger one, consisting of 100 villages, which would roughly correspond to the modern Tehsil or Taluka. The district, which according to Manu was to consist of a thousand villages, would include ten Tehsils. The *Mahābhārata* suggests some variation in this decimal system of administrative units and recommends intermediate groups of twenty and thrity villages.[1] A glance at the epigraphical data shows that if not this exact system, its underlying principle was followed in several provinces. During the 8th and 9th centuries there were divisions of Vavullāla and Ruiddha 10 villages, Sihari and Sārakachchha 12 villages and Sebli 30 villages in the districts of Paithan (in Bombay state), Karpaṭavāṇijya, Vaṭapadraka (in Gujarat) and Purigeri (in Karnātak)[2] respectively. Pravareśvara was the headquarter of an administrative group of 26 villages in the Vākāṭaka kingdom in the 5th century.[3] Tanukūpa, Ghaḍahaḍika and Khattaḍūā were the headquarters of a group of 12 villages in Rajputana, Gujarat and Bundelkhand respectively during the 11th and 12th centuries ;[4] Nyāyapadraka group contained 17, Makkāla 42 and Varakheṭaka 63 villages[5] in Mālwā during the same period. Divisions containing 84 and 126 villages are also known.[6] These units seem to have been known after the name of the important towns situated in them.

A number of these village groups constituted something like modern Tehsil or Taluka, which was known as *pāthaka*, *peṭā*, *sthalī* or *bhukti* in the different provinces. *Kharvaṭaka* and *droṇamukha* consisting of 200 and 400 villages[7] respectively were also sub-divisions of *vishayas* corresponding to modern Tehsils. An official like Tehsildar or Mamlatdar must have been in charge of its administration, appointed by the Central

1. XII. 87. 3 ff
2. *Rāshṭrakūṭas*, p. 138
3. *E. I.*, XXIV. p. 264
4. *E. I.*, II. p. 109 ; *I. A.*, VI. pp. 193-4; *E. I.*, IV. p. 157
5. *E. I.*, XVIII. p. 322 ; *E. I.*, III. p. 48
6. *I. A.*, XIX. p. 350; *E. I.*, I. p. 317
7. *Arthaśāstra*, Bk. II. Chap

Government. He must have wielded powers similar to those of the *vishayapati*, but of course on a smaller scale.

The Tehsildars of the Central Government carried on the administration of their areas with the help of hereditary revenue officers, at least in the Deccan. They were known as *nāḍgāvuṇḍas* in Karnāṭak and *deśagrāmakūṭas* in Mahārāshṭra.[1] Deshapandes, Sardeshpandes and Deshmukhs of the Maratha period were their descendants. Whether there existed similar hereditary Tehsil officers in northern India is not known at present.

Whether the sub-divisional officers in charge of the *pāthakas*, *peṭhas* and *bhuktis* were helped and guided in administration by popular councils is the next point to be considered. There were such councils to help the district administration as shown already ; they formed a salient feature of the village administration, as will be shown in the next chapter. There is therefore nothing improbable in similar councils having functioned for the sub-divisions or Talukas also. We, however, get evidence of their existence only in Tamil country during the Chola period. How they were constituted is not yet fully known ; the Leyden grant of Animaṅgalam, however, suggestes that they included the representatives of the villages included in the *nāḍū*. The *nāḍu* assembly took active part in the periodical assessment of the land revenue as well as in the classification of land ; we find even chieftains requesting the future *nāḍus* to respect the revenue assignments made by them.[2] It also took suitable steps to secure relief in land tax when there was a case to justify it.[3]

Like the village councils, the *nāḍu* councils gave donations of their own and administered charitable endowments given by others. Numerous cases are on record of the *nāḍu* assemblies deciding cases of accidental homicides not amounting to murder, usually requiring the culprits to endow a perpetual lamp in a

1. *Rāshṭrakūṭas*, pp. 178-80
2. *S. I. E. R.*, No. 356 of 1924
3. *Ibid*, No. 556 of 1919

local temple, no doubt for the spiritual benefit of the innocent men accidentally killed by them.[1]

The last and most important link in the administration was the village. As the problems connected with it are numerous and important, we shall deal with the topic in a separate chapter to follow. We shall conclude this chapter with an account of the town administration, which yet remains to be surveyed.

Town Administration

In the modern times, the administrative organisation of a metropolitan city like Bombay differs considerably from that of an unimportant town in the moffusil. There are no doubt certain common principles underlying the constitution of the Bombay Corporation and that of a town municipality, but the former discharges many more functions and requires many more sub-committees for that purpose than is the case with the latter. The same was the case in ancient India.

We have very little information about the cities and their administration in the Vedic period. The civilisation was mostly a rural one, and towns and cities did not form its important feature. Very little is known about the town life of the period of the Later Saṁhitās and Brāhmaṇas.

When, however, we reach the historic period proper, we find that the Punjab was studded with a large number of towns and cities on the eve of the invasion of Alexander the Great. Most of them were autonomous to a great extent, being governed by their own councils. How these councils were constituted is not, however, described ; very probably experienced elders were coopted on them by a general consensus of public opinion. The chief officer of the town was called Sarvārthachintaka by this time.[2]

We get more detailed information of the administration of ordinary towns from the Gupta period onwards. It was

1. *S. I. E. R.*, No. 217 of 1926 ; No. 411 of 1912

2. नगरे नगरे चैव कुर्यात्सर्वार्थचिन्तकम् । *Manu*, VII. 121

usually presided over by an officer of the central government usually called *purapāla*. If the town was the headquarters of a district, the district officer usually discharged this duty as well. If the town was also a fort, it used to have another imperial officer called *koṭṭapāla*, who had under him a number of commandants.[1] Very often the *purapālas* were themselves military captains, as was the case with ministers and district officers as well; thus Rudrapayya, who was the prefect of the town of Saravṭura in Karnāṭak, was a bodyguard of the Rāshṭrakūṭa emperor Kṛishṇa III.[2] Mahādeva and Pātāladeva, the joint prefects of Badāmī under Jagadekamalla in 1140, were both *daṇḍanāyakas* or military captains. Sometimes, however, the *purapālas* were selected from among scholars as well, some of whom were interested in promoting the study of 'the everlasting six systems of philosophy.'[3] It is quite possible that they might have combined the literary qualifications with military ability as well.

The *purapāla* or the governor was assisted by a non-official committee, variously called as *goshṭhī*, *pañchakula* or *chaukaḍika*[4] in the different parts of the country. All classes and interests were represented on the committee. Sometimes towns were divided into wards and each ward sent its own members to the committee. Thus in the town of Ghaplop in Rajputana, there were eight wards, known as *wāḍās*, each of which used to send two representatives.[5] How the representatives were selected, we do not know. Very probably elderly persons, who had earned the regard of the residents by their experience, character and ability, must have been sent to the council by a general consensus of public opinion.

The *pañchakula* usually consisted not necessarily of five but often of a larger number of representatives thus sent by the different wards. It used to have an executive of its own for the speedy and convenient dispatch of business. The

1. Such was the case at Gwalior in *c.* 875 A. D.; *E. I.*, I. pp. 154-60
2. *I.* A., XVII. p. 258
3. *I. A.*, XV. p. 15
4. At Ghalop in Rajputana; *E. I.*, XI. p. 39
5. *Ibid.*

executive was called *vāra* in Rajputana and Central India during the Pratīhāra period.[1] Prima facie, this appears to be a queer name ; but it was probably given to the executive because it used to change by turn (*vāra*). An 11th century record from Bhinmal refers to a gentleman as the *vārika* of the current year.[2] This suggests that the executive committee changed annually at the city. At Siyadoni the same persons are seen to have been *vārikas* both in 967 and in 969 A.D.[3] It appears that the executive was elected at this city for a period which was longer than one year.

The number of members of the executive committee must naturally have varied according to the needs of each case. At Siyadoni they were only two but at Gwalior they were three. It was their duty to look after all the executive work, the collection of taxes, the investment and recovery of public funds, the administration of trust funds, etc.

The *vārikas* were assisted in their work by a permanent office and staff. The former was called *sthāna* in Rajputana and used to keep carefully all records of important documents[4]. Thus when the horse dealers of Pehoa decided to give a voluntary cess, they passed a formal resolution and deposited its copy in the office (*sthāna*) of the municipality, so that it might be enabled in the future to collect the dues according to the agreed scheme. A permanent secretary (*karṇaika*) was in charge of the records and correspondence of the committee. Important documents were carefully drafted by him under the instructions of the committee. He must have had a sufficient clerical staff under him. An officer called *kauptika* used to be appointed for collecting the market dues, which probably formed the main stay of the local finance. Sometimes the dues of the Central government in customs duties were collected by the town committee on its behalf; thus the pilgrim tax at Bāhuloda in Gujarat,

1. *E. I.*, I. p. 154 and pp. 173-79
2. वर्तमानवर्षवारिकजोगचंद्र । *B. G.*, I. i. p. 43
3. *E. I.*, I. 154; pp. 173-79
4. लिखितं स्थानानुमतेन करणिकसर्वहारिणा । *E. I.*, I. p. 79

which amounted to several lakhs, was collected in the 12th century by the local municipality on behalf of the central government.[1]

The instances of town-councils given so far all hail from Gujarat and Rajputana ; but it should not be supposed that these bodies did not exist elsewhere. At Nāsik in Mahārāshṭra there was a town council (*nigamasabhā*) in the 2nd century A.D. ; all documents creating or transferring rights in landed property were registered in its office.[2] The council of Koṭivarsha in Bengal has been already described in connection with the district administration. At the town of Guṇapura in Koṅkan, the prefect was assisted by a committee consisting of one Brāhmaṇa, one merchant and two bankers.[3] The city of Aihola in Karnātak had its own corporation throughout the Rāshṭrakūṭa and Chāulukya periods. The town of Mulunda of the same province was divided into five wards. As the inscription referring to this topic is fragmentary, no definite conclusion can be drawn ; but it is not unlikely that the division into wards may have a reference to the representation on the committee, as was the case with the eight wards of Ghalop referred to above (p. 221). The town committees, therefore, were a common feature of the ancient Indian administration.

We shall conclude this chapter with a brief description of the corporation of Pāṭaliputra during the 4th and 3rd centuries B.C.[4] Being imperial capital, thronged with foreigners, its constitution was somewhat different, but it followed the same general principles which governed the constitution of ordinary town committees. It consisted of a body of 30 members divided into five sub-committees. Out of these sub-committees, the one dealing with foreigners, watching their movements and providing for their needs, must have existed only in big capitals or busy ports, where they resided in large numbers. The second committee, dealing with vital statistics and registering carefully the births and deaths, is not referred to in any later inscriptions

1. *Prabandhachintāmaṇi*, p. 48
2. *E. I.*, VIII p. 73
3. *E. I.*, III. p. 260
3. Based on the *Arthaśāstra* and Megasthenes' account

or Smṛitis. Probably it was a Mauryan innovation and did not become popular in later times. The third committee, which supervised over the manufacture of articles, must have usually existed only in industrial towns and cities. The fourth and fifth committees dealt with the fixation of fair wages, the supervision of the market, the supply of pure and unadulterated goods and the collection of the different dues and taxes from the merchants. These duties were discharged by most of the town and village boards throughout Indian history. We miss the public works committee, usually known in Tamil country as the tank or the garden committee in later times, probably because Pāṭaliputra, being the imperial capital, its needs in this connection were met by the officers and departments of the Central Government. None of the sub-committees is seen administering trust funds for the benefit of the community, as was invariably done by the town councils and village committees in later times. Probably this work was done by some purely non-official bodies, as indicated by the *Arthaśāstra*. The Greek writers do not inform us about the constitution of this board and its different sub-committees, whether they were official or non-official, elected or nominated. Pāṭaliputra being the imperial capital of a big empire, it is but natural that many officials must have been appointed on the board like the superintendents of the markets, tolls, weights and measures etc. referred to in the *Arthaśāstra*. There is, however, no direct evidence on the point. The board of moffiusil towns consisted mostly of non-officials, as shown already.

CHAPTER XI

VILLAGE ADMINISTRATION

Since earliest times, the village has been the pivot of administration in India. Its importance was naturally very great in an age when communications were slow and industrialisation unknown. Town played a relatively unimportant part in ancient Indian life ; the Vedic hymns frequently pray for the prosperity of villages[1], but rarely for that of towns and cities. While describing the prosperity of a kingdom, Jātakas proudly give the large number of prosperous villages included in it, but are altogether oblivious to the existence of towns and cities that may have flourished in it. In the Vedic age, as shown already, states were small and this circumstance further enhanced the importance of the village. In later times, even when kingdoms became large, there was no change in the situation, because the village was the natural pivot of administration in a rural society. In modern times, governors often convene a conference of collectors to discuss important questions of administrative policy ; in ancient times kings like Bimbisāra used to convene a meeting of village headmen for similar purpose.[2] There is no doubt that villages were the real centres of social life and important units in the country's economy. They sustained the edifice of national culture, prosperity and administration.

The Village Headman

The village government was usually carried under the supervision and direction of the village headman. He is called *grāmaṇī* in the Vedic literature and figures frequently in the Jātakas. The *Arthaśāstra* attests to his important part in

1. *R. V.*, I. 114. 1; I. 44. 10
2. *Mahāvagga*, V. 1

the administration and inscriptions of almost all the provinces[1] refer to him during the first millennium of the Christian era. He was called *grāmika* or *grāmeyaka* in northern India,[2] and *mununda* in the eastern Deccan[3] in the early centuries of Christian era and *grāmukūṭa* or *paṭṭakila* in Mahārāshṭra, *gāvunda* in Karnatak and *mahattaka* or *mahantaka* in U.P.[4] between *c.* 600 and 1200 A.D.[5]

Normally speaking there was only one headman for each village.[6] His post was usually hereditary, government having the right to nominate another scion of the family if the succession of the son was not approved. By caste, he was usually a non-Brāhmaṇa. He was the leader of the village militia, and therefore he may have often belonged to the Kshatriya caste. Sometimes Vaiśyas too aspired for and obtained the office.[7]

The headman was the most important officer of the village administration. His order was represented on the council of *ratnins* in the Vedic period and he appears almost like a village king in the Jātakas. He figures at the head of the village officers mentioned in the inscriptions of the first millennium of the Christian era. Gāhaḍawāla rulers are often seen[8] consulting the village headman when making land grants.

Defence of the village was the most important duty of the village headman ; he was the officer in charge of its militia[9]

1. Very often government used to alienate village revenues in favour of military captains or Brâhmaṇa scholars. The alienees in such cases were often called *grāmabhoktṛis* or *grāmapatis*. The village headman is not to be confounded with such allienees of government revenues.

2. *E. I.*, I. p. 387 ; *I. A.*, V. p. 155 ; *C. I. I.*, III. p. 256

3. *E. I.*, IX. p. 58 ; *I. A.*, XVIII. pp. 15-7 ; *E. I.*, II. pp. 359-61

4. A. S. Altekar, *Rāshṭrakūṭas*, p. 189

5. *I. A.*, XVIII. pp. 15-17 ; XIV. pp. 103-4; XII; p. 271, etc.

6. Sometimes we come across more than one village headman ; some villages in Karnâṭak had as many as six or even twelve headmen (*Rāshṭrakūṭas*, pp. 189-90). This was probably due to the necessity of accommodating the claims of the nemuerous branches of the original family. Usually, however, claims were adjusted by alloting the office to each branch by rotation.

7. *T. S.*, II. 5.4.4. shows that the office of the *grānmaṇī* as often the goal of the ambition of a Vaiśya.

8. *E. I.*, II. p. 395-61

9. See Kulâvaka and Kharassara Jâtakas for the early period ; for the later period, compare ;—

यथा स्वसैन्येन सह ग्रामाध्यक्षादिसैन्यं सर्वाध्यक्षस्य भवति ।

Sāṅkhyattvakaumudī, p. 54 (Jha's ed.)

and watch and ward. Life was much more unsettled in ancient times, and owing to slow communications the help of the Central Government could not be always expected at the nick of time when there were sudden raids of bandits and robbers. The villagers therefore had to be self-reliant in defence.[1] We often come across the headman and members of the village militia laying down their lives while defending their village.[2]

The collection of the government revenue was the next important duty of the village headman. He was the custodian of the necessary records and used to carry out the work of collection in consultation with the village council. The headman was also the ex-officio president of this body and used to guide its deliberations and activities in the various spheres of the village government and life. He was usually remunerated by rent-free land and could also get a number of petty dues in kind, which the villagers had to pay to the government.

The village headman was the most influential person in the village. The *Śukranīti's* observation that he was like the father and the mother to the villagers is substantially true.[3] Though responsible to the central government, he was generally a man of the people and keen to protect their interests. He was as much indispensable to the people as to the government.

The village office had to keep records of rights and transfers of the village lands, as also papers connected with the government dues and their realisation. Correspondence had to be carried on with the district authorities and central government and the decisions and resolutions of the village council had to be duly recorded. All this work was entrusted to another village officer, known as village accountant. His post also was hereditary in most provinces and he also was paid rent-free land. In Tamil country, however, he was appointed by the village assembly.[4]

1. *Arthaśāsrtra*, Bk. II. Chap. I
2. *Saptaśatī*, VII, 31 ; *E. C.*, VIII, Sorab No. 445 ; *I. A.*, VII. p. 104; *S. I. E. R.*, Nos. 479 and 753 of 1916
3. II. 343
4. In some cases the Assembly reappointed the accountant annually ; No. 89 of 1932, *S. I. E. R.*, 1932

The village headman and the accountant were the two usual officers of the village government. The *Śukranīti* refers to four more, *sāhasādhipati* or magistrate, *bhāgahara* or revenue collector, *śulkagrāha* or toll collector and *pratīhara* or the gate-keeper. They are not however referred to in other Smṛitis or mentioned in inscriptions. Possibly they may have existed in big villages, their functions being performed by the headman and the accountant in smaller ones.

Probably all respectable householders were entitled to become the members of the Primary Assembly of the village. We have rather vague evidence on this point about early times and about northern India. There are, however, some indications showing that in Mahārāshṭra, the Primary Village Assembly consisted of all the householders.[1] There can be no doubt that such was the case in Karnāṭak and Tamil country from *c.* 600 A.D. Numerous inscriptions from Karnāṭak show that the number of the Mahājanas (Great Men of the village) was very large, sometimes 200, sometimes 420, sometimes 500, and sometimes even 1002.[2] There is clear evidence to show that they included all the village householders.[3] All villagers were invited by the beat of the drum for the meeting of the Village Assemblies in Tamil country.

All respectable householders of the village had thus an inherent right to become the members of the Primary Village Assembly. It is interesting to note that the different terms by which they were known, *mahattamas* in U. P., *mahattaras* in Māhārāshṭra, *mahājanas* in Karnāṭak and *perumakkāl* in Tamil country, all mean the same thing, Great Men of the Village.[4]

Great Men of the Village, being so large a body, could obviously have carried on the administration only through an executive committee or council, which was known as Village Panchāyat in later times. Let us now see what was its constitution.

1. *E. I.*, XIV. p. 150
2. *I. A.*, IV. p. 274; *E. I.*, p. 274; XIII. pp. 33-4
3. A. S. Altekar, *Rāshṭrakūṭas*, pp. 199-201
4. The term *mayahara* in Prākrit has a similar significance

Jātakas inform us that neither the village headman nor the village accountant ruled over the village community according to the their sweet will. They were both of them guided in the administration by the opinion of the village public, which made itself felt through the village elders, who formed a kind of informal council since very early times. We have shown already how the *sabhā* of the Vedic period was both a village social club as well as a village council ; at its meetings, the members discussed social topics, played indoor games and also transacted the business of the village government.[1] Jātakas inform us that villages transacted their business themselves.[2] They do not attest to the existence of any regular council or standing committee evolved for this purpose. Initiative was usually left with the headman, but if he acted unreasonably or against the the established customs of the locality or realm, the village elders could set the matter right by pointing out his mistake to the headman.[3] In the Mauryan period villages used to organise works of public utility and recreation, settle the disputes between their residents and act as trustees for the property of minors.[4] But they had not yet evolved regular councils ; for the *Arthaśāstra* refers to village elders acting as trustees, and not to any village council[5] or its sub-committee.

The village councils appear to have evolved into regular bodies in the Gupta period at least in some parts of India. They were known as *pañchamaṇḍalīs* in Central India and *grāma-jānapadas* in Bihar. A large number of the sealings of the different village councils (*jānapadas*) have been discovered at Nālandā, which doubtless sealed the letters sent by them to the administrators of the Nālandā University.[6] It seems almost certain that the village councils in Bihar had developed into formal bodies, meeting regularly to transact administrative business

1. *Ante*, Chap. VII.
2. Kuṇāla Jātaka.
3. Pāniya Jātaka. Here the headman cancels his order prohibiting the sale of strong drinks and slaughter of animals, when the villagers pointed out to him how these were time-honoured customs of the village.
4. *Arthaśāstra*, Bk. III. Chap. 10
5. प्रयोजकासंनिधाने ग्रामवृद्धेषु स्थापयित्वा । Bk. III. Chap. 12
6. *M. A. S. I.*, No. 66, pp. 45 ff.

and communicating their decisions to outsiders in formal and sealed communications.

Village elders known as *mahattaras* functioned in the Pallava[1] and Vākāṭaka[2] kingdoms (*c.* 250-550 A.D.), but we do not know whether they had developed a regular council. Inscriptions from Gujarat and Deccan,[3] however, show that from *c.* 600 A. D. the village elders used to appoint a formal executive committee of their own, variously known as *mahattarādhikārins* or *adhikārimahattaras*, either expression meaning 'village elders in office or power'. Inscriptions show a similar development in contemporaty Rajputana also, where the executive of the Village Assembly was known as *pañchakula* ; it worked under the guidance of a headman known as *mahanta*.[5] It was undoubtedly a very important body, for donations made even by royal personages were announced in its formal meetings.[6] Gāhaḍawāla records often refer to the village elders, described as *mahattaras* or *mahattamas*[7]; but we do not know whether they had developed a regular executive council of their own.

Inscriptions of the Chola dynasty (*c.* 900-1300 A.D.) enable us to present a more detailed picture of the constitution and functions of the Village Assemblies and their executive committees in Tamil country.[8] The Primary Assembly of the villages was known as *ur* in the case of ordinary villages and *sabhā* in the case of *agrahāra* villages, mostly tenanted by learned Brāhmaṇas. Sometimes both these Assemblies are seen

1. *E. I.*, VIII. p. 145
2. *E. I.*, XIX. p. 102
3. सर्वानेव राजसामन्त···ग्राममहत्तराधिकारिकान् । *I. A*, XIII. p. 177
   सर्वानेव राष्ट्रपतिग्रामकूटायुक्तकानियुक्तकाधिकारिकमहत्तरादीन् ।
   I. A., XIII. p. 15
   See also, A. S. Altekar, *Village Communities in Western India*, p.p. 20-1
4. *E. I.*, XI. p. 58; B. G., I. I. pp. 474-5
5. *E. I.*, XI. p. 56
6. *E. I.*, XI. pp. 49-50
7. *I. A.*, XVIII. pp. 34-5 ; *E. I.*, III. pp. 266-7
8. See K. A Nilkantha Sastri, *The Cholas*, Chap. XVIII.
   K. A. Nilkantha Sastri ; *Studies in Chola History and Administration*, pp. 73-163
   S. K. Aiyangar, *Administrative Institutions in South India*, Chap. V.

functioning in the same village ; this probably happened when the new Brāhmaṇa colony was a small one.[1]

As observed already, the Primary Village Assembly of the Tamil country consisted of all the village residents. Its meeting was usually summoned by the beating of drum.[2] One of the most important work of the Assembly was to elect the village executive ; it was chosen after obtaining the consent of all the villagers assembled at the *ur* ;[3] but how exactly this was done we do not know. The consent was probably given in an informal manner by the villagers expressing their approval of the proposals made by the influential members of the village community. The executive body was known as *āḷungaṇam*, the ruling group, but its numercial strength is not known.

The information which we get about the constitution and functions of the Village Assemblies (*sabhās*) and their executive is much more detailed and complete in the case of the *agrahāra* villages, mostly consisting of Brāhmaṇa residents. These constituted the most cultured and educated section of the community and the residents of some of these *agrahāras* have immensely helped the historian of ancient India by describing in detail the constitution of the executive of their Assemblies. The most detailed picture of the working of the executive committees of the Village Assemblies (*sabhās*) is to be obtained from the famous inscriptions at Uttaramerur, a village still flourishing in Chingleput district with only a slightly changed name, Uttaramallur.[4]

The Government of this village was carried on by five sub-committees of the *sabhā*. All members worked in the honorary capacity and held office for one year. They could, however, be removed earlier, if found guilty of misconduct. It was felt that all experienced and qualified residents of the village should get an opportunity to serve on the various sub-

1. Such was the case with Tiruverumbūr (Nos. 112 and 123 of 1914), Tiraimur Nos. (201 and 216 of 1917), etc.
2. *S. I. E. R.*, Nos. 553 of 1921, 85 of 1896, 72 of 1914, 103 of 1897.
3. *Ibid*, No. 89 of 1932.
4. For the text of the inscriptions, see K.A.N.Sastri, *Studies in Chola History*; see also *A. S. I. A. R.*, 1904-5; pp. 131-145.

committees ; one of the rules, therefore, provided that a member who had served once on a sub-committee was not to be re-appointed to it during the next three years. Persons whose character was loose, or who had been found guilty of misappropriation of public funds, were debarred from membership as also their near relatives. The bar against the latter was obviously intended for increasing the volume of public opinion against those who were guilty of defalcation of public funds. Members were to be neither too young nor too old ; their age was to be above 35 but below 70. These negative qualifications, however, were not sufficient. Candidates were required to own a house and at least $\frac{1}{4}$ *veli* (about two acres) of tax-paying land. It was felt that those who deal with public funds should be persons above need. But the property qualifications were halved in the case of those who were good scholars either of the Vedic learning, or of Smṛitis, or of *bhāshyas* (philosophy). It was but natural that an *agrahāra* community should be anxious that its representatives on the different village committees should be, as far as possible, well-to-do scholars, of good character and known rectitude. It is worth noting that no government officers were included in these committees. *Mahattarādhikārins*, who formed the village council in the Deccan, are also sharply distinguished from regular government officers in the inscriptions hailing from that province.

It is not to be supposed that these rules about the qualifications of members were of rigid and universal application even in the case of the *agrahāra* villages. The village *sabhās* had gradually evolved out of popular gatherings of the earlier periods which discussed social, religious and political matters indiscriminately at their meetings, as there was hardly any distinction made in such matters at that time. In the light of experience gained, rules were gradually framed in the course of time. Inscriptions begin to refer to them only from about the end of the 8th century A. D. Each *sabhā* had as a rule its own constitution, though of course, it did not very widely differ from the normal type. Thus, for instance, in some cases the minimum age qualification for members was 35, in others

40. In some cases members became re-eligible for election after three years, in others after five or even ten years. Some assemblies held that even the near relatives of persons once elected should not be permitted to seek re-election for the next five years.[1] The number and functions of the sub-committees also differed according to the needs of the situation and the locality.

Each *sabhā* was usually the architect of its own constitution. The earliest known constitution, that of the *mahāsabhā* of Mānanlainallūr, was framed by that body itself at a special meeting of villagers convened by a beat of drums.[2] When amendements became necessary in the constitution, they also were usually considered and passed by the *sabhā* itself. Sometimes we find the *sabhās* amending their rules in less than two months' time.[3]

At Uttaramerur members of the different sub-committees were selected by drawing lots. Several nominations were made for each of the thirty wards of the village, the name of each nominee being put on a separate ticket. All the tickets for each ward were put in a pot and a young child, who was quite innocent of what it was called upon to do, was asked to pick up one ticket. That person was declared elected for each ward whose name was on the ticket so taken out. There was no room for canvassing or party politics.

Thirty persons who were thus selected were later assigned to different sub-committees. The first sub-committee was in charge of village gardens and orchards ; the second supervised the village tank and the distribution of its water; the third discharged the important function of settling disputes. The fourth committee was known as the gold committee ; its function was to assay gold for all people impartially. This sub-committee naturally consisted of experts in the art. There was no standard state coinage and so gold that was offered for taxes or prices had to be certified about its fineness. A special procedure was laid down for the selection of the expert mem-

1. *S. I. E. R.*, 1927, II. 28 ; No. 500 of 1925
2. Sastri, *Studies* in Chola History, p. 82
3. *S. I. E. R.*, Nos. 240 and 241 of 1922

bers of this committee. The fifth sub-committee was known as *pañchavāra* committee; its functions are not clear.

When members, who had once served on a sub-committee, became eligible for re-election after the lapse of the prescribed number of years, they were usually transferred to a different sub-committee. This was intended to ensure a wide administrative experience in the different members.

In addition to these five sub-committees, there was a general committee of supervision known as Annual Committee (*saṁvatsara-vāriyam*). Only experienced elders, who had previously served on other sub-committees, were eligible for the membership of this body.

The number and functions of the sub-committes naturally varied according to the needs and circumstances of each village. A land survey committee is disclosed by one record ;[1] its function must have been to survey and clasify lands and see to it that the government assessment was fair and equitable. A temple committee is referred to in another.[2] Some *agrahāra* villages had their own colleges ; they probably had an education committee.

We have shown already how the village assemblies had developed a regular council in Bihar, Rajputana, Central India, Mahārāshṭra and Karnāṭak at least in the Gupta and the post-Gupta periods. Neither Smṛitis nor inscriptions, however, enlighten us as to the manner in which it was constituted. The committee was reconstituted annually in Tamil country, as shown above ; in an inscription from Bhinmal in Rajputana, (dated 1277 A.D.), we find the members of the local committee making a religious grant and observing that though they have made the donation, its merit will belong to all those who may happen to become members of the council in future.[3] This suggests that the members of the village councils

1. *S. I. E R.*, No. 262 of 1913
2. *Madras Epigraphy Report* for 1915-6, p. 115
3. यस्मात्पञ्चकुलः सर्वो मंतव्य इति सर्वदा ।
तस्य तस्य तदा श्रेयो यस्य यस्य यदा पदम् । *E. G.*, I. I. p. 480

used to be periodically changed in the north as well. We, however, have no information about the duration of the tenure of their office. At Uttaramerur, the selection was by lots. It does not seem that election of the modern type giving rise to party jealousies and rivalries was prevailing aynwhere. Persons were periodically elevated to the council by the consensus of public opinion as expressed in a general meeting of all the respectable householders of the village. Caste consideration did not sway in the selection of the council members. Many non-Brāhmaṇas worked on it in the Gupta age ; on the judgments of many village Panchāyats in the Maratha period appear the signatures of not only non-Brāhmaṇas but also of untouchables.

The division of the village council into sub-committees, which prevailed in Tamil country, was unknown to Karnāṭak. Numerous inscriptions from this province show that the Great Men of the village (*mahājanas*) used to manage schools, construct tanks, build resthouses, raise subscriptions for public purposes and act as trustees and bankers, guaranteeing for all time to come the proper utilisation of the trust funds entrusted to their care. One naturally expects that the Great Men should have appointed sub-committees to supervise these different activities, but the inscriptions never refer to them.[3] It would appear that the village *mahājanas* of Karnāṭak used to make only informal arrangements for the discharge of these various duties and responsibilities through their executive council, which is seen to consist sometimes of three and sometimes of five members.[4] The members of the council may have taken the help of other influential citizens of the village community according to the needs of the situation.

Sub-committees of the Chola type did not probably function in northern India as well. Here the village council consisted of five members only ; it is expressly called a *pañchamṇḍalī* in a Gupta inscription[4] and *pañchakuli*, in several medieval re-

1. *Aitihāsika Lekhasamgraha*, XVI, p. 55
2. A. S. Altekar, *Rāshṭrakūṭas*, p. 203
3. *Ibid.*, p. 202
4. *C.I.I.*, III. p. 31

cords.[1] Sub-committees of a small body of five members were obviously impracticable.

Let us now briefly survey the functions of the village council. Several records from south India make it quite clear that the ultimate responsibility for collecting the land revenue was fixed upon the village council. It was this body which negotiated with government for concessions in the usual demand in the case of famine and similar calamities. But when the acount was once settled, the village council had to collect the dues from the land-owners and even proceed to auction their land, if they were in default for a long time. The council had even the power to exempt a piece of land from the taxation of the central government, if its owner deposited with it the capitalised value of the annual tax. The tax was of course paid by the council itself out of the interest of the capitalised fund.

It is doubtful whether the village councils in Karnāṭak, Mahārāshṭra and northern India enjoyed such considerable powers concerning the collection and remission of land revenue, as were possessed by the Chola councils. At any rate inscriptions are silent upon the point.

The ownership of the village waste lands was vested in the village councils. In the Gupta period the Central Government could dispose of them only with the sanction of the local bodies.[2] Numerous Chola epigraphs record the sale of land by the village councils ; probably in many cases these were pieces of waste lands brought under cultivations.[3]

The settlement of the village disputes was one of the most important functions of the village councils.[4] In the first instance, family elders or the guild to which the disputants belonged tried to settle the case ; but if they failed, the village council used to decide the dispute. Serious crimes were naturally excluded from the jurisdiction of the village council ; sometimes capital punishment had to be imposed upon the criminals and it

1. *E. I.*, XI. pp. 49-56 ; B. *G.* I. i. pp. 474 ff
2. *E. I.*, XV. p. 130
3. *S. I. E. R.*, Nos. 312, 319 and 329 of 1910
4. They discharged this function as early as the Vedic period ; *sabhāchara* seen connected with the sacred law in the Vedic literature

was naturally felt that the highest court of the state should be called upon to decide the momentous issue. Cases of accidental homicides not amounting to murder were, however, often settled by the Tehsil councils in the Chola period.[1]

There was, however, no limit to the jurisdiction of the village council as far as civil cases were concerned ; disputes involving rights to properties worth several thousands could be settled by them.

The theory of some early writers that the village councils or Panchāyats owed their judicial powers to the prevailing anarchy,[2] no court of the king being available, is completely disproved by the evidence of the Smṛitis, inscriptions and Maratha records. Smṛitis, observe that the decisions of the village councils, duly arrived at, must be enforced by the state because it has duly invested them with the judicial powers.[3] Several documents of the Maratha period have been found showing how kings like Shivaji, Rajaram and Shahu would refuse to entertain a suit, if directly brought to them ; they would invariably refer it to the village Panchāyat concerned.[4] Even Muslim Kings of Bijapur used to do the same. A suit involving the right to the post of the headman of the village of Masur was decided against one Bapaji Musalman by the Masur Panchāyat, and the decision was confirmed by the Tehsil or Taluka Panchāyat of Karad. Bapaji Musalman then appealed direct to the King Ibrahim Adil Shah, complaining that he had not received proper justice owing to communal prejudice. The emperor refused to entertain the suit in his own court, but ordered its retrial by the Hindu Panchāyat of the famous holy place of Paithan.- When this Panchāyat also refused to reverse the lower decisions, Ibrahim Adil Shah declined to take any further

1. Nos. 64 and 77 of 1900 ; No. 223 of 1903 ; Nos. 257 and 352 of 1909
2. Maine, *Village Comminities in East and West*, p. 68
3. तैः कृतं यत्स्वधर्मेण निग्रहानुग्रहं नृणाम् ।
तद्राज्ञाऽप्यनुमंतव्यं निसृष्टार्था हि ते स्मृताः ॥ *Yājñavalkya*, II, 30
4. A. S. Altekar, *Village Commūnities*, pp. 45-6
Parasnis, *Aitihāsika Lekhasamgraha*, XVI. No. 82

action. These cases will show clearly that it was the considered and deliberate policy of the state to invest the village Panchāyats with extensive judicial powers. Parties to a dispute had no alternative but to submit the case to their decision.

In the light of this later but overwhelming evidence, we may well conclude that the village courts, called Pūga by Yājñavalkya, were functioning during the first millennium of the Christian era in the same way as in later centuries. It is really unfortunate that we should get no evidence about their functioning from contemporary literary or epigraphical sources. The assignment of minor fines, imposed upon the criminals in the village, to the donees of villages in numerous grants, however, suggests that these cases were tried locally and by the village Panchāyats.[1]

In many cases temples had their own separate management committees. When, however, such was not the case, the village councils or one of its sub-committees would supervise the temple administration with a view to see that worship was duly arranged, funds properly utilised and repairs to the templed iligently carried out.[2]

South Indian inscriptions show that the village councils used to transact business as bankers as well. They used to receive perpetual deposits and guarantee the utilisation of their interest according to the desires of the donors.[3] They used to capitalise the value of the government tax of a particular land and make it tax-free on receiving its capitalised value, arranging to pay the tax out of the interest annually accruing. It was always understood that the obligations undertaken on such occasions were binding on the *sabhā* in its corporate capacity, though its membership may change. We have an interesting case of the temple authorities at Uttaramerur demanding in 1215 A.D. the fulfilment of certain of obligations, which the *sabhā* had undertaken three centuries earlier, but which had not been

1. For the working of the village Panchāyat courts, see Altekar, *Village Communities*, pp. 42-51

2. *I. A.*, XII. p. 258 ; *E. I.*, p. 275

3. *I. A.*, XII. p. 120; p. 256 ; *E. I.*, VI. pp. 102 and 253

carried out for some time. The *sdbhā* readily recognised its responsibility and gave fresh undertaking to meet its obligation, though on a somewaht reduced scale.[1]

In the case of calamities like famines, they used to raise a public loan by mortgaging the common lands at least in the Chola period ; we have an instance of one village council mortgaging 8·33 *velis* of common land in order to secure a loan of 1011 *kaḷañjus* of gold and 464 *palams* of silver in order to distribute relief to the famine stricken population.[2] The creditor in such cases was usually the village temple, which used to own extensive properties in most cases.

The village councils used to organise several works of public utility. Efforts were made to bring forests and wastelands under cultivation in order to increase the wealth of the village.[3] Construction, maintenance and repairs of irrigation tanks and canals engaged the serious attention of the village councils of the Chola period, and probably the same was the case in other provinces and centuries as well. Jātakas give us a vivid picture of how villagers used to repair the village roads,[4] and a south Indian inscription shows how roads used to be repaired by village councils ; sometimes they would even widen them by purchasing the adjoining lands.[5] Wells for drinking water were also dug and kept under repairs. Occasionally public halls or rest houses were also built.

We should not, however, suppose that the village councils were interested in promoting only the material comforts and well-being of their residents. We often find them taking steps to promote cultural and intellectual progress as well. The *sabhā* of Uttaramerur gave three endowments on different occasions to promote the study of grammar, the *Bhavishya-purāṇa* and the Yajurveda.[6] *Vedavṛittis* or grants for Vedic studies

1. *Mad. Ep. Rep.*, 1899-1900, p. 20
2. *S. I. E. R.*, No. 67 of 1898
3. *S. I. I.*, III. No. 11
4. Vol. I. p. 199
5. *S. I. E. R.*, No. 9 of 1898
6. *S. I. E. R.*, Nos. 18, 29 and 33 of 1898 and No. 194 of 1923

were given or procured by numerous village councils of south India.[1]

Let us now see how the village councils used to finance these different activities. There is sufficient evidence that the Central Government used to permit the village council to spend a small percent of the revenues collected in the village for financing its own activities. Evidence of the Maratha period shows that the village council was permitted to utilise about 10 to 15 per cent of the village revenues for works of public utility and village defence.[2] Probably the same was the case in the Hindu period, though we have no direct evidence upon the point. Fines imposed by the village court upon the offenders were another source of revenue.[3] Village councils had also the right to impose aditional taxes and cesses. The Assembly of Nalur in Tamil country borrowed 25 *kāsus* from a local temple in the 10th century A. D., and in return assigned to it the right of collecting certain rates from the stall in the bazars near the temple.[4] The residents of Salotgi in Karnāṭak agreed to pay in 945 A.D. certain cesses at the time of marriage and other ceremonies for the maintenance of a local college.[5] The same was done by the villagers of Patan in Khandesh for a similar purpose in 1069 A. D. Northern India also supplies numerous instances of such local cesses levied by the village communities and trade guilds for financing works of public utility.[6]

Religion also considerably helped the village councils by enumerating digging of wells and tanks and founding of poor houses and hospitals among the most approved methods of gaining religious merits. The *sabhā* of Uttarmerur had received two permanent endowments to meet the expenses of removing silt from its big tank.[7] An endowment was also received by this village *sabhā* for digging a well for drinking

1. *S. I. E. R.*, Nos. 481 and 487 of 1917
2. A. S. Altekar, *Village Communities*, pp. 70-72
   H. Mann ; *Land and Labour in a Deccan Village*, Vol. I. pp. 42-50
3. *Arthaśāstra*, Bk. III. Chap. 10
4. *S. I. E. R.*, No. 32 of 1910
5. *E. I.*, IV. p. 66
6. *I. A*, XII. p. 87 ; *E. I.*, I. p. 188
7. *S. I. E. R*, Nos. 69A and 74 of 1898

water.[1] The instances given above are only typical and not exceptional ones.

The Central Government would also occasionally help the village councils by direct grant or by giving the requisite material free or at concession rates.[2] If a project was clearly beyond the means of the local body, it was entirely financed from the central revenues. Such, for instance, was the case with the famous dam at Girnar in Kathiawar.

A few words are necessary about the procedure followed at the meetings of the Primary Village Assemblies and their Executive Councils or Panchāyats and their sub-committees. The meeting place of the Primary Assemblies varied according to local conditions ; sometimes it was the hall of the Assembly, sometimes the pavilion of the local temple, sometimes even a tamarind or a banyan tree. All respectable householders were entitled to attend ; in actual practice about 200 or 300 persons generally participated in the meetings. The Primary Assemblies used to meet when the Village Council had to be constituted. In the Agrahāra villages of Tamil country the executive committees were usually constituted by drawing lots; in other places probably names were previously discussed informally by the leading residents, and when it was felt that they were generally acceptable, they were formally proposed in the Primary Assemblies and accepted by them. It is very unlikely that there was any regular voting as in modern times.

Meetings of the Primary Assemblies were also probably convened when matters of unusual importance like the sale of public land to mitigate the miseries of famine were to be considered. Elderly members alone must normally have taken part in the discussion as in ancient Greece. Occasionally, however, persistent opposition was raised by mischievous persons ; for we have a rule made by one Tamil assembly prescribing a fine of five *kāsus* for persons guilty of this mischief.[3]

1. *S. I. E. R.*, No. 75 of 1898
2. *Arthaśāstra*, Bk. II. Chap. 1
3. *S. I. E. R.*, No. 423 of 1906

It was also customary to convene a meeting of the whole Village Assembly, when donations were to be accepted on behalf of the community. In Karnāṭak in particular, it was customary for the assembly to assure the donor on such occasions that the donation would be used for the purpose intended. The convening of the Primary Assembly on such occasions was no doubt a suitable way of showing the community's grateful appreciation of the donor's action.

Very little is known about the procedure of the meetings of the Village Council or the Panchāyat. Probably the village headman in Northern India and the Deccan and the *madhyastha* in Tamil country presided over the meetings, which were usually held in the village office (*chāvadī*). The village accountant must have kept a record of the proceedings in the village office, especially when grants were accepted or tax exemptions granted. Sometimes the important resolutions on such matters were got engraved on the walls of the village temple; that is how we happen to know about them after the lapse of ten centuries.

We shall now consider the relations between the Central Government and the Village Council. No doubt some Smritis occasionally state that the Village Councils derive their power from the king or the Central Government.[1] This statement however, indicates the greater power of the Central Government, but is not historically true. Most of the dynasties in ancient India used to flourish for about two centuries. The village communities and councils were, on the other hand, of hoary antiquity and derived their powers from immemorial custom and not from any charter or delegation from the Central Government. When the Central Government became more organised and developed, it often sought to control and curtail the powers of the Village Councils. Sometimes king's officers are seen to be present, when the Primary Assemblies met to change their constitution;[2] sometimes the rules are stated to have received the approval of the king himself.[3] These, however,

1. *Yājñavalkya*, II. 30
2. As a Uttaramerur in 919 A. D. *A. S. I. A. R.*; 1904-5, pp. 131-145
3. No. 148 of 1927

were rather exceptional cases; it is not unlikely that king's officers might have been occasionally present because they happened to be in the village, and that the king may have accorded approval to proposals formally submitted to him by the Primary Assembly. A persual of the evidence, however, clearly sugests that usually the village Primary Assemblies themselves determined the constitution of their committees and not the Central Government. The same probably was the case in northern India as well. There the Village Council consisted of only about five persons, who were raised to that body by the general approval of the whole community. There was hardly any scope for the Central Government to dictate any constitution.

Numerous inscriptions from northern and southern India, giving king's orders issued to the village headman and the Village Council, show that the Central Government used to have a general power of supervision and control over the village government. This control was exercised by the occasional summoning of the village headman to the district headquarters to explain and clarify matters, as also by the periodical despatch of inspection officers to villages to supervise their accounts and general administration. Periodical auditing of the village accounts by the inscpecting staff of the Central Government is frequently referred to in Chola records, and it must have been done in all other administration as well. Members of the council were removed for misconduct by the Assembly itself; but sometimes they were also fined by the Central Government.[1] If there was a dispute between two Village Assemblies, the case must have been normally referred to the Central Government; we have, however, an instance on record when such a case was referred to the arbitration of a third Village Assembly.[2]

It will be thus seen that the Central Government exercised only a general supervision and control over the Village Assemblies and their Councils. It left the initiative to the Village Councils which enjoyed large powers. They made effective

1. *S. I. E. R.*, No. 192 of 1915 ; No. 268 of 1910
2. *Ibid.* No. 89 of 1932

arrangements for the defence of the community, collected the taxes of the Central Government and levied their own, settled village disputes, organised works of public utility and recreation, functioned as trustees and bankers, raised public loans to mitigate the miseries of famines, organised schools, colleges and poor houses and arranged for their funds, and supervised the manifold religious and cultural activities of the temples. There can be no doubt that they exercised greater powers than those that are at present enjoyed by the local bodies in most countries, both of the east and of the west. They played an important and creditable part in defending the interests of the villagers and in promoting their material, moral and intellectual progress.

CHAPTER XII

JUDICIAL ADMINISTRATION

Administration of justice is no doubt one of the most important functions of the State according to the modern notions. The average citizen becomes conscious of the existence of the state and of its coercive power when he sees the courts functioning and their decisions enforced both in civil and criminal cases. The court is no doubt the most majestic symbol of the power of the State.

Administration of justice, however, did not form a part of the state's duties in early times. In Europe as well as in India the aggrieved party had itself to take such steps as it could in order to get its wrongs redressed. Distraint of the defendant or the accused by the plaintiff, his sitting before the latter's house and not allowing him to move out till his claim was satisfied or wrong righted (*dharaṇa*) was a well established practice as much in ancient England and Ireland as in ancient India. One of Alfred's laws says, 'Let the man who knows his foe to be home sitting fight not before he has demanded justice of him. If he has power to beset his foe and besieges him in his house, let him keep him there for seven days, but not attack him in his house, if he remains indoors. If then after seven days he be willing to surrender and give up his weapons, let him be kept for 30 days and let notice be given to his kinsmen and friends. But if the paintiff have not the power of his own, let him ride to the elderman, and if the elderman will not aid him, let him ride to the King before he fights'.[1] This will show how king's courts as such hardly existed in England in the 10th century and how the aggrieved party had to rely on the strength of himself and his friends.

In India also we find that an authority like the *Manusmṛiti* recognising the use of the force, strategem and *dharaṇa* by the

1. Maine, *Early Institutions*, p. 303

plaintiff as a normal means of redress, even when the law courts had been established.[1] Even a jurist like Nārada disapproves of force only when the claim is doubtful and the king's permission is not taken previously.[2] The wergeld which the Dharmasūtras (*c.* 400 B. C.) prescribe for the murder of the different classes of individuals also shows that for a long time even murders were not regarded as offences against the state but as simple torts, where mere compensation had to be given to the relations of the party murdered.

It is therefore no wonder that we do not find references to any judicial organisation in the Vedic literature, which is at least a 1000 years earlier than the age of Manu. Vedic literature nowhere refers to the king as a judge either in civil or criminal cases. Offences like murder, theft and adultery are mentioned, but there is nothing to indicate that they were tried by the king or an officer authorised by him. It is only the analogy of later times that may perhaps warrant the conjecture that the king in the Vedic age functioned as a judge in private disputes. It has been suggested that *sabhāpati* of the later Vedic period may have been a judge. But the possibility of his being a governor cannot be excluded.[3] Such slight indications as exist seem to show that normally it was the *sabhā* or the popular village assembly rather than the king who tried to arbitrate when it was feasible to do so. This conjecture is based upon the circumstance that in the Purushamedha sacrifice, a *sabhāchara* is dedicated to Dharma or law. If the terms *praśnin* and *abhipraśnin* really mean plaintiff and defendant, they must be referring to those litigants who submitted their disputes for settlement to the village *sabhā* either voluntarily or because they were too weak to help themselves. *Madhyamasī* was rather an arbitrator than a judge.

1. घर्मेण व्यवहारेण छलेनाचरितेन च ।
प्रयुक्तं साधयेदर्थं पंचमेन बलेन च ॥ VIII. 41

2. अनावेद्य तु योराज्ञे संदिग्धेऽर्थे प्रवर्तते ।
प्रसह्य स विनेयः स्यात्स चास्यार्थो न सिध्यति । I. 46

3. *C. H, I.* I. pp. 131-2

The Dharmasūtras and the *Arthaśāstra* reveal to us a more or less full-fledged and well developed judiciary. The king was at its head and he was to attend the court daily to decide disputes. It was his sacred duty to punish the wrong-doers; if he flinched from discharging it, he would go to hell. The thief was to approach the king with a pestle in his hand and confess to him his offence ;[1] if the king did not take the pestle from his hand and dash his brains out as a punishment, it would amount to a derilection of duty.

The Dharmaśāstra and Nītiśāstra literature regards the king as the fountain source of all justice. His time table required him to spend every day about a couple of hours in adjudication.[2] In theory the king could entertain any suit, but in actual practice he could have looked into only the important cases from the capital. He was often too busy to do even this and used to delegate the work to the chief justice or to some other royal officer.

The king was also the highest appellate court. Nārada points out how an appeal was possible to the city court against the village court decision, and how a litigant could appeal to the king against the decree of the city court. But whether a king decides a case properly or otherwise, there is no appeal against his decision.[3]

The king however was expected to be strictly impartial in deciding the cases or appeals that came before him. He was to decide according to law ; otherwise he would be guilty. Dharma or law in India was not a measure passed by a legislature ; if religious in nature, it was regarded as based upon Śrutis and Smṛitis, which were revered as super-human in origin ; if secular, it was based upon custom of universal validity and authority. One sacred text points out how law is the king of the king ;[4] he could not therefore set it aside.

1. *Baudhāyana D. S.*, II. 1. 17-18
2. *Arthaśāstra*, I. 16
3. ग्रामे दृष्टः पुरे याति पुरे दृष्टस्तु राजनि ।
   राज्ञा दृष्टः कुदृष्टो वा नास्ति पौनर्भवो विधि. ॥ I. 307
4. तदेतत्क्षत्रस्य क्षत्रं यद्धर्मः । *Brih. Up.* I. 4. 14

Prāḍvivāka or the Chief Justice, who deputised for the king during his absence, was naturally a legal luminary of high reputation. He was to be well versed both in substantive law as well as in the law of procedure. He was to be a master in the sacred as well as in the customary law.

The most interesting feature of the judicial administration was the system of jury. Even the king and the chief justice could not begin the trial of a case, if they were not assisted by a panel of three, five or seven jurors.[1] The number of jurors was deliberately kept uneven to provide for the contingency of a difference of opinion. The jurors differed from their modern counterpart in an important respect ; they were to be not only impartial, but also well grounded in the law.[2] They were to be fearless exponents of what they believed to be the correct legal position. A juror keeping prudent silence has been condemned. If necessary, the jurors were to express their opinion, even if it was in opposition to that of the king ; it was their duty to restrain a wilful king going astray and giving a wrong decisions.[3]

A number of famous jurists maintain that the king or presiding judge is to be guided by the verdict of the jury.[4] We may therefore assume that such was actually the case. The only exception was that of a difficult case, where the jurors could not come to any definite decision. In such a case the king exercised his privilege of deciding the point according to his own view.[5] The case of Chārudatta in the *Mṛichchhakaṭika* would further show that the jurors used to give their opi-

1. लोकवेदज्ञधर्मज्ञाः सप्त पंच त्रयोपि वा ।
यत्रोपविष्टा विप्राः स्युः सा यज्ञसदृशी सभा ॥ *Śukra* IV. 5, 26

2. श्रुताध्ययनसंपन्ना धर्मज्ञाः सत्यवादिनः ।
राज्ञा सभासदः कार्या रिपौ मित्र च ये समाः । *Yāj.* II. 2

3. अधर्मतः प्रवृत्तं तं नोपेक्षेरन्सभासदः ।
उपेक्षमाणाः सनृपा नरकं यान्त्यधोमुखाः ॥ *Śukra*, IV. 5. 275

4. सभ्यादिनिभिर्विनिर्णिवतं विधृतं प्रतिवादिना ।
दृष्ट्वा राजानुजयिने प्रदद्याज्जयपत्रकम् ॥ *Śukra*, IV. 5.273

5. निश्चेतुं ये न शक्याः स्युः वादाः संदिग्धरूपिणः ।
सीमाद्यास्तत्र नृपतिः प्रमाणं स्यात्प्रभुर्यतः ।

nion about the innocence or guilt of the accused ; the quantum of punishment was often left to the king.[1]

The Smṛitis are almost unanimous in stating that the *sabhyas* or jurors should be Brāhmaṇas.[2] The study of the Dharma-śāstra was usually cultivated in the Brahmanical circles, and a deep knowledge of the sacred law was necessary for the proper discharge of the duties and functions of the juror. This must be the reason for the usual view of the Smṛitis that the *sabhyas* should be Brāhmaṇas. Where, however, the knowledge of the sacred law was not necessary, as when the case concerned the disputes among the cultivators, merchants and foresters, Dharma-śāstra writers themselves recommended that the cases should be tried with the help of the jurors selected from the castes or the professions of the parties themselves.[3] Manu goes to the extent of declaring that if the jurors did not belong to the caste of the parties, a proper decision would be almost impossible.[4] We have evidence to show that in the Vijayanagar administration, the jurors were Brāhmaṇas, where complicated law points had to be decided ; otherwise they were merchants and agriculturists. Śukra's statement that the *sabhayas* were to be from all the castes seems to be more in correspondence to the usual reality[5] than that of Yājñavalkya that they were to be Brāhmaṇas.

What was the highest court in the republican state can only be inferred. It is not improbable that the President himself might have been the highest judicial authority. Or it might have been vested in one of the members of the Central Cabinet who was in charge of law and justice (see *ante*, Chap. VI). It is quite likely that the lower courts in a republic were similar to those in the monarchy, which would be now described.

1. आर्य चारुदत्त निर्णये वयं प्रमाणं। शेषे तु राजा। Act. IX
2. व्यवहारान्नृपः पश्येद्विद्वद्भिर्ब्राह्मणैः सह। *Yāj*, II. 1
3. कर्षकवणिक्पशुपालकुसीदकारवः स्वे स्व वर्गे प्रमाणम्। *G.D.S.* XX. 23
4. वणिक्शिल्पिप्रभृतिषु कृषिरंगोपजीविषु।
अशक्यो निर्णयो ह्यन्यैस्तज्ज्ञैरेव तु कारयेत्। VIII. 39
5. राज्ञा नियोजितव्यास्ते सभ्याः सर्वासु जातिषु॥ IV. 5. 17

When kingdoms began to be fairly extensive ones after c. 600 B. C., subordinate royal courts began to be constituted for important towns and cities. To judge from the evidence of the *Arthaśāstra*, they were often located in the headquarters of territorial divisions, like Sthāna (which included about 800 villages), Droṇamukha (which comprised 400 villages) and Kharvaṭika, (which was exactly half the size of Droṇamukha)[1]. These courts functioned under the authority of the royal seal and were therefore called *mudrita* in later times. There used to be also circuit courts, which are referred to by Nārada.[2]

During the Mauryan age these provincial courts used to consist of three officers and three jurors. Probably under other administrations, the official element may not have been so strong.[2] We may well presume that these courts continued to function throughout the ancient period. What was the relation of the presiding officer of these courts with the head of the local administration, we do not know.

There were special royal courts of criminal jurisdiction, known as Kaṇṭakaśodhana courts. According to the *Arthaśāstra* (IV. 1-2) these courts took cognisance not only of the serious crimes against the state but also of offences against society. Thus if traders used false weights or sold adulterated goods, or charged excessive prices, if the labour in the factory was given less than a fair wage or did not do its work properly, the Kaṇṭakaśodhana courts intervened to punish the culprits. Officers charged with misconduct, persons accused of theft, dacoity and sex-offences had to appear before the same court.

Popular Courts

In addition to the above official courts, there were a number of popular courts in the ancient Indian polity, which constituted one of its special features. We have already indicated

1. धर्मस्यास्त्रयोऽमात्या जनपदसंधिसंग्रहद्रोणमुखस्थानीयषु व्यावहारिकानर्थान्कुर्युः । III. Chap. 1

2. प्रतिष्ठिता पुरे ग्रामे चला नामाप्रतिष्ठिता ।
मुद्रिताध्याक्षसंयुक्ता राजयुक्ता च शासिता । *Nārada.*

how the *sabhā* of the Vedic age probably functioned as a popular court. The *Arthaśāstra* polity was a highly centralised one, but it left a number of causes to be decided by unofficial courts. Disputes about the boundaries were to be settled by the village elders.[1] Causes concerning the affairs of the temples, Brāhmaṇas, ascetics, women, minors, old and invalid persons were also to be decided by the Dharmasthas or unofficial jurors.[2] What precisely was the nature of these cases, and how and by whom the Dharmasthas were selected and what was their number is not known to us.

Popular courts are for the first time mentioned in *Yājña-valkya-Smṛiti*. They are unknown to the Dharmasūtras as well as to the *Manusmṛiti*. Whether they were not evolved before the Christian era or whether they were not mentioned as being unofficial, it is difficult to say. Probably the latter was the case. Yājñavalkya mentions three types of popular courts, *Pūga*, *Śreṇī* and *Kula* ; his commentator Vijñāneśvara expressly describes them as agencies of adjudication other than the official ones[4]. These same courts are mentioned in the same order by Bṛihaspati, who points out that an appeal will be to the Śreṇi court from the decision of the Kula court and to the Pūga court from the decision of the Śreṇī court.[5] In the Vijayanagar administration these courts were called *amukhya* or secondary courts to distinguish them from the royal tribunals.

Let us now ascertain the nature of these courts. Kula court has been defined by the *Mitāksharā* as consisting of a group of relations, near or distant. Kulas or joint families were often very extensive in ancient India ; if there was a quarrel between two members, the elders used to attempt to settle it.

1. क्षेत्रविवादं सामन्तग्रामवृद्धाः कुर्युः । III. 9
2. देवब्राह्मणतपस्विस्त्रीबालवृद्धव्याधितानां....कार्याणि धर्मस्थाः कुर्युः ॥ III. 20
3. नृपेणाधिकृताः पूगाः श्रेणयोथ कुलानि च ।
पूर्वं पूर्वं गुरु ज्ञेय व्यवहारविधौ नृणाम् ॥ II. 29
4. राजसभातो निर्णायकान्तरमाह याज्ञवल्क्यः ।
5. I. 28. - 30

The Kula court was this informal body of family elders.[1] Or alternatively, it may have been a court taking cognisance of quarrels arising in family units of ten, twenty or forty villages. The Gopa of the *Arthaśāstra* was in charge of such units of villages, and they might well have had an informal court of their own, consisting of family elders.

When the effort at family arbitration failed, the matter was taken to the Śreṇi court. The term Śreṇī was used to denote the courts of guilds, which became a prominent feature of the commercial life in ancient India from *c.* 500 B. .C. They are frequently mentioned in the Buddhist literature and the *Mahābhārata* gives a glorious description of the guild chiefs assembled at the coronation of king Dharma. Śreṇis had their own executive committees of four of five members and it is likely that they might have functioned as the Śreṇī courts also for settling the disputes among their members. Though mentioned for the first time by Yājñavalkya, the Śreṇī court might well be placed a few centuries earlier. There is definite evidence to show that guild courts continued to function down the 18th century in Mahārāshṭra ; probably the same was the case in the rest of the country.

The Pūga court of Yājñavalkya consisted of members belonging to different castes and professions, but staying in the same village or town. If the *sabhā* or the village assembly of the Vedic period was occasionally settling the village disputes, the *sabhā* court would be the earlier prototype of the Pūga court. *Grāmyavādi* of the *Taittirīya-saṁhitā* would be probably a member of that court. The Grāmavṛiddha court of the *Arthaśāstra* would also be the forerunner of the Pūga court. Pūga court later became known as Gota court in Mahārāshṭra, as we have already pointed out in Chapter XI. In Karanāṭak it was known as Dharmaśāsana during the 17th century A. D. ; the Mahājanas (elders) of the village and the twelve village servants were represented upon it and it used to decide private disputes, its decisions being enforced by the State as a matter

1. जातिसंबंधिबंधूनां समूहः कुलम् ।

of course.[1] The popular village court thus played a prominent part almost throughout the long course of Indian history.

For a long time there was a great misconception about the causes that were responsible for the widespread functioning of these popular courts. They were well-known to be functioning down to the beginning of the British rule, and they soon disappeared when it was well established. It was therefore argued by Sir Henry Maine and others that the prevailing anarchy in the country,[2] which did not allow any regular royal courts to function at the village level, was the main cause of their existence. As soon as law and order were established in the country and regular official courts began to function efficiently, these Panchāyat courts naturally died down.

This theory, however, is untenable,. It was the considered and long-established policy of the governments in Ancient India to encourage these popular courts and to enforce their decisions. Though these courts were essentially non-official and pupolar, they had the royal authority behind them. Yājñavalkya describes them as sanctioned by the king.[3] The government has been advised to execute their decrees because the state had delegated these powers to them.[4] In the medieval and Maratha periods of the history of Mahārāṣṭra we come across several cases of kings like Shivaji, Rajaram and Shahu refusing to entertain any cases at the first instance though pressed to do so. Muslim rulers also like king Ibrahim Adil Shah of Bijapur used to do the same, even when one of the parties was a Muslim and complained that there was a prejudice against him on that score.[5] It will be thus seen that it was the considered policy of the Government that these popular village courts should flourish ; it refused to entertain any suits except in appeals against their decisions; it also gave effect

1. See Madaksiri copper plate (Anantpur District) dated Śaka 1578. *Inscriptions from Madras Presidency.*
2. H. S. Maine ; *Village Communities in the East and West*, p. 68
3. See *ante*, p. 250 n. 3
4. तैः कृतं यत्स्वधर्मेण निग्रहानुग्रहं नृणाम् ।
तद्राज्ञाप्यनुमन्तव्यं निसृष्टार्था हि ते स्मृताः । II. 30
5. A. S. Altekar. *Village Communities in Western India*, pp. 45-6

to their decrees. When the British rule was established, the new government began to entertain suits at first instance in its courts. It further declined to execute the decres of the village Panchāyats. The latter, therefore, naturally died down.

Ancient India appreciated and encouraged the village Panchāyats and guild courts for several reasons. They encouraged the principle of self-government. They reduced the burden of the central administration. And above all they helped the cause of justice. The members of a guild or a village Panchāyat have more or less reliable knowledge of the facts in dispute as the parties belonged to their guild or locality.[1] It is difficult for a witness to come to a village court and tell a brand lie in the presence of his compeers whose respect he will be thereby forfeiting.

There was no limit to the jurisdiction of the popular courts in civil matters. They could not, however, try criminal cases of a serious nature. Minor offences, including even accidental homicides, could however, be disposed of by them.

The parties to a suit had to pay 'stamp duties'. It was 10% in the case of the successful litigant and 5% in the case of his opponent. A portion of the income from this source was utilised for the payment to the bailiff and clerk of the court, and a portion was paid as an honorarium to the Panchas.

The *mehjars* or the Panchāyat judgments in Mahārāṣṭra are seen to be signed by about thirty to forty Panchas belonging to different castes and professions, including the village grain-sharing functionaries. It is, however, likely that only a small number of Panchas, who were senior and well acquainted with the customary law, participated in the actual trial. In Vijayanagar administration, there was a different set of Panchas for each case. If the case required a knowledge of law, Brāhmaṇas predominated ; if land tenures were involved, the Mahajanas were coopted. Caste disputes were settled by the heads of the different castes. The cases were

1. अभियुक्ताश्च ये यत्र यन्निबन्धनियोजना: ।
तत्रत्यगुणदोषाणां त एव हि विचारका: । *Śukra*, IV. 5. 24

usually tried in the local temple, whose atmosphere inspired awe and stifled any tendency to tell a lie.

An appeal was possible against the decision of the Panchāyat to the Tehsil or sub-divisional Panchāyat. The final appeal lay to the royal court at the capital.

We may briefly refer to certain fundamental principles that were followed by the Hindu jurisprudence. It insisted that the trial should be in public[1] and that the cases should be normally disposed of serially except in the case of urgency.[2] Laws's delay has been condemned by the Smṛiti writers.[3] The executive was not to interfere with the judiciary.[4] The judges were to be impartial ; during the pendancy of the suit, they were not to have any private talk or relations with the parties.[5] If a judge was guilty of foul play, partiality or harrassment, or did not follow the correct legal procedure, he was to be punished. The clerk of the court, not taking the depositions correctly, was severely dealt with (*A.S.*, III. 20 ; IV, 9). In the sphere of the criminal law also, we have some interesting and important principles enunciated. A crime was regarded as committed, if there was intention to commit it, even if accidental circumstances resulted in the attempt being foiled.[6] Abetment, whether by supplying funds[7] or weapons or boarding and lodging, was also

1. नैकः पश्येच्च कार्याणि वादिनां शृणुयाद्वचः ।
रहसि च नृपः प्राज्ञः सभ्याश्चैव कदाचन । *Śukra*, IV. 5. 6

2. क्रमागतादिवादांस्तु पश्येद्वा कार्यगौरवात् । *Ibid*, IV. 5. 157

3. न कालहरणं कार्यं राज्ञा साधनदर्शने ।
महान्दोषो भवेत्कालाद्धर्मव्यापत्तिलक्षणः ॥ *Ibid*, IV. 5. 167

4. नोत्पादयेत्स्वयं कार्यं राजा वाप्यस्य पुरुषः । *Manu*, VIII. 43

5. अनिर्णीते तु यद्यर्थे संभाषेत रहोर्थिना ।
प्राड्विवाकोऽथ दण्डयः स्यात्सभ्याश्चैव विशेषतः ॥
Kātyāyana in P. M. III. 1. 35

6. सृष्ठश्चेब्राह्मवधेऽहत्वापि । *G. D. S.*, III. 4. 11

7. यः साहसं कारयति स दाप्यो द्विगुणं दमम् । *Yaj.*, II. 231

8. आरंभकृतसहायश्च तथा मार्गानुदेशकः । आश्रयद्रव्यदाता च भक्तदाता विकर्मिणाम् ॥ Kātyāyana in Aparārka p. 821

punishable. In the case of treason, even the desire to rebel or capture forts by force was punishable.[1]

An accused could plead duress,[2] self-defence or minority in his defence. Jurists differ as to the age when minority would cease to be a defence. Some granted absolute exemption till the age of 8, others till the age of 15. Accused was usually entitled to the benefit of doubt.[3]

Fines, imprisonment, banishment, mutilation and death sentence were the punishments in vogue. Fines were most common ; their amount differed according to the crime. Those sentenced to imprisonment were often made to work on roads and in public places, so that there should be a deterrent effect.[4] Mutilation of the hand was often inflicted upon the thief. Banishment was sometimes imposed upon the members of the privileged classes. Death sentence was imposed upon murderers, traitors, dacoits and persons guilty of heinous sex offences. Punishment was to be imposed upon the criminal only ; his relations were not to be victimatised.

When deciding upon punishment, the judge was to take into consideration the nature of the crime, the motive of the accused, his age and status in society. In ancient India punishments often differed with the caste of the accused ; lighter punishments were recommended to Brāhmaṇas and Kshtriyas. In early times the wergeld for the murder of a Brāhmaṇa was a thousand cows, for that of a Kshatriya 500 cows, for that of a Vaiśya 100 cows and for that of a Śūdra only ten cows. In later times fines often varied with the caste of the offenders. This is no doubt a regrettable feature of our jurisprudence. Our jurists recognised that the sin of a Brāhmaṇa would be a hundredfold that of a Śūdra for the same offence. His punish-

1. *Arthaśāstra*, Bk. IV. 11

2. बलाद्दत्तं बलाद्भुक्तं बलाच्च प्रतिपादितम् ।
सर्वान्बलकृतानर्थानकृतान्मनुरब्रवीत् । *Manu*, VIII. 181

3. न च संदेहे दण्डं कुर्यात् । *Ap. Dh. S.*, II. 5. II. 2

4. बन्धनानि च सर्वाणि राजा मार्गे निवेशयत् ।
दुःखिता यत्र दृश्येरन्विकृताः पापकारिणः । *Manu*, IX. 288

ment also should then have been more severe instead of being lighter. We should however not forget that all over the world till the last century, the privileged classes like the nobles and bishops did enjoy similar preferential treatment. Our estimation of our culture would however have been higher, if we could have risen above the prejudices of the times and shown impartiality in the award of punishments.

Jails and jailors are rather rarely referred to. The latter is called Bandhanāgārādhyaksha in the *Arthaśāstra*, where Kauṭilya tells us how he was to be punished if he took bribes from prisoners or belaboured them or did not give them their full rations. Male and female prisoners were kept in separate wards. The jail department was under the charge of Sannidhātā, who was to select sites for their location and build the necessary buildings (Bk. II. 4).

We shall now give a brief description of the judicial procedure. The plaintiff was first to file the plaint stating precisely his case and claim. He was not allowed to vary his pleas. The defendant was then summoned with notice and required to submit his written statement in reply. He could either deny or admit the claim, or plead estoppel or *res judicata*. After considering the plaint and the written statement, the judge would call upon the parties to cite evidence. The evidence could be oral or documentary ; the latter was regarded as more weighty. Possession was also possible to be adduced in proof of a claim.

If all other evidence failed, ordeals were permitted. The ordeal sounds strange to the modern ear, but it continues even in the present courts under the form of a special oath, if the parties agree to it. In the ancient and medieval times, the ordeals were fairly common both in Europe[1] and India owing to the prevailing belief in divine intervention on behalf of the

1. When his hero, though innocent, fails in the ordeal, Scott observes in the *Marmion*, V. 21 :—

> 'Perchance some form was unobserved,
> Perchance in prayer or faith he swerved,
> Else, how could the guiltless champion quail,
> Or how the blessed ordeal fail?'

just and the innocent. The Smṛiti ordeals were not quite irrational. It was only when no other evidence was available, that a party was permitted to establish his case by an ordeal. In the fire ordeal as described in *Yājñavalkya*. II. 103, seven green leaves of *palāśa* were placed on the palm of the party and then, after the recitation of the Mantras, which prayed God Fire to protect the party if he was innocent, a red hot iron ball was placed on the palm of his hand and the party was required to take seven steps and then throw out the ball. His hand was then covered and tied in a piece of cloth, and if after three days, no injury was noticed, he was pronounced to be in the right. An age which believed in divine intervention naturally did not regard this procedure as irrational. The ordeals by water, poison and weighment were of the same nature and allowed reasonable chance to an innocent man to come out successful. For want of space we cannot describe them in details.

When the evidence was over, the judge would in consultation with *sabhyas* or jurors give his decision. A copy of the judgement was given to the parties. The unsuccessful party could appeal to the higher court.

Pleaders rarely figure in the ancient Indian judicial system. It is argued by some that Manu refers to a pleader by the term *Vipra* (Brāhmaṇa) when he points out how the witnesses, the sureties and the judge labour for others and how *Vipra* (Brāhmaṇa), the creditor, the merchant and the king profit in the transaction.[1] This is quite possible, but we cannot exclude the possibility of the *Vipra* referred to here being a member of the jury (*sabhya*), who might have received an allowance. A very clear case of a lawyer pleading for a party for a fee occurs in Asahāya's commentary upon *Nārada-Smṛiti*, where one Smārtadurdhara instigates a party not to pay the debt and undertakes to secure exemption from a law court in this connection, if he is

1. त्रयः परार्थे क्लिश्यन्ति साक्षिणः प्रतिभूः कुलम् ।
चत्वारस्तूपचीयन्ते विप्र आढ्यो वणिङ्नृपः । VIII. 169

paid the fee of a thousand *drammas*.[1] Śukra also refers to the practice of appointing recognised agents in the law courts to defend a case when a party was himself unable to do so owing to his other preoccupations or ignorance of the law. Such agents were known as Niyogins and they were expected to guard the interests of their parties very carefully. If they colluded with the other party, they were punished by the state.[2] The lawyer's fee varied from 6% to ½% according to the value of the property; the larger the corpus of the property, the smaller was the percentage of the fee. It is therefore clear that when the law and legal procedure became complex from about 500 A. D., scholars well trained in Smṛitis were often engaged by the parties to represent their cases. Such cases however were not frequent, and there is no evidence to show that there was a regular class of persons in ancient India, whose profession and status were the same as those of the modern lawyer and whose members were licensed by the state to follow the profession.

ANCIENT INDIAN CONCEPTION OF THE NATURE AND SOURCE OF DHARMA OF LAW

The law courts in ancient India, whether official or unofficial, were administering the law. Let us see what was its source and nature. The Sanskrit word used for law, Dharma, has very wide connotation. It includes religious and ritualistic law as well as rules of morality and prudence. These were not usually enforced by the law courts in India. Dharma, for instance, required a householder to keep Agnihotra and to lead a pious life. Law courts did not move in the matter, if somebody did not follow the rules in these matters. Laws in ancient India were for a long time preserved only in tradition; they are expressly described by the Dharmaśāstra as customary rules, *sāmayāchārika dharmas*, or rules based upon conven-

1. *Riṇādāna*, V. 4
2. व्यवहारानभिज्ञेन ह्यन्यकार्याकुलेन वा।
प्रत्यर्थिनार्थिना तज्ज्ञः कार्यः प्रतिनिधिस्तथा॥
लोभेन त्वन्यथा कुर्वन्नियोगी दण्डमर्हति। IV. 5. 114-5

tions. Such of these rules as pertained to family and social life and personal laws, and created civil and criminal rights, were enforceable in law courts. *Varṇāśrama* rules and rules of personal and family law originally based upon custom were later embodied in Smṛitis. This made them a little inflexible for sometime. Society however was naturally changing and it saw to it that ancient but obsolete rules were replaced by current and acceptable ones embodied in new Smṛitis.

Besides administering the rules embodied in a part of the Dharmaśāstra literature, courts enforced *jātidharmas* (rules of castes) *janapadharmas* (local customs), *śreṇidharmas* (bye-laws of guilds) *kuladharmas* (family traditions), in so far as they created civil and legal rights.[1] Most of this law was based upon tradition, which was changing along with social customs ; *Varṇāśrama-dharma*, which our governments and courts are described as enforcing, was not a scheme of life evolved and determined by priests in their interests, but contained rules which made a liberal allowance for the changes in the customary, civil and criminal law, as sanctioned by popular usage and moulded by state guidance. It was the duty of one of the ministers, called Paṇḍita by Śukra, to make a periodical survey to find out which laws are ancient and which modern, which of them are sanctioned by Dharmaśāstra and which though based upon that authority, are no longer valid and which of them have the approval neither of the Dharmaśāstra nor of popular usage. He was then to lay down a proper policy.[2] It will be thus seen that the laws which the courts administered represented a set of rules, which though embodied in Smṛitis to a great extent, also conformed to the actual social practice and were acceptable to the state.

In the ancient period India regarded her law (*dharma*) as sacred in origin as did ancient Greece, but it was substantially based upon custom ; it cannot be described as institutionalisation of the selfish interests of the Brāhamaṇas and Kshatriyas. Dharma

1. जातिजानपदान्धर्मान्श्रेणीधर्मांश्च धर्मवित् ।
समीक्ष्य कुलधर्मांश्च स्वधर्मं प्रतिपादयेत् ॥ *Manu*, VIII. 41

2. See *ante*, p. 172, n. 3

of ancient India was not consciously made by law-givers or by a ligislature ; it was generally enforced by social approval or the dread of hell and not by the force of the state. It was not static ; it however changed not by the arbitrary will of a king nor the noisy method of legislation but by the slow and prolonged process of change in social customs and practices.

CHAPTER XIII

INCOME AND EXPENDITURE

Sound finances are absolutely necessary for a stable and prosperous state. The importance of this proposition was well realised by ancient Indian political thinkers. They have included prosperous treasury and ample reserve funds among the essential constituents of the state and have declared that any deterioration in this connection would be one of the most serious national calamity.[1]

Vedic literature, owing to its predominantly religious nature, naturally supplies meagre information about the revenues of the state in the contemporary times. In the earliest period, the king's power was not well established and the taxation seems to have been occasional and voluntary, the king probably supporting himself, his retinue and meagre administrative staff out of the proceeds of his own lands, pastures and herds. The term *bali*, originally used to denote voluntary offerings made to gods for securing their favour,[2] came to be applied later to the presents and taxes offered to the king, more or less voluntarily. It is also significant to note that a prayer is often offered on behalf of a king, restored to the throne after an earlier deposition, that Indra may compel his subjects to pay him his dues and taxes,[3] or that he may have the good fortune to see ample presents brought to him by his subjects.[4] These prayers suggests that people were not yet quite accustomed to pay regular taxes to the state as a matter of normal liability.

1. कोशमूलाः कोशपूर्वाः सर्वारम्भाः तस्मात्पूर्वं कोशमवेक्षेत् । *A. Ś.* II. 2
कोशमूला हि राजानः कोशो वृद्धिकरो भवेत् । *Mbh.*, XII. 119. 16
कोशमूलो हि राजेति प्रवादः सार्वलौकिकः । *Kāmandaka*, XIII. 33
2. Cf. *R. V.*, V. 1. 10
3. अथा ते इन्द्रः केवलीः प्रजा बलिहृतस्करत् । *R. V.*, X. 173. 6
4. *A. V.*, III. 4. 3

There was a change in the situation in the course of time. In the coronation ritual of the later Vedic literature, the king is described as the 'eater of his subjects'[1]; this metaphor was obviously suggested by the regular payment of taxes by the people to the king which enabled him and his officers to live in dignity and pomp.

In the Vedic period, Brāhmaṇas were engaged in the unproductive profession of priesthood, and the Kshatriyas were mostly occupied in conquering and annexing new territories ; the Śūdras held no property. The incidence of taxation, therefore, naturally fell heavily on the Vaiśyas who were engaged in the productive profession of agriculture, trade and cattle-rearing. The Vaiśya is, therefore, often described as the payer of tributes and taxes.[2] It is not, however, to be supposed that the other classes escaped altogether ; for the king is often described as taxing all his subjects.[3]

We have already shown in Chapter V how in early times the king was but the president of council of nobles. It is not unlikely that the latter also might have often imposed their own tributes. This conjecture derives some support from a statement in the Brāhmaṇa literature that the weak have to offer tributes to the strong.[4]

Bhāgadhuk, 'the collector of the (royal) share,' and *samāhartā* 'the bringer (of tributes)', who figure as members of the king's council (*ratnis*) at this period were probably concerned with duties of the taxation department. Probably the former collected the taxes and tributes which were mostly in kind and the latter stored them in the royal granary and treasury.

The state derived its revenues from the agriculturists and cattle-breeders. The farmers paid a certain portion of the produce of the crops, the amount of which is not disclosed by the Vedic literature. The cattle-breeders formed

1. विशामत्ता समजनि । *A.Br.*, VII. 29
2. अन्यस्य बलिकृत् । *A.B.*, VII. 29. See also *S.Br.*, XI. 2. 6. 14
3. विशोऽद्धि सर्वाः । *A.V.*, IV. 22. 7
4. *S.Br.*, XI. 2. 6. 14

a much more important class in the Vedic than in the succeeding ages, as the society was then just emerging from the pastoral stage. They paid taxes in the form of cows, bulls and horses,[1] a certain per cent. of the herds being claimed by the state.

Apart from taxes from their subjects, Vedic kings often used to receive tributes from conquered chieftains.[2] Trade and commerce were not held in high esteem in the Vedic age and do not seem to have made any appreciable contribution to the royal exchequer. Whether mines were actively worked and were regarded as state property, we do not know.

Hopkins has advanced the view that the taxation in the Vedic period was oppressive and grinding. Instead of checking the predatory tendencies of the king, the priests of the age, he says, encouraged the king to devour his subjects.[3] This view is however untenable. Hopkins is misled by the phrase *viśāmattā*, 'the eater of the people' used to describe the king. As observed in the *Vedic Index*, this phrase might have had its origin in a custom by which the king and his retinue were fed by the people's contributions, a plan with many parallels'.[4] In the Brāhmaṇa literature, the term *attā* is often used in the sense of the enjoyer ; for instance, in one place the husband is described as the *attā* (enjoyer), and the wife as *ādya*, the object of enjoyment.[5] It would be too far fetched to argue that these terms indicate that the husband was the eater or the oppresser of his wife. The expression 'the eater of the subjects', it must be further remembered, is obviously used metaphorically in a coronation proclamation intended to describe the pomp and power of the king in the most grand-eloquent manner ; "Here comes into existence today the ruler of all people, the eater of the subjects, the breaker of forts, the destroyer of demons, the protector of Brāhmaṇas and *dharma*". We have shown already in Chapter V how the king's position was far from secure in the Vedic period

1. एमं भज ग्रामे अश्वेषु गोषु । *A. V.*, IV. 22. 2
2. *R. V.*, VII. 18. 19
3. Hopkins, *India Old and New*, p. 240
4. *Vedic Index*, under *Rājan*.
5. *S. Br.*, I. 8. 3. 6

and how the Assembly (*samiti*) exercised a fairly effective control over his actions. It is therefore unlikely that people would normally have suffered from grinding taxation in that age.

Very little definite is known about the system of taxation during the post-Vedic and pre-Mauryan period. Jātakas may be presumed to give us a glimpse of this age, but their information is meagre. They tell us how good kings levied only legal taxes and how bad rulers oppressed the subjects so much by illegal imposts that they would often flee to forests to escape from tax-collectors.[1] These statements hardly enable us to have a proper picture of the taxation system.

With the Mauryan period we come on firmer ground. The *Arthaśāstra*, the Dhramasūtras and the Smṛitis supply considerable data, which can to a great extent be checked by the statements of Greek writers and the contents of contemporary state documents preserved in stone inscriptions and copper-plates.

It would be convenient to discuss at the outset the general principles of taxation. Nothing can be more admirable and less flawless than the scheme propounded by the Smṛitis and epics in this respect.

(1) The taxation was to be reasonable and equitable; the king was never to forget that nothing exposed him to greater hatred than oppressive taxation.[2] The gardener plucks fruits and flowers, but does not harm the trees; the bee sucks the honey but does not damage the flower;[3] in the same way the king should collect his taxes, but should not cause any sufferings to his subjects. One who kills the goat can at best get one meal: one who feeds it well can get milk for several years.[4]

1. See *Jātakas*, IV. p. 399; V, pp. 98-9; 101; II, p. 17
The tax collectors are called *balisādhakas* or *balipaṭigāhakas* in the Jātakas, terms reminiscent of *bali*, the Vedic word for taxes.

2. प्रद्विषंति परिख्यातं राजानमतिखादिनम । *Mbh*, XII. 87. 19

3. फलार्थी नृपतिर्लोकान्पालयेद्यत्नमास्थितः ।
दानमानादितोयेन मालाकारोऽङ्कुरानिव । *Pañchatantra*, I. 243

4. अजामिव प्रजां हन्याद्यो मोहात्पृथिवीपतिः ।
तस्यैका जायते प्रीतिर्न द्वितीया कदाचन ॥ *Ibid*, 242

(2) The criterion of equitable taxation was that the state on the one side and the agriculturist or the trader on the other should both feel that they have got a fair and reasonable return for their labours.[1]

(3) In the case of trade and industry, the taxation was to be on net profits and not on gross earnings.

(4) An article was to be taxed only once and not twice.[2]

(5) If increase in taxation becomes inevitable, its hould be gradual and not sudden and steep.[3]

(6) Extra taxation was to be imposed only in times of national calamity after taking comprehensive steps to explain the situation to the people with a view to ensure a willing response. The king was never to forget that it was only an exceptional remedy to be adopted when there was no other alternative.[4]

There can be no doubt that the above principles will be universally recognised as sound, applicable as much in modern as in ancient times. How far they were actually given effect to in the ancient times, we shall discuss later in this chapter.

Equally sound principles have been enunciated about partial or total remission in the normal taxation, when the situation justified such concession. Both the *Arthaāśāstra* and *Śukranīti* recommend that if enterprising persons bring fresh land under cultivation or seek to make it more fertile and productive by irrigating it with water from tanks built by themselves, the state should charge only a nominal tax in the beginning and gradually raise it to the normal rate during a period of four or five years.[5] There is ample evidence to

1. विक्रयं क्रयमध्वानं भक्तं च सपरिव्ययम् ।
योगक्षेमं च संप्रेक्ष्य वणिजो दापयेत्करान् ॥ *Manu*, VII. 127
न हीनसमम्ल्याद्धि शुल्कं विक्रेतृतो हरेत् ।
लाभं दृष्ट्वा हरेच्छुल्कं क्रेतृतश्च सदा नृपः ॥ *Śukra*, IV. 2. 19

2. वस्तुजातस्यकवारं शुल्कं ग्राह्यं प्रयत्नतः । *Śukra*, IV. 2. 111

3. अल्पेनाल्पेन देयेन वर्धमानं प्रदापयेत् ॥
ततो भूयस्ततो भूयः क्रमवृद्धिं समाचरेत् ।
दमयन्निव दम्यानि शश्वद्भारं विवर्धयेत् ॥ *Mbh*, XII. 88. 7-8

4. *Mbh*, XII. 87 26-39; *Śukraniti*, IV. 2. 10

5. *Arthaśāstra*, Bk. VI. Chap. 9 ; *Śukranīti*, IV. 2. 122

show that governments in ancient India were actually following this advice down to the 18th century.[1]

Military villages were exempted from taxation in consideration of the regular supply of recruits, which they ensured for the army.

Exemption from taxation has been recommended also on the ground of incapacity in the case of the dumb, deaf and blind persons, who are usually poor. Students studying at *gurukulas* and hermits practising penance in forests were not earning members of society and were, therefore, not to be taxed. Women in early times could hold only a negligible amount of property and have, therefore, been also recommended for exemption from taxation.[2] When later on their right of inheritance was recognised by society, only poor widows and destitute women must have got the benefit of this concession.

Dumb, deaf and decrepit persons required greater protection from the state. The ancient theory that taxation was a payment for protection would normally result in heavier taxes being imposed upon such persons. But humanitarian considerations were given greater weight than the above theory and persons of these categories were universally exempted from taxation.

Smṛitis further recommended that learned Brāhmaṇas (*śrotriyas*) should be also exempted from taxation.[3] An ideal *śrotriya* was vowed to poverty and was required to impart higher Vedic and Sanskritic education free to all students.

1. *E C.*, III. Seringapattan, No. 148; No. 422 of 1912; *I. M. P.*, Vol. II Madura No. 3A.

2. अकरः श्रोत्रियः। सर्ववर्णानां स्त्रियः। कुमाराश्च प्राग्व्यंजनेभ्यः। ये च विद्यार्थिनो वसंति। तपस्विनश्च ये धर्मपराः। शूद्रश्च पादावनोक्ता। अंधबधिरमूकरोगाविष्टाश्च। *A D. S.*, II. 10. 26. 1-17

E. C., IV. Chamarajanagar, No. 186 and Yelandur No. 2 supply concrete evidence to show that this precept was followed in practice. The latter record states that if a woman lost her living, she should be not only exempted from the payment of five *varāhas* (gold coins), but be given an unemployment bonus of six *varāhas*.

3. म्रियमाणोऽप्याददीत न राजा श्रोत्रियात्करम्। *Manu*, VII. 133

There is ample evidence to show that they were discharging this duty in spirit as well as in letter, and it was but meet that the state should have exempted them from taxation. In many cases, however, revenues of whole villages (known as *agrahāra* villages) were assigned to learned Brāhmaṇas for their maintenance; when such was the case, they were usually required to pay a quit rent.[1] This was but fair, for they could no longer put forth the plea of poverty. If, however the share which Brāhmaṇa scholars obtained in the revenue was very small, they were often granted full exemption from taxation.[2] But such cases however were exceptional.

The whole of the Brāhmaṇa class, however, has been recommended for exemption from taxation by some Smṛitis.[3] Opinion seems to have been divided on this point, for the *Mahābhārata* emphatically declares that those among the Brāhmaṇas, who were holding lucrative appointments in the government service, or those who were following the money-making professions like trade, agriculture and cattle-rearing, were to be charged usual taxes and cesses at their full rates.[4] When Brāhmaṇa writers themselves differed on this point, it is but natural that all states should not have regarded the recommendation as binding. We do get occasional cases of the entire Brāhmaṇa class being exempted from certain taxes. Thus a record of king Somasiṁhadeva of the Paramāra dynasty,[5]

1 Thus the *agrahāra* village of Dindugura had to pay a revenue of 100 *nishkas*, and that of Keśavapura 350 *nishkas*. *E. C.* V. Channarayapattana Nos. 173 and 179.

2. *I. M. P.*, I. 73 In this case, however, we find that the full exemption given to Brāhmaṇas was not respected by some of the succeeding rulers.

3 Cf. for instance, ब्राह्मणेभ्यः करादानं न कुर्यात् । ते हि राज्ञो धर्मकराः ।

Vishṇu, III. 25-26

4. येजाविमहिषाणां च वडवानां च पोषकाः ।
वृत्यर्थं प्रतिपद्यन्ते तान् (विप्रान्) वैश्यान्संप्रचक्षते ॥ ४ ॥
ऐश्वर्यकामा ये चापि सामिषाश्चैव भारत ।
निग्रहानुग्रहरतांस्तान्द्विजान्क्षत्रियान् विदुः ॥ ५ ॥
अश्रोत्रियाः सर्व एते सर्वे चानाहिताग्नयः ।
तान्सर्वान्धार्मिको राजा बलिं विष्टिं च कारयेत् ॥ ७ ॥

Mth., XII. 76. 4-7.

5. *E. I.* VIII. p. 208.

another of king Achyutarāya of Vijayanagar[1] and two epigraphs from Guntur district[2] describe how taxes were remitted in the case of Brāhmaṇas in medieval times ; but they also prove that the exemptions were new and unusual ones. The available evidence shows that such exemptions were not the rule, but the exception ; hence the great credit claimed for them by the kings concerned.

This is clearly proved by some concrete cases from south India, where we find the lands of Brāhmaṇa owners being sold away for the non-payment of the government dues. One record (*c.* 1229 A. D.) shows that even the Brāhmaṇa donees of *agrahāra* villages had to pay interest on the land tax remaining in arrears. The state, however, did not wait for more than three months ; at the end of this period it would sell away the shares of the defaulters.[3] Another record shows that the period of waiting was often extended to two years,[4] at the end of which the sale could not be stopped except by the full payment of the state dues. We have no such cases recorded in northern India, but we shall not be far wrong in stating that the exemption from taxation seems to have been enjoyed by the entire Brāhmaṇa community only on rare occasions. As a general rule all Brāhmaṇas had to pay taxes, excepting those who were learned and poor and had received no state patronage.

Temples, which owned extensive lands, were naturally not exempted from taxation. Sometimes, if their income was small, only a quit rent was charged ; but usually the full rate was in operation. We have cases of temples selling part of their lands in order to pay the government revenues due from them;[5] sometimes we even find their lands being sold away by government for default in the payment of land tax.[6]

Let us now survey the field of taxation. Land tax was, as in later times, the main stay of the government revenue.

1. *I. M. P.*, Vol. III. Nos. 768 and 946
2. *I. M. P.*, I. p. 22
3. *E. C.*, V. Arsikera, No. 128
4. *I. M. P.*, II. p. 1245
5. No. 07 of 1890
6. *I. M. P.*, II. p. 1322

It is referred to in inscriptions, sometimes as *bhāgakara* and sometimes as *udraṅga*. Smṛitis lay down no uniform rate of taxation ; the percentage they recommend varies from eight to thirty-three.[1] This variation must be due partly to the quality of land ; it is clear for instance, that Manu could not have the same types of land in his view when in the same breath he recommends that the land taxation should be either 8 or 12 or 16 per cent.[2] Kulottuṅga Chola is known to have divided land into eight classes for the purpose of taxation.[3] The non-agreement among the Smṛitis must be partly due also to the varying practices of the different states or to the different rates charged by one and the same government at different times to meet its varying needs.[4] The normal procedure, however, was to charge one-sixth of the produce as the land tax ; the tax collectors were often called *shasṭhādhikṛitas*, as in Bengal and Bundelkhand.

Land tax at 16% was, however, found insufficient for their needs by states which had chalked out a policy of imperial expansion. The testimony of the *Arthaśāstra*[6] and the Greek writers[7] shows that the Mauryan state charged 25% tax on agricultural incomes ; the concession, which Aśoka showed to the inhabitants of Lumbini, because the Buddha was born in their village, consisted in the reduction of this usual percentage to half.[8] Under the Cholas in the 11th century, the taxation was 20% ; a *veli* of land, yielding 500 *kalams* of paddy was taxed 100 *kalams* ; sometimes, however, wet lands were charged 33%.[9]

1. *Manu*, VIII. 130 ; *Gautama*, X. 24-27 ; *Arthaśāstra*, V. 2

2. धान्यानामष्टमो भागः षष्ठो द्वादश एव वा । VII. 130

3. *I. M. P.*, I. pp. 125-130.

4. षड्भागमुपलक्षणं यावता प्रजानां पीडा न स्यात् तावदेव प्रजापालनस्यावश्यकत्वात् ।। *Smṛitiratnākara*, p. 62

5. Sen, *Inscriptions from Bengal*, No. 1

6. Bk. V. Ch. 2

7. Megasthenes, I. 46

8. Cf. हिद भगवं बुधे जातेति लुंबिनिगामे उबलिके कटे अठभागिये च । Rumindei Inscription
The *Rāmāyaṇa*, III. 16. 14 also suggests 25 per cent tax.

9. *Rāshṭrakūṭas*, p. 22. See also, *E. C.* X. Mb. Nos. 44 (a) and 107

In the reign of Rājādhirāja the temples are seen paying a quit rent of 10% ; the charge on the land of ordinary cultivators must, therefore, have been higher, probably varying from 20 to 30%.

It is difficult to state whether the percentage of the land tax, mentioned above, refers to gross or net produce. The Jātaka literature shows how the government agents were present on the fields when the yield of the crops was garnered ; so the share they claimed must have been of the gross produce.[1] There is, however, no definite evidence to show that the government did not make an allowance for the cost of agriculture, when it was charging a tax as high as 25% or 33%. The *Śukranīti*, which permits 33% taxation, definitely states that the cultivator should get as his net income twice the amount which he spends by way of the land-tax and the cost of production.[2] This would show that the share claimed by the state would be about 16% of the gross produce and 25% of the net income.

When the cultivator suffered owing to an adverse change in the circumstances, e.g. the land becoming sandy due to the encroachment of the sea, the state used to remit or reduce the tax as demanded by the situation.[3] In all cases, however, an automatic relief was obtained to a certain extent, for the dues were usually collected in kind ; if the yield was less, the state naturally got less.

The evidence to show that the land tax was usually paid in kind is overwhelming. The very term used to denote it, *bhāgakara*, the tax in the form of a share, suggests that it was paid as a part of what was actually produced in the field. In the Jātakas the tax collecting officer is called *droṇamāpaka*, 'the measurer of the corn by the *droṇa* measure'. They also narrate the stories of overscrupulous land-owners regretting

1. II. p. 378
2. राजभागादिव्ययतो द्विगुणं लभ्यते यतः ।
कृषिकृत्यं तु तच्छ्रेष्ठं यन्न्यूनं दुःखदं नृणाम् । IV. 2. 115
3. *I. M. P.*, I. p. 136

their conduct in casually taking a handful of rice blades from their own fields, because the king would not thereby get a share in that part they had thus removed earlier;[1] the *Arthaśāstra* imposes a fine for such a conduct.[2] State used to have huge granaries at different centres, where the corn collected in taxes was stored. Officers in their charge used to dispose of it before its quality started to deteriorate on account of the action of time or insects.[3]

A few records, however, show that the land tax was in some localities collected in cash after about the 9th century A. D. A 10th century Gurjara Pratīhāra record from the U. P. assings 500 *drammas* for a temple out of the revenues of a certain village.[4] An inscription from Orissa of about the same period records the gift of a village yielding 42 *rūpyas* or silver coins.[5] Two 11th century inscriptions in the Rājarājeśvara temple record the amount of the government revenue from 35 villages ; in the case of 30 of them, the taxation was levied in kind at the rate of 100 *kalams* of paddy per *veli* ; but in the case of 5, it was collected in cash at the rate of 10 gold *kalanjus* per *veli*.[6] It thus appears that cash taxation was introduced in some cases from about the 9th century A. .D. These, however, appear to be exceptional cases.

When the land tax was collected in kind, the annual dues must naturally have been recovered at least in two instalments at the time when the autumn and spring crops were garnered.[7] A Gujarat record, however, shows that it was sometimes collected in as many as three instalments under the Rāshṭrakūṭa administration.[8]

There was no permanent settlement of the land tax. The large variation in percentage permitted by the Smṛitis naturally rendered its enhancement possible, when required by

1. *Ibid*, II. p. 378
2. Bk. II. Ch. 2
3. *Śukranīti*, II. 26 29
4. *I. A* , XVI. p. 174
5. *E.I.*, XII. p 20
6. *S. I. I.*, Nos. 4 and 9
7. This practice has been recommended by Bhaṭṭasvamin at *Arthaśāstra* II, 1 and Kullūka at *Manu*, VIII. 307
8. *I.A.*, XIII. p. 68

the exigencies of the state finance. On the other hand, when canals irrigating certain fields dried up, their taxes had to be reduced. An inscription from Banavāsi (Karnāṭak) shows that the state in ancient times did not fail to grant the needed relief on such occasions.[1]

When the land-owner failed to pay the land-tax, his land was sold away after a certain period, which varied from place to place and time to time. Under Rājendra Chola the period of grace extended to three years,[2] but it was reduced to two by Kulottuṅga.[3] Interest was often charged on the amount in arrears. We have shown already how this principle was allowed to operate even in the case of lands belonging to Brāhmaṇas and temples. It is, however, rather surprising to find that Smṛitis should nowhere refer to the state's right to confiscate the lands of the defaulting owners. Was this right claimed only after *c.* 900 A. D. ?

It would be convenient to discuss here the question about the ownership of cultivable land. For, if we regard the state as its owner, the amount which the cultivator paid would be land revenue and not land-tax ; if on the other hand, the ownership vested in private persons, the same amount would be a land-tax.

It is but natural that in ancient as in modern times opinion should have differed on this important point. A verse in the *Manusmṛiti* states that the king is the owner of the treasures buried under ground, because he is the owner of the land;[4] this suggests state ownership of all land, including the cultivable one. Bhaṭṭasvāmin, the commentator on the *Arthaśāstra*, quotes a verse averring that private ownership can have no application in the case of land, tanks and water pools.[5] Diodorous states

1. *E. C.*, VIII. Sorab. No. 83
2. *S.I.I.*, Vol. III. No. 9
3. *I. M. P.*, Vol. II. p. 1245
4. निधीनां तु पुराणानां धातूनामेव च क्षितौ ।
अर्धभाग्रक्षणाद्राजा भूमेरधिपतिर्हि सः ॥ VIII. 39
5. राजा भूमेः पतिर्दृष्टो शास्त्रज्ञैरुदकस्य तु ।
ताभ्यामन्यत्तु यद्द्रव्यं तत्र स्वाम्यं कुटुंबिनाम् ॥ Bk. II. Chap. 24

that land in India is the property of the crown and no private individual is permitted to own it. As against these three authorities, the testimony of none of whom can be regarded as conclusive on the point,[1] we have the definite evidence of the *Pūrvamīmāṃsā* stating that a king cannot dispose of the lands of private individuals, when he is called upon to gift away all his possessions in charity at the end of certain sacrifices.[2] The *Arthaśāstra* also clearly differentieates between the crown lands and private lands.[3] Nārada points out that it would be highly iniquitous if the king proceeded to interfere with the ownership and possession of houses and lands, for it would result in utter chaos.[4] Nīlakaṇṭha definitely declares that although an emperor is the lord of the entire earth, the ownership in different fields belongs to their several private owners, and not to the state.[5]

In pre-historic times, however, the ownership in land was regarded as vested in the whole community. This is suggested by the view of some authorities, which hold that the transfer of land can become valid only if assented to by the entire body

1. Manu may have put forth the theory of the state's ownership of the entire land merely to find an argument for its claim to hidden treasures. The verse quoted by Bhaṭṭasvāmin may be interpreted merely as a general claim to all land and water; it may be compared to the sovereignty in land, sea and air, which is claimed by the modern state. Greek writers may have generalsed from the crown lands.

What was Yuan Chwang's impression about the ownership of land is difficult to make out from his few observations at vol. I. p. 176

2. Śabara comments as follows :—

न भूमिः स्यात्सर्वान् प्रत्यविशिष्टत्वात् ॥ VI. 7. 3

य इदानीं सार्वभौमः स तर्हि भूमिं दास्यति । सोऽपि नेति ब्रूमः । कुतः । .... । सार्वभौमत्वे त्वस्यैतदेवाधिकं यदसौ पृथिव्या सभूतानां व्रीह्यादीनां रक्षणेन निर्दिष्टस्य कस्यचिद्भागस्येष्टे न भूमेः ।

3. Bk. II, Chap. 23

4 गृहक्षेत्रे च द्वे दृष्टे वासहेतू कुटुंबिनाम् ।
तस्मात्ते नाक्षिपेद्राजा ते हि मूले कुटुंबिनाम् ॥ Chap. XI. 42

5. तत्तद्ग्रामक्षेत्रादौ स्वत्वं तु तत्तद्भौमिकानामेव । राज्ञां तु करग्रहणमात्रम् । अत एव इदानींनपारिभाषिकक्षेत्रदानादौ न भूदानसिद्धिः । किंतु वृत्तिकल्पनामात्रमेव । *Vyavahāramayûkha*, Svatvāgama Chapter.

of villagers, agnates and castemen.[1] The communal ownership of land did not, however, permit the state to dispossess an individual of the land he owned; it merely restricted his power of its disposal, lest an unwanted or undessirable person should be introduced in the village community to disturb its peace. It is interesting to note that in the Vedic age even the king was permitted to gift a piece of land only when the adjacent residents agreed to the proposal.[2]

The theory of the communal ownership of land, that was accepted in pre-historic times, has left its trace and influence only in two matters in the historic period. The state's claim to eject the land owners, who do not pay the land-tax, is similar to that of the land-lord to evict a tenant, who does not pay the rent of his house. It clearly pre-supposes the state's ownership in land. The ownership in waste lands, forests and mines, which the state claimed in historic times, was originally based upon its claim to the entire land in the realm.

There is conclusive and overwhelming evidence to show that at least from *c.* 600 B.C. the ownership of private individuals in their arable land could not be affected by the action of the state, except when there was a failure to pay the land tax. People could freely gift away, mortgage or sell their lands. Ambapallī and Anāthapiṇḍaka gave extensive plots of land to the Buddhist *saṁgha* at Vaiśālī and Śrāvastī. In the Jātakas, we find a Brāhmaṇa of Magadha giving away his portion of land to another.[3] Inscriptions also record numerons gifts of land made by private individuals without any let or hindrance from the state.[4]

It is no doubt true that some state grants recorded the gifts of entire villages to Brāhmaṇas or temples; but this procedure does not support the theory of the state ownership of the arable land. For what the grants assign in most of these cases is the

1. स्वग्रामज्ञातिसामन्तदायादानुमतेन च ।
हिरण्योदकदानेन षड्भिर्गच्छति मेदिनी ॥ *Mitākshharā* on *Yāj.*, II. 113
2. *S.Br.* I. 7. 3. 4; VIII 1. 1. 8
3. IV., p. 281
4. *E.I.*, VIII, Nasik, No. 9

state's right to receive the various taxes, including the land-tax; they never effect any chage in the private ownership of the landed property included in the village. The grant never calls upon private owners of the lands situated in the village to surrender their property to the donee; it simply exhorts them to show him proper courtesy and respect and pay all the state taxes in cash and kind, not to the state officers but to the new grantee. Future kings are requested to desist, not from taking possession of the village land, but from receiving the various taxes due from them.[1]

We have also many records which transfer full ownership in land to the donee. In such cases, however, not the entire land in the village, but certain small pieces situated in it, often detached, are usually transferred. Thus Dhruvasena I of Valabhi wanted to give 360 *pādāvartas* of land to a temple in his kingdom; he gave four pieces of land situated to the north-west and four others situated to the north-east of the village, eight together measuring 300 *padavaratas*; and two other fields, both irrigated by wells.[2]

The donee in this case would certainly have preferred to get one entire connected piece of land measuring 360 *pādāvartas*, and the king also would certainly have given such a piece, were he the owner of the entire cultivable land in the village. If he gave disconnected pieces, the reason must be that the state possessed only a few fields in the village, the ownership of which had accrued to it, either through failure of heirs or through the non-payment of the land tax. As in modern days so in ancient times, state used to acquire ownership in some such pieces of land in most villages; they have been expressly described as *rājyavastu* or state property in some records.[3] When kings

1. Cf. ते यूयं समुचितभागभोगकरहिण्यादिप्रत्यायोपनयनं करिष्यथ आज्ञाश्रवणविधेयाश्च भविष्यथ ॥ *C. I. I.*, III. p. 118

See also Khoh copperplate grants, *Ibid*. pp. 126, 133; Pali grant, *E. I.*, II. p. 304; Barah grant, *E. I.*, XIX. p. 19

2. E. I., III. p. 321

3. चेंडल्रग्रामे राज्यवस्तु भूत्वा स्थितं क्षेत्रं ब्राह्मणाय प्रदत्तम् । *E.I.I.*, I. p. 239.

wanted to donate, not land revenues but landed property, they used to give such small and usually disconnected pieces under their ownership.[1] Sometimes when kings did not own any land, they used to purchase the piece they wanted to give; thus we find a Vaidumba king (*c.* 950 A. D.) purchasing three *velis* of land from a village assembly in order to assign them to a temple. Some Chola records also expressly refer to the previous purchase of the rights of the former owners and hereditary proprietors, when the state wanted to assign, not land revenue but land itself, in villages where it possessed none of its own.[2]

Some records, however, supply still more convincing evidence on the point. Thus the emperor Amoghavarsha of the Deccan (*c.* 850 A.D.) is seen donating the village of Taleyur and also a flower garden, 500 × 150 cubits in dimension, *situated in the same village.*[3] King Govindachandra of the U.P. (*c.* 1150 A. D.) is found giving the village of Lolisapāda *along with the field named Tiyayi situated in it.*[4] If the donation of a village had meant the transfer of the ownership of the entire land situated in it, it would not have been necessary to specify the further gift of certain gardens or fields in it.

We thus possess conclusive evidence to show that in the post-Buddhist period at any rate the ownership in cultivable lands was vested in private individuals ; the state could not interfere with it except for the non-payment of the land-tax. What is claimed from the average cultivator was thus not a land rent but a land tax.

Let us now proceed with our survey of taxation. Trade and industry had to bear their own burden like agriculture. Traders had first to pay octroi duties that were levied on most of the articles imported in the town or village at varying rates. The state justified these duties on the ground that it had to spend

1. For other instances of the gift of small pieces of land see, *I. A.*, IX. p. 103 (Andhradeśa, 3rd century *A. D.*) ; *E. I.*, III. pp. 260-62 (M. P., 9th century) ; *I. A.*, VI. p. 36 (Tamil country, 6th century) ; *E. I.*, VI. p. 56 (Mysore, 10th century) ; *I. A.*, VI. p. 203 (Gujarat, 13th century).

2. *S. I. I.*, III. p. 104-6

3. *E. I.*, VI. p. 29

4. *Ibid.* VII. pp. 203-4

considerably for the up-keep and protection of roads on which the merchandise was carried.[1] The duties were usually collected at the gate of the town or village by customs house officers usually as *śaulkika*.[2] They had to be paid sometimes in cash and somtetimes in kind according to the local usage. The rules in the Smṛitis suggest that the payment was usually in kind;[3] sometimes we come across inscriptions stating the actual quantity of ghee, oil, cotton, betel leaves etc., that was collected as customs dues in different places.[4] Cash collections also were not unknown, and they must have been usual in the case of the imports of gold, silver and jewels. Assignments in cash against the income of the toll houses, which we sometimes come across in inscriptions,[5] show that probably people had the option to pay the customs dues in cash as well, if they so liked.

Customs duties varied according to the commodities as in modern times. Manu recommends a 16 per cent duty on fuel, meat, honey, ghee, scents, medicines, flowers, vegetables earthen pots and leather goods.[6] The *Arthaśāstra*, however, recommends a lighter tariff of 4% to 5% on medicines, fuel, leather goods and earthen pots. Cotton stuff also paid the same duty, but wines and silken pieces were charged a higher duty varying from 6½% to 10%.[7] It is clear that the tariff differed from province to province and age to age according to the needs and policy of the different governments. There is ample epigraphical evidence to show that most of the articles mentioned in this connection by the Smṛitis had to pay the customs duty, though we are not usually informed about its incidence.[8]

1. मार्गसंस्काररक्षार्थं मार्गगेभ्यः फलं हरेत् । *Śukra*, IV. 2. 25
2. *I. A.*, XXV. p. 18 (Kumaon, 5th century); Sen, *Inscriptions from Bengal*, No. 1 (Bengal, 8th century).
3. आददीताथ षड्भागं द्रुमांसमधुसर्पिषाम् ।
गंधौषधिरसानां च पत्रमूलफलस्य च । *Manu*, VII. 131
Cf. also *Śukra*, IV. 2. 121; *Arthaśāstra*, II. 22
4. *E.I.*, III. p. 36
5. *E. I.*, I. No. 16
6. VII. 131-2
7. *Arthaśāstra*, II. 22
8. *E. I.*, I. p. 6; XV. p. 41

Kauṭilya recommends that commodities intended for religious ceremonies and Sanskāras like sacrifices, marriages etc., as also presents given to the bride, should be exempted from octroi duties (II, 21).

Jewellry intended for the Hindu and Buddha images could be also imported tax-free. There are some indications that priests and monks were sometimes not above the temptation to be in collusion with crafty traders, who would urge them to carry it with them and declare that it was intended for divine images.[1]

Along with the customs duty, we may refer here to the ferry tax that had to be paid for passengers, goods, cattle and carts. As a general rule it was a small impost.

In addition to the customs duties and ferry tax, trade had to bear some other burdens as well. Some states used to test and stamp weights and measures and charge a small free for the same.[2] A shop tax, which is to be rarely met with in Smṛitis, is frequently referred to in inscriptions. It existed in the Deccan under the Yādavas;[3] its rate in South India was six *paṇams* per annum under the Pāṇḍyas and two *vimośpakas* per month under the Gurjara-Pratīhāras.[4] It appears that it was a small impost levied upon shops in small villages and towns. The 10% tax on sale proceeds referred to by Megasthenese is unknown to the *Arthaśāstra* or the Smṛitis; very probably the Greek ambassador confounded the customs dues with the sales tax.

Let us now consider the taxes payable by industry. As far as petty artisans like smiths and carpenters wrere concerned, it appears that they were usually required to work one or two days a month for the state.[5] The Central Government usually transferred the right to receive the labour tax to the local bodies which could utilise it in carrying out their schemes of works

1. *Śramaṇeraṭikā*, Chap. II (unpublished)
2. *Arthaśāstra*, Bk. II. Chap. 19
3. *I. A*, XII. p. 127
4. *E. I.*, III. No. 36
5. Earlier authorities like Manu (VII. 138) and Vishṇu (III. 32) prescribe the monthly liability of one day only; later ones like Śukra double the number of days.

of public utility. Inscriptions refer to this tax as *kārukara*, 'the tax on artisans'. It may have also included small imposts realised from barbers, washermen, goldsmiths and potters.

Weavers used to pay a tax of 1½ *paṇam* per loom under the Vijayanagar administration;[1] it is not unlikely that a similar cess might have been levied upon them in earlier centuries as well.

Trade in wine was under strict state control. It was manufactured partly in state distilleries and partly by private agency; the wine prepared by the latter had to pay an excise duty of 5%.[2]

All mines were regarded as state property. Some of them were worked by the government, but others were often leased out as well. When such was the case, the lessee had to pay a fairly heavy excise duty. According to Śukra it was to be 50% in the case of gold and diamonds, 33⅓% in the case of silver and copper and 16 to 25 per cent in the case of other metals.[3] A two per cent tax on gold, mentioned in the Smṛitis,[4] is probably the customs duty and not the excise duty.

Excise duty was levied on salt. Salt deposits could be worked only by the state or its licensees. Copper plate grants donating villages usually invest the donee with the right to dig for salt and metals without the payment of any fee.[5]

Cattle breeding was an important trade, especially in earlier times, and it had to bear its own share of taxation. When Manu requires a cattle breeder to pay 2% of the herd as the tax,[6] he obviously thinks of the corpus of the herd. When Śukra imposes a duty of 6 to 12%, he probably refers to the increase in the herd effected during the year. Inscriptions on the other hand refer to a third method of taxation at a certain cash rate per head per cow, sheep or she-buffalo.[7]

1. *I M.P*, I. p. 50
2. *Arthaśāstra*, Bk. II. Chap. 25
3. IV. 2. 118-19
4. *Eg*., *Vishṇu*, III. 24
5. *Eg*., *I. A* XVIII. pp. 34-5
6. VII. 130
7. Under Vīrapāṇḍya (*c*. 1250 A. D.) a tax of one *paṇam* per annum was evied on 50 sheep or 10 cows or 5 buffalloes. *Paṇam* was probably a silver coin, equal to a six-anna piece.

Customs and excise duties, so far dealt with, are often referred to in inscriptions by a comprehensive term *bhūtopātta-pratyāya*,' a tax on what has come into existence (*bhūta*) *i.e.*, has been manufactured, and on what has been imported (*upātta*).[1] Some times the simple word *śulkika* is also used for the customs duties.[2]

Vishṭi or forced unpaid labour was fairly common in ancient times. Poor people could afford to pay a tax neither in cash nor in kind, but it was felt that they also should pay something to the state in return for the protection they got from it. This they could do most conveniently by offering free service to the state. They were not usually employed all through the month and it was therefore felt that it would be but equitable to require them to work for the state free for one or two days in the month.[3] The state was of course to feed them during this period.[4]

The state could usually utilise its right to this free service only during the visit of its officers on tour in the moffusil.[5] Otherwise it would authorise the local bodies to exact this labour on its behalf in order to carry out their public works programmes.

Forced labour is always an unpopular liability. Yuan Chwang found it non-existent in some places and sparingly exacted in others.[6] The visits of inspecting officers were not every-day events ; the right to free labour therefore eventually benefited the village communities themselves, as it enabled them to get the help and cooperation of a number of labourers, carpenters and smiths in building and repairing roads, rest-houses and tanks.

1. *E. I.*, VI. p. 29; *I. A.*, XII. p. 161; Vol. V. p. 150; Altekar, *Rāshṭrakūṭas*, pp. 228-9
2. *I. A.*, XII. p. 264 ; XVI. p. 24
3. *Gautama*, II. 1. 31 ; *Manu*, VII. 138 and *Vishṇu*, III. 32 prescribe only one day's free labour, while Śukra lays down two days' liability
4. भक्तं च तेभ्यो दद्यात् । *G. D. S.*, II. 1. 35
5. *Skandhaka* tax mentioned in some northern Indian inscriptions probably refers to the liability of labourers to carry the luggage of the touring officers upon their shoulders, see *E. I.*, III. p. 266
6. Watters, I. p. 176

It would be convenient to refer here to certain contributions which villagers had to make when inspecting officers or members of the police force visited the village on duty. They had to be provided with free boarding and lodging out of the subscriptions raised for the purpose.[1] Fodder had to be supplied to their horses. Relays of draught animals had also to be provided to enable them to reach the next destination.[2]

Apart from the usual taxation, the state was naturally empowered to levy extra cesses to meet unforeseen calamities, or to finance costly works of public utility, or to carry out its plans of ambitious expansion. The *Mahābhārata* is reluctant to sanction extra taxation even on such occasions, but it admits that there is often no alternative to it. It however urges the state to send out special messengers to the people to explain the gravity of the situation and to win their willing assent to the new taxation proposals.[3] The *Arthaśāstra* describes these extra contributions as *praṇayas* or benevolences and lays down that the farmers may be called upon to pay about 25% and merchants from 5 to 50% according to their circumstances.[4]

Epigraphs often refer to these benevolences and extra taxes. Rudradāman (*c.* 150 A.D.) proudly states that he carried out the huge project of the Sudarśana lake without troubling the people either with forced labour or benevolences. It is clear from this that extra levies were normal when such huge works were undertaken. Virarājendra is known to have levied a special tax of one *kalañju* of gold per *veli* to finance his war against the Chālukyas of Veṅgi.[5] The *turushka-daṇḍa*, which was levied by the Gāhaḍawālas throughout their kingdom, was a special tax, the proceeds of which were most probably intended to meet the cost of extra military forces and preparations to meet the danger of the Muslim invasions.[6]

1. राजसेवकानां वसतिदंडप्रयाणदंडौ न स्तः । *I. A.*, XIV. p. 319
2. Cf. अपारंपरगोबलीवर्दः । in Vākāṭaka plates.
3. XII. 87. 26-39
4. Bk. V. Chap. 2
5. *S. I. E. R.*, No. 520 of 1920
6. Eg., *E. I.*, XIV. p. 193

It would be convenient here to consider how far the taxation in ancient India was fair, equitable and reasonable in actual practice. The general principles, which most of the Smṛitis prescribe in this connection, are all very admirable, as we have shown already. But the question we have to answer is how far they were actually followed in practice. We have to point out that the data in this connection are very poor and meagre. Royal panegyrists naturally represent the subjects as happy, contented and prosperous ; on the other hand we often get clear evidence in literature and inscriptions to show that taxation very often pressed oppressively on the people. One Jātaka describes the pitiable condition of the people of a village, who had deserted their homesteads *en masse* to live in forests in order to escape the tyranny of the tax-gatherers.[1] King Lalitāditya of Kashmir is said to have recommended to his successors that they should tax the agriculturists so heavily that they should have with them corn just sufficient for the current year.[2] Under king Śaṅkaravarman of that kingdom we are told that the taxation was so heavy that people were left only with air to live upon.[3] Instances are on record of the agriculturists of some villages in Tanjore district giving up all cultivation as a protest against heavy taxation.[4] Under Kulottuṅga III, a feudatory of his imposed an unjust tax even on waste lands ; the protests of the Assembly were of no avail. Members of the village council were imprisoned for failure to pay the dues and were released only when the amount was paid by selling away some land of the Assembly.[5] Even the grantees of Brahmadeya villages often suffered from high-handedness and were made to stand in the sun or in water, and could get no relief against such ill-treatment.[6]

1. Vol. V. p. 98
2. *Rājataraṅgiṇī*, VI. 344 ff.
3. कायस्थप्रेरणादेतैर्देवेनाद्य प्रवर्तितैः ।
आयासैः श्वासशेषैव प्राणवृत्तिः शरीरिणाम् ॥ *Rājataraṅgiṇī*, V. 184
4. Nos. 96, 98 and 104 of 1897
5. No. 202 of 1912
6. No. 159 of 1895

We should not, however, attach any undue importance to these cases. Kashmir kings referred to above were exceptional tyrants ; Śaṅkarvarman, Diddā and Harsha were a class by themselves. The last mentioned king not only spoliated temple property, but also defiled and confiscated divine images. We cannot therefore regard these rulers as normal representatives of their order. As regards south India, we have hundreds of inscriptions detailing arrangements about the revenue collections. It is indeed surprising that we should have so few references to fiscal oppression. Most of the cases referred to above relate to the closing decades of the Chola dynasty, when there was a distinct deterioration in administration.

Evidence is available to show that people could successfully oppose the levy of unjust taxes and imposts imposed by the state. We get an instance of the Assemblies of some *nāḍus* in Tanjore district meeting and resolving that they will pay only legitimate dues and resist all other demands.[1] Another Assembly in Karnāṭak met and resolved that the taxation on cows and she-buffaloes was not sanctioned by the usage of the district since immemorial times and should not be therefore paid. The Assembly further specified the rates at which it was going to pay the land tax.[2] These records show how people often tried to declare and protect their rights against undue encroachments. They might not have been successful in their efforts, when kings were tyrannical and self-willed; but there can be no doubt that they had strength enough to press their claims successfully when kings and their officers were of the normal type. The absence of a popular body like the Vedic *samiti* at the centre during the first millennium of the Christian era no doubt tended to increase the number of oppressive demands from the centre ; but the village assemblies and their executives were usually strong enough to resist encroachments on their legitimate rights and interests.

Let us now proceed to consider the items of state revenue other than taxation. The important ones among these were

1. *S. I. E. R.*, Nos. 96, 98 and 104 of 1897
2. *E. C.*, X. Mb. 44 (a)

the income from state properties, the profits of the state industries and other similar undertakings, proceeds of fines and the tributes from feudatories. We shall now consider these one by one.

State property consisted of crown lands, waste lands, forests, mines, treasure-troves, natural tanks and reservoirs and it yielded considerable income. As shown already, the ownership in arable lands was vested in private owners in historic times, but their lands would often lapse to the state on account of the absence of heirs, or the non-payment of state taxes or the commission of heinous crimes involving forfeiture of property. In most villages, the states in ancient times, as in modern days, possessed their own detached pieces of arable land, which they cultivated either through temporary labourers or by leasing them out to private tenants. To supervise over the administrative arrangements of the state lands was the work of a special officer called *sītādhyaksha* in the *Arthaśāstra*. What his designation was in later times we do not know.

Waste-lands, being under nobody's occupation, were naturally regarded as state property. Steps were taken to induce enterprising persons to bring them under cultivation by by guaranteeing a total or partial exemption from the land tax for the first four or five years.[1] The administration of waste lands was often left to the local bodies ; in the Gupta administration their sale was usually effected with their consent and approval.[2] It appears that in South India the village assemblies not only administered these lands, but also claimed their ownership. We often find them selling or mortgaging common lands to tide over calamities like famines or floods.[3]

As in almost all times and climes, the ancient Indian state claimed ownership in mines and their products. When villages were granted, the donees were usually invested with the right to work all the mines that may have been situated within their boundaries. Mines always included salt deposits

1. *Arthaśāstra*, Bk. VI. Chap. 9
2. *E. I.*, XV. pp. 129 ff.
3. *S. I. E. R.*, No. 679 of 1898

and sometimes stone quarries as well.[1] They were an important source of income, if they happened to be of precious metals. How they were worked has been already explained in chapter IX, pp. 201-2.

The state claimed ownership in treasure troves also, either because it claimed to be the heir to heirless property or because it regarded them as similar in nature to the mineral yields, both being recovered from the bowels of the earth. If the treasure trove was discovered by a Brāhmaṇa, he was however allowed to take the whole of it ; in the case of other persons, the finder was naturally permitted to have one half of the find and the state would take the other half.

Forests were an important item of state property. A portion of them was reserved for breeding elephants, so important for the army. Another portion was reserved for the king's game. The remaining area was utilised for fuel and timber.[2] Their administration has been already described at p. 199.

Grants of only the Gāhaḍawāla dynasty invest the donee with the proprietary right in mango and *madhūka* trees.[3] It is however very doubtful whether the state ever claimed ownership in these trees growing on private lands. Probably mango and *madhūka* groves on waste lands are intended, as hinted by one record.[4]

We have shown already in Chap. IX (pp. 198-202) how the state in ancient India used to organise several industrial concerns. It used to have a weaving department to produce cloth. It had its own distilleries for manufacturing wines. It had its own slaughter houses and used to rear herds of sheep, buffaloes, goats, cows and elephants. It would often mint money for private individuals after charging a small fee. It would sometimes engage or license goldsmiths to manufacture silver and golden wares and ornaments for the public. It would hire

1. Cf. सपाषाणखनिः in a grant of Manthavadeva (U. P., 11th century) *I. A.*, XVIII., 234-5.

2. *Arthaśāstra*, Bk. Chaps. 1-2

3. *Eg.*, *I. A.*, XV. pp. 103-4

4. Cf. समधूकाम्रवाटिका in Chandravati plates, *E. I.*, XVI. p. 193

its boats for transporting the merchandise of private individuals and charge also a ferry tax for taking men, goods and cattle across the rivers. It would license and control gambling and prostitution. All these activities brought considerable income to the state treasury.

Tributes formed a considerable source of income in the budget of imperial states. Its amount however was uncertain ; it could be regularly received only as long as the feudatory kings were too weak to refuse it and the imperial army strong enough to enforce its payment.

Fines were naturally one of the items of state's income. It appears that petty fines imposed for small offences tried by village courts were usually assigned to the headman or to the village community. In the case of crimes tried in the state courts, the fines may have gone to the central treasury. The officer in charge of their collection was called *daśāparādhika* in the province of Kumaun.[1]

Ownerless and heirless property was naturally claimed by the state. At a time when widows were not recognised as heirs to their husbands' property, the state would take the whole of it, of course sanctioning a reasonable maintenance to the widows.[2] The recognition of widow as an heir adversely affected the state's interests ; we find many administrations refusing to countenance the reform down to the 12th century,[3] though it was advocated by jurists as early as the 3rd century A. D. The tax on persons dying without a son mentioned in some Chālukya and Yādava records[4] was no doubt a kind of compenstion claimed by the state for recognising the new right of the widow.

Let us now consider the items of ecpenditure in the state

1. *I. A*, XXV. p. 18

2. अदायिकं राजगामि . . . . . .
अन्यत्र ब्राह्मणात्किंतु राजा धर्मपरायणः ।
तत्स्त्रीणां जीवनं दद्यादेष धर्मः सनातनः ।। *Nāradasmṛiti*, XIII. 52

3. In Gujarat the right was not recognised till the 12th century ; see *Kumārapālabratibodha*, Act III

4. *I. A.*, XIX. p. 145 ; *E. I.*, III. No. 36 ; Pool *Kolhapoor*, p. 333

budget. We possess very little reliable information on this topic. Neither the *Mahābhārata* nor the early Smṛitis throw any light upon the point. Inscriptions and copperplates are also usually silent.

The *Arthaśāstra* is a little more helpful. It gives us different items of the state expenditure. They, however, mostly refer to the royal establishment and throw very little light on the moneys spent on the different state departments. It does not also tell us what percentage of the state income was spent on each item of expenditure included in the royal household. Kauṭilya also gives us the salaries of ministers and some other officers of his ideal State. But we do not know its income, and so can form no idea about the reasonableness of the emoluments received by different officers. It is further almost certain that states in ancient India usually paid their officers either by the grants of land or by the assignement of land taxes. Cash pay was rather an exception.

Śukra is the only writer who gives us some difinite idea of the percentage of the state income devoted to the different items. According to this authority the state income was to be spent as follows[1] :—

1.	Fighting forces (*balam*)	50%
2.	Charity and donations (*dānam*)	$8\frac{1}{3}$%
3.	People (*prakṛitayaḥ*)	$8\frac{1}{3}$%
4.	Civil administration (*adhikārinaḥ*)	$8\frac{1}{3}$%
5.	Privy purse (*ātmabhoga*)	$8\frac{1}{3}$%
6.	Reserve Fund (*kosha*)	$16\frac{2}{3}$%

Elsewhere (IV. 7. 24ff.), he gives us the budget of a feudatory having an income of 1,00,000 a year as follows :—

Privy purse	18,000 or 18%
Prakṛitis	3,600 or 3.6%
Lekhaka	1,200 or 1.2%
Queens and princes	3,600 or 3.6%
Scholars	2,400 or 2.4%
Army	48,000 or 48%

1. I., 316-7

Elephants, horses and guns	4,800 or 4.8.%
Reserve Fund	18,000 or 18.%

A comparison of the two budgets shows that the smaller a kingdom, the greater was the percentage of the state revenues spent on the king and his court and retenue. The percentage of the revenue spent on the works of public utility was small. It is possible to argue that the item Prakṛiti in the first budget may refer to the people in general, and might have thus covered the expenditure on the works of public welfare like the building of roads, digging of wells and tanks, maintenance of rest houses, etc. But the word has also the meaning of ministers and officers and the 16% revenue spent on Prakṛitis would then be the expenditure on the civil administration. At several places in his book, Śukra has used prakṛitis in the sense of ministers and officers and *praja* in the sense of people or subjects. Only the item charity (*dānam*) of the budget which included grants for *sattras* (poor houses), hospitals, monasteries and temples; catered for the works of public utility. The two last mentioned institutions used to run schools and hospitals in many cases.[1] The Brāhmaṇa donees of *agrahāra* villages also used to promote the cause of education and culture by imparting free education to deserving students.

The budget of the normal state provided an allotment of 8% for the social, cultural and nation-building activities of the state. But the actual amount spent was somewhat larger; for the amounts spent by the local bodies out of the revenues assigned to them by the Central Government are not included in the above budget.

According to Yuan Chwang (II, 176) Harsha spent 50% of the land revenue on general administration and fifty percent on rewards for high intellectual eminence and gifts to various sects. Even after making here some allowance for exaggeration, we may conclude that enlightened rulers used to spend much more than 8% on patronage of learning, Mathas, wells, rest houses, poor relief etc.

The privy purse at 8⅓% cannot be regarded as too high. 10% was the ideal that was placed before the rulers of the

1. Altekar, *Education in Ancient India*, (4th Ed.) pp. 104-144

Indian states by the British Government, and the Union Government has generally accepted it in its recent policy of mergers and unions.

The military expenditure at 50% of the central revenues is undoubtedly very high. From about 500 A. D. militarism was rampant and warfare common. If a state wanted to live and maintain its independence,, it had to spend heavily on its fighting forces. It must be, however, noted that every pie of this huge expenditure was spent within the country and that the heavy military budget went a long way not only in fostering martial spirit but also in indirectly encouraging trade and industry.

Reserve fund or treasury claimed $16\frac{2}{3}$% of the revenues. It has been observed by a number of Muslim authors how it was customary for Hindu rulers to have large treasures handed down by their predecessors, which they would touch only on very grave occasions. Public or state loans were unknown, and the state could tide over a crisis only if it had a rich treasury and full and overflowing granaries. The huge booties which Alaud-din and Malik Kafur obtained in the Deccan show that, as mentioned by Muslim historians, Hindu states used to set apart a large percentage of their revenues as reserve fund to be kept in their treasuries for the purpose of emergencies.

Treasuries in ancient Indian states were of two types, public and secret. The locality of the latter was known only to a select few and it could not be normally touched. At the time of the foundation of Vijayanagar, the Minister Vidyāraṇya is stared to have buried for the king a treasury consisting of 96 crores of Varāhas. The figure may be an exaggerated one but there can be no doubt that such treasuries did exist in most the ancient Indian states. The other type of the treasury may be conveniently called the public treasury, the contents of which were entered into the usual state documents and could be utilised at any time for normal current expenditure.

CHAPTER XIV

INTERSTATE RELATIONS

In a work primarily intended to describe the state and government organisation, problems connected with the interstate relations can be described only in their broad outlines. The subject divides itself into two parts : interstate relations in war and the same in peace. Further, we shall have to discuss separately the relations between sovereign states and their numerous feudatories.

We possess very little information about interstate relations of the Vedic period. States were still to a great extent tribal and for a long time they were engaged in subjugating the non-Aryans. Their mutual relations were therefore generally peaceful. Aryans, however began to become envious of one another owing to the difference in success achieved by the different tribes to which they belonged. We therefore sometimes find them fighting among themselves, often taking the help of non-Aryan chiefs. Such occasions, however, were few.

In the later Vedic period small Aryan tribes became fused into bigger territorial states. Their normal size, however, was still not very large. Most of the states, for instance, included in the 16 Janapadas of the early Buddhist works were not bigger than a Commissioner's Division of the modern time.

The status and prestige of the different states differed according to their resources and the leadership of their rulers. Titles like *svarāṭ*, *ekarāṭ*, *samrāṭ* and *adhirāṭ*, that were taken by the different rulers, indicate clearly a difference in status, but what exactly its nature was it is difficult to determine at present. Some of these rulers, e.g. *samrāṭs*, were probably enjoying a much higher status than the rest, but whether they were ruling as emperors over feudatories, we do not know. It is likely that the weaker states might have paid a tribute to the stronger ones.

The religion and culture of the later Vedic period placed the ideal of the emperorship before the Aryan king. The *aśvamedha* sacrifice was to be performed by one who wished to be the king of kings, and the *vājapeya* by one who wanted to become an emperor. This naturally introduced a principle of instability in the interstate relations. A *vijigīshu* or ambitious king could at any time launch a campaign of conquest. We should further note that there were no natural boundaries to separate a state, for instance, like Kauśāmbī from another like Kāśī or Kośala ; when one of them became strong , it was natural for it to seek expansion at the cost of its neighbours.

Smṛitis also declare that when a king feels that his army is strong and kingdom prosperous, and notices that the case is reverse with his opponents, he is at liberty to declare a war against them.[1] Surprise is often expressed that Smṛitis should have thus countenanced a war of unprovoked aggression. If, however, we look to the realities of the situation, we shall have to admit that all over the world states which have grown strong and powerful have been attacking their weaker neighbours in all ages, primarily because the latter were weak, though often they used to put forth spacious and philanthrophic motives for their action. Why did Akbar, Shahjahan and Aurangzeb attack the Sultans of the Deccan though they were their co-religionists? Why did the British declare war against the Marāthās in 1802? Simply because they felt that they were stronger than their opponents and could grab their territories. Why did the last two world wars break out? Simply because the different combatants felt that the time had come for the realisation of their visions of the world domination or for the defence of their empires. It is, therefore, no use to blame the Smṛiti writers for countenancing a course of conduct which is the order of the day in the international world even to-day.

Of course it is possible to argue that the Smṛitis and Nīti-writers should have been ahead of their age and advocated like Aśoka a total cessation of interstatal wars, at least for aggressive purposes. It is not, however, always easy to ascertain which state is the aggressor ; each party to the strife can

1. *E. g.*, *Manu*, VII. 171

put forth a plausible defence for its action. The ideal of total abandonment of war was too high to be realised, as we know from the efforts unsuccessfully made by Aśoka. The prevailing insecurity rendered it absolutely necessary that there should be a class in society powerful enough to defend it against aggression. The Kshatriya community supplied the band of fighters necessary for this purpose, which regarded it a disgrace to die on the bed.[1] War was its natural profession ; to taboo it would have left it without a calling. It was, therefore, but natural that Smṛitis should have felt themselves powerless to recommend an ideal inconsistent with Kshatriya life and too difficult of realisation, not only in ancient India but also in the modern world.

It would be, however, wrong to suppose that ancient Indian thinkers, while striving for harmony within the states, were indifferent for its realisation among the comity of nations. Almost all of them point out to the ambitious king that the appeal to the arms should be avoided as far as possbile;[2] an unrighteous war brings disgrace in this life and procures hell thereafter.[3] The protracted negotiations between the Kauravas and the Pāṇḍavas and the readiness of the latter to be content even with five villages, will show that wars were not declared in hot haste in ancient India.

The ancient Indian thinkers knew that war could not be altogether tabooed ; they therefore tried to minimise its chances by advocating a judicious balance of power among the different states with which the country was studded. The

1. अधर्मः क्षत्रियस्यैष यच्छय्यामरणं भवेत् । *Śukra*, IV. 7. 305

2. साम्ना दानेन भेदेन समस्तैरथवा पृथक् ।
विजेतुं प्रयतेतारीन्न युध्येत कदाचन ॥ Manu, VII. 198
नाशो भवति युद्धेन कदाचिदुभयोरपि ॥ *Kāmandaka*, IX. 11.
वर्जनीयं सदा युद्धं राज्यकामेन धीमता । *Mbh.* XII, 69. 23
जघन्यमाहुर्विजयं युद्धेन च नराधिप ॥ *Mbh.* XII. 94. 1

3. नाधर्मेण महीं जेतुं लिप्सेत पृथिवीपतिः ।
अधर्मविजयं लब्ध्वा को नु मन्येत भूमिपः ॥
अधर्मयुक्तो विजयो ह्यध्रुवोऽस्वर्ग्य एव च ॥ *Mbh.*, XII. 96. 1-3

well-known *maṇḍala* theory of the Smṛiti and Nīti writers is based upon this principle.[1]

The *maṇḍala* theory presupposes the division of the country into a number of small states and the presence of an ambitious conqueror, anxious to establish his hegemony over them. Both these assumptions were true of ancient Indian polity and they have not become antiquated even in the modern world, in spite of the presence of the United Nations Organisation. The theory lays down that the immediate neighbouring state in front should be assumed to be enemical. The enmity between France and Germany, between Poland and Russia, between China and Japan was largely due to their contiguity, which often caused conflicts of interests. The state which is the neighbour of one's neighbour is assumed to be a friendly ally. The temporary alliance between Germany and Russia in 1939 and between England and Poland in 1937 show the general truth of this assumption. Next to *ari* (enemy) and *mitra* (ally), *arimitra* (enemy's ally) *mitramitra* (one's ally's ally) and *arimitramitra* (enemy's ally's ally) will figure in the *maṇḍala*. All this follows the natural assumption of the probable enmity between neighbours. The kings in the front enumerated above are five in number.

The kings in the rear of the conqueror are given different names by the political writers, but their presumed relationship is similar. The immediate neighbour in the rear is called *pārshṇigrāha*, one who attacks in the rear, and the next one is called *ākranda* (ally in the rear) ; then come *pārshṇigrāhāsāra* (ally of the rearward enemy) and *ākarandāsāra* (an ally of the rearward ally). The kings in the rear are thus four in number.

There were however some kings who were not interested in these rivalries going on around them. A king who was contiguous to both the conqueror and his enemy and capable of helping both the kings whether united or disunited or of resisting either of them individually was called *madhyama* or indifferent. A king with similar potentialities, but not conti-

1. *Arthaśāstra*, Bk. VI. Chap. 2 ; *Kāmandaka*, VIII. 45 ff.

guous to the conqueror, his enemy or *madhyama*, was called *udāsīna*. The 12th member of the *maṇḍala* was the *vijigīshu* himself.

The twelve kings mentioned above were regarded as constituting the *maṇḍala* of kings. A monarch was advised to be watchful about their motives and movements in order to secure peace and safety for his dominion and if possible, its expansion, by a system of judicious alliances. The emphasis laid upon proper alliance brings to our mind the development in the contemporary world politics since the second world war, when each of the two blocks is seeking to strengthen its position by roping as many states as possible within its own sphere of influence.

Aśvamedha and Vājapeya sacrifices being prescribed by the Vedic religion, even the idealistic school of the political thinkers could not disapprove of an expedition of conquest; it, however, tried to humanise it as much as possible. The king, who was out for a *dharmavijaya*, was to remain content with the formal recognition of his suzerainty and the payment of a tribute by the conquered king;[1] he was not to annex his kingdom or disturb its administration. If the defeated king died in war, or if he was living but unwilling to continue on the throne, a suitable successor was to be installed in his place. If annexation became inevitable, the established laws and customs were to be respected and the new subjects were to be treated as kindly as the old ones.[2]

There is sufficient evidence to show that this policy was generally followed. In their expeditions of conquest, the Pāṇḍava heroes were content with submission and tribute ; there was

1. गृहीतप्रतिमुक्तस्य स धर्मविजयी नृपः।
श्रियं महेन्द्रनाथस्य जहार न तु मेदिनीम् ॥ *Raghu*, IV. 43
Kauṭilya however disapproves even the exaction of tribute in धर्मविजय ; cf. तेषामभ्यवपत्या धर्मविजयी तुष्यति । ...भूमिद्रव्यहरणेन लोभविजयी । पुत्रदारप्राणहरणेन असुरविजयी । XII. 1

2. स्थापयेत्तत्र तद्वंश्यं कुर्याच्च समयक्रियाम् । Manu, VII. 202
See also *Vishṇu*, III. 30 ; *Śukra*, IV. 7. 373 ; 397-98

no annexation. The Jātakas hardly know of any wars of annexations. When the king of Kośala invaded Kāśi, the minister of the latter kingdom said to his king, "Sir, you need not be afraid; there will be no molestation; your kingdom will continue to be yours; only you will have to submit to the suzerainty of the invader."[1] The Muslim travellers of the 8th and 9th centuries were also struck by this peculiarly human method of conquest that they saw in the Deccan. "When a king subdues a neighbouring state," says Sulaiman, "he places over it a prince belonging to the family of the fallen king, who carries on the government in the name of the conqueror. The inhabitants will not suffer it to be otherwise."[2]

The advice to refrain from annexation after conquest is easy to give but difficult to follow; a survey of the ancient Indian history, however, shows that it was more frequently followed than disregarded. We have very little authentic information about the internal condition of the Mauryan empire, but it is not unlikely that it left untouched the autonomy of the powerful republics of the Punjab and Rajputana. In the Gupta empire, there flourished a number of feudatories even in Magadha itself. The Nāga rulers, who were overthrown by Samudragupta, continued to serve as imperial officers of the government in the Doab. Samudragupta annexed the kingdoms of some kings, but their number was smaller than the number of those who were restored and allowed to rule in the feudatory capacity. The empire of Harsha also contained a number of feudatory states. The same was the case with the Pratīhāra empire of northern India. The Deccan kingdoms of the Sātavāhanas, the Chālukyas, the Rāshṭrakūṭas and the Yādavas had a large number of feudatories, who enjoyed considerable autonomy. *Digvijaya* being inevitable, it was possible only to strive for the preservation of the local autonomy

1. मा भायि महाराज नात्थि ते परिपथो तव रज्जं तवेव भविस्सति केवलं मनोजरञ्ञो वसवती होहि। *Jātakas*, V. p. 316; cf also p.-391

2. Elliot and Dowson, *History of India*, Vol. I, p. 7; see also *Account of China and India*, p 33

and culture of the conquered states. It cannot be denied that ancient India did succeed in doing this to a great extent. This success was partly due to the uniformity of culture and religion that prevailed in the states, temporarily at war with each other. Normally in peace time their relations were not embittered by religious or cultural divergences or animosities, and so the war did not spur the combatants to bring about the utter destruction of each other. Internal autonomy was easily conceded.

The usual causes for which states went to war with each other were :- (1) the desire to attain the imperial status, (2) the necessity of self-preservation, (3) the acquisition of more territories or tributes, (4) the restoration of the balance of power, (5) the retaliation for raids and (6) the rescue of oppressed populations. It will be seen that these are the normal cause of war in all times and climes. It is unnecessary to illustrate how these motives were at the bottom of the different wars in ancient India.

Interstate war being found inevitable in actual practice, ancient India thinkers tried further to mitigate its evils by recommending a high code of honour on the battlefield. It is doubtful whether this code governed the warfare of the Aryans with the *dasyus* in the Vedic period. Indra is represented as trampling them under his feet in the caves and the Vedic Aryans might have done the same. The Vedic literature also refers to the use of poisoned arrows in warfare.[1] The Smṛitis, however, are emphatic in condemning their use. They further lay down[2] that the enemy should not be struck unawares or when he is not properly armed and ready, or when he is at a disadvantage. Quarter must be given when asked ; prisoners were to be treated well and given medical treatment if necessary.[3]

We may well assume that these rules were actually followed in practice as long as the opposing states were evenly

1. *R. V.*, I. 117. 16 ; VI. 75. 15 ; *A. V.* VI. 6. 7
2. *Eg.*, *Manu*, VII. 90 ff.
3. भग्नशस्त्रो विपन्नश्च कृतज्ञो हतवाहनः ।
चिकित्स्यः स्यात्स्वविषये प्राप्यो वा स्वगृहं भवेत् ।
निर्व्रणश्च स मोक्तव्य एष धर्मः सनातनः । *Mbh.*, XII. 95. 13-14

matched and annexation did not follow the defeat. Megasthenes was surprised to notice that warfare in India did usually not interfere with the agricultural operations ; combatants on either side waging the conflict made carnage of each other, but allowed those engaged in agriculture to remain quite unmolested. Yuan Chwang was also struck by the fact that wars, though not infrequent, produced little harm to the country.

It seems that as long as annexations were rare, these humane rules of warfare were followed as a general rule. When, however, empires became the order of the day, and the feudal yoke became more and more oppressive, the desire for self-preservation naturally got the upper hand ; and all means began to be regarded as fair, which were likely to ensure self-preservation or victory. Kauṭilya gives the commonsense advice ; if a state has immense superiority over its opponent, it should follow the chivalrous code (*dharmayuddha*) ; otherwise it should have recourse to all methods of warfare, whether fair or foul.[1] The view of Bhīshma (*Mbh.* XII. 140) is the same. Śukra concurs with his two predecessors.[2] In the epic we find both Kauravas and Pāṇḍavas violating the rules of righteous warfare, when hard-pressed. In 1945, America used the atom bomb to ensure speedy victory and save the lives of half a million of her soldiers.

The rules of *kūṭayuddha* permitted attack at any time and under all circumstances; the enemy country was to be devastated, trees were to be cut, and crops and stores were to be burnt down ; civilians were to be taken into captivity. Many of these calamities occurred when Aśoka conquered and annexed Kaliṅga and we may well assume that they were to some extent inseparable from all warfare in the post-Christian period. Scores of medieval inscriptions from Karnāṭak refer to the practice of Kūṭayuddha at the time. *Mānasollāsa*, written in c. 1140 A. D., refers to several varities of the Kūṭayuddha. In Deśanāśaka warfare villages were burnt down; in Janāṅgachhedaka warfare enemy subjects were mutilated ; in Gograha warfare

1. बलविशिष्टः प्रकाशयुद्धमुपेयात् । विपर्यये कूटयुद्धम् । Bk. X. Chap. 3
2. धर्मयुद्धैः कूटयुद्धैर्हन्यादेव रिपुं सदा । I. 350

cattle were carried away; in Dhānyaharaṇa warfare, corn was plundered; in Bandigrāha warfare traders and wealthy men were imprisoned; in Sthānadāha warfare houses and palaces were burnt (II. 1038-82). There can, however, be no doubt that there was a constant effort made to follow the higher ideal as far as possbile; otherwise the high Rajput code of chivalry could not have survived till the medieval times.

It would not be out of place to point out that even the rules of *kūṭayuddha*, referred to above, will appear as humane when compared to the atrocities that disfigured the warfare in the Ancient Middle East. No ancient Indian king is known to have boasted of having built a wall with human skulls or having flayed the enemies and covered the city gates or fort-walls with their skins, as Thutmoses III and Asurnazerpal are known to have done.

There were definite rules about quarters to be given to the enemy. One who laid down arms and threw himself on the mercy of the conqueror was not to be slain, so also one who was wounded or fleeing away from the battlefield. Prisoners of war, if wounded, were to be treated by the army doctors. Among the Aryans they were usually not sold into slavery[1], but allowed to return home at the end of the war.[2]

There were also regular rules about the booty. Treasures, valuables, weapons, provisions, etc., belonging to the defeated king could be seized by the victor.[3] All immovable property belonging to private persons could be temporarily occupied and utilised.

We have very little information as to the intercourse between the two countries waging war with each other. Since we find passports necessary for foreigners entering the country in normal times, it is quite likely that all communications might have been stopped with the declaration of war. States must

1. म्लेच्छामानदोषः प्रजां विक्रेतुमाधातुं वा । *Arthaśāstra*, III. 13
The slave captured on the battlefield is, however, referred to by Nārada; he was, however, permitted to secure his release by offering a substitute.

2. *Agnipurāṇa*, Chap. 240

3. *Manu*, VII. 96-7; *Śukra*, IV. 7. 380

have naturally taken care to see that merchandise and provisions of their own country did not pass into the possession of the opponent to strengthen his fighting power. When, however, frontiers were extensive and administration inefficient, some amount of trade might have continued stealthily. There was blockade by sea and enemy ships were seized, as happened at Kalyan in the Śaka-Sātavāhana war.

Let us now pass on to consider the relations between sovereign states in time of peace. It is doubtful whether there were permanent resident embassies in vogue in ancient times. Megasthenes resided at the court of Chandragupta Maurya and Deimachos at that of Bindusāra. It is quite likely that the Mauryas might have sent their own ambassadors at the Seleukidan court, especially because the Buddhist missionaries had been dispatched there to preach *dharma*. We, however, do not know whether the Greek ambassadors lived for a few months or whether their embassies were permanent. Heliodorus was residing at Vidiśā, the capital of Mālwā, as the ambassador of Antialkidas, the Greek ruler of Taxila, but it is not unlikely that he might have stayed only for a few months and for a particular mission. The embassies were received at the court of Samudragupta form the king of Ceylon and at the court of Chālukya ruler Pulakeśin II (*c.* 630) from the king of Persia ; but they were for specific purposes only. The Indian embassies that went to China or Rome were also something like the modern missions of good will, making some presents to the kings concerned and requesting some commercial concessions. In Europe too regular permanent embassies started only late in the medieval period. The Sanskrit word for ambassador, *dūta*, literally means a messenger and suggests that he visited the foreign court for a particular purpose or mission. The instructions given to the *dūta* in the *Arthaśāstra* (Bk.I, chap.16) show that he was to reside in the foreign court only till he felt that there was still a possibility of his mission succeeding ; otherwise he was to return.

Heads of the missions sent to foreign countries were classified into three categories. *Nisṛishtārtha* ambassador was one who had the full powers of negotiations and *parimitārtha* was one who could not deviate from his instructions. *Śāsanahara-dūta* was merely to deliver the message and take back the reply ; he could not negotiate at all.[1] In ancient as in modern times, the ambassador was a licensed and open spy ; during his stay at the foreign court, he was to cultivate friendly relations with the officials with a view to get a clue to the real policy of the government. He was also to see that the terms of earlier treaties were observed by the king to whose court he was accrediated and also to impress upon him how his own king was very strong and had rich resources. He was to guage the general situation, estimate the state's resources in men and money and get a first hand information from his own spies about the condition of the defences and forts of the country. He was to send his reports home in a cipher code (*gūdhalekha*)[2].

The person of the ambassador was regarded as inviolable in ancient as in modern times. *Dūta* is a mere messenger, says the *Rāmayāṇa*, delivering his master's message, and so he should not be punished even if he is provoking.[3] The *Mahābhārata* declars that a king who kills an ambassador will go to hell along with all his ministers.[4] Even when hostilities start, the *dūta* and his entourage are not to be touched.[5] If, however, he misbehaved, he could be branded or disfigured, as was done by Rāvaṇa in the case of Māruti.

Even when occasional embassies were not on visit in a neighbouring state, spies were always at work to fish out useful information. Some of them lived in the guise of students and others in that of ascetics or merchants. Prostitutes and dancing girls were also extensively employed; many of them used to manage to get service as betel-bearers or umbrella bearers in the court and so manage to be nearest to the king with a view to find out what was passing in the innermost circles of government.

1. *Arthaśāstra*, Bk. I. Chap. 16
2. *Ibid.*
3. ब्रुवन्परार्थं परवान्न दूतो वधमर्हति ।
4. दूतस्य हंता निरयमाविशेत्सचिवैः सह ॥ X. 85. 26
5. *Nitiprakāśa*, VII. 64

There was free intercourse between neighbouring states in time of peace. Passports were of course necessary for entry, but when they were procured, further movements were unrestricted. Foreign merchants visiting the country regularly were not required to procure a passport for every visit. Suspicious looking persons were arrested at ports and were not allowed to proceed.[1] The state kept a watchful eye over the foreigners and noted their movements and actions carefullty with a view to find out whether they were functioning as spies. There was no restriction on the imports and exports of goods; of course the necessary customs duties had to be paid.

Ships that touched the harbours on their way elsewhere had to pay port dues. If they were weather-beaten or damaged, all facilities were offered to them for repairs and re-equipment.[2] Sometimes some states used to confiscate all articles on such ships, if they touched at places other than regular ports; but this practice was not usually approved. Kākatīya king Rudradeva claims the credit of having stamped out this practice.-

RELATIONS WITH FEUDATORIES

Feudatory or semi-independent states existed in large numbers in ancient India. We have seen already how the conqueror was expected not to annex the territories of a king defeated by him, but to allow his state an autonomous existence under his overlordship. This gave rise to a large number of feudatory states. Their number was further increased when the senior posts of Divisional or Provincial governors began to become hereditary and their incumbants began to be invested with the feudatory titles like *mahārāja*, *sāmanta*, *mahāsāmanta* or *maṇḍcaleśvara*. Under the Deccan administrations like those of the Yādavas or the Chālukyas, it becomes very difficult to state whether a particular *mahāmaṇḍaleśvara* was a real feudatory or a provincial viceroy with the feudatory's titles. The confusion becomes more confounded by the prac-

1. *Arthaśāstra*, Bk. II. Chap. 28
2. *Ibid.*
3. *E. I.* XII. p. 165

tice prevailing in several localities of appointing defeated feudatories as provincial officers in the empire of the conqueror.

Till recently some of the larger Indian feudatory states like those of Hyderabad, Baroda and Kolhapur had their own feudatories ; the same was the case in ancient India. Thus king Māṭrivishṇu of Eran (*c*. 480 A. D.) was a subordinate of king Suraśmichandra, who in his turn was a feudatory of the emperor Budhagupta.[1] In 813 A. D. Govinda III was the Rāshṭrakūṭa emperor ; his nephew Karkka was his feudatory, ruling over southern Gujarat and Sri-Budhavarsha of Salukika family was governing Siharikā 12 as a sub-feudatory, to which position he was raised by the younger brother of Karkka.[2] It will be thus seen that the feudatories could create their own sub-feudatories, probably with the previous permission of the emperor.

Naturally, therefore, the status and powers of the feudatories were not the same, a circumstance which reminds us of the Indian polity under the British rule in which the different Indian princes enjoyed different privileges. The important feudatories were entitled to the use of feudal throne, fly whisk, palanquin and elephants. They were also authorised to the use of five musical instruments, *śriṅga* (horn), *śaṅkha* (conch), *bherī* (drum) *jayaghaṇṭā* (bell of victory) and *tamaṭa* (?), a privilege that was guardedly conferred by the imperial power. They were usually styled as *mahārājas*, *sāmantas*, *mahāsāmantas*, or *maṇḍasleśvaras*.

Śukra (I. 183 ff.) gives an interesting account of the grades and incomes of the different feudatories. Lowest in the rung of the ladder, Sāmanta, had a revenue of a lakh of silver Karshas, roughly equal to Rs. 40,000 of modern days. Then came Māṇḍalika with a revenue of 10 lakhs, Rājā with a revenue of 20 lakhs, Mahārāja with a revenue of 50 lakhs, Samrāṭ with a revenue of a crore, Virāṭ with a revenue of 10 crores and Sārvabhauma with a revenue of 50 crores. The scheme seems to be a theoretical and ideal one ; it seems to be based more on the decimal calculations than on the realities of life. When terms like Virāṭ were in use, terms like Sāmanta and Māṇḍalika were non-exis-

1. *C. I. I.*, III. p. 89
2. *E. I.*, III. p. 53

tent, as also the currency in silver. Śukra's account however would give us sufficient evidence to show that several grades of feudatories existed with varying powers and incomes.

A representative of the imperial power stayed at the court of feudatory rulers to watch its interests. He exercised power of general control and supervision, similar to those of the Residents or Political Agents under the British rule. They were received, as merchant Sulaiman informs us, with profound respect due to the representatives of the imperial power. They had a large number of spies under them to detect whether the feudatory kings were contemplating sedition or revolt against the imperial power. The feudatories, on the other hand, used to appoint a representative of their own at the imperial court to keep themselves in touch with its latest trends and developments. Thus Bankeya, the feudatory governor of Banavāsi, had a representative of his named Gaṇapati at the court of the Rāshṭrakūṭa emperor Amoghavarsha I (*c.* 850 A. D.).[1]

The control, which the paramount power exercised, naturally varied with the status of the feudatory and its own capacity to check him. General obedience to imperial orders was expected and exacted. The feudatories were usually required to acknowledge their subordinate position in the official charters they issued by mentioning the name of the emperor first. They could not issue their coinage. Attendance at the imperial court was required not only on ceremonial occasions, but also at periodical intervals ; epigraphs and literary works usually describe the imperial courts as teaming with feudatories come to pay personal homage to the emperor. A regular tribute had to be paid ; sometimes it was sent to the imperial capital ; sometimes emperors used to collect it during their tours.[2] Special presents were also expected on the occasions of festivity in the imperial household like marriage or the birth of a son. The feudatories were also expected to offer their daughters in marriage, in case the emepror was inclined to wed them.

1. *E. I.*, VI. p. 33
2. *I. A.*, XI. p. 126

Under the Gupta administration kings, who had been reduced to the feudatory status after a conquest, used to be granted imperial charters regranting them their territories under such conditions as were agreed upon.[1] Whether such a procedure was followed under other administrations, we do not know.

As in medieval Europe, the feudatories had to supply a certain number of troops to their feudal lord to participate in his imperial campaigns. Kalachūri prince Soḍhadeva (*c.* 850 A.D.) participated in the Bengal campaign of his suzerain Mihira Bhoja;[2] Narasimha Chālukya (*c.* 910 A. D.) of southern Karnāṭak is seen fighting in U. P. against the Pratīhāra emperor Mahīpāla on behal of his overlord, the Rāshṭrakūṭa emperor Indra III.[3] The Chālukyas of Veṅgi had to supply forces to the Rāshṭrakūṭas in their wars against the Gaṅgas of Mysore during the 9th century. Nāgarasa, a feudatory of the Gaṅgas, had, at the bidding of his sovereign, to participate with his own forces in a feud between Ayyapadeva and Vīramahendra, wherein he lost his life.[4] Many such instances are known; the above are mere typical ones.

The measure of internal autonomy varied according to circumstances. Bigger feudatories like the Uchchakalpas, the Parivrājakas and the Varmans under the Guptas, the Gujarat branch rulers under the Rāshṭrakūṭas, and the Śilāhāra kings under the Chālukyas and the Yādavas enjoyed large amount of internal autonomy. Some of them like the Uchchakalpas do not even refer to the Imperial power in their land-grants; but this procedure was rather exceptional. Subject to the payment of a certain amount of tribute, they enjoyed full internal autonomy. They could create their own sub-feudatories and appoint their own officers. They could assign taxes, alienate villages and even sell them without any reference to the imperial power.[5]

1. Allahabad Pillar Inscription of Samudragupta
2. *E. I.*, XII. p. 101
3. *Rāshṭrakūṭas*, p. 265
4. *Ibid.*, pp. 91-4
5. *I. A.*, XIII. p. 136 ; *E. I.*, III. p. 310
The Uchchakalpa, Parivrājaka and Gujarat Rāshṭrakūṭa charters were usually issued without the sanction of the imperial power

How slender was the control which the proud feudatories were generally disposed to tolerate can be judged from the following extract from a letter of Akkham, the Lohana chief of Brahmanabad, to Chacha, who called upon him to recognise his sovereignty; 'I have never shown you opposition or quarrelled with you. Your letter of friendship was received and I was much exalted by it. Our friendship shall remain and no animosity shall arise. I will comply with your orders. You are at liberty to reside at any place within the territory of Brahmanabad. If you have resolved to go in any other direction, there is nobody to prevent you or molest you. I possess such power and influence that I can render you aid.[1]

Smaller feudatories naturally enjoyed far less freedom. Nārāyaṇa Mahārāja and Śatrughna Mahārāja, who were Vākāṭaka feudatories, Rudraṭa who was a feudatory of Vainyagupta, Paramagula, a subordinate ruler of Gaṅga king Śivamāra and Bhānuśakti, who owed allegiance to the Kadambas,—all felt the necessity of securing imperial sanction for alienating the revenues of some villages in their own states.[2] When Budhavarsha, a feudatory of the Rāshṭrakūṭa emperor Govinda III, desired to grant a village to counteract the evil influence of Saturn, he had to supplicate for the permission of his feudal lord.[3] Śaṅkaragaṇa, a feudatory of the Rāshṭrakūṭa emperor Dhruva, is seen to take the imperial permission when making a village grant.[4] The Kadambas also exercised a similar control over their feudatories. In the Gurjara Pratīhāra empire feudatories even in the distant provinces like Kathiawar had to take imperial permission for the alienation of land or land revenues, which was usually given through the resident Political Agents, who are often seen signing the copperplate charters on behalf of the imperial power.[5] The same practice prevailed also under the Paramāras[6] and was followed in the 7th century in Kashmir.[7]

1. Elliot and Dowson, I. p. 146
2. *C. I. I.*, III. p. 236; *I. H. Q.*, VI, p. 53; *E.C.*, X, Gd.47; *I.A.*, VI, pp.31-2
3. *I. A.*, XII. p. 15
4. *E. I.*, IX, p. 195
5. *E. I.*, IX. 9
6. *J. A. S. B.*, VII. pp. 736-9
7. *I. A.*, XIII. p.98

Third rate feudatories were subjected to still greater control and interference. Their feudal overlords and even the latter's premiers are often seen granting away villages in their kingdoms. Thus the Rāshṭrakūṭa emperor Kṛishṇa II gave a village in the jurisdiction of a Gujarat feudatory of his, king Chandragupta.[1] The Paramāra king Naravarmā gave twenty 'p oughs' of land in a village of his feudatory Rājyadeva.[2] A feudatory of the Chālukya emperor Someśvara is seen agreeing to pay five gold coins for a certain charity, because he was commanded to do so by the prime-minister of the Emperor.[3] Gaṅgadeva, a feudatory of the Paramāra king Jayavarman, is seen making a land grant at the dictate of his sovereign.[4]

Feudatories, who had rebelled and were defeated in war, were subjected to a number of indignities. Kumārapāla (*c.* 1150 A. D.) defeated and dethroned Vikramasiṁha, a feudatory of his, and put the former's nephew upon the throne.[5] Sometimes greater humiliations were in store for them ; they were often compelled to sweep the stables of the conqueror.[6] They had to surrender their treasures, horses and elephants as a punishment for their disloyalty. Often their states were taken over or annexed, usually for a short period.

If the Central Governement became weak, the feudatories used to become practically independent. During the decline of the Gurjara Pratīhāra empire, a number of its feudatories quietly assumed the imperial title *mahārājāhdirāja-parameśvara.*[7] They would discontinue mentioning the emperor's name in their charter, or refer to it only in a casual manner. Their tributes would become more and more irregular. The imperial power, having become weak, would require their military support, and they could dictate their own terms when giving it. Thus Rāmapāla of Bengal had to pay a heavy price for getting the support of his feudatories to win the throne. If

1. *E. I.*, I. p. 89
2. *P. R. A. S. I. W. C.*, 1920-1, p. 54 ; *Bhandarkar's List*, No. 180
3. *I. A.*, I. p. 141
4. *E. I.*, IX. pp. 120-3
5. *Kumārapālaprabandha*, p. 42
6. *E. I.*, XVIII. p. 248
7. *E. I.*, II. p. 193 ; III. pp. 261 7

there was a war of succession, their position would be still stronger; they could then take sides and try to put their own nominee on the throne, thus playing the role of the king-makers. On such occasions they could pay off their old scores by imposing their own terms on the new successors ; the latter could hardly get or expect the same obedience to his orders from the feudatories who were his erst-while benefactors. If the emperor was very weak, a war would start among the feudatories for succeeding to the imperial position. At the decline of the Chālukya power, the Yādavas , the Kalachūris and the Hoysalas started a race for the hegemony of the Deccan, in which the first mentioned power eventually succeeded. Such a phenomenon occurred towards the end of almost all the empires.

The policy to permit defeated kings to rule as feudatories no doubt protected vested interests and favoured local autonomy. But it also introduced a permanent element of instability in the body politic. Naturally the feudatories were always cherishing the hope of throwing the imperial yoke one day, and the imperial power had to keep a vigilant watch over their actions and intentions. It could not disarm them, because it needed their forces for its own purposes also. Very often the feudatory and the imperial power were in a state of armed neutrality ; the imperial power could maintain its position as long as it managed to keep a balance of power among its feudatories and its own effective hold over all of them. The consequences of this permanent condition of instability will be discussed in the course of the last chapter.

CHAPTER XV

HISTORICAL SURVEY OF ADMINISTRATIONS

PART I

FROM THE VEDIC TO THE MAURYAN AGE

During the course of the last fourteen chapters, we have described the conceptions and ideals of the ancient Indians about the state and its nature and functions and described the different branches of its administration. While dealing with the latter, we isolated the different parts of the administrative machinery like the king, the ministry, the secretariat, etc. and discussed their characteristic features and history in the different periods. This treatment must no doubt have enabled the reader to trace the origin and development of the different institutions and offices very clearly. It is, however, equally desirable that he should have the picture of the government machinery as a whole from age to age, so that he may understand the main administrative features and developments of the successive ages. In this and the next chapter, we therefore propose to survey the administration as a whole from age to age.

The student of ancient Indian institutions like the caste, the marriage, the Āśramas etc. has sufficiently ample material to trace their development from age to age. The same is not the case with the student of ancient Indian polity and administration. We can give a picture only in broad outlines of the government in the Vedic age. The developments that took place during the next thousand years or so are more or less concealed from our view owing to the lack of original sources,. When the curtain rises with the Mauryan period, we find a fully developed administration, undertaking a vast number of ministrant functions of the state. The different stages of development by which the state, which in Vedic age was performing only a few essential functions, began to undertake a number of ministrant activities, are more or less concealed from our view. The State machinery and administration, of which we get so full a picture in the Mauryan period, become stereotyped later and we can hardly notice much development and variation in later centuries.

SECTION I

ADMINISTRATION IN THE RIGVEDIC PERIOD

The State of the early Vedic period was a small one like the city states of ancient Greece, being hardly more extensive than a modern district. In most cases it was also tribal in origin; its residents were or believed themselves to be the descendants of some famous traditional ancestor like Yadu, Puru or Turvaśu. The governing class consisted of the patriarchs of the different families. A number of these families formed a *viś* or canton, presided over by a *viśpati*; and a number of *viśas* formed a *jana*, presided over by a *janapati* or king.

In the Aryan society kingship had evolved from the institution of the joint family, and like the head of the latter, it was usually hereditary. We have definite evidence upon the point in the *Ṛigveda*, where in some cases we can trace the line of succession for four generations; *e. g.* Vadhryaśva, Divodāsa, Pijanava and Sudās; Durgahaṇa, Girikshit, Purukutsa and Trasadasyu. There are a few traces of kingship being elective also; one passage in the *Ṛigveda* refers to *viśas* electing the king.[1] These cases however were rather the exception than the rule.

The *Ṛigveda* does not associate any divinity with the king. Nor is the king seen performing any public sacrifices for the state as a whole. The kingship in ancient India had no connection with the priesthood, as far as its origin is concerned. Nor is the king described anywhere as having any magical or medical powers. The Vedic king seems to have been the hereditary head of a council of *viśpatis*, and originally he owed his position to his qualities as a military leader. There were frequent wars with the non-Aryans; nor were the Aryan states

1. X. 124. 8; see *ante.*, p. 80

at peace with one another for a long time. The military leadership would single out a Viśpati for the leadership of the tribe and the post would tend to become hereditary in course of time. It is quite likely that when the heir was a child or incapable of military leadership, the choice might have fallen upon a senior relation or even a different person. These cases however must have been rare.

The Ṛigvedic king had the simple title *rājā* ; more ambitious titles like *adhirāṭ* and *samrāḷ* were unknown to the age. The king lived in a residence, probably built in mud and not very imposing. He wore glittering dress and golden ornaments, and had a respectable retinue. He is usually described as *gopā janasya* or the protector of the people. His other functions can be merely conjectured. Adjudication is nowhere referred to as his function ; it is not unlikely that the *sabhā* and the *samiti* were more concerned with the settlement of disputes than the king. The principle of self-help had an extensive scope at this time both in civil and criminal cases. Even for murder there was the system of the wergeld or blood money.

The main source of the king's income in time of peace was the income of the crown-lands and *bali* or gifts from the people, which were originally voluntary but subsequently became obligatory. In time of war, the king used to get a large share of the booty as also of the land conquered from the enemy.

The *Ṛigveda* mentions very few government officers ; only three of them are referred to, *senānī i.e.* general, *grāmaṇī i.e.* the village headman or military captain and *purohita i. e.* the royal priest. *Senānī* was the deputy commander of the military forces and went to the battle along with the king, leading the state troops which fought with arrows, spears and lances. It appears that the king and the nobles wore armours and rode in chariots, while the ordinary soldiers fought as foot soldiers. *Grāma* means both a village and a group; *grāmāṇī* might have been the headman of the village or a captain in the army. *Purohita* was no doubt mainly concerned with the sacrifices to be offered to gods. But his knowledge and skill were believed to be very valuable to gain victory ; he would acccompany the king in the battlefield to help the army by the spiritual force of his prayers and the mystic powers of his charms. The role of Viśvāmitra and Vasishṭha will give us an idea of the great influence that the priest exercised over the king.

As observed already, the king was originally a president of the council of peers or elders ; his powers were not extensive. There were two popular bodies in the Ṛigvedic age, *sabhā* and *samiti*, which exercised considerable control over the king. We have discussed their nature and functions already (pp. 141-4).

There is some evidence to show that a few of the Ṛigvedic states were republics. Their nature has been already indicated (pp. 116-7).

SECTION II

ADMINISTRATION IN THE PERIOD OF THE LATER SAṀHITĀS, BRĀHMAṆAS AND UPANISHADS

During the period of the Later Saṁhitās and Brāhmaṇas the size of the state increased considerably. There was amalgamation of tribes; the Kurus and the Pañchālas are known to have formed a federation and the same might have been done by some other tribes as well. The average kingdom at this period was probably of the size of a modern commissioner's division. Some kings of this period are styled as Mahārājas and Samrāṭs; a few are described as great conquerors, who celebrated their victories by performing sacrifices like Vājapeya and Aśvamedha. What precisely was the extent of their kingdom is difficult to state. It is unnecessary to observe that the state had long ceased to be a tribal one ; it was now everywhere territorial.

Traces of elective kingship occur in the *Atharvaveda*, as also in the *Śatapatha Brāhmaṇa*; but election disappeared in course of time as shown already(pp.80-81). In some cases, as in the case of the Sṛiñjaya family, the kingship was hereditary for as many as ten generations. It was but natural that the coronation ceremony (Rājasūya) should become elaborate and pompous.

The king was clad in ceremonial garments fit for his rank, was annointed by the priest and stepped on the tiger-skin to attain the invincible power. There was a chariot race, in which he came out successful, as also a mimic cattle raid.

KING AND MINISTRY

The growing power of the king is illustrated by the tendency to attribute divinity to him. In the *Atharvaveda* the king Parīkshit is described as a god among men and the *Śatapatha Brāhmaṇa* describes the king as the visible symbol of god Prajāpati himself. At the time of the coronation the priest made the king *adaṇḍya*, above ordinary punishment. The king still figured as the chief military leader ; the *Aitareya Brāhmaṇa* points out how Indra was elected as king among the gods because of his military leadership. The king's growing power is indicated by the description of the Vaiśya and Brāhmaṇa as liable to be expelled at will. Probably he controlled the land of the state and his crown estates became more extensive. He could rely upon regular taxation for the upkeep of his administration and could supplement it with occasional extra exactions ; the Vaiśya has been described as liable to be devoured i.e. taxed heavily. The king probably got a lion's share in the war booty. His judicial powers seem to have increased, especially with reference to criminal cases. The disappearance of the *sabhā* and the *samiti* removed an important check upon the royal power.

The government was getting more and more complex as is indicated by a large number of officers being referred to in this period. The king was assisted in the administration by a council of *ratnins* consisting partly of his relations, partly of courtiers and partly of the heads of the departments of the administration (see *ante*, pp. 161-2). Some of the latter like Saṁgrahītā and Bhāgadhuk appear to have corresponded with Adhyakshas like Sannidhātā and Samāhhartā of the later age mentioned in the *Arthśāastra*, II. 5-6. The commander-in-chief, the tax-collector, the treasurer, the chamberlain and the village headman are the principal officers that are mentioned in this period.

The charioteer and superintendent of dicing also belonged to the king's entourage.

A relatively extensive kingdom presupposes district and local officers, but very few of them are mentioned ; one of these is Grāmaṇī or the village headman and another is Sthapati, who is presumed to be a governor or chief judge.

Grāmaṇī was probably at the head of the village administration and exercised both civil and military functions. The post carried considerable prestige and is described to be the object of the highest ambition of a Vaiśya. The king exercised his powers over the village through the medium of the Grāmaṇī. The art of writing had not yet become common ; the king could establish contact with the villages either by personal tours or by sending messengers. The collection of the taxes must have been the function of the tax-gatherer and the treasurer must have stored and distributed them.

ROLE OF SABHĀ AND SAMITI

Sabhā and *samiti* continued to be powerful checks over the king to the end of the Atharvavedic period. The worst curse which the *Atharvaveda* can pronounce against a king is that his *samiti* may not agree with him. As the period advanced, both *samiti* and *sabhā* lost their importance owing to factors that cannot be easily understood now. They are hardly referred to in the Brāhmaṇa literature. We hardly come across any systematic discussion of the aims and ideals of the state. Incidental observations, however, enable us to know that like god Varuṇa, the king was expected to be *dhṛitavrata*, the upholder of law. He was also to promote the material and moral well-being of his subjects. The *Atharvaveda* (xx. 127) glorifies king Parīkshit because people thrived merrily in his kingdom ; every one felt safe and secure in his house and corn was plentiful.

Side by side with the monarchy, which was the prevailing type of the state, there also existed republics in this age. They were known as *vairājya* or kingless states. The republican assemblies probably consisted of the patriarchs and heads of *viśas*, who used to elect a president of their own. When this office became hereditary, kingship came into existence ; when it remained elective, the state continued to be republican.

Consolidation of the power of monarchy, the rise of different forms of the state like the Bhojya, Sāmrājya, Vairājya, etc. and the emergence of the republics may be regarded as the chief features of the age.

SECTION III

MAGADHA ADMINISTRATION BEFORE *c.* 320 B. C.

Magadha began gradually to expand its power and territory from the time of Bimbisāra, *c.* 520 B. C. Aṅga, Videha, Kāśī and Kośala were incorporated in Magadha by *c.* 450 B.C. At the time of the invasion of Alexander the Great, the whole of the Gangetic plain, consisting of the modern Uttara Pradesh, Bihar and Bengal, was under the Nanda suzerainty. How the administration of this fairly big empire was carried out is but imperfectly known. In the time of Bimbisāra and Ajātaśatru the provinces were usually under royal viceroys. The central government, however, used to keep direct contact with the villages ; for we hear of Bimbisāra convening a meeting of 80,000 village-headmen in his kingdom. The Nandas believed in the centralisation of the administration, as would appear from their titles Samrāṭ and Ekarāṭ. We may well presume that the Nanda empire was divided into provinces, and the latter into divisions and districts, as was the case later under the Mauryas. The high judicial, executive and military officers were known as Vohārika Mahāmātras, Sabbathaka Mahāmātras and Senānāyaka Mahāmātras respectively . The Nanda state was famous for its riches and was maintaining a fairly huge army consisting of 3,000 elephants, 20,000 cavalry and 2,00,000 infantry.

SECTION IV

THE MAURYAN ADMINISTRATION

We have seen above how we get only a very dim and fragmentary picture of the administration of the Vedic and post-Vedic periods. The case, however, is quite different with regard to the Mauryan administration. Here also the picture is far from complete ; we would have liked to have more light and information on a number of important administrative details, practices, institutions and offices. But when compared to the earlier and later periods, the historian has to admit with gratitude that the Mauryan sources enable him to give a remarkably satisfactory picture of the administration. This is mainly due to the richness of the original material available for utilisation. We have not only important indigenous contemporary sources like the *Arthaśāstra* of Kauṭilya and inscriptions of Aśoka but valuable though fragmentary accounts given by several Greek writers, some of whom had direct and first hand knowledge of the country and its government.

REPUBLICS

At the time of the invasion of Alexander the Great, there were a large number of republics in the Punjab, eastern U. P. and northern Bihar. We get only occasional references to them in the *Arthaśāstra*. It is not impossible that all these republics were integrated into the Mauryan empire, and that Kauṭilya's references are rather to what was the reality before the establishment of the new empire, of which he was the distinguished Chancellor. It is, however, more likely that several of the republics continued to exist as separate political units, but as feudatories of the new power. The provincial governors may have supervised over them as they did over feudatory kings. An account of their administration has already been given in Chapter VI.

MONARCHY

Monarchy was the prevailing form of government in the Mauryan period and it had become hereditary. There are no references to any election of kings in contemporary records, either indigenous or foreign. Usually the eldest son succeeded to the throne. Considerable care was taken to train him properly in the art of government and administration. He was well acquainted with the traditional culture as embodied in the

Vedic lore (*trayī*) ; but the *Arthaśāstra* emphasises that he should be an expert in economics (*vārtā*) and science of government (*daṇḍanīti*). For this purpose special effort was made to train him in drafting, public accounts and various military tactics and exercises. He was to attend upon elderly statesmen and imbibe from them their accumulated experience (I. 2). The *Arthaśāstra* and the *Mahābhārata* are particular about describing in detail the qualities that a king was to cultivate and the training he was to receive. It appears as if they were anxious that the head of the monarchical state, which was now becoming popular, should possess all the necessary qualities to make monarchy more acceptable to the people than the republic.

Kauṭilya (I. 21) and Megasthenes refer to the extremely busy daily time table of the king which permitted him hardly six hours rest at night. Only a small part of his time was spent in bath, meal and rest. Almost throughout the day he was busy either in receiving reporters and officers or in participating in the meeting of the ministry, or in surveying the military parades or in judging causes and suits. The *Arthaśāstra* recommends that above all a monarch should be quick in action and remarkable in energy (*adīrghasūtrī mahotsāhaḥ*). Aśoka tells us in his inscriptions that he never felt satisfied that he had done his utmost for his government (*nasti hi me toso utthanamhi, R. E. VI*) and instructs the official reporters to come to him even when he was dining or resting in order to report upon people's business. The Mauryan kings showed untiring energy in the prompt dispatch of official business ; this was one of the secrets of the success of the Mauryan administration.

The king was no doubt the fountain source of all governmental activity. The army and treasury, the keys to all power, were under his immediate control. He was guided by his council of ministers, but he could set aside its advice, if he deemed it necessary in the public interest. He could issue edicts prescribing a definite course of conduct, prohibiting slaughter of animals or announcing administrative innovations. Nevertheless the Mauryan emperors did not degenerate into selfish autocrats. They followed the advice of the *Arthaśāstra* and regarded the welfare and interest of their subjects as more important than their own.[1] Aśoka observes in one of his inscriptions that all his subjects were to him like his children and that his one anxiety was to promote their spiritual and temporal well-being.

There is no evidence to show that queens were taking any active part in the administration in the Mauryan and pre-Mauryan periods, as they began to do during the Gupta and post-Gupta periods.

The Mauryan king ruled over one of the biggest empires known to the contemporary times, and his court had naturally a pomp and grandeur of its own. The audience hall was a big structure, 150′×120′ in dimension, resting on tall, artistic and beautifully polished pillars. It was surrounded by tanks. The king had a strong body-guard and was protected by a platoon of 24 elephants when out on hunting or inspection. The royal procession on such occasions was majestic; attendants used to carry in their hands silver censors; they used to perfume with incense all the roads. The king was dressed in fine muslin embroidered with purple and gold. Naturally all precautions were taken to protect the person of the king, the roads being carefully guarded. In the palace also there were a number of secret and subterranian passages as a precaution against a sudden rising or attack.

MINISTRY

Ministry formed an important limb of the Mauryan body politic. The *Arthaśāstra* points out that it is as reasonable to expect an administration to function efficiently with king alone unaided by a ministry, as to expect a chariot to move on one wheel only (I. 3). The evidence of the *Mudrārākshasa* shows how very often the prime minister counted much more than the king. Tradition asserts that the great king Aśoka had to bow down before his ministers and stop his extravagant

1. प्रजासुखे सुखं राज्ञः प्रजानां च हिते हितम्।
नात्मप्रियं हितं राज्ञः प्रजानां तु प्रियं प्रियम्॥ 1. 19

charity to Buddhist Sangha and had eventually to content himself by presenting only half an Āmalaka fruit to it.

The political thinkers differed widely as to the strength of the ministry. The Mānava school recommended a ministry of 12, the Bārhaspatya of 16 and the Auśanas of 20. Kauṭilya was averse to lay down any rigid rule ; he recommends the appointment of as many ministers as may be necessary. His statement (I. 15) that a king with a small council lacks an important source of power and that Indra is called thousand-eyed because his council of ministers had a thousand members, would suggest that he was rather in favour of a large council. Secrecy of policies becomes difficult to maintain with such a large body. Kauṭilya therefore suggests (I. 11) that while the council may be large, normally speaking the king should consult only three or four ministers, whose portfolios may be connected with the topic under consideration. In the Mauryan administration very probably there was an inner cabinet of four or five persons, consisting of the Yuvarāja, Prime-minister, the Purohita, the Commander-in-Chief and the Treasurer.

It is rather strange that neither the *Arthaśāstra* nor the inscriptions of Aśoka give us an idea of the portfolios of the different ministers. It appears that the heads of the departments (*adhyakshas*) were not always differentiated from ministers ; hence probably the *Arthaśāstra* does not separately mention the ministerial prortfolios.

The ministry was in the charge of the entire administration. It was to initiate new policies and review the old ones, especially in the light of the resources available in men and money. The proper time and place for action was to be determined and steps were to be taken to meet all possible difficulties (*A. S.* I. 15). Kauṭilya is naturally particular that the Council of Ministers should be associated with all important formal functions. The king is advised to summon its members when, for instance, foreign ambassadors were to be received or formal durbars were to be held on auspicious or important occasions.

Ministers were to be personally present for the council meeting ; if one was unaviodably absent a letter was to be sent inviting his opinion. The council met at fixed intervals; if, however, there was an urgent matter, a special meeting could be held. Normally the opinion of the majority prevailed, if there was no unanimity. The king could, however, decide in favour of the minority view, if it was his conviction that it would be in the interest of the realm.[1]

From Aśoka's Rock Edict VI, it appears that the Council of Ministers continued its normal meetings even when the king was out on tour. In the absence of the king ministers often felt it difficult to pass final orders on difficult and delicate issues ; Aśoka had left instructions that they should be immediately reported to him for decision. Conversely the oral orders issued by the king on tour were sometimes passed in hurry, and they came to the Council for final recording; very often the Council would on such occasions respectfully suggest a variation in the proposed course or even its abandonment.[2]

It was also the duty of the central government to secure a uniformity of administration. Aśoka was particular to bring it about by issuing a number of edicts to guide the subordinate officers.

PROVINCIAL GOVERNMENT

The Mauryan empire covered a territory certainly as wide as India and Pakistan put together. It was naturally divided into a number of provinces; unfortunately the *Arthaśāstra* does not mention what they were. The Aśokan inscriptions refer to three viceroys stationed at Taxila, Tosali (in Kaliṅga) and Brahmagiri (in Mysore); Buddhist tradition refers to a fourth viceroy at Ujjayinī. A later Śaka inscription incidentally refers to a fifth viceroy with Girnar in Kathiawar as his headquarters. We may well presume that very probably there

1. अनासन्नैः सह मंत्रप्रेषणेन मंत्रयेत् । आत्ययिके कार्ये मंत्रिणो मंत्रिपरिषदं चाहूय ब्रूयात् । तत्र यद्भूयिष्ठाः कार्यसिद्धिकरं वा ब्रूयुस्तत्कुर्यात् । 1.15

2. Rock Edict VI

was a viceroy for Eastern Punjab and Northern U. P. with his capital at Ahichchhatra, another for Southern U. P. and Kośala with his capital at Kauśāmbī, a third for Telangana with his capital near Maski. Mahārāshṭra and Bengal were also probably under separate viceroys.

The viceroy at Brahmagiri is expressly described as a Kumāra or prince in the Aśokan inscriptions; Buddhist tradition mentions Aśoka and Kuṇāla as viceroys at Taxila and Ujjayinī. It is therefore clear that some important provinces had princes of the blood royal as their viceroys. The viceroy in Kathiawar under Chandragupta was a Vaiśya named Pushyagupta and the one under Aśoka was a Yavana (Parthian] named Tushāshpa. It is thus clear that some viceroys were commoners, but belonging to the official cadre. It is quite likely that some of the viceroys may have been selected from among the members of the ex-ruling families or of the executive councils of the Punjab and Sindh republics.

Like the king, the provincial viceroy was also assisted by a council of ministers. The people of Taxila, who had risen in rebellion, pleaded in extenuation that they were not at all disloyal to the king-emperor ; only they could not tolerate the tyranny of the local ministerial clique. In Brahmagiri edict of Aśoka, the wishes of the emperor are communicated to the local administration at Isila not through the Prince-viceroy alone but through the Prince-viceroy-in-Council. Aśoka addressed his second Kaliṅga edict to the Prince-viceroy and the Mahāmātras, who formed his council. We may, therefore, well conclude that the provincial viceroys of the Mauryan empire were generally assisted by a council of ministers, who were of the status of the Mahāmātras.

The precise work of the provincial government has not been expressly described, but it will not be difficult to conjecture about its nature. It had to maintain law and order, collect the taxes for the central government, cooperate in the work of its different departments and keep a watch over the feudatories and frontier people. It reported the general situation to the centre and received instructions from the latter, which it used to transmit to the district headquarters, as was done by the viceroy at Suvarṇagiri. What amount of local autonomy was enjoyed by the provinces is not disclosed by the available evidence.

DIVISIONS, DISTRICTS, CITIES AND VILLAGES

Provinces were subdivided into Divisions and the latter into Districts. The officers over the former were probably known as Prādeśikas and those over the latter as Rajjukas[1]. Both were assisted by a large number of subordinate officers known as Yutas or Yuktas. The Prādeśikas of the Aśokan inscriptions appear to be the same as the Pradeshṭāraḥ of the *Arthaśāstra*, who were directly responsible to the Samahartā and were to supervise the work of the superintendents of the various departments, probably within their own territorial spheres.[2]

The Pradeshṭṛi was charged with the executive, revenue and judicial functions. Whether he was assisted by any advisory council, official or popular, we do not know.

Pillar edict IV gives us a vivid idea of the duties and responsibilities of the Rajjukas. They were appointed over many hundred thousands of people; obviously their charge must have been at least as large as that of a district. Originally they were revenue officers, but they exercised judicial functions also. Aśoka had granted them greater freedom both in investigation of crimes and their punishment. They could also grant remission in punishment in deserving cases. They were to devote themselves to the welfare and happiness of the people in their charge and to confer favours upon them. The position of the Rajjukas was to a great extent similar to that of the collector in the modern administration. They had to collect the land-revenue, maintain proper roads, promote trade and industry and carry out public works like roads and irrigation. It would appear from the Sarnath, the Rupanath and the Brah-

1. Rock edict III mentions Yuktas, Rajjukas and Prādeśikas in the ascending order; so Prādeśikas seem to be superior to Rajjukas.

2. *A. S.* IV. 9

magiri records that Āhāra was the name of the territorial division corresponding to the modern district in charge of the Rajjuka.

The district was subdivided into a Sthānīya usually compressing of about 800 villages. Each of the latter consisted of two Droṇamukhas having 400 villages each. The next territorial division was Khārvaṭika consisting of 200 villages. The latter consisted of 20 Saṅgrahaṇas each having 10 villages.[1] The head of these divisions exercised the revenue, the judicial and executive functions. The officers of the subordinate grades working under them were known as Yuktas. The officer over Saṅgrahaṇa, who supervised ten villages, was called Gopa (*A S.*, II. 35).

Greek historians refer to a number of cities in the Punjab which were governed by their own magistrates. They are called Nāgarakas in the *Arthaśāstra* and *Nagalaviyohālakas* in Aśoka's inscriptions. They were exercising executive, revenue and judicial functions. They had to keep a watch over inns, *serais* and places of entertainments, especially to find out the arrival of foreigners and persons of bad character. Superintendents of trade and commerce, weights and measures worked under them. Stringent action was taken against persons committing nuisance, throwing rubbish on roads, or helping the outbreak of fire by their negligent action.[2] For administrative purposes, cities were divided into a number of wards. The city had its own court of justice, where the judge was assisted by a number of non-official jurors. In some big cities like Pāṭaliputra, the City Superintendent was, according to Megasthenes, assisted by a board of thirty members divided into five sub-committees, whose functions have been already described earlier p. 223. Some cities like Taxila, Tripuri and Ujjayini enjoyed the privilege of issuing their own coins, a number of which have been discovered.

Cities were well protected by moats and fortifications. The moat round Pāṭaliputra, the capital, was 600 feet wide

1. *A. S.*, II. 1
2. *A. S.*, II. 36

and 30 feet deep ; the water of the Śoṇa was made to flow through it. There was a palisade surrounding the city with 64 gates and 570 towers. Towers were 75 yards apart and the archers posted in them could effectively prevent a hostile force from attacking the city at any intervening point.

The village administration was under a Grāmaṇī or headman assisted by an informal council of village elders (*gramavriddhās*). The office work was done by the Gopa, who used to keep careful records about the numbers of the houses and their inmates, the extent, boundary and ownership of fields and gardens, crops grown upon them, the taxes due from them and the condition of roads, water courses, inns, temples, etc. Village elders used to settle petty civil disputes ; others were decided by a court consisting of three officials and three jurors.[1]

DEPARTMENTS OF GOVERNMENT

We shall now consider the different departments of the Mauryan administration. The second book of the *Arthaśāstra* supplies us valuable data upon the point.

Palace department was under the charge of a controller who looked after the needs of the royal household. He had to pay special attention to the kitchen to see that no poisoning was done. Gardens and pleasure canals, furniture and decorations also engaged his attention. There was Dauvārika or Chamberlain who issued passports and controlled entrance and exit. A special bodyguard was always in attendance to ensure the safety of the king's person.

Army department was an extensive one, as the fighting forces of the Mauryan government consisted of 6,00,000 infantry, 30,000 cavalry and 9,000 elephants. The *Arthaśāstra* refers to the camel and ass corps also (IX. 11). Apart from these fighting forces, the army must have had a huge compliment of labourers, transport workers, scouts and sappers and miners. The ambulance corps with doctors carrying their medicines and surgeons their instruments helped by bands

1. *A. S.* II. 35

of nurses carrying balms and bandages is also referred to by Kauṭilya (X. 3).

Soldiers were recruited partly from hereditary fighting classes, partly from the militias of guilds and partly from forest tribes. Some soldiers were professionals, willing to fight for any government which could engage their services. The military equipment for the ordinary soldier was bows and arrows, swords and spears, shields and armours.

The war chariot was drawn by four horses and carried six men. Two of these controlled the horses, two carried shields and two discharged arrows, usually standing on either side of the chariot (Curtius, VII. 14). The cavalry usually faught with lances; each horseman carried two lances and one bucler.

The infantry, the cavalry and the elephant force and the war chariots were welded into common units at the time of fighting. A Pādika commanded not only a force of 200 infantry, but also of 10 elephants, 10 chariots and 50 horsemen. According to Kauṭilya Senāpati was an officer over 10 Padikas and a Nāyaka over 10 Senāpatis (X. 6). Probably the designations of these officers may not have been uniform during the Mauryan period ; Kauṭilya himself uses the term Senāpati elsewhere (II. 33) in the sense of the commander-in-chief.

According to Megasthenes the administration of the army was controlled by a council of 30 members, divided into six boards in charge of Infantry, Cavalry, Chariots, War-elephants, Transport and Admiralty. The *Arthaśāstra* does not mention these boards but refers to several superintendents. One of these, Rathādhyaksha, was in the charge of the organisation and manufacture connected with war chariots, another named Hastyadhyaksha looked after the capture and training of the war elephants. Aśvādhyaksha supervised the organisation of cavalry. Fort commanders (Durgapālas) and armoury officers (Āyudhāgarādhyakshas) must obviously have worked under the military department. The same probably was the case with Antapālas (wardens of the marches), who had to watch the frontiers. The department of passport and spies must have worked in close cooperation with the military department and the foreign department. Ascetics, jugglers, bards, prostitutes, fortune-tellers etc., were employed as spies.

Foreign department must have been a very busy branch of administration under the Mauryas, who had to keep in touch with a large number of kingdoms in and outside India. Megasthenes was the Greek ambassador in the time of Chandragupta ; Daimachus came in the next reign. Chandragupta must have himself sent his own ambassadors to the court of Seleukos, but we have no definite information on the point. Aśoka is known to have sent religious missions to the kingdoms of Antiochus, Ptolemy, Antigonos, Magas and Alexander. We shall not be wrong in assuming that these religious missions must have been working in close cooperation with the political embassies. Full fledged ambassador was called *nisrishṭārtha-dūta* by Kauṭilya ; *Parimitārtha-dūta* could not go beyond his instructions in negotiations. *Sāsanāhara-dūta* was only a special messenger. The foreign policy was regarded as dictated by *lobhavijaya* when the enemy kingdom was annexed, as was the case with Kaliṅga. *Arthavijaya* policy permitted the imposition of an indemnity and *dharmavijaya* allowed merely the imposition of a nominal suzerainty. Officers in charge of foreigners, who registered them and looked after their comforts and needs when sick, must have worked under this department.

Revenue department was in charge of Samāhartā, who was naturally a very important officer. He supervised over the collection of all revenues, both in cash and kind, revenues from land, irrigation, customs, road cesses, shop tax, ferry tax, forests, mines, pastures, crown-lands, fees from craftsmen, etc. The land tax varied from 16 to 25%; the inhabitants of Lumbini were shown the concession of a tax at 12½% because the Buddha was born in the village.

It was the duty of the Samāhartā to arrange for the working of old mines and the prospecting of new ones. He arranged for the supply of labour and seeds for the crown lands and kept a record of rain fall. Treasury officer *Sannidhātā* worked in close co-operation with him. Grain, cash, precious metals like gold and silver, that were sent to the treasury in payment of government dues, were received by him and stored in carefully built and strong buildings (II. 5). He was to change old grain for new one, when the former showed signs of deterioration. Census of men and cattle, which used to be taken in the Mauryan administration, was probably organised by this department. It was the duty of one of its subordinate officers, the Gopa, to keep records of the number of villagers, cattle and fields in his charge.

Commerce and Industry was another big department of the Mauryan administration. It controlled retailed and wholesale prices of commodities and tried to ensure their steady supply through its market superintendents. It prohibited the entry of banned articles. Products of state industries were offered by it to the market. It controlled and checked weights and measures in order to prevent frauds upon the public. It levied the usual customs duties and granted exemption for articles intended for temples, sacrifices, marriages, and deliveries. It had a big spinning and weaving establishment, which distributed cotton to people and collected the yarn from them. Breweries, both state and private, were under its control and supervision through the *surādhyakshas*. It supervised the slaughter houses. Harbours were under its management, and arrangements were made to offer asylums to weather-worn ships. River traffic also was under its control. Superintendent of mint probably worked under the direction of this department. He was in charge of issuing the copper and silver punch-marked coins, which were the state currency of the Mauryan empire.

Law department was in charge of the administration of justice. Civil courts described as *dharmasthīyas* by Kauṭilya, decided cases relating to contracts, agreements, gifts, sales, marriages, inheritance, boundary disputes. etc. Criminal courts called *kaṇṭakaśodhanas* used to entertain cases of thefts, robbery, murder, sex offences, etc. The supreme court was at the capital presided over by the king or the chief justice. There were subordinate courts at the headquarters of provinces, divisions and districts. *Dharmasthīya* courts were assisted by nonofficial juries also. The villages had in addition popular courts also which consisted of village elders ; they used to try minor cases.

Jails were probably under the management of this department. There used to be jail deliveries every year on the occasion of the anniversary of the royal coronation. Aśoka refers to 25 such deliveries in his Pillar Edict No. 5. Probably criminals guilty only of minor offences were released. Capital punishment was in vogue under Aśoka even after his conversion to Buddhism ; only the condemned criminals were given a respite of three days to perform religious ceremonies and give money in charity to secure welfare in the next life.

Purohita or the royal priest was the head of an important department. He was in charge of Vedic and Smārta sacrifices to be performed in the palace for the well-being and prosperity of the king and the kingdom. He was to take steps against possible calamities by using the charms prescribed in the *Atharvaveda*. The temples in the kingdom were under his supervision and the charity of the king was under his guidance. Dharmamahāmātras, whose posts were created by Aśoka in the 14th year of his reign, probably worked in co-operation with the Purohita. They tried to bring about harmony among the different sects, to promote morality and righteousness in the public, to establish a concord between masters and servants, to help the poor, the aged and the destitute, to offer succour to families of prisoners and secure their release, if possible.[1]

SUPERIOR SERVICES

The Mauryan administration with its so varied and multifarious activities must have required a big staff of civil servants. How was it recruited ? Diodorus, Strabo and Arrian agree with one another in stating that the administrative service was manned by councillors of state, who deliberated on public affairs. We are told that it was the smallest class looking to the numbers but the most respected one on account of the high character and wisdom of its members; from their ranks were the Advisors of the king taken, as also treasurers of the State and the arbiters who settled disputes. Arrian tells

1. Rock edicts 7 and 12 and Pillar edict VII

us that on account of their superior wisdom and justice, they enjoyed the privilege of choosing governors, chiefs of provinces, deputy-governors, superintendents of treasury, generals of the army, admirals of the navy, controllers and commissioners, who superintended agriculture (*India*, XI—12).

These councillors of the Greek historians were not members of any caste but corresponded to the class of the Amātyas of the *Arthaśāstra*, members of which were to be of noble extraction and high training, mature judgment and keen intellect, quick decision and remarkable energy, sterling integrity and unquestioned loyalty (I 5). The *Arthaśāstra* informs us that Mantrins or ministers were selected from among them,[1] as also all the members of the Adhyaksha class,[2] and the higher officers in the secretariat who drafted important documents.[3] The judicial officers in the moffiusil courts were also recruited from the Amātya class.[4] In one place Kauṭilya avers that *amātyavyasana* is a very serious one, because all important government activities proceed from them, e.g. successful carrying out of projects, protection against internal and external enemies, precautions against calamities, colonisation, recruiting of the army and collection of the revenue.[5] It is thus clear that the Amātyas of Kauṭilya were discharging most of the functions of the councillors of the Greek historians; their position was similar to that of the I. C. S. or I. A. S. officers who fill posts in most of the departments of Indian Government.

It appears that in Aśoka's time the senior Amātyas were called Mahāmātras, which term seems to be but a variation of Mahāmātyas. In the Aśokan administration Mahāmātras were members of the central[6] as well as provincial cabinets[7]

1. *A. S*, I. 5
2. अमात्यसंपदोपेता सर्वाध्यक्षाः शक्तितः कर्मसु नियोज्याः । II. 9
3. तस्मादमात्यसंपदोपेतो. . . . .लेखकः स्यात् । II. 10
4. धर्मस्थास्त्रयस्त्रयोऽमात्याः.......व्यवहारिकानर्थान्कुर्युः । III. 1
5. अमात्यमूलाः सर्वारंभाः । जनपदस्य सिद्धयः...व्यसनप्रतीकारः शून्यनिवेशोपचयो दण्डकरानुग्रहश्च: । VIII. 1
6. Rock edict, VI.
7. Separate Kalinga edict No. 2

heads of the district administration[1] and judges of the city court.[2] When appointed to promote religious harmony, piety and charities they were called Dharmamahāmātras, when charged with the work of frontier administration, they were called Antamahāmātras,[3] and when entrusted with the work of promoting the welfare of women, granting them relief when destitute or in child bed, they were called Strīadhyaksha-mahāmātras.[4] This last term would indicate that Adhyaksha and Mahāmātras were officers of the same cadre.

It is only in the case of the Mauryan administration that we have definite information about the salaries of officers. The *Arthaśāstra* V. 3 supplies us interesting information upon the point. The Prime Minister, the Chief priest, the Commander-in-chief and the Crown-Prince each received 4,000 Paṇas a month. The same allowance was given to the Crowned Queen, the Dowager Queen, the preceptor and the sacrificial priest. The chamberlain Dauvārika), the overseer over the harem, the revenue minister (Samāhartā) and the treasurer (*sannidhātā*) each received 2,000 Paṇas a month. Ordinary members of the ministry and superintendents of departments recieved 1,000 Paṇas a month. The army commandant (Nāyaka) and the warden of the marches received the same amount. Officers in charge of elephants, chariots and cavalry received $666\frac{2}{3}$ Paṇas a month. The foot soldier received $41\frac{2}{3}$ Paṇas a month.

There is some difference of opinion as to whether the Paṇas were the silver or copper coins. Most probably they were copper Paṇas. In that case the salary of the Prime-minister of 4,000 Paṇas in copper would be equal to 250 Paṇas in silver. Its purchasing power would be equal to that of Rs. 600. If we assume the Paṇas to be silver coins, then the equivalent of the salary of Prime Minister would be about Rs. 9,600.

The picture of the Mauryan administration as given above refers to the periods of all the great Mauryan emperors.

1. Brahmagiri edict.
2. Separate Kalinga Edict No. 1
3. Pillar edict I.
4. Rock edict XII.

It may not be out of place to draw attention here to the innovations introducted by Aśoka. He popularised the paternal theory of the Government and regarded his subjects as his children and officers as midwives. The king owes a debt to his subjects which he can pay off only by securing their moral and material welfare. His deep faith in non--violence made him adumbrate the theory of the renunciation of violence and war. It is interesting to note that even Jain kings like Mahāpadma Nanda had not tabooed war. Buddha had tried to stop it with varying success, but had not preached its formal abandonment in his sermons. Aśoka believed in the great importance of constant exertions both by the king and his officers and particularly exhorted the latter to undertake tours of inspection at fixed intervals of three or five years. This was probably to counteract the possible evil effects of the principle of decentralisation, which he had decided to follow when it was settled that the Rajjukas should be invested with greater powers in judicial matters. It is interesting to note that the principle of Ahimsā, which induced the emperor to abjure war, did not make him champion the cause of the abolition of the capital punishment. The only innovation he introduced was to give to the condemned criminal a respite of three days, which could be utilised for securing his spiritual welfare in the next world by making it possible for gifts being made on his behalf by his friends or relatives.

In order to carry out the policy of moral regeneration of his subjects he created a new class of officials, known as Dharmamahāmātras, who among other things were to preach Dharma during their tours and direct charity into proper channels. Moral welfare of the subjects alone did not satisfy Aśoka. He took active steps to build roads and rest houses, to dig wells and to organise hospitals. He regarded the animal world also as falling within the scope of royal duties and responsibilities. He therefore built veterinary hospitals also to relieve the sufferings of the animal world. He was a realist and therefore did not stop completely the slaughter of animals for food ; but he prohibited it on certain days of the months, which were regarded as holy by the Hindus and the Buddhists.

A WELFARE STATE

A survey of the nature and scope of the activities of the Mauryan state will show that it was largely a welfare state. It regarded itself as the trustee of the population as a whole and tried to harmonise the conflicting interests of its different classes. It tried to keep the scales even between the employer and employee by laying down that the former should pay the agreed wages even when no work was done, if it had to be stopped for no fault of the employee. On the other hand the labourer was punished if he neglected the work or committed theft or destroyed the raw material (III. 14). It protected the consumer by preventing merchant princes from cornering commodities and raising their prices. It regulated the prices of articles in the interest of the general consumer (II. 16), but while doing so, gave full consideration to the cost of the raw material and manufacture, and the toll and transport expenditure. Fraud on the customers was sought to be minimised by making the use of standardised and stamped weights and measures compulsory; traders using unauthorised measures were punished (II. 19). Merchants selling adulterated goods were also severely dealt with (VI. 2). The state, however, tried its best to help the traders and industrialists also by laying out roads, by ensuring the safety of traffic, and by constructing emporiums. Merchants were compensated for articles lost through any thefts in transit (VI. 13). The state no doubt took land tax, but it also financed irrigation works to help agriculture. It helped community projects by granting tax-exemption for four or five years to those villagers who constructed or repaired village dams, canals and roads. Material like timber and stone was also supplied free to the villagers for their works of public utility.

The Mauryan state recognised its responsibility to the destitute and diseased. It offered doles to the orphans, the aged and the infirm, as also to poor women in the family way (II. 1 . It also supplied work to persons in temporary difficulty; its spinning department supplied cotton to women whose guardians were away and later collected the yarn after paying for it (II. 23). Persons were not allowed to embrace asceticism without providing for their dependants; they were fined if they failed to maintain their children or minor brothers or sisters, when they were capable enough to do so (II. 1).

The welfare state of the Mauryan period paid full attention to public hygiene. Every house was to have a dunghill and an outlet for refuse water (III. 8); throwing of refuse or dirt or a carcass on the road was an offence (II. 36). It further safeguarded the health of the citizens by penalising adulteration of grains, oils, salts and medicines (IV. 2). It took adequate measures against epidemics. When a famine broke out, state granaries were utilised for providing relief and seeds; an extra taxation was imposed upon the rich in order to relieve the poor (IV. 3). Government agencies were alert against fires breaking out and tried to mitigate the damage of monsoon floods (IV. 3).

The moral welfare of the subjects was also a concern for the state; gambling, drinking and prostitution were under rigorous control. Literature and education were encouraged; articles required for sacrifices and temples were exempted from customs duties.

All these activities presupposed a full treasury. The state, therefore, was keen in increasing its resources by working mines, organising factories, developing forests and encouraging colonisation of waste lands. The state had, however, a mixed economy like the present Indian republic; for private enterprise was also allowed a large scope, of course, under the general regulations of the government.

An impartial observer will have to admit that the Mauryan administration was not only a very efficient and successful one, but also much in advance of its time. During the ancient Indian period, India was perhaps most efficiently administered under the Mauryas.

CHAPTER XVI

HISTORICAL SURVEY OF ADMINISTRATIONS: PART II : POST-MAURYAN PERIOD

SECTION I

THE DARK PERIOD, 200 B. C. TO 300 A. D.

We do not possess detailed information about the different kingdoms that flourished in India from *c.* 200 B. C. to 300 A. D., and so can give only a very imperfect picture of their administration. There were a number of Indian dynasties ruling at this time like the Ailas, the Śuṅgas, the Kaṇvas and the Sātavāhanas ; there were also foreign houses like those of the Indo-Greeks, the Indo-Scythians, the Indo-Parthians and the Kushāṇas. But the administrative structure of the latter did not differ in any vital and important points from that of the former. Foreign rulers came under the powerful influence of the Indian political thought ; Rudradāman, the 3rd ruler of the Scythian house of Western India had assiduously studied the Indian science of polity (*arthavidyā*); he asserts that his officials were possessing the necessary qualifications of *amātyas* (*amātyaguṇas*) and is proud to point out that he had refrained from the imposition of benevolences *praṇaya*) and forced labour (*vishṭi*). It is clear that though a foreigner, Rudradāman had completely assimilated Indian political theories and was anxious that his administrative structure should conform to the traditional Indian type.

The institutions of the foreigners had, however, some influence upon the Indian administrative usage. Chandragupta and Aśoka were content to call themselves mere Rājās ; the Mauryan queens like Chāruvākī were known as mere Rāṇīs ; Kanishka on the other hand styled himself as Mahārāja-

1. Kanishka of the Ara inscription had taken the title *kaīsora*, it did not become popular in India.

rājatirāja-devaputra.[1] Queens began to be called *agramahishīs* and *mahādevīs*. Hindu kings and queens did not adopt these titles during this period. The title *devaputra* shows how the theory of the divinity of the king was making a rapid progress under the Kushāṇa auspices ; the emperors of this dynasty started building temples at Mathurā in honour of their dead predecessors, following the Roman practice on the bank of the Tiber. Manu, who flourished during this period, describes the king as a great deity (*mahatī devatā*).

An interesting practice popularised by the Scythian rulers was the system of *dvairājya*. This practice was not unknown to the Hindu polity (see *ante* p. 38) but was rather rare. Under the Śakas and the Parthians, the king and the heir-apparent both ruled with almost equal powers. As instances of this *dvairājya* we may refer to the joint rule of Spalyrises and Azes, Hagāṇa and Hagāmasha, Gondopharnes and Gad and Kanishka II and Huvishka. Under the Western Kshatrapas, the father usually ruled as Mahākshatrapa simultaneously with his heir-apparent as Kshatrapa, both issuing coins in their own names. In the *dvairājya* administration, the junior member seems to have exercised greater powers than those conceded to Yuvarāja by the Hindu polity. Some queens like Nayanikā of the Sātavāhana dynasty used to act as regents during the minority of their sons.

The powers of the king were on the increase ; there was no revival of a popular assembly like the *samiti* of the Vedic period. In the centre, the power was vested in the king and the ministry, the latter being responsible only to the former. Ministers were known as *matisachivas* and *karmasachivas* under Rudradāman I. Among the specific ministers only the treasurer known as *Koshṭhtāgārika* or *Bhāṇḍāgārika*, figures in our records.[1] Others of course must have existed, though they do not figure in our records. The secretariat continued to function as in the earlier period and used to serve as the link between the Central Government on the one hand and Provincial and District administrations on the other. It received the reports from the latter, and after

E.I. XX.28 ; *Lüder's List*, No. 1141

considering them, used to communicate to them the decisions of the former.

The general machinery of the provincial, district and town administrations remained the same. The foreign rulers changed the designations or titles of some offices ; thus the provincial governor was called Kshatrapa or Mahākshtrapa under the Śakas and the Kushānas, the district officer probably as *meridarh* and the military commandant as *strategos* under the Greeks. These designations however did not become popular in India, for the foreign rulers themselves were being rapidly Indianised. Rudradāman, the 3rd ruler of the Śaka house in Western India, took pride in his ability to write elegant and chaste Sanskrit.

There was not much departure from the earlier tradition in the general administrative structure. Senior officials continued to be known as Mahāmātras and Rajjukas ; the Sātavāhanas had a Śramaṇa-mahāmātra at Nasik and the Rajjukas were working in Central India under the Śuṅgas and in Karnātak under the Chūtu Sātakarṇis.[2] The cadre of the Amātyas, corresponding to the present I. A. S., continued to supply high officers in the different departments of the administration. Ayama, the minister of Mahākshatrapa Nahapāṇa, was an Amātya, as also Kuplaipa, the viceroy of Gujarat under Rudradāman. Under the Sātavāhanas private secretaries to kings and treasures were also Amātyas.[5] The officers in charge of Govardhana and Māmala districts belonged to the same cadre.[6] The royal donor of the gift of a tank and monastery at Banavāsi had entrusted the work of the execution of her project to Amātya Khadasati, who probably belonged to the engineering department, as he is expressly described as the superintendent of works (*kammāntika*).[7] The Amātyas were as

1. *Lüder's List* No. 1144
2. *Ibid*, Nos. 416, 1195
3. *Ibid*, No. 1174
4. *Ibid*, No. 965
5. *Ibid*, No. 1141
6. *Ibid*, Nos. 1105, 1125
7. *Ibid*, No. 1186

ubiquiotous in the administration at this period as they were in the Mauryan age.

To return to territorial divisions, Rāshṭra or Deśa denoted the province and Āhāra or Vishaya the district. But sometimes these terms were used indiscriminately; thus *Sātavāhanī rāshṭra* was also called *Sātavāhanī-āhāra*. The chief officer over Rāshṭra was called Rāshṭrapati or Rāshṭrika ; he belonged to the cadre of the Amātyas. Sometimes, however, he used to belong to the military cadre, as was the case with Mahādaṇḍanāyaka Srīdhara, the governor of Mālwā under the Western Kshatrapas. The special designation of the district officers does not occur ; they are referred to merely as Amātyas to whose cadre they belonged. Sometimes however they were military officers, as was the case with Sātavāhanī-Āhāra at the end of the Sātavāhana rule.[1] It may however be noted that the members of the Amātya cadre also supplied military and naval officers under the Mauryas. Probably a certain amount of military training was compulsory for all the members of the Amātya service.

Grāma or village continued to be the smallest administrative unit; its headman was known as Grāmani, Grāmika, or Grāmeyaka or Grāmabhojaka. He was assisted in the administration by a council of elders, Grāma-mahattaras, as in the earlier period.

Bhāga (land tax), *śulka* (customs) and *bali* (extra impositions) are the main taxes referred to in the Junagad inscription of Rudradāman. They were paid in cash or kind. Benevolences (*praṇaya*) and forced labour (*vishṭi*) were resorted to by less scrupulous rulers. The army, the general administration and the royal household must have required the lion's share of the state revenues. There is however evidence to show that a considerable part of the state's income was spent on charity to temples and monasteries, help to learned men and the construction of the works of public utility. The extensive charities of Ushavadāta, the son-in-law of king Nahapāṇa, are a pointer in this direction.

1. Mykadoni Inscription, *E. I.*, XIV, 155

Republics reasserted themselves during this period on the downfall of the Mauryan dynasty. The evidence of the coinage show that the Kuṇindas, the Yaudheyas, the Arjunāyanas and the Mālavas became independent by *c.* 150 B. C. The central executive of the republic was however tending to become hereditary, especially during the times of stress and strain. The Nāndasā Yūpa inscription shows how the family of Śri-Soma, who succeeded in recovering the independence of Mālwā by overthrowing the power of the Western Kshatrapas, was at the helm of affairs at least for three generations.[1] In some cases the head of the republic used to have the title of the Mahārāja, as in the case of the Sanakānīkas in Central India. In other republics, as in the case of the Mālavas, though the headship had become hereditary, the royal title was not permitted. No republican president was however allowed to issue coins in his own name; the coin legends like *Malavānāṁ jayaḥ*, *Yaudheya-gaṇasya jayaḥ* show that the coinage was in the name of the republic and not in that of its head.

The above picture of the administrative machinery of the period, 200 B. C. to 300 A. D. is undoubtedly very incomplete, but it is so because it takes account of only those facts that are accidentally revealed by the short and often fragmentary inscriptions of the period. Unfortunately no ruler of the period issued administrative edicts like Aśoka; no writer of the age wrote a book like the *Arthaśāstra*; nor was the country visited by an inquisitive foreigner like Megasthenes, whose writings have been handed down to us. We may however well presume that under the bigger kingdoms of the period like those of the Śuṅgas, the Sātavāhanas and the Kushāṇas, the state discharged most of the ministrant functions referred to in the *Arthaśāstra* and had an administrative machinery almost as extensive and varied as that of the Mauryas.

SECTION II

THE ADMINISTRATION IN THE GUPTA AGE

We shall now survey the administrative structure in the Gupta

1. समुद्धृत्य पितृपैतामहीं धुरम् । Nandsa inscription, *E. I.* XXVII. p. 252.

period (*c.* 300 to 550 A. D.). Our account will be based mainly upon the Gupta inscriptions, but it will be supplemented here and there by the records of the contemporary dynasties as well.

REPUBLICS

Only a few republics lingered in the Gupta period in the Punjab and Rajputana. The principal ones among them were the Madras in the Central Punjab, the Kuṇindas in the Kangra valley, the Yaudheyas in the south-eastern Punjab, the Arjunāyanas in Agra-Jaipur tract and the Mālavas in Central Rajasthan. The Prārjunas, the Sanakānīksas, the Kākas and the Abhīras flourished in Central India ; they were very small in size. The Lichchhavis had probably a republican constitution, but it had almost glided into monarchy by *c.* 300 A. D. The head of the Sanakānīka republic had the title Mahārāja. The head of the Yaudheya republic also, who was its commander-in-chief as well, enjoyed the title of Mahārāja, but he was elected.[1] No republic of the age permitted its head to put his name or bust upon its coinage.

The republics completely disappear from our view after c. 400 A. D. The circumstances responsible for this development have been already explained before (pp. 137-8).

MONARCHY

Hereditary monarchy was the prevailing type of government during this period. The title Mahārājādhirāja adapted from the Kushāṇa title Rājātirāja, became well established during this period in the case of mighty rulers of northern India. Early Gupta kings like Gupta and Ghaṭotkcha were designated simply as Mahārājas ; from the time of Chandragupta I the higher title of Mahārājadhirāja began to be claimed. Early rulers in the Maukhari dynasty use the simple title Mahārāja; from the time of Iśānavarman, however, they adopt the grander epithet Mahārājādhirāja. In south India this title did not become very common ; it is on rare occasions that the Pallava kings

1. यौधेयगणपुरस्कृतस्य महाराजमहासेनापतेः । *C. I. I.* III. p. 252.

use the title Mahārājādhirāja or its variant *Dharmamahārājādhirāja.*

The doctrine of the divinity of the king became more popular in this period. Samudragupta is described as God come to live upon this earth,[1] and the Kadmaba and Sālaṅkyāyana rulers as fifth Lokapālas or divine protectors.[2] No king, however, could claim either infallibility or autocratic powers on account of their divinity. Smṛitis and inscriptions of this period emphasise that a king can become a successful ruler only if he waits upon the elders, studies the art of government and cultivates righteousness. Haughty, irreligious and tyrannical kings are held to public opprobrium in the records of our period.[3] Gupta inscriptions are silent about the nature of the training given to the prince, but the Kadamba inscriptions tell us how an ideal king was expected to have his body well built by various military exercises including riding horses and elephants, and his intellect sharpened and view-point liberalised by the study of different science.[4] The eldest son, trained on the above lines, was usually selected as Yuvarāja; on rare occasions the choice fell upon a younger son. Junior princes were usually appointed governors; thus Govindagupta, probably a younger brother of Kumāragupta I, was his governor in Mālwā. It was only on rare occasions that the kingdom was divided to accommodate the conflicting claims of contending princes. This probably happened in the case of the Gupta empire during the latter half of the 5th century and in the case of the Vākāṭaka kingdom after the death of emperor Pravarasena I *c.* 325 A. D. In both cases the consequences were far from beneficial.

In the Gupta administration, the Yuvarāja had his separate establishment, both civil and military. We may presume

1. लोकधाम्नो देवस्य, Allahabad *praśasti*, *C. I. I.* III. 8
2. *I. A.*, V. 15; *E. I.*, VIII. 234
3. आविर्भूतावलपैरविनयपटुभिर्लंघिताचारमार्गे
मोहादैदंयुगीनैरपशुभमतिभिः पीड्यमाना नरेन्द्रैः । *C. I. I.*, III. 146
4. अनेकशास्त्रार्थतत्वविज्ञानविवेचनविनिविष्टविशालोदरमतिः हस्त्यश्वारोहणप्रहरणादिषु व्यायामिकीषु भूमिषु यथावत्कृतश्रमः । *I. A.*, VII. 37

that he could issue orders to the heads of the provincial governments with the consent of the emperor. If the king was old, a good deal of the administrative work would fall upon the heir-apparent, as was the case towards the end of the reign of Kumāragupta I.

Queens and princesses do not seem to have taken any active part in the administration. Kumāradevī was probably a regnant queen, but does not seem to have taken any active part in the administration of her husband Chandragupta I. The same seems to have been the case with Dhruvadevī, the famous crowned queen of Chandragupta II. Dowager queens however were often assuming the reins of administration during the minority of their sons; the instance of Prabhāvatīguptā, the daughter of Chandragupta II and queen of the Vākāṭaka king Rudrasena II, is a well known one in our period.

POWERS OF THE KING

Kings were, as usual, the centre of all military, political, administrative and judicial powers. They no doubt governed with the assistance of a ministry, but the ultimate responsibility of a final decision rested with them. They were often their own commanders-in-chief and used to lead important military campaigns, as was done by Samudragupta, Chandragupta II and Skandagupta. All viceroys, governors and important military and civil officers were appointed by, and responsible to them. The secretariat at the capital worked under their personal direction and supervision, and the provincial governors and their officers were under their control and guidance. They distributed titles and favours in recognition of meritorious service or literary and artistic works of distinction. To all appearance, kings were thus almost autocratic rulers, but in reality the case was considerably different. They shared their powers with ministers and other high officers who, though not theoretically responsible to the people, were expected to control the king, if he was acting against the established laws and customs.[1] Large powers were also delegated to local bodies like the village Panchāyats and town councils, which became fairly efficient and powerful after *c.* 400 A. D. Almost all functions of the government, except that of determining foreign policy and declaring and terminating a war, were discharged through the agency of the local bodies, where the representatives of the locality had a powerful voice. No doubt, there was no central popular assembly like the modern parliament; nevertheless people did not suffer from the evil consequences of autocracy owing to the above delegation of large powers to the local bodies. Smṛitis and epigraphs of our period emphasise that a good king should be particularly careful in winning popularity among his subjects by respecting their wishes and promoting their welfare,[2] and there is every reason to believe that the rulers lived up to this ideal. The Chinese pilgrim Fa-hien seems to be paraphrasing the language of some of the inscriptions of our age when he describes how the people under the Gupta rule were virtuous, happy and prosperous, and had no occasions to complain against the autocracy or high handedness of the government.

CENTRAL GOVERNMENT.

The Gupta records throw very little light on the nature of the machinery of the Central Government. We may, however, well presume that it was under the general supervision of a Chief Secretary called Sarvādhykasha in the contemporary Pallava, Vākāṭaka and Kadamba administrations. The secretariat in the capital accommodated a number of departments. Each office had its own seal with which its communications were invariably stamped for authentication. We have discovered the seals of several officers like those of Kumārāmātyas, Daṇḍanāyakas, Balādhikaraṇikas, etc. The routine business was transacted by each minister on his own responsibility, but important matters were referred to the whole council presided

1. Purohita (chief priest), Senapati (eommander-in-chief), ministers, ambassadors and spies are referred to as constituting 'The Great Five-fold Group' in early Tamil literature, *Muduraikkanji*, II. 499, 510. They must obviously have exercised considerable influence over the king.

2. Cf. प्रजासंरंजनपरिपालनोद्योगसंततसत्रदीक्षितस्य । *I. A.*, V. 51
I. A., V, 51; see also *E. I.*, VII, 235

3. Cf. Legge: *A Record of Buddhist Kingdoms*, Chap. XVI with verses 6, 21-23 of the Junagadh inscription of Skandagupta, *C. I. I.*, III, 58. ff.

over by the king. Orders were issued by the government in writing. When on tour kings often used to pass oral orders, but they were noted by private secretaries on duty and communicated to the central secretariat for proper recording and appropriate action. The Gupta period term for private secretary Rahasi-niyukta looks like an exact translation of the corresponding English word. People seeking audience were ushered in by officers known as Pratīhāras or Mahāpratīhāras who were in charge of the court ceremonial.

The military department was the most important department under the direct charge of the king or the Yuvarāja. There were a large number of Mahāsenāpatis working under the king, probably posted in the different parts of the empire. Mahādaṇḍanāyaka, who belonged to the next lower grade, appears to have corresponded to the Lieutenant-General of the modern age. Daṇḍanāyakas were probably of the rank of colonels. The army had different quarter masters, (Raṇabhāṇḍāgārikas) and seals of some of them have been found. The fighting force was divided into infantry, cavalry and elephant corps; the officers of the latter two branches were known as Aśvapatis Mahāśvapatis, Pīlupatis, Mahāpīlupatis. Soldiers were provided with armours and fought with weapons like arrows, swords, battle axes, spears, etc. Our records do not refer to the ambulance corps, but it must have existed. The general structure of the military administration did not differ much from that of the Mauryan age.

The foreign minister figures in several Gupta records; he however appears under a new name Mahāsandhivigrahika, which is no doubt more majestic than the old title Dūta. He worked in close cooperation with the military department. He must have been the busiest minister in the early Gupta period when Samudragupta and Chandragupta were planning their campaigns in the north, the south and the west. Which kingdoms were to be annexed and which were to be permitted to remain in the feudatory status was to be determined by this department. Mahāsandhivigrahika had several Sandhivigrahikas under him to assist him in the work.

The designation of the head of the police department is not known. Daṇḍapāśikas, referred to in the seals from Vaiśāli, were probably officers of the police of the status of the modern police superintendents. Ordinary members of the police force were probably known as Chāṭa and Bhaṭa.

The Revenue department was in charge of the collection of taxes and revenues, which were paid partly in cash and partly in kind. The government had to maintain big granaries at several places. Forests and mines, which were state properties, were probably administered by the Revenue department. The administration of the waste lands, which also were owned by the state, was left in charge of the municipal boards or the village councils in whose jurisdiction they were situated.

The Judicial department is not mentioned in contemporary records, but its remarkable development during our period can be inferred by the evidence afforded by Smṛitis like those of Nārada and Bṛihaspati, written at about this time. Rules about plaints, written statements, relative importance of documentary and oral evidence, *res-judicata* etc., as disclosed in these works, are more developed and advanced than those in the *Arthaśāstra*. The Judicial department was presided over by the Chief Justice who was assisted by a number of city and town judges. The seals of the office of the Nyāyādhikaraṇa, Dharmādhikaraṇa and Dharmaśāsanādhikaraṇa that were found at Nālandā and Vaiśāli obviously belonged to the courts of these judges.

The Ecclesiastical department was in charge of another minister, probably called Purodhā or Paṇḍita. This officer does not figure in our records, but his subordinates Vinayasthitisthāpakas are known from their seals. They seem to have discharged functions similar to those of the Dharmamahāmātras of Aśoka, *viz.* regulation of public morals, supervision of charity and temples and promotion of education.

Trade and industry department was under another minister. He is not mentioned in our records, but his subordinate officers Drāṅgikas figure in contemporary inscriptions. This department was probably in charge of roads and rest-houses also.

SUPERIOR SERVICES

The Guptas had a superior civil service, corresponding to the I. C. S. and I. A. S. of the modern times. The members of this service were known as Kumārāmātyas. Scholars had once thought that Kumārāmātyas were ministers to the princes of the blood-royal, but a careful analysis of the epigraphical evidence shows that such was not the case. Harisheṇa, the foreign minister of Samudragupta, and Śikharasvāmin and Pṛithivīsheṇa, the ministers of Kumāragupta I, were working directly under the emperors, but are still described as Kumārāmātyas. District officers in Puṇḍravardhana were styled as Kumārāmātyas ; nay, sometimes they are seen to be the subordinates of Mahādaṇḍanāyakas also. It is clear that Kumārāmātyas worked sometimes as the district officers, sometimes as government secretaries and were often promoted to the posts of ministers and generals. They thus resembled the Amātyas of the Maurya and Sātavāhana administration who filled similar posts. Why the term Kumāra was prefixed to their designation in this period is difficult to understand. They were so called probably because they were Amātyas since their youth, i.e. since the time of joining service. They were thus members of a superior service since recruitment and corresponded to the officers of the I. C. S. and I. A. S. grades of the modern time. Seals refer to Yuvarājapadīya-Kumārāmātyas and Paramabhaṭṭārakapadīya-Kumārāmātyas; they seem to be the officers of this cadre attached to the office of the heir-apparent and the emperor. The designation Kumārāmātya became fairly popular ; we find the officers of this designation existing in Kathiawar under the Maitrakas of Valabhi and in some local dynasties of Orissa[1].

PROVINCIAL AND DISTRICT ADMINISTRATIONS

Provinces of the Gupta empire were known as Deśas[2] or Maṇḍalas. Three of these are referred to in our records, Surāshṭra, Mālwā and Antarvedī (the territory between the Yamunā and the Narmadā). We may well presume that Pañchāla, Kāśī,

1. *C. I. I.*, III. 165; *E. I.*, XXIII. 201; XI. 287.
2. Cf. सर्वेषु देशेषु विधाय गोप्तॄन् । *C. I. I.*, III. 66

Kośala, Magadha and Vaṅga may have been among the remaining provinces of the empire. The Junagad inscription of Skandagupta shows that the viceroys of the provinces were appointed by the emperor himself. They had to maintain law and order and protect their territory against outside attacks. They were to develop their provinces by constructing and repairing works of public utility like tanks and roads and strengthen the foundations of the empire by promoting public confidence by their good and efficient administration. They could appoint their subordinate officers. Probably they had branches of almost all the departments working at their centre. Whether they had provincial ministries as under the Mauryas, we do not know.

Provinces were divided into Bhuktis which appear to have comprised of two or three districts; the latter were called Vishayas. Puṇḍravardhana-bhukti included the districts of Bogra, Dinajpur and Rajashahi in northern Bengal, Magadha-bhukti of the districts of Gaya and Patna ; Tīra-bhukti included most of the Tirhut division of the present day. Bhuktis were in charge of officers known as Uparikas, who were appointed by and responsible to the emperor himself. They often had the title Mahārāja, probably when they were scions of the earlier ruling families. Vishayas were governed by Vishayapatis who were appointed sometimes by the Uparaikas, and sometimes by the emperor. Several sealings of the officers of the Vishayas and Bhuktis have been found, which had once sealed confidential despatches sent from their offices. It is difficult to state whether in the Gupta empire there were any administrative divisions intervening between the Vishaya and towns and villages comprised within it. They are not mentioned in Gupta inscriptions, but figure in later records. We have already seen that they existed in the the Mauryan administration. Their non-occurrence in Gupta records is probably accidental.

The subordinate staff of the district administration consisted of officers described as Yuktas, Niyuktaś, Vyāpṛitaś, and Adhi-

1. The first two of these designations were in use under the Mauryas also, as shown already.

kṛitas in our records; they served as links betwen the district and the village. Officers of the police, forest and trade departments probably worked under them.

There is ample evidence supplied by the Damodarpur plates to show that the office of the Vishayapati was well organised and used to keep careful records and files. The officer in charge of the records was called Pustapāla ; his records could show the precise dimensions of bands, both cultivated and uncultivated, situated within his jurisdiction. Even when waste lands were proposed to be sold by the central government, the district authorities had to be consulted. In some cases copper plates granting such lands bear the seals of the district administration as a proof of its concurrence.

NON-OFFICIAL DISTRICT COUNCILS

There was no body like the Central Parliament in the Gupta administration to voice the views of the people at the capital. But there is evidence to show that there were district councils to advise and assist the district administration ; this seems to have been an administrative innovation of the age. This council consisted of the chief banker, the chief trader, the chief artisan, the chief Kāyastha (writer) and several other members. The Faridpur plate III shows that the district council often consisted of about 20 members, some of whom like Kulasvāmin and Śubhadeva were Brāhmaṇas, some like Ghoshachandra and Guṇachandra were non-Brahmins. Members of this non-official council were called Vishayamahattaras. Seals of the councils of Vishaya-mahattaras have been found at Nālandā.

How the members of the Vishayamahattara council were selected or elected is not stated in the Gupta records. The terms Prathamaśresthin and Prathamasārthavāha suggest that very probably the guilds of the bankers and traders were represented by their presidents. As far as the remaining members of the council are concerned, it would appear that different classes were represented by those persons among them who had acquired a pre-eminent status by their age, experience and character.

THE VILLAGE AND TOWN ADMINISTRATION

The village administration was in charge of a headman designated as a Grāmeyaka or a Grāmādhyaksha. He had a clerk to work under him to keep the records. The headman was assisted in his work by a non-official council. The members of this body were known as Mahattaras under the Vākāṭakas and Pallavas and probably had the same designation under the Guptas. The village councils were known as Janapadas in the Gupta administration. A large number of village janapada seals have been found at Nālandā belonging to the Gupta period. Letters sent to outsiders communicating the decisions of the village councils were usually stamped with their seals. There is no indication as to how the members of the village Janapadas were selected ; the term Mahattara would suggest that senior persons of the different classes, who had acquired a pre-eminent status by their character, experience and age, were elevated to the village council by general approval.

The village council looked after the village defence, settled village disputes, organised works of public utility, acted as a trustee for minors, collected government revenues and paid them into the treasury. Village lands were carefully measured and the boundaries were accurately fixed. Villages were protected by walls and ditches. Agriculture was the main occupation of the villagers, but each village had its own complement of weavers, potters, carpenters, oil-pressers and gold-smiths.

An officer named Purapāla was in charge of the town administration; he corresponded to the Nagaravyavahārkas of the Mauryan age. He often belonged to the cadre of the Kumārāmātyas. Very probably he also was assisted by a popular council similar to the village council in composition and functions. Gupta records show that the townsmen of the age were particular about water supply, town halls, recreation gardens, etc.[1], and the town councils took the necessary steps to satisfy their expectations. Most of the towns were protected by walls and moats.

1. *C. I. I.*, III. p. 75

TAXATION

It is unfortunate that Gupta records should supply very little information about the taxation. We may, however, well presume that the taxes current under other contemporary dynasties like the Vākāṭakas and the Kadambas were also imposed by the Guptas. Land tax was the main source of government revenue. It was known as Bhāgakara in some localities and Udraṅga in others ; its incidence varied from 16 to 25%. It was usually collected in kind. Octroi duties were another important source of revenue; they were collected both in kind and cash. Excise taxes had to be paid on oil, cloth and similar commodities. States claimed ownership in waste lands, forests, pastures and mines and derived considerable income by letting them out or selling their produce. When the touring officers of the state visited villages, the public had to provide them the necessary rations and transport free of cost.

GENERAL REVIEW

The Gupta administration was on the whole well organised, both at the centre and in the provinces. The central secretariat worked efficiently and could keep itself well informed about the happenings in the districts and villages. Oral orders of kings given during tours were verified and recorded. Lands were carefully measured and there was an accurate record of their ownership.

Gupta government could secure safety to its subjects both from foreign invasions and internal disturbances for a long time. As observed by the Chinese pilgrim, Fa Hien, it did not put restrictions on the movements of people unless they endangered public safety. In the administration of criminal law there was a happy combination of justice and humanity; criminals were punished promptly but the punishments were not inhuman.

Apart from maintaining law and order, the government developed the resources of the country as well. Its trade department no doubt collected octroi duties, but also promoted commerce by securing safety of roads and by establishing a gold currency of international standard. Mines and forests were developed. Agriculture was promoted by the construction and repairs of tanks and reservoirs; and the state afforded facilities by bringing waste lands under cultivation. Its activities were probably as diverse as those of the Mauryan state. The non-mention of some of the Mauryan departments seems to be accidental. Thus the superintendent of the mint (*Lashaṇadāyaksha*) of the *Arthaśāstra*, does not figure in Gupta records, but no student of numismatics can dissent from the view that the mint department of the Guptas, which issued the most artistic coins of the ancient period, must have been much more extensive and well organised than that of the Mauryas, which issued only the punch-marked coins.

Government, however, was not content merely with promoting material prosperity of its citizens ; it tried to promote their moral and spiritual welfare also by appointing sepecial religious inspectors. Donees of Brahmadeya villages were particularly required to set high moral standards, so as to become an example to others. State extended its patronage impartially to Hinduism, Buddhism and Jainism. Though there is no direct evidence upon the point, we can well presume that the Gupta state tried to keep an even balance between the conflicting interests of the different classes.

There was no central parliament to control the king and ministers, but traditional rules about their duties and the high ideals that were placed before them in semi-religious works were sufficiently effective to curb tyrannical tendencies. Government, moreover, was remarkably decentralised, and most of its functions were transferred to the district administration. In the district headquarters, the officers of the central government were assisted and controlled by popular councils of Mahattaras, whose concurrence was necessary even if the state wanted to sell the waste land of its own. Villages had their own councils, which functioned as corporate bodies and administered all the branches of its administration, including the settlement of civil disputes and the collection of taxes.

People were virtuous, rich and prosperous ; cities were teeming with population. The poor and the sick were offered free relief and medicine in hospitals and charitable institutions. Peace and prosperity secured by the government led to rich and remarkable development of art, literature, philosophy and science. The administration had thus promoted both moral and material progress of the people.

SECTION III

In the post-Gupta period, India became divided into a number of small kingdoms and it is not possible to review their administrations separately in a book of the present size. Nor is it necessary to do so, for the administration became more or less stereo-typed after *c.* 500 A.D. We shall first give a brief account of the administration of Harshavardhana during *c.* 600 to 650 A. D. and that of the Rāshṭrkuṭas for the Deccan during *c.* 750 to 1000 A. D. and then give a general picture of north Indian and south Indian administration of the later period.

ADMINISTRATION UNDER HARSHAVARDHANA

For getting a glimpse of the administration under Harsha, we have to rely mainly upon the account of Yuan Chwang and the narrative of Bāṇa in the *Harṣhacharit.* Both these, though good in their own way, are seriously inadequate from the view point of the historian of the administration. Only two official inscriptions of this king have been found so far.

The king continued to be the pivot of the administration. Like Aśoka and Kauṭilya, Harsha held that the head of the state must constantly exert himself in order to keep the administration efficient. Yuan Chwang says that Harsha was indefatiguable and the day was too short for him, and we can well believe his statement. The Chinese pilgrim's observation that the king's day was divided into three periods of which one was devoted to the affairs of the state and two to those of religion was probably true of the evening of the king's life only ; during his youth, when he was engaged in incessant wars, things must have been quite different.

Like Aśoka, Harsha believed in the utility of inspection tours ; if there was any irregularity, observes the Chinese pilgrim, 'in the manners of the people of the cities' he went amongst them.[1] His inspection tours, however, were not confined to the urban areas only ; rural areas received equal attention. The king naturally suspended his inspection work during the rainy season, when it is difficult to tour ; in the fair weather, he visited as many places as possible, not residing long at any one place, but having temporary buildings created for his residence at each place of sojourn. During these halts the local gentry and villagers had easy access to the king and used to report their grievances and press for their local needs.[2]

Pomp and glory continued to be associated with royalty. When the king was on march, he was accompanied by a long retinue carrying golden drums, one strike being beat at every step. The royal chamberlain regulated the audience.

The king continued to be assisted by a council of ministers. This is not referred to in the inscriptions of Harsha, but the Chinese pilgrim describes how the vacant Maukhari throne of Kanauj was formally offered to Harsha by its ministers. A special meeting was held for the purpose at which the premier, while addressing his colleagues said, 'The destiny of the nation is to be fixed today. I propose that Harsha assume the royal authority ; let each one give his opinion on the matter, whatever he thinks'. When an agreement was reached upon this point, Harsha was offered the crown with these words, 'Reign then with glory over the land, conquer the enemies of your country, wash out the insults laid on your kingdom'. This incident will show that ministers exercised considerable powers and authority in the Maukhari administration, especially when there was a break in the government and we may well presume that ministry wielded considerable influence under Harsha also. Unfortunately, however, our sources give us no information about the ministry of Harsha and its functioning.

As usual, there was a well organised secretariat at the capital. The Inspector General of the Government Records figures in

1. Watters *On Yuan Chwang*. I. p. 344
2. *Harshacharit*. tr., p. 208
3. Watters, I, p. 343

the Bansekhra plate as *Mahākshapaṭalādhṛita*. The superior civil service was probably manned by Kumārāmātyas, from whose cadre the district and secretariat officers and ministers were selected. The centre had its own inspecting officers. Its communications were carried by royal messengers, who are described as *dīrghādhvagas* in the *Harshacharit*. This work refers to an officer called *sarvagataḥ*;[1] he was probably a member of the secret service department, which figured so prominently in the Mauryan administration. It appears that most of the senior officers were paid not in cash but by assignments of lands, villages and cities. 'Ministers of state and common officials,' says Yuan Chwang, 'all have their portion of land and are maintained by cities assigned to them'; government servants of the lower grades were paid in cash or land according to their work.[2] Harsha's administration thus was the forerunner of the feudal system that became popular in northern India a little later.

Our original sources supply information only about two of the departments of the government; the Foreign department and the Army department; the chief of the former department was known as *Mahāsandhivigrahādhikṛita* and its incumbent was a person named Avanti at the time when the *Harshacharit* was written. This office must have been very busy in the early days of Harsha, when he was engaged in incessant warfare. The latter presupposed a strong military force. The army consisted of the infantry, the cavalry and elephant and camel corps. According to Yuan Chwang 'Harsha's cavalry was 1,00,000 strong and the elephant corps consisted of 60,000 elephants'. The latter figure seems to be exaggerated, for even the Maurya empire possessed an elephant corps of 9,000 only. The horses for the cavalry were recruited from Sindh, Persia and Kamboja. The infantry must have been several lakhs strong; its exact strength is not referred to in our records. Ordinary soldiers were called *chaṭas* and *bhaṭas*, cavalry officers,

1. *Harshachari*, p. 57.
2. Watters, I, 176-7.

bṛihadaśvavāra and infantry officers, *balādhikṛitas* and *mahābalādhikṛitas*. The commander-in-chief was called *mahāsenāpati*.

The kingdom of Harsha was divided into provinces, divisions, districts and sub-divisions. Neither the number of provinces nor the designations of their governors are known. The *Harshacharit* probably refers to them in a vague way when it refers to the appointments of governors of people (*lokapālas*) in different directions.[1] Provinces were divided into Bhuktis; the Bhukti of Ahichchhatrā is referred to in the Madhuvan and Bansekhra plates of Harsha and it probably comprised of modern Rohilkhand. In the kingdom of Harsha, as in the Gupta empire, the Bhukti corresponded to the modern Commissioner's division.

Bhukti was subdivided into Vishayas, which were probably of the size of the modern district. The Vishayas of Kuṇḍadhāni and Angadiya were included in the Bhukti of Ahichchhatrā. The Vishayas comprised of a number of Pāthakas, which probably corresponded to the modern Tehsil or Taluka. Whether any smaller division intervened between the Pāthaka and the village we do not know. The village government was in the charge of a headman called Grāmākshapaṭalika, who was assisted by a number of clerks designated as Karaṇikas. The village council is not referred to in our records, but its non-occurrence is probably accidental.

We get little information about the taxation of the period. Harsha's copper plates refer to three taxes, *bhāga*, *hiraṇya* and *bali*. The first of these is obviously the land tax paid in kind, the second refers to taxes paid in cash, whether by the farmers or by the merchants. What particular taxes are referred to by the term *bali*, it is difficult to say. The long-established ferry tax was in vogue. Taxes on merchandise varied with its weight and measure. The Chinese pilgrim states that the taxation was light and forced service was sparingly used. But when one considers how Harsha was for a long time engaged in warfare and was maintaining a huge army, one is inclined to doubt the literal truth of the above statement.

1. दिशाप्रमुखेषु परिकल्पिता लोकपालाः ।

It appears that Harsha's government was not keeping that kind of elaborate register of men and cattle, which was maintained by the Mauryan administration; for Yuan Chwang states that families were not registered. The statement of the Chinese pilgrim, 'As the government is generous, official requirements are few ... Everybody keeps to his hereditary occupation and attends to his patrimony' seems to suggest that the government of Harsha was following a *laisses faire* policy, as compared to the Mauryan administration.

We may well believe Yuan Chwang when he states that Harsha was just in his administration and punctilious in the discharge of his duties.[1] It appears that the cultural activities received generous patronage; for the Chinese pilgrim states, 'Of the royal land, there is a fourfold division. One part is for the expenses of the government and state worship, one for the endowment of great public servants, one to reward high intellectual eminence and one for acquiring religious merit by gifts to various sects'.[2]

The efficiency of Harsha's government does not compare favourably with that of the Mauryan or Gupta administration. Yuan Chwang no doubt states that as the government was honestly administered, the people lived together on good terms and that the criminal class was small.[3] But this appears to be a somewhat courtly compliment, because the Chinese pilgrim himself was captured by robbers not far from the capital and escaped being offered as a sacrifice through an accidental natural phenomenon; a sudden black tempest broke at the nick of time, which frightened the robbers. The law against the crime was severe; prisoners received harsh treatment; they were not allowed to shave; they used to have hairy faces and matted beards. Punishments were more sanguinary than under the Guptas; 'For offences against the social morality and disloyal and unfilial conduct, the punishment is to cut off the nose, or an ear or a hand or a foot or banish the offender to another

1. Watters, I. p. 343
2. *Ibid*, I. p. 176
3. *Ibid*, I, p. 171

country or into wilderness.'[1] Fines were imposed for minor offences. The severity of the criminal administration no doubt helped to keep down the crime.

The government of Harsha promoted moral and material progress of the people, but it appears that on the whole it was neither as efficient as the Gupta administration nor as many-sided in its activities as the Mauryan one.

SECTION IV

THE RĀSHṬRAKŪṬA ADMINISTRATION.

As compared to the Gupta period, we have more considerable epigraphical material to reconstruct the picture of the Rāshṭrakūṭa dynasty, which was ruling over the Deccan between *c.* 750 to 977 A. D. As the administration had become considerably stereotyped by this time, we shall refer only to the salient features of the Rāshṭrakūta government. The reader can get its detailed picture from Part II of my work, *The Rāshṭrakūṭas and Their Times*, pp. 135-268.

The king continued to be the centre and fountain source of all power in the state. His titles were growing more and more pompous; in addition to the imperial titles like *Mahārājādhirāja*, *Paramabhāṭṭārka*, etc., he began to assume certain personal titles like *Dhārāvarsha* (raining good things upon the subjects in torrents), *Akālavarsha* (raining good objects when least expected), *Suvarṇavarsha* (raining gold), *Vikramāvaloka* (of victorious look), *Jagattuṅga*, (lofty peak of the world), etc.

The royal court and the machinery of the central administration were permanently established at the capital. The emperor used to attend the court regularly, when he was not absent on some expedition. Pomp and grandeur befitting a mighty empire characterised the appointments at the reception hall. In the courtyard outside, military captains were on duty with their select platoons of infantry, cavalry, and the war elephants; very often elephants and horses captured from the defeated enemies were exhibited there as a visible proof of the

1. Beal, *Life of Yuan Chwang*, p. 73

imperial might. Visitors were admitted only by express permission of the royal chamberlain; feudatories and ambassadors had to wait in the ante-room until they were ushered in by the court officials. The visitor found the emperor seated on an imposing throne, wearing a number of costly jewels and ornaments. There was a bodyguard always in attendance. Dancing girls added to the charm of the court ; they often gave skilful performances of music and dances to which the elite of the capital were invited. Prominent among those regularly present in the court were vassal chiefs, foreign ambassadors, high military and civil officers, poets, doctors, astrologers, merchant-princes, and guild representatives.

Kingship as before was hereditary and the crown usually passed to the eldest son, who used to be formally installed as Yuvarāja, when his training of the type already described earlier (p. 85) was over and he had come of age. Usually the eldest son was selected as heir apparent, but sometimes, as in the case of Govinda III, a younger son was selected if he was found to be abler. The fact that Govinda's accession was challenged by his elder brother Stambha and led to a big rising, would show that the selection of the eldest brother was regarded as normal. We have however some cases of younger princes like Dhruva and Govinda IV deposing their elder brothers after the latter's succession.

Yuvarāja usually stayed at the capital and helped his father to carry on the administration. He used to accompany him on important military expeditions ; sometimes he was himself entrusted with them, as was the case with Govinda II in 770 A. D. Other princes used to be appointed to the posts of provincial governors, as was the practice also under the Mauryas and the Guptas. Under the Rāshṭrakūṭa administration princesses are rarely seen occupying government posts. The only known instance is that of Chandrabelabbā, a daughter of Amoghavarsha I, who was administering the Raichur Doab in 837 A. D. Under the later Chālukyas, the practice of appointing princesses to high government posts became very common. Mailādevī, one of the queens of Someśvara I, Akkādevī, an elder sister of

Jayasiṁha III and Lakshmīdevī, the chief queen of Vikramāditya VI, were holding important administrative charges. Under the Rāshṭrakūṭas, we get one instance of a crowned queen, Śīlabhaṭṭārikā making a land grant without any permission of her husband Dhruva. Probably the omission of king's permission is accidental. There is no reason to believe that either Śīlabhaṭṭārikā or any other crowned consort was a regnant queen.

Succession was frequently accompanied by political upheaval in the Rāshṭrakūṭa administration; this seems to be the reason why male relatives are usually seen acting as regents during minority and not dowager queen-mothers.

The emperor carried on the administration with the help of a council of ministers. Our records do not supply the names of the portfolioe of the various ministers, but to judge from the contemporary evidence, it is clear that the ministry must have consisted of the prime minister, the foreign minister, the revenue minister, the treasurer, the chief justice, the commander-in-chief, and the Purohita or royal chaplain. In the modern administration, a minister is a member of government, quite distinct from the official who is the head of the department ; in ancient times the two posts were often held by the same person. Our records are silent about the qualifications of ministers and the manner in which they were selected, but we can safely conclude that they must have been chosen for their general competence and proficiency in political and military matters. Most of the ministers were usually also military officers. Some of them, like Dalla, the foreign minister of Dhruva,[1] enjoyed feudatory status, and were also assigned *jāgīrs*. There was, as a rule, complete confidence between the emperor and his ministers; the latter are often described as the right hand of the former.[2]

Rāshṭrakūṭa records so far discovered do not refer to any members of a superior civil sercvice like that of the Amātyas under the Mauryas or the Kumārāmātyas under the Guptas.

1. *E. I.* X, 89
2. तस्य यः प्रतिहस्तोऽभूत्प्रियो दक्षिणहस्तवत् । *E. I.* IV, 60

This absence of reference is probably accidental. There is no information available about the manner in which the central government exercised supervision over the outlying districts and provinces. But we shall probably be not wrong in assuming that there were officers of the central government under the Rāshṭrakūṭas, as there certainly were under the earlier administrations, who used to go on tours of inspection in the interior. Feudatories and district officers were often called to the capital to give explanation of their conduct. Secret service agents were stationed all over the empire to keep the central government informed of the intentions and actions of provincial and territorial administrators.

The Rāshṭrakūṭa empire consisted partly of vassal states and partly of directly administered areas. Important feudatories like the rulers of Southern Gujarāt enjoyed almost complete autonomy; they could even alienate villages without the imperial sanction; they had also their own sub-feudatories. The latter had very little independent power and often were called Rājās by the merest courtesy. They had to secure higher sanction before they could alienate revenues or grant villages.[1] Feudatories had to obey the orders of the sovereign and to attend his court at periodical intervals to offer assurances of personal loyalty and to give such explanations as might be required by the imperial secretariat. They were bound to pay regular tribute and also to supply an agreed quota of fighting troops. Very often they had also to participate with their forces in the military campaigns of their feuadal lords. They were obliged to entertain an imperial resident at their courts and used to keep their own representatives at the imperial capital to watch there the trend of events.[2] If they rebelled, they were subjected to a number of indignities after the defeat. They had to surrender their treasures, elephants, and horses and sometimes had to engage themselves in menial work at the arbitrary dictation of the emperor.

Directly administered areas were divided into Rāshṭras and

1. *I. A.* XII, 15; *E. I.* IX. 195
2. *E. I.* VI, 33

Vishayas, roughly corresponding to modern divisions and districts. The number of villages comprised in a Vishaya varied from 1,000, as in the case of Puṇaka, (the modern Poona), to 4,000 (as in the case of Karhāṭaka, modern Karad). The Vishayas were subdivided into Bhuktis consisting of 50 to 70 villages, and named after the headquarter towns.[1] The Bhuktis were further subdivided into smaller groups of 10 to 20 villages each.[2] The village itself was the smallest administrative unit.

The Rāshṭrapati was at the head of the administration of the Rāshṭra, which was usually equal to four or five modern districts. He was in charge of both the military and the civil administration. He had to maintain peace and order and keep a watchful eye on smaller feudatories and officers; if the latter became refractory, they were to be immediately dealt with by a punitive expedition.[3] Naturally the Rāshṭrapati had a sufficient military force under his command and was usually himself a military officer. Very often he used to enjoy the status and titles of a vassal. His position was similar to that of the Uparikas in the Gupta administration.

Like the modern commissioners of divisions the Rāshṭrapatis were in charge of the fiscal administration and were responsible for the prompt collection of the land revenue. They had to keep careful records of local rights and privileges and to note the villages whose revenues had been granted to temples and Brāhmaṇas. They could not themselves alienate any revenues without royal permission. Nor had they the power of appointing district and sub-divisional officers.

Vishayapatis or district officers and Bhogapatis or tahsil officers exercised the same functions as Rāshṭrapatis within their smaller jurisdictions. Some of them also had titles of small feudatory rulers.

Appointments to the above posts were usually made either in recognition of administrative ability or as a reward for military

1. *I. A.*, XI, 111
2. A. S. Altekar, *Rāshṭrakūṭas*, p. 138
3. *Ibid* p. 179
4. *Ibid*, pp. 175-6

services. In some cases the posts became hereditary, especially when the original officers had sons who had proved their worth on the battlefield or in the secretariat.

Vishayapatis and Bhogapatis carried on the revenue administration in cooperation with hereditary revenue officers called Nāḍgāvuṇḍas or Deśagrāmakūṭas, who seem to have discharged functions similar to those of the Deshmukhas and Deshpandes under the later Muslim and Marāṭhā administrations. These officers were remunerated by the grant of rent-free lands.[1] It is interesting to add that hereditary revenue officers for districts are so far not known to have figured in any north Indian ancient administration.

The village administration was carried on by the village headman and the village accountant, whose posts were usually hereditary. The headman was responsible for preserving law and order in the village and used to have a local militia at his disposal to assist him in carrying out his duties. The peace of the villages was disturbed not so much by thieves and dacoits as by the rebellions of feudatories and the rivalries of adjacent villages. Headmen had to discharge the duties of military captains on such occasions and had often to lay down their lives, while defending the hearths and homes of fellow villagers. They were also responsible for the collection of the village revenues and their payment into the royal treasury and granaries. They were remunerated by rent-free lands and the assignment of some petty taxes paid in kind. The village accountants worked as their assistants.[2]

How far the popular voice influenced the administration is a question naturally uppermost in the mind of the modern reader. As far as the administration of the villages and towns was concerned, the popular element was fairly effective. Each village in Karnāṭaka and Mahārāshṭra had a popular council on which every adult householder was represented. There were no formal elections held as in the Tamil country, but the

1. *Rāshṭrakūṭas*, pp. 178-79
2. *Ibid*, pp. 168-9

elders of the villages (Grāma-mahājanas or Grāma-mahattaras) used informally to appoint sub-committees to manage local schools, tanks, temples and roads. They would also receive trust properties and administer them according to the conditions laid down by the donors. These sub-committees worked in close co-operation with the village headman and received a fair percentage of the village revenue for financing the various public welfare schemes. Civil suits were also decided by the village council and its decisions were enforced by the government. Towns had similar popular councils discharging similar functions.[1]

Rāshṭrakūṭa records refer on rare occasions to Vishaya-mahattaras (elders of the district) and Rāshṭramahattaras (elders of the province), suggesting the existence of popular bodies at the district and provincial headquarters, discharging functions probably similar to those of the councils of village elders (Grāma-mahattaras) in villages. We have, however, no direct evidence to show that the elders of the district or the province had actually a council of their own, regularly meeting at intervals and discharging important administrative functions. It may be that the absence of a reference to the council of Rāshṭramahattaras and Vishyamahattaras in our records is accidental and that the district non-official councils functioned under the Rāshṭrakūṭas in the Deccan, as they did under the Guptas in Bengal.

A popular assembly or parliament at the Rāshṭrakūṭa capital is nowhere referred to, and probably no such body existed. In former days when communications were difficult, the regular meeting of a popular assembly at a distant capital was not easy to arrange. In the Rāshṭrakūṭa administration, the popular voice could not make itself effectively felt in the central but only in the village administration. We must, however, remember in this connection that the village councils of this period discharged many of the functions of the provincial and central governments of modern times ; the popular element could effectively control the administration by having a decisive voice in these local bodies.

1. *Rāshṭrakūṭas*, pp. 200-1

A few words are necessary about the military forces of the Rāshṭrakūṭas. The emperors cherished constant ambitions to extend their territories and were always trying to translate these into reality ; therefore the Rāshṭrakūṭa military machine was both powerful and efficient. The administration always maintained a large army, but unfortunately we have no data to enlighten us on the exact strength of its infantry, cavalry and elephant corps. We may however well presume that the Rāshṭrakūṭa army could not have been less than half a million strong, as was the case with the army of Harsha. A considerable portion of the army was concentrated at the capital. But there used to be also an army of the South, usually under the Banavasi viceroy, and an army of the North, probably commanded by a prince of the blood ròyal. The standing armies were maintained for the protection of the empire from external enemies ; they used also to carry out aggressive expeditions when these had been decided on by the central government. The army was famous for its infantry divisions, though cavalry also played an important part. Some battalions consisted of men from military castes, the soldiers of which followed their profession as a matter of heredity; these usually enjoyed the reputation of crack divisions. Some battalions were supplied by feudatories and provincial governors. These used to be summoned when an important military venture had to be undertaken. Troops of the military castes received professional training in their villages before they joined the colours ; others were trained and led by adventurous mercenaries or *condottieri*, who were paid directly by the government for their work in this connection. The commissariat was organised with the help and cooperation of wealthy merchants. The army consisted of persons from all castes ; even Brāhmaṇas and Jains were represented on it. It is rather surprising to find that many of the famous Rāshṭrakūṭa generals like Baṅkeya, Śrīvijaya, Mārasiṁha, etc. were Jains by religious persuasion. They probably felt that the doctrine of Ahimsā in its extreme form was intended in practice for recluses and not for ordinary laymen.

Let us now enquire what were the main sources of revenue

in the Rāshṭrakūṭa empire. The financial resources consisted of tribute from feudatories, income from government properties, and the proceeds of taxation. Of these the first has been referred to already. Under the second category came the income from mines, forests and waste lands, the ownership of which was claimed by the state. The ownership of arable lands, however, was vested in private individuals and families. The state could confiscate them only if the revenue demand had not been complied with.

The taxation structure under the Rāshṭrakūṭas was more or less similar to that in northern India. Land-tax, variously called as Udraṅga or Bhogakara, was the sheet anchor of the government finance. Its incidence was about 25% and it used to be generally collected in kind in two or three instalments. Lands given as grants to Brāhmaṇas and temples were taxed at a lower rate. Remissions in land tax were granted in the case of calamities like famines. Petty taxes in kind were collected on fruits, vegetables, etc.; they were called Bhogakara and were usually assigned to local officials as part of their pay .

Octroi and excise duties were levied on a number of articles: these were collected sometimes in cash. Villagers had also to arrange for the free boarding, lodging and transport of the inspecting and investigating officers.

SECTION V.

North Indian Administration in the post-Harsha period[1]

We get ample epigraphical and literary evidence to reconstruct the picture of the administration from *c.* 700 to 1200 A. D. Northern India was divided into a number of dynasties during the greater part of this period, and we shall give here a composite picture based upon the evidence supplied by their records and by contemporary works on polity. This would give an insight into the nature of the general administration of the period, although the whole of it may not be true of any particular dynasty.

1. Largely based upon a portion of the thesis written by my daughter, Dr. Mrs. Padma Udgaonkar.

Kingship had now become hereditary; we have shown already how the theory of king's election is ridiculed by Kalhaṇa, the Kashmir historian(p.84). Crown prince was probably selected formally even in the earlier periods, but epigraphical records of this period refer more frequently to his selection. Thus we find that Gāhaḍawāla records expressly refer to the selection of Madanapāla, Govindachandra and Āsphoṭachandra as crown princes by their fathers. The same was the case with Tribuvaṇapāla and Rājyapāla of the Pāla dynasty and several rulers of other houses. A younger brother or a nephew was selected as crown prince in the absence of a son. Women rarely became *de jure* queens. Sugandhā of Kashmir and Tribuvanamahādevī, Daṇḍamahādevī and Dharmamahādevī of the Kara dynasty of Orissa were really regents and not queens. Diddā of Kashmir was a real queen and ruled over the land effectively for 22 years. But this woman of extraordinary ability and energy had to a wait for a number of years after her husband's death and work for the removal of three kings before she could get the coveted throne.

The theory of the divinity of the king was becoming more widely acceptable; kings were now often conceived as incarnations of God. King Lantigadeva in Rajputana is known to have built a temple for his own image.[1]

Coronation ritual of this period was more Pauranic than Vedic; a number of Vedic Mantras were recited, as we gather from the Rājadharma of the *Kṛityakalpataru*, but they were not connected with any details of coronation. Owing to the ascendancy of astrology great interest was attached to the selection of a proper auspicious day. King's body was rubbed with earth brought from a number of places; right hand, for instance, by the dust dug by an elephant, and the left hand by the sand adhering to the horns of a bull. This procedure had an obvious symbolical element. The king was then given a bath by people of all four castes with water fetched from several holy rivers. A number of Śāntis or propitiatory rites were performed like Aindrī-śānti, Grahaśāntī and Vināyakaśāntī to ward off evil influence. Then followed worship of Gaṇesha, Brahmā, Śiva and

1. *E.I.* IX, 79-81

Vishṇu. The king was then seated on a throne covered with tiger's skin with umbrella-bearers and chauri-bearers by his side. He then gave audience to his subjects and then the coronation procession started. There was jail delivery also.

In this description we miss any reference to any oath. The coronation ceremony had now hardly any constitutional signifance. Records of this period refer to the coronation of the crown prince also. Gāhaḍawāla prince Jayachandra is expressly described as *Yauvarajābyishikta* in one record (E. I. IV. 118).

The growing influence of religion manifests itself also in another direction. Owing to the greater hold of the theory of Samnyāsa some kings are seen abdicating their throne in their old age. Such was the case with Vigrahapāla I, father of Nārayanapāla of the Pāla dynasty, king Jayavarman of the Chandella dynasty, Bhalladitya and Jhoṭa of the Pratihāra dynasty, Durlabharāja of Chaulukya dynasty and Anma of Varman dynasty of Kanauj. Religious suicide was recommeneded by some Smṛitis in extreme old age; Jainism also permitted it under its *sallekhanāvrata* vow. Chedi king Gāṅgeyadeva and the Chandella ruler Dhaṅga are known to have drowned themselves in the Triveṇī at Allahabad.

Records of our period show that queens normally took no part in the administration. They are sometimes seen making land-grants, but usually they did so with the permission of their husbands the ruling kings. Thus when queen Nayanakelidevī of Govindachandra wanted to make the grant of a village to the royal priest, she had to get the sanction of her husband.[1]

Crown princes were playing important part in the administration; they could often make a land grant themselves.[2] Sometimes our records refer to the rule both of the king and the crown prince; thus the Sevadi inscription refers both to Mahārājādhirāja Aśvarāja and Yuvarāja Kaṭukarāja.[3] Younger princes often acted as governors.

The ministry continued to be an important limb of adminis-

1. *E. I.*; IV. 108. See also *E. I.* II. 187-188; V. 117-8
2. *I. A.*, XIV, 101-4; *E. I.*, IV. 118
3. *E. I.* XI. 29-30

tration during our period. In Chap. VIII (p. 186) we have given a number of instances showing how ministers were highly respected by the kings and how they would often control his arbitrary actions. Ministers would often sacrifice their lives to save that of their king. We have, however, equally numerous instances of kings disregarding the advice of their ministers. Mahīpāla of Bengal spurned the advice of his ministers and was ruined. Kings' love affairs often disgusted their ministers, but they could do nothing even when the sweethearts of the rulers belonged to the untouchable classes. Whether ministry had become more impotent in our period, it is difficult to say, because we have instances of either type. The roles of the king and the minister varied with the personal ability and temperament of either party.

The qualifications of ministers were the same as those in the earlier periods. Qualities prescribed for ministers in our epigraphs are similar to those laid down by Kauṭilya, Manu or Kāmandaka. Very often ministry was hereditary in one family: we have quoted one example in the Chandella dynasty on p. 179; another instance from the Pala dynasty may be given here. From Badal *praśasti* we learn that Garga and his four descendants, Darbhapāṇi, Someśśvara, Kedāra Miśra and Gaurava Miśra were ministers of Dharmapāla and his three successors. Ministry was probably hereditary in several families in other dynasties also. About the working of the ministry during this period, we may refer the reader pp. 176-7.

Epigraphs of our period refer to a number of new official designations like Khola, Hiraṇyasamudāyika, etc.; the precise meaning of these expressions is not yet clear. Similarly we come across some new territorial divisions smaller than a Vishaya like Vīthi, Vṛitti, Chāturikā, Pattalā, etc., but their precise extent is still somewhat uncertain. The last mentioned division Pattalā seems to have corresponded with a Taluka or Tehsil of the modern period.

The working of the secretariat was similar to what it was

1. Ghoshal, *Beginnings of Indian Historiography* p. 418.

in the last period. As compared to the earlier age, copper plate grants become much more numerous in our period. When the letters of the old plate became blurred, new ones were issued (*E. I.*, XIX. 15). Sometimes grants were forged and then they were pronounced as frauds by the secretariat officers. In one case, however, recorded in the Tarachandi inscription (*E. I.*, XIV, 182) we find an officer of the Gāhaḍawāla king himself issuing an unauthorised charter to some Brāhmaṇas after receiving some bribe from them; Government officer Japila investigated into the case and pronounced it to be fraudulent.

Growth of feudalism was a marked feature during this period. Kings used to assign fiefs liberally to their relatives and officers, as was done by king Avantivarman of Kashmir.[1] The Paramāras, the Chaulukyas and the Chāhamānas also encouraged the feudal system by making liberal land and village grants to their relations and officers.[2] Chāhamāna Pṛithvīrāja, Kalachūri Karṇa, and Chaulukya Kumārapāla had 150, 136 and 72 Sāmantas or feudories under them.[3] Kings thus became direct rulers over their feudatories and not over their subjects. These feudatories, even when small, had their own courts and secretariats.

We come across instances of a feudatory of 84 villages having his own court and foreign minister.[4] These rapidly increasing courts had to be maintained by the common cultivator, whose burden naturally became heavier.

When Kumārapāla prohibited slaughter of animals on certain days, the feudatories imposed different scales of fines. One feudatory imposed a fine of four Drammas; another prescribed a fine of five Drammas on ordinary persons and of one Dramma only on members of royal families.[5] The imposition

1. विभज्य बंधुभृत्येभ्यः बुभुजे पार्थिवः श्रियम् । *Rājataraṅgiṇī*, V. 21
2. These were known as Sejas in Rajasthan.
3. *Prabandhachintāmaṇi*, p. 33
4. *E. I.* XIX No. 10
5. *Prakrit Sanskrit inscriptions*, Kāvyamālā Series, pp. 206-7

of different fines on different persons by different feudatories show that feudalism had become a law unto itself and a source of oppression to the population.

Apart from the Sāmantas, royal relations like the queens, crown princes, and junior princes also received feudal grants, known as Rājakīyabhoga under the Gāhaḍavālas and Grāsabhūmi under the Chāhamānas. Usually they had no full proprietary rights over these assignments. The extent of these assignments varied with the resources of the kingdom. We find the Chāhamāna prince Kīrtipāla enjoying twelve villages as his fief.[1] Princes Lakhaṇapāla and Abhayapāla were together enjoying only one village in 1177 A. D.[2]

The abnormal growth in the number of the feudatories was a source of oppression, as far as the ordinary man was concerned. He had now a large number of superiors to deal with, each of whom was anxious to grow richer at the cost of the former.

We get greater information about the constitution and administration of the army during this period. The army was far from being an integrated force. It consisted partly of imperial, partly of feudatory and partly of hereditary forces. Some brought their own weapons, while others used the weapons supplied by the Government. Some sections brought their own officers, others were supplied officers by the government. Mercenary forces were common; one epigraph describes the Pāla forces as consisting of Mālava, Khaśa, Lāṭa and Karṇāṭa soldiers.

In a well-trained army officers were appointed over ten, hundred, a thousand and ten thousand soldiers, known as Gaulmikas Śatānīkas, Sahasrānīkas and Āyutikas. Regular drill was taken and half-trained soldiers were paid less. The army had its office establishment, which kept account of the weapons, provisions, salaries, etc. Such well-trained and well-officered forces formed, however, only a small section of the total army. Great attention was paid to the construction and proper equipment of the different types of forts.

1. *E.I.* IX, 68
2. *Ibid*, XI, 50
3. See *Śukranīti*, Chap. II, 140 ff.

We need not devote more space to other aspects of the administration, because they were more or less the same as in the age of Harshavardhana.

SECTION VI

South Indian Administration[1]

We propose to survey here the general features of the administration of South Indian kingdoms like the Chola, Kerala, Pāṇḍya, Pallava, Chalukya, Hoysala, and Vijayanagar. Neither the literary nor the epigraphical data are ample except for the treatment of the Local Government, which we have already dealt with in Chap. XI.

The position of the king and the conceptions about his duties and responsibilities in South India were similar to those in North India already described in Chap. V.

The Council of Ministers was as constant a feature of the south Indian administration as that of the north Indian one. The *Kural* of the Sangam age points out :—

> The king with none to censure him
> Bereft of safeguards all,
> Though none his ruin work,
> Shall surely ruined fall.

We have frequent reference to Amātyas in the Sātavāhana records and also in the Pallava ones (*E.I.*, VIII. 218). There is no doubt that in some cases these were district officers. but in others they were the advisers or ministers of the king. The Kadambas of Banavāsi had a council of ministers which was consulted when the king made land grants (*J.B.B.R.A.S.* IX. 275,284). The Pallava king Nandivarman had a ministerial council which has been referred to in the Vaikuṇṭha Perumal inscription (*S.I.I.* IV. 135) One Kālidāsa was a minister of war of the Chālukya king Jagadekamalla. Eastern Chālukya records also refer to Mantrins and Pradhānas. The official advisers of high status that are referred to in the *Śilappadikaram*

1. For a detailed account, see Dr T. V. Mahalingam, *South Indian Polity*. Madras University, 1953.

and the *Maṇimekalai*, often 18 in number, were probably of the ministerial status.

We rarely get information about the portfolioes of the different ministers, or the way in which the council of ministers transacted its day-to-day business. Pradhānas, Mantrins, Sachivas, Purohitasand Senāpatis are some ministers that are often referred to. Their names suggest their functions. Some ministers used to have the charge of several portfolioes in the south as in the north ; the Prime Minister was very frequently the Foreign Minister or the War Minister. Thus under Hoysal king Narasiṁha, Lokamaya was the Prime Minister as well as the War Minister.

The qualifications laid down for the ministers in works like the *Kural* or *Āmuktamālyada* are similar to those recommended by North Indian writers. The latter work recommends that the king should be always watchful of the actions of his ministers with the help of his spies, lest they should launch upon unnecessary and unprofitable works. It is quite possible that this precaution may have been taken in several administrations.

The effectiveness of the advice of ministers largely depended on the character of the king and their own reputation. Kṛishṇadevarāya was a powerful ruler with a forceful personality ; we find him declaring war against Bijapur inspite of the opposition of his ministers. But in one of his soliloquies we find the same king saying, 'I am sitting upon the throne but the whole world is ruled by ministers ; who listens to my words ?'[1]

Reference has already been made to some aspects of the working of the secretariat under the Cholas (Chap. IX, p. 189) We do not get any information about this institution during the earlier period. The graphic description of the Vijayanagar secretariat by Abdur Razzak may give us some further idea about the secretariat. 'On the right hand of the palace there is the Diwankhana or ministers' office, which is extremely large and consists of a forty pillared hall, and in its front runs a gallery

1. *Journal of the Telugu Academy*, II, 30

higher than the stature of a man, thirty yards long and six yards broad, where the recrods are kept and scribes seated.[1] We may well presume that in the secretariat of the Pallavas and the Cholas also there were similar arrangements though perhaps on a smaller scale.

There were officers to take down the oral orders of the king and the decisions of the king-in-council respectively known as Tiruvakkelvi and Tommandira Olai. One section of the secretariat used to issue the orders of the central government and another used to reply to the enquiries made by local officers. There was also a board of inspectors to tour the kingdom, the members of which were known as Karnams. The centre also periodically took the work of land survey, which was done very meticulously. An inscription in the Bṛihadīśvara temple reveals how a piece of land as small as 52,428,800,000 th part of a Veli was measured and assessed to revenue (*S.I.I.*, II. 62).

Let us now consider the administrative divisions. In the early period the kingdoms of the south were usually small; but what may be called the provincial administration was not developed even in the Sātavāhana empire, whose inscriptions refer only to Āhāras or districts. The Rathikas, the Mahārathikas, the Bhojakas and the Mahābhojakas in the Sātavāhana empire were not provincial governors but feudatories. Provincial administration had not developed under the Pallavas, the Kadambas and the Gaṅgas, whose kingdoms were small. The Maṇḍalas under the Cholas usually consisted of about two or three modern districts; their number was nine when the Chola power was at its zenith. But from their extent and dimensions the Maṇḍalas appear to be more like Commissioners' Divisions than like provincial administrations.

The Maṇḍalas were usually divided into Valanāḍus and the latter into Nāḍus, which were also known as Kurrams and Kottams. Between the Nādu and the village was the division known as Melāgram, theoretically consisting of 50 villages. Epigraphs, however, refer to Sthalas consisting of 53,26, 14 or 11 villages.

1, Elliot and Dowson, IV, 107

In northern India also there were similar divisions consisting of varying number of villages (*ante*, p. 218).

The governors of the Maṇḍalas were sometimes royal princes, sometimes senior officers and sometimes also defeated kings, who had promised to become loyal and were kept under strict control. Maṇḍala governors had their own armies and courts. In the course of time, their posts tended to become hereditary and then they could not be distinguished from feudatory governors. Each of them had to entertain an imperial representative at his court, who acted like the Resident or the Political Agent under the British rule. He saw to it that the feudal chief entertained no treasonous ambitions and sent military contingents to help the emperor in his military undertakings. In order to keep himself in touch with the events and trends at the imperial capital, the feudatory governor also used to keep his own representative in the court of the emperor. He was required to be personally present to offer his greetings, presents and loyalty on the occasions like the coronation, marriage or the birth of a son or a daughter.

Village councils were a special feature of the south Indian administration. Their early history is, however, shrouded in obscurity. Some early Pallava inscriptions show that villlages were organised under the leadership of the village leader called Grāmakeya or Mutaka, to whom the royal orders were usually addressed. The village government was transacted at the village Manram, which was an open place under the shade of a large tree. Popular courts were held here and matters of common interest discussed. Early inscriptions, however, hardly give any information about the village Sabhā or council.

We begin to get detailed information about the village councils and their constitutions and functions only after the 9th century A.D. They were called Sabhās, when the villages were mostly inhabited by Brāhmaṇas and Urs, when they contained a very large section of non-Brahmin population. The full information about these two types of village councils has been already given by us in Chap. XI, pp. 231-5.

The king was the fountain source of justice in the south

as in the north. Some kings like Maṇunitikaṇḍa Chola used to hang the bell of justice at the palace door, which could be rung by any aggrived party who wanted justice from the king himself. The king was assisted by the Chief Justice, who also held his court in the capital. Provincial governors deputised for the king in the provinces and so naturally held their own courts of justice. Popular courts also coexisted with the royal courts throughout the ancient period. In the Sangam age they were known as Manrams, Avais and Avaikkulams. They continued under Vijayanagar also. Their constitution and functions have been already described in Chap. XII, pp. 250-5.

Taxation in south India did not differ very much from that in North India. The land tax was the principal source of revenue ; it varied from 25 percent (on dry crops) to 50 percent (on wet crops under tanks). Village Sabhās or Urs were responsible for its collection in majority of cases. They could grant exemptions under suitable circumstances to individual land holders ; in such cases their share of tax was distributed over other holders. Village Sabhās would also grant perpetual exemption from the land tax on receiving the capitalised value of the tax due. Members of the Sabhā were personally responsible for the tax collection; in case of default the officers of the central government would make them stand in water or under the burning sun as a punishment.

South Indian inscriptions show that there were taxes imposed upon the smiths, goldsmiths, shepherds, fishermen, weavers, toddy-drawers, etc. Smṛiti writers have recommended that the artisans should be made to work free for the state once or twice a month; in later times this liability seems to have been converted into a regaular tax in south India.

Octroi dulties were collected at market places, ghats, rest houses and city gates.

As in the north, there was a tendency to increase the demands of the state towards the end of the ancient period. There is a case on record showing how in the reign of Rājarāja a woman committed suicide because an ordeal was imposed upon her in connection with an unjust tax (*S.I.E.R.*, 1907, para 42). Villages and their Sabhās however used to organise a united opposition to unjust demands and were often successful. Under Rājarāja III the assemblies of five adjoining Nāḍus resolved to authorise the people to pay only those taxes that were legitimately due (*S.I.I.*, VI, Nos. 48,50 and 58). In the reign of Kulottuṅga I people decided that the government's share was one fifth of the dry crop and one third of the wet crop under the tank (*E. C.* X, Mb. 49 a). Another record says, 'Because we were unjustly taxed, we were about to run away. Then we realised that because the whole country was not united in a body, we were unjustly dealt with. Hereafter we shall pay what is just and in accordance with the yield of the crop (*S.I.E.R.*, 1918, para 68). If the Government did not yield, the people used to threaten to migrate in a body and even a mighty monarch like Kṛishṇadevarāya used to be perturbed by such a possibility. In his *Āmaktamālyada*, he says, 'That king is never prosperous who has an officer who does not call back the subjects who leave the state on account of suffering (IV. 237).

The available evidence thus shows that the taxation had a definite tendency to be oppressive from *c.* 900 A. D. and that people could save themselves only by organising a systematic and united opposition. Whether the government would succeed in realising its oppressive demand or whether people would succeed in resisting it depended largely upon their relative strength.

We should however also note that there are cases on record of the Government granting relief in order to enable the tenants to overcome natural calamities like floods, famines, pestilences, etc. When in 1402 A. D. the Kāverī overflowed its banks and deposited heavy amount of silt, farmers were unable to carry on the cultivation and had to abandon the area as uncultivable. Government, however, soon took steps to rehabilitate the agriculturists by granting them various types of concessions in the rate and collection of land taxes (*S.I.E.R.*, No 629 of 1923). If a village suffered by plunder or civil war, a concession in the land tax was usually granted for a specific period.

Unfortunately we have no sufficient statistical data to show whether the cases of oppressive taxation were more numerous than those of concessions to mitigate calamities.

The items of expenditure in the south Indian administration were similar to those in the north Indian one. The royal court took a lion's share. Administrative posts were tending to become hereditary and were often paid by land or village assignments; so the cash expenditure on civil list did not appear to be very heavy. Wars between the different states were very frequent and so the expenditure on the army was considerable. It was held that 'the money which is utilised in buying elephants and horses, in feeding them, in maintaining soldiers, in the worship of gods and Brāhmaṇas and in king's own enjoyment could never be called an expenditure' (*Āmuktamālyada*, IV. 262). The Cholas and the Pāṇḍyas were maritime powers also and used to maintain a fairly strong navy. It is therefore very likely that the army and the navy together must have consumed about 50% of the state revenues, as is permitted by the *Śukranīti*. A number of Chola records show that the temples, like the Rājarāja shrine at Tanjore, enjoyed a number of grants made to them by the Government. There were a large number of temple colleges in the South, where students were not only taught free but were also given stipends for a number of years. Chairs or *adhyanana-vṛittis* were also maintained at a number of temples. The huge temples, which are a legitimate source of pride to South India, must also have meant a heavy demand on the public exchequer. South Indian administrations must have allotted quite sizeable sums to gods, temples, Brāhmaṇas, education and charity. If the Vedic scholarship of South India is a source of envy to North India or the so-called Āryāvarta, the credit must be largely given to the Sourth Indian states, which fostered Vedic scholarship and Sanskrit studies with admirable solicitude.

As in the north, South India also used to set apart about 25 percent of the anual revenue to meet unexpected demands or calamities. This formed the so-called secret treasury, which was normally not to be opened or touched.

CHAPTER XVII

A GENERAL ESTIMATE

We have now finished our survey of the Ancient Indian Polity. We have studied its different features and surveyed the administrative systems under the different dynasties. We shall now proceed to form a general estimate about the merits and limitations of the Ancient Indian Polity. While doing so, we shall take an impartial standpoint. We should not however forget that ancient thought and institutions cannot be judged by standards then not known anywhere. We shall have to make due allowance for the circumstances and surroundings in which the ancient Indian polity and thought were developed and then form our estimate about them. We shall also discuss the lessons taught by our general survey and estimate; the study of the past becomes more useful and interesting, if it can be made to bear on some of the problems of the present as well.

Several types of states like republics, oligarchies, diarchies and monarchies were prevailing in India in ancient times, but eventually monarchy became the order of the day. This phenomenon was not peculiar to ancient India; it repeated itself in ancient Europe also where we find the republics in Greece and Italy being gradually supplanted by monarchies and empires. Representative government was not known both to the ancient East and West, and so republics could function only when the state was small and frequent meetings of its Assembly consisting practically of all the senior members of its privileged order were possible. As in the ancient republics of Greece and Italy, political power was vested not in the whole population, but in the members of a small privileged order, mostly consisting of Kshatriyas and perhaps of the Brāhmaṇas also in a few cases. The Hindu polity worked in a society that had accepted the principle of the caste system, which laid down that government was primarily the function and duty of the Kshatriyas, assisted to some extent by the Brāhmaṇas. Franchise in the ancient

Indian republics could, therefore, not be extended to the whole population. In the modern age, which does not believe in the predetermination of one's functions by birth, it will naturally have to be extended to all. The constitution of republican India has already done so.

Democracy is the order of the day at present and we have already established a full fledged republic in India in 1951. It will be, therefore, necessary to understand the causes that led to the disappearance of the republics in ancient India. Generally speaking republics could function successfully in ancient India in small states. They also presupposed a kind of tribal unity in the governing class; republics failed to develop into a purely territorial state of large dimensions. Distances are annihilated now; the principle of representative government has been discovered and is in universal practice. Tribal stage has passed away long ago and we have now developed a national consciousness. There is therefore no reason why India should not function and flourish as a large republic in the modern age.

Growing veneration for a hereditary ruler fostered by the principle of the divinity of king was also partly responsible for the disappearance of the ancient republics. When presidents, generals and members of the executive council became hereditary in republics, their polity could not be much differentiated from monarchy. Divinity of king is now a dead doctrine and we need not apprehend that it will prejudice the development of the republican spirit or institutions in the modern times. It is interesting to note that some members of the old feudal order are taking part in the working of the new democracy as members of the Parliament, ministers or deputy ministers.

A study of ancient Indian history and polity shows that our republics flourished as long as there was harmony and concord among the members of their Assemblies. There was, however, a tendency among them to quarrel. In some republics every member of the Assembly was given the title of *rājā*; often he was not inclined to accept the leadership of a fellow member because it presupposed his own inferiority. Neighbouring kings used to send spies to foment quarrels and dissentions among the members of the republican bodies. Groups and parties were often formed in the republican Assemblies and they spent their time and energy in bringing each other's downfall and incidentally paving the way of an outside conqueror. Many of the ancient Indian republics were destroyed by the neighbouring kings and emperors by encouraging feuds and dissensions among the members of their Assemblies. The party defeated in the Assembly would often seek outside help and thus seal the ruin of the state. Modern India, which seeks to develop republican traditions and institutions, may well carve on the gate of its Parliament House the prophesy of the Buddha about the Lichchhavi republic. The republic of the Lichchhavis, said the Buddha, would prosper as long as the members of their Assembly met frequently, showed reverence to age, experience and ability, transacted the state business in concord and harmony and did not develop selfish parties engaged in unending wrangling for their narrow and selfish ends.

In the course of time, monarchy became the order of the day owing to the causes already explained. It cannot be denied that our political writers placed the highest possible ideals before the kingly order; they can be hardly improved even in modern times. The king was to be *dhṛitavrata*, pledged to maintain and defend law, order, justice and morality; he was not above the law, but subject to its jurisdiction. He was to be something even more than a trustee for his subjects; a trustee has merely to abstain from taking any undue advantage of his position, while promoting the interest of the trust; the king, according to the ancient Indian ideals, has to sacrifice his own personal comforts and interests in order to secure the prosperity of the kingdom. Divinity was conceded not to the *person* but to the *office* of the king. The theory that a king can do no wrong and is accountable to none but God was almost unknown to ancient India. Attention of the king was pointedly drawn to the great necessity of a proper training, the absence of which was sure to land him into numerous pitfalls, that do not come across the path of an ordinary individual. The doctrine of the divinity of the king's office was intended merely to inspire respect for authority and not to encourage autocracy or irresponsibility in the kingly order.

It must be however admitted that in actual practice many kings failed to live up to the ideal. The percentage of vicious or tyrannical kings in ancient India was however by no means higher than in medieval Europe. It would be however useful to understand the causes that were responsible for the non-realisation of the ideal of kingship in a large number of cases.

Failure to develop proper secular and constitutional checks on the power of the king was the main reason for the kingly ideal not being frequently realised in practice. Like some medieval political thinkers of Europe, most of our ancient Indian thinkers did no doubt not say that a bad king was accountable to God alone. Nevertheless, in actual practice the fear of hell was the only effective deterrent in the case of a tyrant. Our writers no doubt permit subjects to migrate *en masse* from the country, if the king became oppressive; ancient inscriptions supply some instances of kings being brought to their senses by this method. This remedy, however, is a very impracticable one and could not be easily resorted to. They also sanction regicide in extreme cases. Regicide, however, presupposes an open and successful rebellion; as a remedy against day to day petty cases of tyranny, it is altogether impracticable and inapplicable. Ancient Indian polity failed to develop secular and practicable remedies which could control the actions of a king who was inclined to disregard the ideal and become tyrannical.

This failure was largely due to the disappearance of the *samitis* or Popular Assemblies in the post-Vedic period. As long as these Assemblies functioned, they could effectively control the actions of the king in the day to day administration. The Vedic literature makes it quite clear that a king could succeed in maintaining himself on the throne only so long as his *samiti* or Popular Assembly was in agreement with him. If there was a disagreement, the views of the Assembly generally prevailed, and kings had to submit or abdicate and go into exile.

Central Assemblies, however, gradually disappeared in the

post-Vedic period, not because democracy became more and more unsuitable to the Indian temperament, but because the state became bigger and bigger in size, rendering the meetings of a Central Assembly more and more impracticable. Had Aśoka, Chandragupta or Harsha revived the Central Assembly, its members would have had to spend several weeks in reaching the capital in order to attend the Assembly meetings, and an equally long time in returning to their homes. The principle of representation was also unknown in those days both in the East and in the West.

At the attainment of Independence in India in 1947 there were a number of ruling princes in the country, and it was possible to trv the experiment of the limited monarchy in their states on the Vedic lines. Things however moved with a lightning rapidity and most of the ruling princes agreed to merge their states in the Indian Republic. For a few years about half a dozen members of the princely order functioned as hereditary Rājapramukhas, but all of them disappeared in that capacity when the recommendations of the States Reorganisation Committee were given effect to in 1956. The days of even limited monarchy are thus over in India.

Effective popular central Assemblies not being found practicable in the case of larger kingdoms, ancient Indian political thinkers tried to protect the interests of the people by recommending and bringing about a great decentralisation of the functions of the government. Large powers were vested in the district, town and village administrations, which could be effectively supervised and controlled by local non-official councils. In the Gupta period, the sale of even the waste lands owned by the state required the sanction of the popular district council. The powers of town and village councils in ancient India were probably more extensive than those of similar bodies in any other polity, eastern or western, ancient or modern. They collected the revenues on behalf of the Central Government, refused to collect oppressive taxes, settled village disputes, organised works of public utility, and often maintained and financed hospitals, poor houses and educational institutions. It would be worth while to entrust larger and larger powers to the district boards and local and village councils. A word of warning, however, must be given. The village councils worked successfully in the past because the people had a high regard for truth and character and were instinctively inclined to respect age, experience and ability. Members of the village councils were not elected; they were raised to that position by the consensus of public opinion. Democracy of the modern type involving voting and party alignments did not exist, and is new to India. It presupposes wide spread of education, which must be immediately brought about. Fear of God and hell, which has now disappeared, must be replaced by the sense of civic duty, which alone can now induce our elected representatives to place the good of the people they represent above everything else.

Village Panchāyats of ancient India exercised wide judicial powers. They decided practically all cases excepting those of serious crimes. Life in ancient times was simple; judicial disputes were usually confined to local parties and transactions and the law to be administered was known to and understood by all. Modern law is complex and complicate and presupposes technical knowledge and assistance; parties to a dispute may often belong to distant places. Village Panchāyats in modern times cannot, therefore, successfully exercise that wide civil jurisdiction which they did in the past. A beginning has been made by investing them with a limited civil jurisdiction. It will be difficult for witnesses to tell brand lies in the presence of their fellow residents in the Panchāyat courts, with reference to events and transactions well known to the locality. The revival of the village Panchāyat courts will also secure speedier justice. There will be, however, some uphill wrok. The faith in God and the dread of hell that helped the cause of justice in ancient times are rapidly dying out. Party factions are cropping up in villages due to illiteracy and selfishness. So until a proper sense of civic duty and responsibility is developed to replace the faith in God and fear of hell, there will be some difficulty in the successful working of the village Panchāyats.

Ancient India sought to solve the problem of the finance of the local bodies by localising a part of the land revenue. Most of the villages could get back about 15 to 20% of the proceeds of the land-tax from the government of the day. If the state governments, which are benefiting by the abolition of the Zemindari, set apart a part of the additional income from this or other sources to meet the needs of the village Panchāyats, the financial hurdle in their successful working may be removed.

There can be no doubt that ancient Indian political thinkers had evolved excellent principles for taxation. The grounds on which remissions were sanctioned and exemptions granted were also as a rule sound. All will agree that the state should gather the taxes like the bee, which sucks the honey without damaging the flower, that the trade and industry should be taxed not on gross earnings, but on net profits, that an article should not be taxed twice, that the rise in taxation, when inevitable, should be gradual, and so on. The principles of exemption were also sound. The dumb, the deaf, the blind and the widows were exempted from taxation, as they were usually poor. Students studying at the Gurukulas (educational institutions) were also given the same concession, as also teachers, if they were poor and imparting education free. These principles are well worth considering by a modern welfare state of the socialistic pattern.

The taxation was usually determined by the local customs and traditions. In the later times, however, when the *samiti* disappeared from the scene, governments would often impose high and arbitrary taxes. We often find tugs of war between the central governments, which wanted to levy new and oppressive taxes and the village Panchāyats, which would refuse to collect them. Very often, however, power prevailed and justce went to the wall; we find villagers migrating *en masse* to escape unbearable taxation. There can be no doubt that in later times, the interest of the average man in the sphere of taxation was not adequately protected when a greedy tyrant was on the throne. This however happened primarily because there was no *samiti* or popular assembly in later times. The importance of a strong and vigilant popular Assembly as a champion of popular rights and interests cannot be overemphasised.

The ancient Indian state was not merely a tax-gathering corporation, interested only in preserving law and order. It is pleasing and surprising to find that the state in ancient India should have interested itself in a number of ministrant activities of the nation-building type, which are being undertaken by the modern governments only in relatively recent times. Private agencies, trade guilds and state departments worked side by side to promote national welfare without mutual jealousies. Mines were worked both by the state and private enterprise; guild banks and organisations often inspired greater confidence than the state treasuries. Private and guild concerns received subsidies, if they promoted national welfare. The state regarded itself as a trustee for the population as a whole, and usually contented itself by harmonising the conflicting interests of the different classes. It tried to keep the scale even between the capital and the labour, the employer and the employee, the producer and the consumer and the merchant and the purchaser by laying down suitable and stringent regulations for curbing the greed of the former and protecting the interests of the latter. Free India has embarked on the pattern of the mixed economy, as was the case with ancient India. We have however to see to it that the growing sphere of state socialism does not eliminate or cripple private and corporate enterprise. If the state runs the key industries and controls the rest, if it encourages the local bodies and city corporations also to enter the field of production and constructive nation-building activities, we shall have an economic structure, more or less similar to that in ancient India and likely to meet the needs of the time.

The ideals of the ancient Indian state were undoubtedly very high and all comprehensive. It sought to promote the moral, material, aesthetic and spiritual progress of the whole community. Human ideas about the progress in these different spheres go on changing from age to age, and it is no wonder that we may not be able to agree with all that the state in ancient India did or countenanced in order to achieve progress in this fourfold field. For instance, it gave a general support to the *varṇāśramadharma*, which was undoubtedly iniquitous, especially to the Śūdras and untouchables. We must not, however, forget that a state is but the spokesman of the society it represents ; if certain iniquitous practices were tolerated by the state in ancient India, the society is as much to blame as the state. We should not judge ancient customs and institutions by modern standards and ideals. People in those days had a burning and living faith in the doctrine of Karma. Even the Śūdras and untouchables believed that they were born in their particular caste as a natural result of certain sins committed by them in past lives. As a further consequence of the same, some classes have certain religious and social disabilities imposed upon them in this life as well, under the sanction of the divine śastra. It was impossible for the ancient Indian state even to think of disallowing these disabilities, much less of removing them. Equality of all citizens before the law, therefore, did not exist in ancient India to a great extent. It is no doubt a sad spectacle. We would all have felt prouder of our civilisation if the Smṛiti writers had imposed a higher punishment on the Brāhmaṇa culprit than on the Śūdra one, since they recognised the sin of the former to be greater than that of the latter. We should, however, not forget that such iniquities and inequalities existed in all civilisations, eastern and western, and have not completely disappeared even in modern times. If the fine for murdering a Śūdra is lighter than that for murdering a Brāhmana, we should not forget that the wergeld for the head of a slave or a serf was much smaller in Europe than that for the head of a knight or a landlord. Limited exemption from taxation sometimes sanctioned by the ancient Indian state to the Brāhmaṇas had its counter part in the European polity, where the church and nobility enjoyed many unjust exemptions down to the 18th century. Ancient Indian state did no doubt not belive in affording opportunities to the son of a cobbler to become a premier ; but such a phenomenon rarely occurred in ancient times, both in the West and the East. It will have to be admitted, however, by every impartial critic that the ancient Indian state was not solicitous only for the interests of the Brāhmaṇas ; it tried to promote the material and moral interests of all the castes; only it did not encourage one profession to trespass on the field of another ; for society honestly believed that these fields were predetermined by birth.

The ideal of an all-India state under an emperor ruling over the territories from the Himalayas to the sea was recognised, as early as *c.* 1000 B. C., if not earlier. There were, however, only few occasions in ancient Indian history when it was actually realised. The recognition of this ideal was probably a natural consequence of the realisation of the fundamental unity of India,—geographical, religious and cultural. The ancient Indian polity, however, laid down that the empire should not be at the cost of local autonomy, culture and institutions ; it therefore laid down that the *chakravartin* or the emperor should remain content, if his imeprial status is recognised by the offer of a suitable tribute. He was not to annex the local, provincial or district kingdoms ; even if the heads of the latter had been defeated or had died fighting, some relations of theirs were to be put on the throne on condition that they were willing to recognise the conqueror's suzerainty. Local laws, customs and tradition were never to be interfered with by the conqueror.

An all-India state powerful enough to bring about the unity of the country and to defend it from foreign aggression through a cooperative effort under the aegis of the Central Government, but generous and considerate enough to permit the existence of local governments following their own customs and traditions and fostering their own culture and customs was thus the ideal of the ancient Indian polity. Curiously enough it is very much similar to our present ideal of a strong and united India with full autonomy to states. Let us therefore analyse a little more closely this ideal and find out its strong and weak points as disclosed by our ancient history.

The insistence of the political thinkers that conqueror

should allow the conquered king or state to retain his or its individuality in the feudatory capacity, undoubtedly produced many good results. It permitted local culture, traditions and political institutions to develop more or less unhampered. It toned down provincial and dynastic jealousies and animosities; for an ambitious province or kingdom could at most aim at imposing its more or less nominal suzerainty over its neighbour; it could never aim at crushing its culture or wiping out its separate existence. Warfare also tended to remain humane; neither side had the danger of being completely wiped out, if it was defeated; it therefore did not generally stoop to unchivalrous and unapproved methods to avert a defeat or win a victory.

While recognising that this ideal of an empire with a number of composite units governed by feudatory kings or republics had many good points about it, we cannot remain oblivious to certain injurious results that sprang from it. The recommendation to recognise local autonomy by permitting the conquered king or state to continue in the feudatory capacity eventually stood in the way of effective unification of India. Most of the ancient Indian empires were merely loose federations of a number of feudatory kingdoms held together by masterful personalities for a few decades. Many of his feudatories were usually entertaining imperial ambitions; for the political thinkers recognised that it was but a natural thing that each feudatory should aspire to the imperial status for himself. As a consequence big kingdoms and empires in ancient India were never in a state of equilibrium for a long time. There was a constant tussle going on for the coveted position of a Chakravartin. It was the duty of each king to secure the expansion of his kingdom by attacking his neighbours when they were weak. Feudatories were therefore usually on the look out for an opportunity to rebel against the imperial power. Ninety percent of the wars in Indian history would have been avoided if the ideal of the Chakravartin had not been recommended to every feudatory, and if its successful realiser had not been prevented from annexing the conquered state and compelled to permit it to continue to rule in the feudatory capacity.

Ancient Indian political thinkers probably thought that there was nothing wrong in this ideal. Probably they felt that each king, state or province should have a sporting chance to be the leading state in the country at one time or another. Frequent wars no doubt thus became inevitable; they were perhaps felt to be necessary to keep up the martial spirit and traditions of the Kshatriyas. It did not matter very much whether Pāṭaliputra, Kanauj or Avanti was to be the imperial capital of India. Whatever province may be at the head of the empire, the culture, religion and language of the subordinate provinces did not suffer; for the conqueror was expressly required to respect and preserve local traditions, cultures and institutions.

Ancient Indians began to become growingly indifferent in the course of time to the necessity and desirability of a strong and stable central state. As monarchies became the order of the day from *c.* 400 A. D., the interstate struggles became dynastic wars for hegemony; people were not much interested in them because they knew that their local culture, laws and institutions would not be much affected, whatever might be the outcome of the struggle. Contending armies also fought not so much for their states as for their kings. There was hardly any patriotism in the real sense of the word. This ideal of federal-feudal empire, with full liberty to each constituent state to strike for the imperial status but without permission to forge a unitary empire after the conquest, thus produced a state of continuous instability in ancient India. There were frequent wars, but they did not lead to the emergence of a strong and unitary state. The energy of the nation was unnecessarily wasted in interminable feuds, which only weakened the combatants. The country as a whole became weak and fell an easy prey to the Greek, Scythian and Muslim invaders.

A glance at our history shows that India has prospered only when it had succeeded in evolving a strong central government. In the age of Aśoka, Chandragupta II and Akbar India was able to make good progress, because it had a strong Central Government. The same fact is at the root of the progress made during the last 100 years.

It is a matter of satisfaction that the new Indian constitution recognises this fact and provides for a strong central government. Ancient India was keen that there should be full freedom for the cultural development of each state, even if it was conquered by its neighbour. Luckily now there is no longer any possibility of one state in India being defeated or conquered by another and the principle of state autonomy guarantees a fair amount of freedom for the development of local culture, language, literature and industry.

State jealousies, however, can creep up owing to linguistic differences and conflicting economic interests. There were several languages in ancient India, but Sanskrit was cultivated as the official *lingua franca* even by the states of the south, whose regional languages were of Dravidian stock. Vijayanagara issued its official charters not in Canarese, but in Sanskrit. There is therefore nothing wrong in the effort to have a national language. We should however not forget that Sanskrit did not stand in the way of free development of the different vernaculars like Bengali, Marathi, Gujarati, Telugu, Tamil, etc. The development of Hindi as a national language should not in the same way be an impediment to the full and free development of the regional languages.

Economic conflicts and jealousies between the states would be another impediment in the emergence of a strong Indian nation. But these can be solved without much difficulty in our national forum, the Central Parliament. We cannot and should not forget that union is strength; the U. S. A. and the U. S. S. R. have become great world powers because the different states which constitute them have agreed to merge themselves into a Federal State to watch the common welfare of the federating units. Had this happened in Western Europe, the once powerful and flourishing states of that region would not have been thrown into the background by Russia and America.

If the states in India effectively check separatist or fissiparous tendencies in order to develop a strong Union Government at the centre, and if the latter shows a genuine concern for fostering the cultures, languages and economic development of the former, our Union Government will be powerful enough to defend the motherland against external aggression, to promote an all-round economic development and capable enough to make India once more a mighty and flourishing country, whose voice and views will count in the comity of nations.

Oṁ tatsadbrahmārpaṇamastu.

APPENDIX I

Bibliography

Original works in Sanskrit, Prakrit and Pali.

Ṛigveda
Yajurveda
Atharvaveda
Kāṭhaka Saṁhitā
Tattirīya Saṁhitā
Aitareya Brāhmaṇa
Śatapatha Brāhmaṇa
Pañchaviṁśa Brāhmaṇa
Taittirīya Brāhmaṇa
Bṛihadāraṇyaka Upanishad
Apāstamba Dharmasūtra
Gautama Dharmasūtra
Vasiṣṭha Dharmasūtra
Baudhāyana Dharmasūtra
Vishṇu Dharmasūtra
Rāmāyaṇa
Mahābhārata
Manusmṛiti
Yājñavalkyasmṛiti
Nāradasmṛiti
Kauṭilīya Arthaśāstra, edited by Dr. Shamshatri
Kāmandakīya Nītisāra
Nītimayūkha by Nīlakaṇṭha
Rājanītiprakāśa by Mitramiśra
Rajanītiratnākara by Chaṇḍeśvara
Śukranīti
Bārhaspatya Arthaśāstra
Agnipurāṇa
Mārkaṇḍeyapurāṇa
Dighanikāya
Chullavagga
Divyāvadāna
Jātakas
Achārāṅgasūtra
Pratijñāyaugandharāyaṇa by Bhāsa
Mrichchhakaṭika
Raghuvaṁśa
Mālavikāgnimitra
Pañchatantra
Rājataraṅginī
Kathāsaritsāgara
Āmukhamālyada of kṛishṇadevarāya

Modern works on Ancient Indian Polity

K. P. Jayaswal, Hindu Polity, Calcutta, 1924.

J. J. Anjaria, The Nature and Grounds of Political Obligation in the Hindu State, Longmans Green & Co., 1935.

H. N. Sinha, Sovereignty in Ancient Indian Polity, London, 1938.

Beni Prasad, The Political Theory in Ancient India, Allahabad, 1927.

Beni Prasad, The State in Ancient India, Allahabad, 1928.

A. K. Sen, Studies in Ancient Indian Political Thought, Calcutta, 1926.

N. C. Vandyopadhyara, Development of Hindu Polity and Political Theories, Calcutta, 1927.

P. C. Basu, Indo Aryan Polity, Pioneer Press, Lucknow.

N. N. Law, Aspects of Ancient Indian Polity, Oxford, 1921.

" " Studies in Ancient Indian Polity, Longmans Green. & Co.

" " Law, Interstate Relations in Ancient India, (Calcutta). 1920.

Vishvanathan, International Law in Ancient India, Longmans Green & Co., 1925.

D. R. Bhandarkar, Some Aspects of Ancient Indian Polity, Banaras Hindu University, 1929.

T. V. Mahalingam, South Indian Polity, Madras, 1955.

V. R. R. Dikshitar, Hindu Administrative Institutions, Madras, 1929.

V. R. R. Dikshitar, Mauryan Polity, Madras, 1932.

R. C. Majumdar, Corporate Life in Ancient India, Calcutta, 1922.

R. K. Mookerji, Local Self-Government in Ancient India, Oxford, 1920.

A. S. Altekar, History of the Village Communities in Western India, Bombay, 1926.

U. N Ghosal, A History of Indian Political Theories, Calcutta, 1923.

U. N. Ghosal, Hindu Revenue System, Calcutta, 1923.

U. N. Ghosal, History of Public Life in Ancient India, Vol. I, Calcutta, 1944.

R. Pratapgiri, Problem of Indian Polity, Bombay, 1935.

K. V. Rangasvami Aiyanger, Some Aspects of Ancient Indian Polity, 2nd Edition, Madras, 1935.

P. V. Kane, History gf Dharmaśāstra, Vol. III. Chap. I-X.

J. Mathai, Village Government in British India, London 1915.

Verma V. P., Studies in Hindu Political Thought and its Metaphysical Foundations, Motilal Banarasidass, Delhi 6, 1954.

Journals

Epigraphia Indica.

Indian Antiquary.

OTHER WORKS

Epigraphia Carnatica, Edited by Rice, Banglore.

South Indian Inscriptions, 5 Vols, edited by Hultzsch.

South Indian Epigraphical Reports, published by Madras Government annually.

Fleet, Corpus Incriptionum Indicarum, Vol. III (Gupta Inscriptions), Calcutta, 1888.

Hultzsh, Corpus Inscriptionum, Indicaium, Vol. I, Aśoka Inscriptions, Oxford, 1925.

V. Rangacharya, Inscriptions from Madras Presidency, 3 Vols. Madras, 1919

Archeological Survey of India, Annual Reports.

M'crindle, Invasion of India by Alexander the Great, West Minister, 1896.

M'crindle, Ancient India as described by Megasthenese, Arrian etc., Calcutta, 1906.

Watters, On Yuan Chawang's Travells in India, London, 1904.

Elliot and Dowson, History of India as told by her own Historians, Vols. I-III.

Rhys Davids, Dialogues of the Buddha.

A. S. Altekar, Rāshṭrakūṭas and Their Times, Poona, 1932.

A. S. Altekar, Education in Ancient India, Banaras, 1943.

A. S. Altekar, Position of Women in Hindu Civilisation, Banaras, 1938.

A. S. Altekar, Village Communities in Western India, Bombay, 1927.

Fick, Social Organisation in North-Eastern India at the time of the Buddha, tr., by S. K. Maitra.

R. C. Majumdar, History of Bengal, Vol. I, Calcutta, 1943.

R. C. Majumder and A. S. Altekar, The Age of the Vākāṭakas and the Guptas, Lahore, 1946.

K. A. Nilkantha Sastri, Studies in Chola History and Administration, Madras, 1932.

R. N. Mehta, Pre-Buddhist India, Bombay, 1939.

Macdonell and Keith, Vedic Index of Names and Subjects, 1912.

APPENDIX II

Chromological Table of Authors, Kings and Periods referred to in State and Government in Ancient India.

(For the guidance of general readers)[1]

Agnipurāṇa, *c.* 400 A. D.
Agnimitra, Śuṅga king, *c.* 150 B. C.
Ajātaśatru, king, *c.* 490-470 B. C.
Amoghavarsha II, Rāshṭrakūṭa king, 814-878 A. D.
Arthaśāstra of Kauṭilya, *c.* 300 B. C.
Aśoka, emperor, *c.* 273-232 B. C.
Atharvaveda age, *c.* 2000 B. C.
Azilises, king, *c.* 25 B. C.
Āchārāṅga Sūtra, *c.* 300 B. C.
Bārshapatya Arthaśāstra, *c.* 900 A. D.
Bhoja, Paramāra king, 1015-1045 A. D.
Bhoja, Pratīhāra king, *c.* 840-890 A. D.
Brāhmaṇa works, time of, *c.* B. C. 1500 to 800 B. C.
Buddha, time of death of, *c.* 487 B. C.
Chāhamāna dynasty, *c.* 1000-1200 A. D.
Chālukya dynasty of Badāmī, *c.* 550 to 750 A. D.
Chālukya dynasty of Kalyaṇī, *c.* 977-1150 A. D.
Chālukya dynasty of Veṅgi, *c.* 615-1270 A. D.
Chandella dynasty, *c.* 900-1200 A. D.
Chandragupta II, Gupta king, 380-414 A. D.
Chandragupta, Maurya king, *c.* 320-295 B. C.
Chaulukya dynasty, *c.* 950-1300 A. D.
Chedi dynasty, *c.* 950-1200 A D.
Chola dynasty, *c.* 900-1200 A. D.
Chullavagga, book, *c.* 400 B. C.
Dharmasūtras, time of, *c.* 600-200 B. C.
Dīghanikāya, book, *c.* 450 B. C.

1. In many cases dates are approximate; in some they are conjectural.

Gāhaḍavāla dynasty, *c.* 1050-1203 A. D.
Gaṅga dynasty of Mysore, *c.* 400-1100 A. D.
Gondopharnes, king, *c.* 20-45 A. D.
Gupta age, 300-600 A. D.
Gupta dynasty, *c.* 310-550 A. D.
Gurjara-Pratihāra dynasty, *c.* 775-1000 A. D.
Greek dynasties in India, *c.* 190-50 B. C.
Hagāmasha, Scythian king, *c.* 25 B. C.
Hagāna, Scythian king, *c.* 25 B. C.
Harshavardhana, king, 606-648 A. D.
Jātakas, age of, *c.* 300 B. C.
Kadphises, II, Kushāṇa king, *c.* 60-78 A. D.
Kālidāsa, author, *c.* 400 A. D.
Kāmandakanītisāra, book, *c.* 500 A. D.
Kanishka, king, *c.* 78-104 A. D.
Kaṇva dynasty, *c.* 75-25 B. C.
Khāravela, king, *c.* 150 B. C.
Kushāṇa dynasty, *c.* 50-250 A. D.
Lichchhavi republic, *c.* 600-480 B. C.
Mahābhārata battle, *c.* 1000 B. C.
Mahābhārata, time of the book, *c.* 300 B. C.
Maukhari dynasty, *c.* 550-606 A. D.
Maurya dynasty, *c.* 320-185 B. C.
Megasthenes, Greek ambassador, *c.* 300 B. C.
Menander, king, *c.* 150-130 B. C.
Nahapāṇa, king, *c.* 90-120 A. D.
Nanda dynasty, *c.* 400-325 B. C.
Nārada Smṛiti, *c.* 500 A. D.
Nibandha works on Dharmaśāstra, *c.* 1000-1600 A. D
Patañjali, author, *c.* 150 B. C.
Paramāra dynasty, *c.* 950-1200 A. D.
Persian invasion, *c.* 515 B. C.
Purāṇas, age of, *c.* 400-100 A. D.
Pūrvamīmānsā, work, *c.* 150 B. C.
Pushyamitra, Śuṅga king, *c.* 185-150 B. C.
Rājataraṅgiṇi a work, 1150 A. D.
Rāmāyaṇa, a work, *c.* 50 B. C.

Rāshṭrakūṭa dynasty, *c*. 750-977 A. D.
Ṛigveda, age of, *c*. 2000 B. C.
Rudradāman, Śaka king, *c*. 130-160 A. D.
Śaka dynasty of Western India, *c*. 100-400 A. D.
Śākya republic, *c*. 500 B. C.
Śukranīti *c*. 800 A. D.
Śuṅga dynasty, *c*. 185-75 B. C.
Sātavāhana dynasty, *c*. 200 B. C. to 200 A. D.
Saṁhitās, Later, Age of, *c*. 1500 B. C. 1000 B. C.
Upanishads, age of, *c*. 1000-600 B. C.
Vākāṭaka dynasty, *c*. 270-500 A. D.
Vedic age, early, *c*. 2000-1500 B. C.
Vedic age, later *c*. 1500-1000 B. C.
Yādava dynasty, *c*. 1090-1210 A. D.
Yājñavalkya Smṛiti, *c*. 200 A. D.
Yaudheya republic, *c*. 150 B. C. to 350 A. D.
Yuan Chwang, Chinese traveller, 629-644 A. D.

SUBJECT-INDEX

N. B.—Numbers refer to page numbers

P. 198, at the end of the first para :

Apparently it did not play any effective part in Indian history. India has no doubt a long coast, but it has no natural harbours. As is the case with Greece and Scotland, we have no rugged coast line with a number of islands near the coast, which encourage enterprise at sea. So our navy did not become powerful even in peninsular India or in Bengal.

P. 323 Add a footnote on Kharvaṭaka and Droṇamukha.

The terms Kabbaṭa (Kharvaṭaka) and Doṇamuha (Droṇamukha) occur in the Mallijñāta, a Jain work (which is being edited by my student Dr. Roth), as the names of territorial divisions along with Kheḍa, Madamba, etc. Abhyayadevasūri, a 12th century commentator, explains Kabbaṭa as a *kunagaram* or a small or insignificant town and Doṇamuha as *'jalapatha-sthalapathayuktam*, a place which has both land and water approaches. This explanation apparently supports the *Arthaśāstra* according to which Droṇamukha was bigger than Kharvaṭaka.